SEPTEMBER 11

a testimony

SEPTEMBER 11
a testimony

Published by **Pearson Education**

New York • London • San Francisco • Toronto • Sydney • Tokyo • Singapore
Hong Kong • Cape Town • Madrid • Amsterdam • Munich • Paris • Milan

PEARSON EDUCATION LIMITED

Head Office:
Edinburgh Gate
Harlow CM20 2JE
Tel: +44 (0)1279 623623
Fax: +44 (0)1279 431059

London Office:
128 Long Acre
London WC2E 9AN
Tel: +44 (0)20 7447 2000
Fax: +44 (0)20 7240 5771
Website: www.business-minds.com

Cover art photographer: Ray Stubblebine
Cover photo copyright © 2001 Reuters

In compiling this book, thanks go to many people. At Reuters: Nancy Bobrowitz, Steve Crisp, Izabel Grindal, Elaine Herlihy, Gary Hershorn, Stephen Jukes, Peter Morgan, Peter Millership, Paul Mylrea, Jessica Persson, Alexia Singh, Irina Stocker and David Viggers. At Prentice Hall PTR: Tim Moore, Jim Boyd, Sophie Papanikolaou, Patti Guerrieri, Bryan Gambrel, Maura Zaldivar, Allyson Kloss, Jerry Votta, Anthony Geaimellaro, Gail Cocker-Bogusz and Meg Van Arsdale. At Pearson Education: Hannah Cottrill, Helena Dahlstrom, Martin Drewe, Susan Drummond, Peter Marshall, Ian Roberts and Richard Stagg. At Pearson Plc: Rebecca Seymour.

First published in Great Britain in 2001

© Reuters 2002

ISBN 1903 68433 1

British Library Cataloguing in Publication Data
A CIP catalogue record for this book can be obtained from the British Library

10 9 8 7 6 5 4 3 2 1

Printed and bound in Great Britain by The Bath Press, Bath

The Publishers' policy is to use paper manufactured from sustainable forests.

We dedicate this book to our six colleagues
from the Reuters family that we lost at the World Trade Center.

It contains a collection of harrowing images that capture the
destruction of September 11, 2001, but that also reflect acts of
great heroism and compassion and the resilience of the human spirit.

It also shows the exceptional work and talent of Reuters photographers.

Tom Glocer
CEO
Reuters

———◆———

These remarkable pictures record the events of September 11th in a way
that words cannot. They reveal the horrors and they exalt the heroes. They
remind us that we are all involved in this tragedy and that the resilient
spirit and the common purpose we saw on that day are the qualities that
will see us through.

We're proud to be publishing this book
with Reuters to honour those whose lives were lost
and those who fought to save lives.

Marjorie Scardino
Chief Executive
Pearson Plc

At 8:47 a.m. on September 11, 2001, American Airlines Flight 11 slams into the north tower of Manhattan's World Trade Center. Sixteen minutes later, United Airlines Flight 175 plows into the south tower, exploding upon impact. Workers are desperately trying to escape and rescuers are rushing to their aid, when the two towers of the World Trade Center—one of the most imposing symbols of U.S. prosperity—collapse. Thousands of people are buried in the wreckage of the buildings, which were brought down by suicide hijackers at the controls of the two fuel-laden Boeing 767 airliners. Blamed by the U.S. government on Saudi-born Osama bin Laden and his al Qaeda network, the attacks bring comparisons with the December 7, 1941, Japanese assault on Pearl Harbor that left more than 2,300 dead and thrust America into World War II. In the next hour, a third hijacked plane—American Airlines Flight 77, a Boeing 757—is flown into the Pentagon defense headquarters near Washington, D.C.; and a fourth plane—United Airlines Flight 93, a Boeing 757—crashes into a field in Pennsylvania after passengers rush the hijackers.

SEPTEMBER 11

a testimony

Sean Adair

Sean Adair

Sean Adair

(far left) Hijacked United Airlines Flight 175 flies toward the World Trade Center south tower just seconds before slamming into it at 9:03 a.m. September 11, 2001. The north tower burns after being struck at 8:47 a.m. by American Airlines Flight 11. (middle) Flight 175 explodes upon impact as it plows into the south tower. (right) Seconds later, the south tower is engulfed by flames.

Sean Adair

Sean Adair

Sean Adair

(far left) Black smoke billows from the damaged north tower as the south tower continues to burn. (middle) Glass and rubble spill from the building in the seconds after impact. (right) The north tower weakens in the immediate aftermath of the coordinated attack.

Flight 175 explodes on impact with the south tower of the World Trade Center at 9:03 a.m. as the north tower burns. The Brooklyn Bridge is in the foreground. Television cameras filming the aftermath of the first attack broadcast the second attack live to a stunned nation.

Sara K. Schwittek

People standing on a nearby street point in disbelief at the destruction taking place before their eyes.

Richard Cohen

The twin towers of the World Trade Center pour plumes of black smoke into the sky, casting a shadow over New York City.

Brad Rickerby

People hang out of windows as the north tower of the World Trade Center burns. Rescue workers are powerless to save them. Shortly afterwards, the tower collapsed.

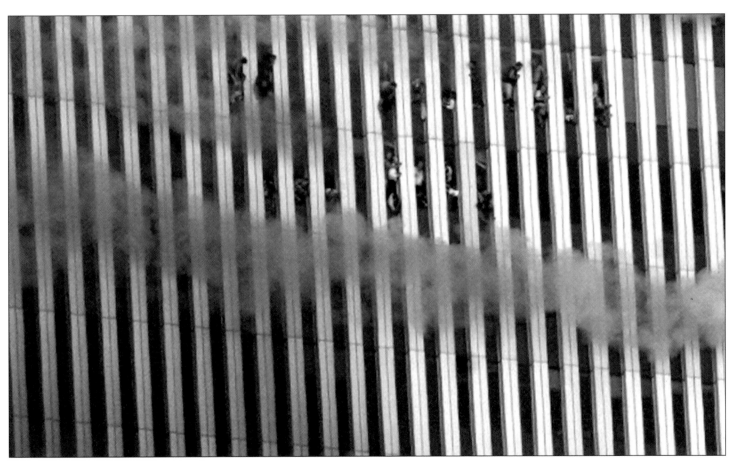

Jeff Christensen

White House Chief of Staff Andrew Card notifies U.S. President George W. Bush of the unfolding disaster. The president, who was at a reading seminar in a Sarasota, Florida, elementary school, gives a brief statement at 9:28 a.m. vowing to hunt down the perpetrators. Bush subsequently declares a global war on terrorism and launches a U.S.-led military campaign against Afghanistan for harboring bin Laden.

Win McNamee

Shocked workers emerge from the World Trade Center. Rescue workers evacuate thousands of people from the complex before the towers buckle.

Shannon Stapleton

One of the towers dissolves in a mushroom cloud of smoke, dust, and rubble.

Jeff Christensen

One of the towers plunges to the ground.

Shannon Stapleton

People flee in panic from the towering cloud of dust and debris that races up the street behind them.

Kelly Price

A man runs down Broadway to escape the choking cloud.

Kelly Price

Black smoke and dust billow through surrounding buildings as the second tower collapses at about 10:30 a.m.

Ray Stubbleb·ne

Rescue workers remove a colleague from the wreckage of the World Trade Center.

Shannon Stapleton

A law enforcement officer expresses her anguish after the collapse of the first World Trade Center tower.

Shannon Stapleton

A dazed man carrying a briefcase and coat is caked in dust after the attacks.

Shannon Stapleton

The smoldering ruins of the World Trade Center provide a nightmarish backdrop as a man hurries past a New York subway stop.

Peter Morgan

A solitary firefighter cuts an eerie figure as he picks his way through the rubble.

Peter Morgan

The Stars and Stripes flies in the face of the devastation.

Peter Morgan

Mangled vehicles and shattered buildings in what comes to be known as "ground zero" near the base of the destroyed World Trade Center.

Peter Morgan

Firefighters carry out the harrowing task of combing the wreckage for signs of life. The rubble smolders for more than a month after the unprecedented attacks.

Peter Morgan

Firefighters are dwarfed by the scene of massive devastation.

Peter Morgan

Just outside Washington, D.C., at 9:38 a.m., less than an hour after the first New York attack, American Airlines Flight 77 slams into the southwest side of the Pentagon. A rescue helicopter surveys damage to the five-sided symbol of American military might as firefighters battle flames.

Larry Downing

The impact of the Boeing 757 on the Pentagon creates a gaping hole in the building. The attack kills 125 people in the Pentagon and 64 people aboard the plane, including five hijackers.

William Philpott

As President Bush inspects the blackened and gutted west side of the building, rescue workers on the roof of the Pentagon unfurl a U.S. flag. Workers break out into a spontaneous chorus of "God Bless America." Flags appear on cars, houses, and businesses around the country in a wave of patriotism as the nation mourns.

Kevin Lamarque

Seen here at sunrise on September 16, is the damaged area of the Pentagon with the U.S. Capitol building in the background.

Larry Downing

Accompanied by Secretary of Defense Donald Rumsfeld, President Bush, also Commander-in-Chief of the armed forces, speaks in front of the Pentagon on September 12. The president says America will not be cowed by terrorists and vows to bring those responsible to justice.

Kevin Lamarque

A U.S. Army helicopter hovers before landing in front of the damaged Pentagon on September 17.

Larry Downing

As New York and Washington reel from the attacks, United Airlines Flight 93 crashes just after 10 a.m. in rural Pennsylvania after passengers try to overpower the hijackers. Forty-four people, including four hijackers, die. Smoke rises behind investigators as they comb the field of debris near Shanksville, Pennsylvania, on September 12.

Tim Shaffer

Investigators search for the flight data recorder near a huge crater carved in the ground by the crashing plane.

Tim Shaffer

Under the watchful eye of a state trooper, travelers are evacuated from Boston's Logan airport where Flight 175, which hit the World Trade Center, originated. The U.S. Federal Aviation Administration grounds all flights departing from U.S. airports just before 10 a.m. on September 11. This is the first U.S. nationwide grounding of aircraft.

Brian Snyder

A sign flashes that all flights are cancelled from Los Angeles International Airport. The planes that hit the World Trade Center and the Pentagon were both fully laden with fuel and bound for Los Angeles. The plane that crashed in Pennsylvania was bound for San Francisco.

Jim Ruymen

As the nation grinds to a halt in reaction to the attacks, a sign over the New Jersey Turnpike in New Brunswick, New Jersey, warns travelers that bridges and tunnel crossings into New York City are closed as part of emergency security measures.

Jim Bourg

With a nation united in grief, a construction worker stands amid a patchwork of patriotic signs, American flags, and other messages hung from the scaffolding of a Times Square construction site in tribute to the victims.

Gary Hershorn

Weary firefighters leave ground zero in the early hours of September 12.

Mike Segar

New York City firefighters douse bent girders, broken concrete, and other debris at ground zero.

Mike Segar

A firefighter looks up at the remains of the World Trade Center.

U.S. Navy Photo by Photographer's Mate 2nd Class Jim Watson

New York City firefighter John Cleary wipes soot from his face while taking a break from rescue work. Cleary helped in the rescue of two trapped Port Authority workers. Only five people were pulled alive from the rubble despite the extensive rescue effort.

Brad Rickerby

New York firefighters continue to battle blazes at ground zero on September 19.

Andrea Booher, Federal Emergency Management Agency

A firefighter calls for more rescue workers to burrow into the rubble on September 15.

U.S. Navy Photo by Journalist 1st Class Preston Keres

Firefighters work to dampen smoke and clear the site on September 19.

Tom Sperduto–U.S. Coast Guard

A bird flies over the ruins of the World Trade Center as a giant American flag hangs in the background, September 19.

Kai Pfaffenbach

Firefighters are winched up in a basket after going deep under the surface at the site of the World Trade Center disaster.

Tom Sperduto–U.S. Coast Guard

Mechanical excavators methodically clear the site at ground zero, September 26.

Mike Segar

A police officer and a rescue worker look at the crushed and burned hulk of a fire truck.

Shaun Best

Workers suspended from a crane hover near what is left of the World Trade Center. Heavy excavation equipment arrives on the scene about ten days after the disaster to clear the smoldering wreckage as hope fades of finding survivors.

Kai Pfaffenbach

Smoke rises from the base of the site on September 16, five days after the attack.
Some ragged sections at the base of the World Trade Center are still standing.

Shaun Best

Risking their lives in search-and-rescue
sweeps, firefighters descend deep
into the rubble, September 14.

U.S. Navy Photo by Photographer's Mate 2nd Class Jim Watson

Workers cut through steel as they clear the site. Over them, a banner expressing the feelings of New Yorkers reads, "We will never forget."

Kai Pfaffenbach

A rescue dog is transported out of the debris with pulleys and ropes in the exhaustive search for survivors, September 15.

U.S. Navy Photo by Journalist 1st Class Preston Keres

A group of rescue workers, wearing masks and goggles to protect them from the dust, leaves ground zero accompanied by two working dogs, September 29.

Jeff Christensen

Captain Robert Blume of the New York City Fire Department is hugged by his two-year-old son Brian after being promoted to battalion chief in a ceremony on September 16. One hundred and sixty eight firefighters are promoted to replace those lost in the collapse of the World Trade Center.

Ruben Sprich

A night view of the Manhattan skyline shows the smoke and glow replacing the once distinctive outline of the landmark twin towers.

Chief Brandon Brewer–U.S. Coast Guard

President Bush's eyes fill with tears while speaking of the victims in the Oval Office on September 13. "I'm a loving guy and I'm also someone, however, who has a job to do and I intend to do it," says Bush, who also warns that America's attackers "made a terrible mistake; they have roused a mighty giant."

Kevin Lamarque

Bowing their heads in prayer, President Bush, First Lady Laura Bush, former President George Bush, his wife Barbara Bush, former President Bill Clinton, Senator Hillary Rodham Clinton, and their daughter Chelsea Clinton (left to right) attend a service at the National Cathedral in Washington, D.C., on September 14. As candlelight vigils take place across the country, Bush leads grieving Americans in prayer. "This nation is peaceful, but fierce when stirred to anger," Bush says in the service.

Kevin Lamarque

President Bush (center) talks with New York City Mayor Rudolph Giuliani (left) and New York Governor George Pataki at ground zero. As Bush tours the site on September 14 to see the devastation first hand, rescue workers cheer the president and chant, "USA! USA!" He replies, "The nation sends its love and compassion."

Win McNamee

President Bush talks to retired firefighter Bob Beckwith (right) at ground zero.
After shaking hands with weary rescuers in hard hats, Bush climbs on top of the
soot-covered remains of a fire truck and tells the throng through a bullhorn,
"I can hear you, the rest of the world hears you, and the people who knocked these
buildings down will hear all of us soon."

Win McNamee

President Bush joins Vice President Dick Cheney (left), Counselor to the President Karen Hughes, and Deputy Chief of Staff Joe Hagin (right) on the South Lawn of the White House in a moment of silence on September 18.

Larry Downing

President Bush and his wife Laura sit with two members of the military at an October 11 ceremony for the victims of the Pentagon attack, exactly one month after the plane struck.

Kevin Lamarque

Three-year-old Alana Milawski waves an American flag as she sits on her father Craig Milawski's shoulders at a candlelight vigil to honor the dead, held in Las Vegas on September 12.

Ethan Miller - Las Vegas Sun

Members of a church choir prepare backstage with the American flag as a backdrop during "A Prayer for America" memorial in Miami, September 18.

Colin Braley

Thousands of people gather for an impromptu memorial at the U.S. Capitol in Washington, September 12. Investigators believe the Capitol could have been a possible target of the hijacked planes.

William Philpott

A man sits in front of flowers left in tribute at the Seattle Center International Fountain on September 16.

Anthony P. Bolante

(from the left) Megan Riley, Kristen Jackson, and Elizabeth Kramer join crowds of people at the Washington candlelight vigil.

Win McNamee

A woman is overcome by emotion as she looks at posters and photographs of the missing in Union Square in New York City on September 18, one week after the attacks on the World Trade Center.

Kai Pfaffenbach

A man leans against a wall showing photographs of missing people outside Bellevue Hospital in New York on September 16.

Russell Boyce

A flower placed on a wall showing photographs of missing people outside Bellevue Hospital in New York, September 16.

Russell Boyce

A cardboard box containing a victim's shoes and a moving message becomes a makeshift shrine at New York's Union Square memorial site.

Kai Pfaffenbach

A simple note torn from a pad is laid at the Union Square memorial, along with flowers.

Jeff Christensen

A lone man looks at a wall displaying photographs of missing people outside Bellevue Hospital in New York, September 16.

Russell Boyce

People along the Hudson River waterfront in Jersey City, New Jersey, light candles for the victims of the attacks as smoke pours out of ground zero across the river, September 16.

Ray Stubblebine

A note is left next to a group of candles at a service held in New York's Washington Square Park on September 12.

Jeff Christensen

A man holds a candle and a U.S. flag at a vigil at Harrison and Greenwich Streets in lower Manhattan, just blocks from ground zero, on September 14.

Mike Segar

A man places a candle at a memorial on the sidewalk outside a firehouse in New York City in the early hours of September 14. More than 300 firefighters die in the World Trade Center attacks.

Gary Hershorn

Firefighters stand by the casket of New York Fire Department
Chaplain Rev. Mychal Judge at a funeral service at St. Francis of Assisi Church on
September 15.

Kevin Coombs

Firefighters and priests watch as the casket of New York Fire Department Chaplain Rev. Mychal Judge leaves the funeral service. Judge is eulogized as a man who ushered firefighters through life, helped the homeless, and kept vigil at the bedsides of sick children.

Kevin Coombs

Firefighters embrace outside St. Francis of Assisi Church after the service for NYFD Chaplain Rev. Mychal Judge.

Rick Wilking

Doris Gadeaille weeps on the street outside St. Francis of Assisi Church after the funeral of NYFD Chaplain Rev. Mychal Judge, September 15.

Rick Wilking

New York City Mayor Giuliani (right) watches as firefighters carry the casket of New York City Fire Department Chief Peter J. Ganci into St. Kilian Church.

Mike Segar

Mayor Giuliani bows his head as firefighters carry the casket of New York City Fire Department Chief Peter J.Ganci, a 33-year veteran of the fire department and its highest ranking uniformed officer, who died while trying to save people at ground zero.

Mike Segar

New York Port Authority police officers salute outside the Our Lady of Assumption Church in the Bronx area of New York City, September 19, at the funeral of officer Dominick Pezzulo.

Mike Segar

A woman holds a teddy bear as she cries outside a memorial service at St. Patrick's Cathedral in New York City on September 17.

Shaun Best

People mourn at a memorial mass for New York City Fire Department Assistant Chief Gerard Barbara outside St. Patrick's Cathedral in New York, October 1.

Shannon Stapleton

A fire truck containing the casket of New York City Fire Department
Chief Peter J. Ganci passes a line of firefighters on its way to his funeral on
September 15, 2001.

Mike Segar

United Airlines worker Alyson Robichaud (left) is comforted by American Eagle pilot Chuck O'Hare (right) at an interfaith prayer vigil on September 13 in Boston. The American and United flights that crashed into the World Trade Center both took off from Boston.

Brian Snyder

Peggy Ogonowski (center), wife of American Airlines pilot John Ogonowski, receives an American flag from Lieutenant Colonel James Ogonowski, the late pilot's brother, after a memorial service in Massachusetts, September 17. Ogonowski was the pilot of American Airlines Flight 11, which was hijacked and flown into the World Trade Center.

Brian Snyder

A police officer, wearing a protective mask, stands guard near the New York Stock Exchange building, which is draped with a giant American flag one day before its reopening on September 17. The four-day hiatus caused by the attacks is the longest shutdown of the New York Stock Exchange since the Great Depression.

Kevin Coombs

A New York shopkeeper vacuums dust from a store near ground zero as he tries to get back to business as usual. The entire area is blanketed with a layer of dust that rose from the site.

Shaun Best

A police officer gazes into the waters off lower Manhattan as he travels on a ferry carrying commuters from Staten Island to Manhattan on the day that the New York Stock Exchange reopens.

Ruben Sprich

In a high-profile example of heightened security, a U.S. soldier in a military vehicle patrols the financial district as people return to work prior to the opening of the New York Stock Exchange on September 17.

Dylan Martinez

As the United States tries to get back to normal, members of the New York City emergency services ring the opening bell at the New York Stock Exchange, September 17. The exchange observes a moment of silence to honor the victims of the September 11 attacks. Also in the picture are New York Senators Charles Schumer and Hillary Rodham Clinton and Governor George Pataki.

Jeff Christensen

New York Stock Exchange traders hold a "God Bless America" sign during a moment of silence to honor the victims.

Peter Jones

Jim Lawlar, a firefighter from Bridgeport, Connecticut, shoulders the American flag outside the Nasdaq in Times Square in New York on September 17.

Kai Pfaffenbach

Commuters leaving Times Square subway station pass posters of people missing after the September 11 attacks.

Peter Morgan

Passersby gaze and take pictures at ground zero while returning to work in New York's financial district on September 17. Some New Yorkers wear masks because of the acrid smell around the site.

Mike Segar

New York City police officers stand close to a wanted poster printed by a New York newspaper depicting Saudi-born Osama bin Laden, named as Washington's prime suspect in the attacks.

Russell Boyce

With the return of baseball seen as another potent symbol of recovery from the attacks, players of the Colorado Rockies and the Arizona Diamondbacks hold a giant American flag prior to the resumption of major league baseball at Coors Field in Denver, September 17. Major league baseball games were cancelled after the attacks.

Gary C. Caskey

Philadelphia Phillies pitcher David Coggin (third from left) holds a U.S. flag during a memorial ceremony before the start of the Phillies versus the Atlanta Braves game in Philadelphia, September 17.

Tim Shaffer

New York Mets catcher Mike Piazza, wearing a New York City Police Department hat, waits for the start of the Mets game with the Pittsburgh Pirates in Pittsburgh, September 17. The Mets players wear baseball caps bearing the logos of the NYPD and the New York Fire Department to honor the victims.

David DeNoma

Players of the Los Angeles Dodgers and the San Diego Padres and members of the Los Angeles Police and Fire Departments stand united in the outfield of Dodger Stadium. They hold a huge American flag during a moment of silence to honor the victims on September 17.

Adrees Latif

Singer Liza Minnelli sings "New York, New York" as city firefighters and police officers clap and do a shuffle step with her during the seventh inning stretch of the New York Mets game against the Atlanta Braves at Shea Stadium in New York on September 21. This is the first baseball game to be held in New York since September 11, and many of the 35,000 fans wave American flags during emotional ceremonies that pay tribute to the victims and rescue workers.

Mike Segar

A fan waves an American flag from the upper deck at New York's Yankee Stadium as a giant version of the Stars and Stripes is unfurled in center field during a pre-game ceremony to honor the victims. The game against the Tampa Bay Devil Rays on September 25 was the first home game for the Yankees since the attacks.

Shannon Stapleton

New York City Mayor Giuliani (left) is embraced by New York Yankees' manager Joe Torre on the field at Yankee Stadium prior to the game against the Tampa Bay Devil Rays.

Mike Segar

Strangers reach across aisles to hold hands as part of the "A Prayer for America" memorial service at Yankee Stadium on September 23. Mourners in the stadium hear prayers from the world's major religions. It is broadcast on large screens in Brooklyn and Staten Island and run live on several television and radio stations.

Shaun Best

A woman holds a red rose to her forehead as she prays during the "A Prayer for America" service held at Yankee Stadium in New York on September 23.

Shaun Best

At the Yankee Stadium ceremony, Carmine Davila (left) comforts her nephew Daniel Lopez, Jr., and his sister Brittany Lopez of Brooklyn, New York, over the loss of their father, Daniel Lopez.

Jim Bourg

Frances Ortega (right) of the Bronx, New York, hugs her nine-year-old daughter Quasha and cries at Yankee Stadium. Ortega was scheduled to have a job interview at the World Trade Center on September 11 when the crash occurred, but it was rescheduled shortly before the disaster.

Jim Bourg

A police officer waves
an American flag at
Yankee Stadium.

Shaun Best

Across the Hudson River in New Jersey, a separate event for that state's victims is held in a park with views of the scarred Manhattan skyline. In this picture, a woman writes a message on a wall for victims before the start of the New Jersey Victims Memorial.

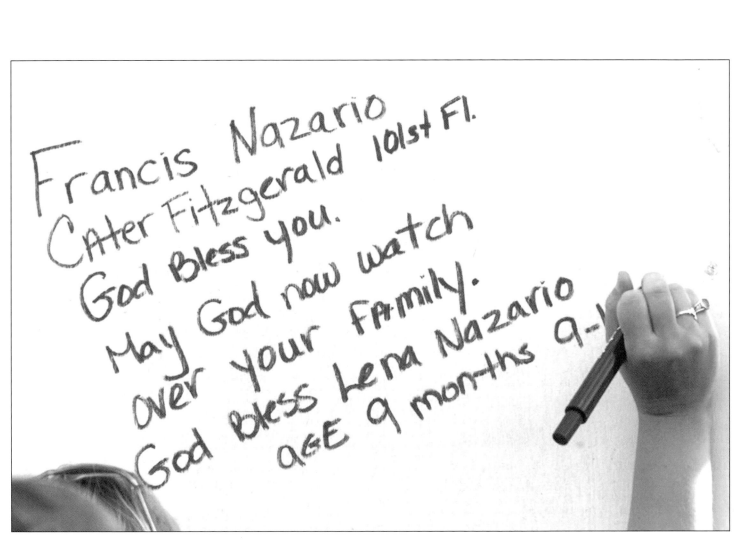

Rick Wilking

With the Statue of Liberty in the background, firefighter Bill Bergner
takes part in the opening prayer at the start of the New Jersey memorial service.

Mike Segar

Britain's Queen Elizabeth leaves St. Paul's Cathedral in central London with American Ambassador William Farish on September 14.

Ferran Paredes

Britain's Prince William signs the condolence book at the American Consulate in Edinburgh for the victims of the attacks on the United States, September 21.

Jeff J. Mitchell

Win McNamee

President Bush holds up the badge of Port Authority police officer George Howard while addressing a joint session of Congress in Washington on September 20. Bush says he will carry with him the shield that belonged to Howard, killed trying to help others at the World Trade Center, and which is given to the president by the officer's mother. "This is my reminder of lives that ended and a task that does not end," says Bush. "I will not forget this wound to my country or those who inflicted it."

Shannon Stapleton

Arlene Howard waves a flag to hundreds of law enforcement representatives at the funeral of her son, George, at St. Ignatius Roman Catholic Church in Hicksville, Long Island, September 19. She sent her son's badge to President Bush.

Lisa Beamer (center), widow of Todd Beamer, as she is welcomed during an address by President Bush in the U.S. Capitol building on September 20. In the minutes before United Airlines Flight 93 went down, Todd Beamer called from a phone on board and told the air phone operator that a group of passengers was going to try to stop the hijackers. He recited the Lord's Prayer with the operator and was then heard saying, "Let's roll." A short time later the plane crashed.

Brendan McDermid

New York Governor George Pataki (right) and New York City Mayor Rudolph Giuliani (second right) clasp hands as they are applauded on Capitol Hill after Bush pays tribute to them during his address. The two men jump to their feet when Bush vows "we will rebuild New York City." First Lady Laura Bush and British Prime Minister Tony Blair (left) are also present.

Shaun Best

Senate Majority Leader Tom Daschle grips Bush in a warm bear hug following his address to a joint session of Congress in Washington on September 20. In the address, Bush says, "Our grief has turned to anger, and anger to resolution. Whether we bring our enemies to justice, or bring justice to our enemies, justice will be done."

Shaun Best

President Bush strides through the grand foyer on his way to a news conference in the East Room of the White House on October 11. Bush tells journalists the acts were "an attack on the heart and soul of the world." It is the first prime-time presidential news conference to be held since 1995.

Win McNamee

President Bush stands shoulder to shoulder with his staunchest ally, British Prime Minister Tony Blair, after a meeting at the White House on September 20.

Larry Downing

Israeli Prime Minister Ariel Sharon (right) and Foreign Minister Shimon Peres observe a moment of silence for the victims of the attacks on America at a weekly cabinet meeting in Jerusalem on September 16.

Natalie Behring-Chisholm

President Bush listens to the translation as Russian President Vladimir Putin speaks during a news conference following their meeting at the Asia Pacific Economic Cooperation (APEC) meeting in Shanghai, October 21.

Alexander Natruskin

United Nations Secretary-General Kofi Annan signs a book of condolences in the lobby of the U.N. headquarters, September 24.

Jeff Christensen

French President Jacques Chirac pauses after laying a bouquet of flowers at a memorial in Union Square in New York on September 19. The first foreign head of state to visit ground zero, Chirac praises Mayor Giuliani for his leadership, "I said from the bottom of my heart that I want to say, 'Bravo,' thank you. You did that for the New Yorkers but also for the free world, for the dignity of all the mankind, and we know that and we are beside you."

Dylan Martinez

One day after the attacks on the United States, Palestinian President Yasser Arafat donates blood for the victims in a Gaza hospital. Arafat sends his condolences to President Bush and condemns the hijackings. "We were completely shocked. It's unbelievable," says Arafat.

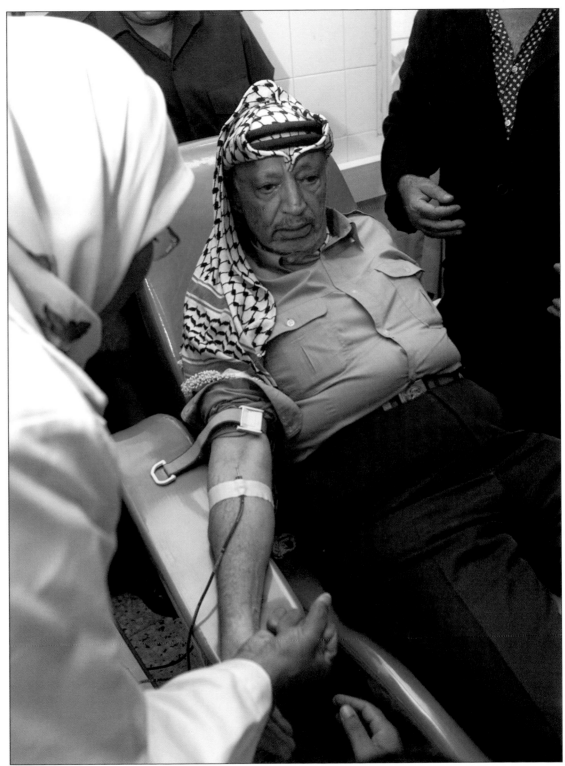

Ahmed Jadallah

President Bush and Pakistan President Perez Musharraf shake hands after a joint news conference in New York on November 10.

Larry Downing

A satellite image of Manhattan taken at 11:43 a.m. on September 12 by Space Imaging's IKONOS satellite shows a column of white dust and smoke where the World Trade Center once stood.

SpaceImaging.com

Wreckage of the World Trade Center smolders on September 15.

New York Office of Emergency Management

Aerial view of ground zero on September 26, 15 days after the attack.
Emergency workers are busy on the ground as the rubble still smolders.

U.S. Customs Photo by James Tourtellotte

The World Trade Center during the
final phase of its construction in
December 1970.

Slim Roomussaar

Enrique Shore

The lower Manhattan skyline is shown in an August 30 photograph, with the twin towers at center, and in a view from roughly the same site on September 27 with the towers missing.

Mike Segar

A New York City firefighter places flowers and mementos from family members of the victims amid the wreckage after a memorial service held on October 28.

Mike Segar

The Photographers

Sean Adair

was born in New York City in 1959. He was educated in New Zealand and has traveled to over 40 countries. He specializes in art, stock, and assignment freelance photography, alongside a career in video and film production. When the morning news of the first plane strike came on the television, Sean rushed up to the roof of his 20th Street, New York City apartment with his camera, telephoto lens, and tripod for a clear view of the smoking tower.

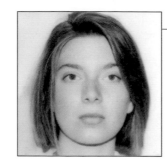

Natalie Behring-Chisholm

was born in 1972. She received her Bachelor of Arts degree in History, began her work with Reuters, Beijing, in 1997, and has since worked for Reuters in China, Israel, and the Palestinian territories. She is currently based in Jerusalem.

Shaun Best

was born in 1968 in Canada. He has been a Reuters staff photographer based in Montreal, Quebec, since February 2001. He previously worked for Reuters for six years as a contract photographer. Prior to that, he was a staff photographer at the *Winnipeg Sun*.

Jim Bourg

was born in Washington, D.C., in 1964. He started his career at the age of 16 when he began photographing for *The Washington Post*. He began shooting for UPI in 1982 before joining Reuters in 1988. He has covered a myriad of political, sporting, and general breaking-news events. He also covered the first bombing of the World Trade Center in 1993.

Russell Boyce

was born in 1962. He joined Reuters 1989 and has covered such events as the Genoa G8 summit, the Sydney Olympics, British paratroopers in Kosovo, Princess Diana, and the Gulf War.

Colin Braley

is based in Miami, Florida. He is a veteran photojournalist who continues to cover international news and sporting events throughout the U.S. and Caribbean for Reuters. His work has been published in numerous books, newspapers, and magazines throughout the world.

Gary C. Caskey

was born in 1947. He studied at the University of Michigan in Ann Arbor. From the Olympics to papal visits, Gary has numerous major event assignments to his credit. He has been a contract photographer for Reuters since 1994. A former UPI Bureau Manager, stringer for both UPI and AP, and newspaper photographer, Gary has been a photojournalist since 1975.

Jeff Christensen

was born in Duluth, Minnesota, in 1958. His first job as a photographer was for UPI in Minneapolis, Minnesota. He started working for Reuters as a contract photographer in 1989. In 1991 he moved to New York City and has been working for Reuters as a contract photographer since then.

Larry Downing

first worked as a professional photographer for a Los Angeles newspaper. He had three years of wire staff work at UPI in Washington, D.C., before spending 15 years at *Newsweek Magazine*, covering the White House. He became a staff photographer at Reuters in 1999, again covering the White House. He is currently based in Washington.

Gary Hershorn

was born in Ontario, Canada, in 1958. He worked at United Press Canada until January 1985, and it was then that Reuters hired him as Chief Photographer for Canada, in Toronto. He transferred to Washington, D.C., in 1990, where he is currently based, working as Editor, Pictures, America.

Peter Jones

was born in 1965 and is currently Chief Photographer of Reuters in Canada, based in Toronto. He has worked for Reuters since 1991.

Kevin Lamarque

has been with Reuters for the past 15 years, spending two years in Hong Kong (1987–1989) before transferring to London (1989–1999) where he covered everything from the troubles in Northern Ireland to the funeral of the Princess of Wales. He is currently based in Washington, D.C., covering the White House.

Adrees Latif

was born in Lahore, Pakistan, in 1973. He received his Bachelor of Arts degree in Journalism from the University of Houston. He has been a freelance photographer for Reuters for six years, during which time he photographed the 2000 Olympics in Sydney, The Haj (Pilgrimage to Mecca, Saudi Arabia), and the current crisis in Pakistan. An American citizen, he is now based in Los Angeles, California.

Dylan Martinez

was born in Barcelona to Argentine parents in 1969 and moved to the UK a year later. He began taking pictures for music magazines and record companies and then moved onto *Sygma* and the *Sunday Mirror*. He began freelancing for Reuters in 1991 and was made staff photographer in 1994. He worked in Asia, based in Vietnam, from 1996–1998 and is now Reuters Chief Photographer in Italy.

Brendan McDermid

was born in Buffalo, New York, in 1973. He was published for the first time in *The New York Times*, while still in high school. Brendan worked as a freelance photographer in Buffalo from 1991–1999 where he first worked for Reuters. He moved to Washington, D.C., in 1999, where he worked as a Reuters summer intern and later as a desk editor. He is now a freelance photographer based in Washington, D.C., and covers events at Capitol Hill and the White House, as well as sports and general news.

Win McNamee

was born in 1963 in Washington, D.C. He majored in journalism and graduated from the University of South Carolina in 1985. After working for newspapers for three years and freelancing for two years, he joined Reuters as a staff photographer in Washington, D.C., in 1990. McNamee has covered four U.S. presidents, three presidential campaigns, and the Persian Gulf War, as well as conflicts in the Philippines, South Korea, and Afghanistan.

Ethan Miller

was born in Austin, Texas, in 1971. He studied under Professor Frank Hoy and received a journalism degree from Arizona State University in 1994. While attending college, he worked as an intern for *The Phoenix Gazette* and *The Arizona Republic* newspapers and shot for local music magazines. Since 1995, he has been a staff photographer for the *Las Vegas Sun* and has also freelanced for Reuters, providing coverage primarily for music and boxing events.

Jeff J. Mitchell

was born in Edinburgh, Scotland, in 1970. Jeff's first full-time job in Scotland was as a photographer for the *Helensburgh Advertiser* in 1989. He then moved to the *Edinburgh Evening News* in 1992, followed by the *Herald* in 1994. It was at the *Herald* that he first worked for Reuters. Jeff has attained various prizes in the Nikon awards, the British Picture Editors Guild, and the Scottish Press Photography Awards. He is currently with Reuters in Glasgow.

Peter Morgan

was born in 1955. He received his Bachelor of Science degree in Journalism from Boston University. With the exception of a four-year stint as a staff photographer with the AP in Philadelphia (1982–1986), he worked as a freelance photographer most of his life. First in New England, then in Latin America and New York. Peter started working with Reuters as an independent contractor in New York in 1992 and was hired as Senior Photographer in New York in 1998.

Kai Pfaffenbach

was born in 1970. After studying history and journalism, he began his news photography career in Frankfurt as a freelancer for the German newspaper *Frankfurter Allgemeine Zeitung*. Kai began working for Reuters as a freelance photographer in 1996 before becoming a staff photographer in 2001. He is currently based at Reuters, Frankfurt. He has been part of the team of photographers covering the disaster that struck New York on September 11, 2001.

Kelly Price

works for JP Morgan Chase in the financial district, near the World Trade Center. She watched her office window billow like a clothes-lined sheet from the shock wave after the planes hit, and then she immediately rushed down to the street. Kelly had previously worked for a photo archive and a magazine, so was interested in documenting what was happening. "I didn't believe that I would outrun the wave [of debris] so I stopped and began shooting.... When the cloud of debris entangled me, I was relieved that I was still alive."

Brad Rickerby

was born in 1958. He received his Bachelor of Arts degree in Political Science from Reed College in Portland, Oregon, in 1980. He received his Master of Business Administration degree from Duke University in Durham, North Carolina, in 1989. Brad has worked for Reuters in New York for the past five years and has been a photographer for *Reuters World Magazine*. In addition to working for Reuters, he has shot conceptual advertising and travel stock images for Stone and the Image Bank.

Jim Ruymen

was born in 1943. He has covered the Los Angeles area for 20 years, photographing Hollywood events and awards ceremonies, such as the Oscars; sporting events, including the NBA Finals and the World Series; the criminal trials of O.J. Simpson and Charles Keating; and world news events, such as the Space Shuttle landings. He began stringing for Reuters in January 2001.

Mike Segar

was born in 1961. He received his Bachelor of Arts degree in American Studies in 1985 from Boston University and received his Masters in photojournalism in 1989 from the International Center of Photography. Mike worked as a staff photographer for the Beacon Newspapers chain in Massachusetts. He later joined the Black Star Photo Agency as an associate news picture editor. Mike joined Reuters as a contract photographer in 1991 and has since covered a full range of news, sports, political, and feature assignments throughout the U.S.

Tim Shaffer

resides in Wilmington, Delaware, where he provides photo coverage for the Philadelphia metropolitan area. He has worked 11 years as a freelancer for AP, three years on staff with Independent Newspapers Chain, has been a contributor to *The New York Times*, *The Philadelphia Inquirer*, and the *The Daily News*. He has worked as a contractor for Reuters in Philadelphia since June 1998. Since then he has participated in Reuters coverage of the Republican National Convention in 2000, as well as the 2000 NBA Finals.

Bryan Snyder

was born in 1968. He received his Bachelor of Fine Arts degree and Bachelor of Arts degree from Tufts University. He has covered various U.S. presidential campaigns, the 1994 World Cup, the death of John F. Kennedy, Jr., and the 1994 Women's Clinics shootings. He has been covering assignments for Reuters since 1989.

Ruben Sprich

was born in 1967. His main area of study was publicity photography. He began his career as photographer in Switzerland for the AP, then became a freelancer for Reuters in 1991, as well as working for various other newspapers and magazines. In 1998, he became Chief Photographer for Reuters, Switzerland, based in Zurich. Ruben has covered a variety of events in Switzerland, including the Olympics, soccer, ski, and track and field world championships.

Shannon Stapleton

was born in 1968 in Ft. Bening, Georgia. He graduated from Ohio State University in 1992 and took graduate classes in photojournalism at Ohio University. Shannon started freelancing for Reuters in March 2001. Prior to that, he freelanced in New York City. He has covered assignments including the war in Kosovo, Sierra Leone amputees, and rap artists in the Brownsville section of Brooklyn. Shannon is currently based in New York City.

Ray Stubblebine

was a staff photographer for the AP from 1971–1987, covering sports and news events. Ray was also on the crew that covered the Jonestown Massacre in Guyana, and he covered part of the "Iranscam" congressional hearings for *New York Newsday*. Since 1988, he has been a full-time contract photographer for Reuters, based in New York, where he has covered many sporting and political events.

Rick Wilking

was born in Madison, Wisconsin, in 1955. His first job as a photographer was for UPI in Denver, Colorado. He moved to Brussels in 1982 and was promoted to be UPI's Chief Photographer, Switzerland, in 1983. He joined Reuters in 1985 and was made Senior Photographer for Reuters in Washington, D.C., in 1989. Rick resigned from Reuters in 1998 and moved back to Denver where he is a freelance photographer.

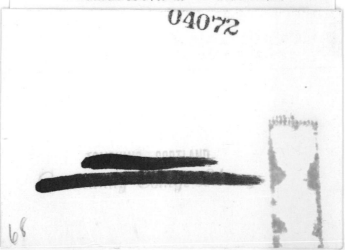

LOST SOLDIERS

The French Army and Empire in Crisis
1947–1962

LOST SOLDIERS

The French Army and Empire in Crisis

1947–1962

GEORGE ARMSTRONG KELLY

THE M.I.T. PRESS

Massachusetts Institute of Technology
Cambridge, Massachusetts

04072

In memoriam

AGNES DICKSON STEWART

1874–1964

PREFACE

The present work should be taken neither as an apology for actions which history has already treated harshly nor as an attempt to fix events in a frozen aspic of political science. I have wanted, above all, to describe and explain the crossing of multiple lines of force without the luxury of *parti pris* or the consolation of righteousness. My active interest in the tensions of the French Army began while I was living in France in 1957; the writing was carried out at intervals while I was a Research Fellow of the Harvard University Center for International Affairs in 1961–1964; some retouchings are more recent. It should be understood that the narrative stops at the close of 1962.

I am sad to be able to offer only collective thanks to many friends for kindnesses of all sorts. However, particular gratitude is due the following, who are responsible for some of my insights but none of my shortcomings:

Stanley Hoffmann, Professor of Government at Harvard University, who shared his vast and fine intelligence with me at many points.

Henry Kissinger, Professor of Government and faculty member of the Center for International Affairs at Harvard, to whom I owe the genesis of an enduring concern for world politics and much else.

Jean Planchais, the brilliant military correspondent of *Le Monde,* whose communications were indispensable on a number of sticky issues.

Daniel Lerner, Ford Professor of Sociology at the Massachusetts Institute of Technology, whose comments on the manuscript led me to useful revisions.

Stephen Graubard, Editor of the American Academy of Arts and Sciences and of *Daedalus,* an old friend and shrewd critic.

Donald Blackmer, Associate Director of the M.I.T. Center for International Studies, whose counsel and experience were of great benefit.

I deeply appreciate the collaboration of Audrey Ball, Sandra Kinyon, Ann James Paden, Janicelee Arvan, and Mary Mitchelson, who, *à longueur d'années,* turned my Linear A into clean copy.

I have been kindly granted permission by the respective editors to incorporate portions of my own articles which have appeared elsewhere, notably: *Political Science Quarterly* (Academy of Political Science), September 1961 (pp. 367–392), and September 1964 (pp. 335–359); *Orbis* (Foreign Policy Research Institute of the University of Pennsylvania), Fall 1960 (pp. 284–306), and Summer 1962 (pp. 311–324); *The Review of Politics* (Notre Dame University Press), July 1963 (pp. 291–308); and *The New Republic,* February 19, 1962 (pp. 12–16).

I am likewise indebted to Editions Inter-Nationales (Paris), publishers of Jacques Dinfreville's *L'Opération Indochine,* for the map appearing on page 50; to Librairie Plon (Paris), publishers of Serge Bromberger's *Les Rebelles algériens,* for the map appearing on page 170; to the editors of *L'Armée* (Paris), successor to *Revue des Forces terrestres,* the publishers of General Tabouis's "La lutte psychologique en Algérie" (April 1957), for the organizational chart shown on page 187; to the Presses Universitaires Françaises (Paris), publishers of *La Défense nationale,* for the long quotation from Colonel Lacheroy's essay "La guerre révolutionnaire," appearing on page 109; to Librairie Gallimard (Paris) for the passage from Albert Camus's *La Peste* which heads my Chapter XVI, page 330; and to the publisher of *Le Monde* for extensive reference to the reporting of that newspaper throughout.

Frances, my wife, deserves to be told once more how much the sanity of her suggestions and the force of her sympathy have meant.

G.A.K.

Cambridge, Massachusetts
April 1965

CONTENTS

CONTENTS

Chaque fois que l'occasion s'en présente, faisons justice.

— P.-J. Proudhon

PART ONE

BEGINNINGS

I

INTRODUCTION:
THE ARMY IN ETERNAL
AND CHANGING FRANCE

La plus belle armée que la France ait jamais connue depuis
Napoléon.
> — *General Charles de Gaulle circa 1957*

L'unité de l'armée ne réside plus que dans le désespérance.
> — *General Maurice Challe, at his trial*

For FIFTEEN YEARS the French Army was torn to its depths by conflicts
it had neither the means nor the luck to surmount, heaped with abuse
it did not merit, and led to react in a way that was aberrant and dangerous but finally understandable. Stung by contradiction and betrayal
and seduced by intemperate demons partly of its own conjuring, this
was both an army of anguished loyalty and a seditious army. The history and rationale of the French Army's conduct are worth the pain to
unravel. Despite some obvious limitations of documentation it seems
important that what these events can teach us should not first be
recounted, years from now, in some quaint dead language of the
archives.

The purpose is not to judge individuals or an institution but rather
to expose the extraordinary push-pull of forces that impelled this army,

3

often unwillingly, toward a political vocation. In pursuit of this objective we begin to get a glimmer of an axiom which the times seem to be erecting: if political involvement is precarious and vitiating for a military group, the circumstances of modern politics permit no reliable rules by which the saving abstinence can be measured. What was once the forbidden fruit becomes, more and more, the daily bread.

"Sedition" is an ugly word. "Treason" is an even uglier one, and Republican France has not hesitated to accuse its citizens of treason in the interrupted hundred years of its existence.[1] But it is easier to charge than to convict, easier to label than to prove. Moreover, sedition and treason are apt to be loose words where "national" values often have difficulty in obtaining a firm national consensus, where the average politician must plod and temporize while the utopians of the permanent opposition dream of Revolution and Restoration. As Raymond Aron has put it: "From the moment when the fatherland is no longer defined in concrete terms, but rather by an ideology, it ceases to function as the supreme instance. It becomes the stake of factional conflicts."[2]

French history is full of examples of the competing demands of legality and legitimacy, of power and sovereignty. According to some jurists, the reign of Louis XVIII dates from 1795, despite the fact that for almost twenty years longer the Convention, the Directorate, and the Emperor Bonaparte held the real power in France. A more cogent and relevant illustration is the debate surrounding the passage of power from the Third Republic to Pétain's "Etat Français" in June 1940, and the questions affecting the legitimacy of de Gaulle's simultaneously created "France Libre." Here, clearly, the different juridical arguments will have in a sense ceded to conviction, to ideology, and to the course of events itself.

The Army in a Spectrum of Protest

The Army has been a unique, peculiar, and powerful instance of the long French tradition of extraparliamentary protest.[3] Its participation in political crisis in the 1950's was not, however, a unique event but rather an aspect of national protest conducted in a unique way. The

[1] As a result of the confused loyalties of World War II, the postwar French government opened 160,000 treason trials, of which 27,000 resulted in acquittal and 45,000 in dismissal of charges. There remained, therefore, 88,000 condemned traitors, of whom 7000 received the death penalty. Taken from statistics given by the *Garde des Sceaux* to the Justice Committee of the National Assembly, February 22, 1949, and cited by André Thérive, *Essai sur les trahisons* (Paris, 1951), p. xxxvii.

[2] Preface to Thérive, *op. cit.,* p. x.

[3] See Stanley Hoffmann, "Protest in Modern France," pp. 69–91, in Morton A. Kaplan (ed.), *The Revolution in World Politics* (New York, 1962).

mediocrity and inertia of the Fourth Republic, its tendency to fabricate consensus where none existed and to sink into continuous crisis when real issues were at stake, foreordained that wide extraparliamentary shock should affront the constitutional system. The sentiment of the *pays réel* was harshly sundered from that of the Assembly, above and beyond the tensions which the normal functioning of that system had engendered.[4] What distinguishes the Army in particular from other disenchanted groups (with some of which it made common cause) was that it had power and that its interests and dissents came to be focused rather sharply.

The personalist rule of today's Fifth Republic — unchallenged in matters of defense and foreign affairs — somewhat conceals the course that French politics has been pursuing for the last generation. The country has moved at least a snail's journey toward a form of corporatism in the sense that major political battles are scarcely any longer decided by parliamentary debate. Even if its members were capable, the Assembly is no longer, in Walter Bagehot's phrase, "in a position of perpetual choice." Rather — de Gaulle's personalism again excepted — this activity became transferred to Councils of Ministers, to conferences of the political groups and labor and agricultural unions, to spontaneous or organized protest movements, to technocratic planning, and to the elite interest groups. The Army's gestures in a political direction have been a part of this larger pattern as well as a consequence of its own exasperation and anguish. While a genuine pluralism has grown up, much richer and more complex than any mere class or occupational pluralism, this variety of aim and interest has found neither representation nor satisfaction within the political structure.[5] It has approached consensus only in horrified reflex to political dilapidation.

If we add to the implications of France's troubled political stability the whole perplexing cycle of "decolonization" and the nervous landscape of the East-West conflict pursued by a variety of means, we begin to establish the context in which the French Army discovered its own special anguish.

The outsider is doomed to the failure of approximation when he attempts to epitomize a military group, for an army is both shadow and substance, belief and performance, matter and spirit. It is com-

---

[4] See Raoul Girardet, *La Société militaire dans la France contemporaine, 1815–1939* (Paris, 1953); Paul-Marie de la Gorce, *The French Army* (New York, 1963); and Lt. Col. Mac-Carthy, "L'Armée française et la politique," *l'Armée,* February 1960, pp. 30–40, and March 1960, pp. 38–48.

[5] An excellent descriptive analysis of this problem can be found in Joseph Rovan, *Une idée neuve: la démocratie* (Paris, 1961).

posed of men arranged in obedience and discipline in what must seem either a useful or an anachronistic order, according to the point of view. Despite the rigor of its professional singularity and the primacy of certain guides to action, an army is itself a petty pluralism, and its conflicts cannot be isolated from the major issues of the nation. Invested with some of the stringency of the religious vocation, the purpose of an army is not to withdraw from the world but to furnish force in support of a certain worldly vision. Nonetheless, the break with civilian thinking can be fairly complete.

Organization

The French Army is not a simple affair. It is men and material and doctrine and combat. It involves the often hyperdramatic lives of men — their outward foes and inner demons, their accordance to and withdrawal of loyalty from leaders and principles. Their feeling is frequently best conveyed in memoirs and conversations, or in novels, like those of Hubert Bassot, Jean Lartéguy, and Georges Buis, where casern and mess hall, desert and jungle, attack and suspense become tangibly interwoven into the destinies of characters created for the purpose.

In concrete detail, this is a force — regulars, reserves, and conscripts — that rose gradually to a total of close to a million men (including Muslim troops) at the height of the Algerian War, a collection of lives gathered from all the departments of France and her overseas territories.

Organizationally, this mechanism was complex. In the French language the word *armée* refers to the idea of "military establishment." Thus there is the conventional tripartite division into army (*armée de terre*), navy (*marine* or *armée de mer*), and air force (*armée de l'air*). I shall be referring generally to the military establishment as a whole, though with greatest emphasis on the land army and with little or no reference to the naval forces. It is the danger of this linguistic confusion, rather than a perverse Hegelianism, that accounts for my capitalization of the word "Army" throughout.

In addition to the three traditional branches of the military service, which are known as "third category" troops and are under the orders of the Interservice Chief of Staff, the Minister of the Armed Forces (formerly the Minister of National Defense), and the Premier, there are two other varieties of troops which must be mentioned.

"First category" troops comprise the regular police, the so-called Gardes Républicaines and the Compagnies Républicaines de Sécurité. These are used, respectively, for normal processes of criminal investigation and apprehension, for ceremonial duties, and for the maintenance of public order. They are at the disposition of the Minister of the Interior.

"Second category" troops comprise the Gendarmerie Nationale, which is divided into territorial and mobile units. These troops have both police functions and the mission of internal territorial defense. They are normally commanded in peacetime by the Minister of the Armed Forces and amalgamated with specified third-category troops in an administrative network called the Défense Intérieure du Territoire (DIT). The latter becomes active rather than purely administrative only when martial law is decreed. Gendarmes may be loaned to other agencies of the government (such as Finance and Justice) as specific occasions demand. The confusion of assignment between the various types of troops was to lead to some of the most deplorable incidents of the Algerian War, and to create morale problems and bad blood between them.

Finally, in the *armée de terre* exclusively, there has been a distinction between the "colonial" and "metropolitan" branches, implying different terms of enlistment, different military units and tours of duty. The rivalry between the two sorts of service, as well as a higher and more tragic irony, is well expressed in the remark made by General Raoul Salan in the preliminary declaration of his trial in May 1962: "As opposed to the man who is asking your permission to kill me [that is, de Gaulle], I served most often outside the *métropole*. I wanted to be a colonial officer, and I became one." [6] However, since virtually all of the regular Army saw service in both Indochina and Algeria, this distinction need not be elaborated here.

What emerges most clearly from these discriminations is that the Army (military establishment) must be understood as a social organism dwelling in and drawing breath from the national milieu. Neither, as some partisans have charged, has it been an overseas mercenary force nor is it a mirror of France or of French political cleavage. It is a complex pluralist group, anxious to ensure its own rights and solidarity of action. Shaken to its roots in 1940 and torn again by struggles between conscience and consistency in November 1942, when the North African landings raised a new question of choice, the French Army's main concern from then on has been for its own fragile unity and *esprit de corps*. General Paul Ely, its former Chief of Staff, was the living symbol of this delicate balancing. With the Challist putsch of April 1961 this cycle, in a sense, came to an end.

[6] *Le Procès de Raoul Salan* (stenographic reproduction; Paris, 1962), p. 76.

Unity and Anguish

Many factors threatened the Army's unity in the decade and a half that I shall survey. But significantly there was one new tension that had an ambivalent cause-and-effect relationship with the widening cleavage between French military and civilian society. This was the Army's reanimated interest in politics, a result of dissatisfaction and disgust at the conduct of the civilian ruling groups, the experience of defeat in colonial wars, psychological alienation, and the very vitiation of forceful democracy in France that I have just touched upon.

The military man by nature forms a rather strict image of function and command. As he would expect a superior officer to fulfill the requirements of this image, he expects no less of the nation he serves and its civilian leadership. But in France the professional officer perceived a vision of chaos and loss of responsibility; he balked at serving this blurred image and sought to bring it into focus again. This, in simple terms, is an explanation for the Army's intervention in politics.

But the matter is very far from simple and is not, in its origin, a political issue at all. Desperation, which led in a significant number of instances to political interplotting, was born from the very nature of the military problem posed for the Army in Indochina and later in Algeria. The Army believed that this was not an insoluble problem but held that the personnel and conduct of the regime were rendering it insoluble. Stated very simply, the Army construed itself as being under orders to accomplish a mission that the regime was progressively thwarting through vacillation, ignorance, and duplicity. Since 1947 the French Army had been doggedly engaged in wars in which it had neither allies nor the active sympathy of many of the French people. The government had given orders to fight these wars, and presumably to win them; what the government had not furnished were the means or the compatible political direction.

The rest followed inexorably from this germinating bitterness. Once the national political image was recognized as displeasing, the debate over the image was tacitly but actively pursued in certain circles of the Army. Both the frustrations of the experience I have mentioned and the minute examination of the nature of the military struggle itself led to the terrain of doctrinal revision and, in extreme but influential cases, raised the question of ideology itself.

Revolutionary War and "Intoxication"

There is a term that will be recurrent throughout this inquiry, and it is critical enough to deserve mention at this point. Out of the sweat and agony of the Indochina conflict came a notion known as *la guerre révolutionnaire*.[7] It professed to be a way of seeing the world in an integral political and military sense, and it included concepts reputedly borrowed from the Marxist enemy. If the battle as well as the stakes and conditions of the battle could be seen in terms similar to those understood by Communist doctrine, so the argument ran, the enemy's strategy could be frustrated.

La guerre révolutionnaire postulated coincidences of design and strategy between Indochina and Algeria and most of the other low-threshold or subversive outbreaks since World War II — such as Greece, Iran, the Philippine Islands, and Malaya. They were held to be diverse irruptions of a unique disease: the worldwide Communist conspiracy, present and destined to command wherever the traditional positions of the West were being threatened. When the Algerian War took shape — despite the insistence of many that this was an inchoate nationalism struggling for identity — the proponents of *la guerre révolutionnaire* would claim that it was an incarnation of the Soviet menace. Jean Planchais, the military correspondent of *Le Monde,* described this attitude vividly: "General Calliès, Inspector-General of the armed forces in North Africa, scarcely ever moves about without a world map where he has drawn a large black arrow, which, issuing from the depths of Red Asia, pushes its point as far as the Maghreb."[8] Planchais himself wrote, while warning against swallowing the theory whole, "no one can dream of denying that *la guerre révolutionnaire* is a reality."[9]

If, in its most fanatic expression, *la guerre révolutionnaire* seemed unreasonable, it also contained many elements of truth, particularly when it referred to the methods by which the enemy waged war. In some cases, its analytical merits gave a free ride to its ideological follies. There were also precise psychological conditions that made the theory highly compatible with French national needs of morale and prestige. It defied the vast impersonality of nuclear war, in which France had then no capability, and it seemed to justify the formulation of strategies de-

---

[7] Because of its peculiar flavor, this term will often be used throughout the book in its French form, though it is originally owing to French translation from Chinese and English.

[8] *Le malaise de l'armée* (Paris, 1958), p. 54.

[9] "La septième arme doit-elle rester l'apanage des militaires?" *Le Monde,* August 23, 1958.

emphasizing the technical perfection of new weapons and statistical measurements of power. *La guerre révolutionnaire* claimed its essence from the war-politics continuum described by Clausewitz and opposed itself not to general nuclear war but to total peace. Peace, in the usually accepted sense, and *la guerre révolutionnaire* could be, indeed often were, coexistent. In *la guerre révolutionnaire* the judgment of leadership and the resourcefulness of small units became paramount, and this tendency seemed to restore morale by "reglamorizing" war. It became a compliment to the French soldier and his military organization to proclaim this initiative as a specific national aptitude vis-à-vis the atom-intoxicated Anglo-Saxons. As Colonel (now General) Nemo wrote in the *Revue de Défense nationale:* "The French Army is practically the only one to have encountered Communism in action in a vast land war of style and amplitude previously unknown [Indochina]. It can, therefore, open broadly the debate on the form of future war." [10] The doctrine of *la guerre révolutionnaire* was a result both of the analysis of combat experience and of institutional self-justification. And being a "global" theory that excluded nothing, it could not help but lead the Army in a political direction.

In Algeria, the extreme polarization engendered first by the military problem, secondly by the doctrinal observations that it elicited, and thirdly by the extension of these observations to politics in the search for effective means, became a deadly business with increasingly seditious overtones, producing the "psychological" atmosphere which the political scientist Maurice Duverger was later to label and deplore as *intoxication:*

The theories of psychological war repose on a fundamental contradiction. One claims to defend the West and the civilization it incarnates against the Communist totalitarian regime. But to assume that defense one wishes to suppress practically all freedom of thought within the Western camp, giving it the same spiritual unity as the Soviet camp, the same doctrinal uniformity, subjecting it to the same intransigence, the same totalitarianism. What remains then of the liberal and humane values that comprise the very essence of Western civilization? Nothing. What good does it do to fight in the name of a cause if one denies and destroys that which he justifies? . . . It is not a matter of replacing one "intoxication" with another, but simply of putting an end to all intoxication.[11]

Intoxication? Among a small number, certainly — those who became infatuated with the conspiratorial climate of Algiers or, beyond all immediate political design, with the mechanism so profoundly described in Dostoevsky's *Notes from Underground,* where "man . . . like a

[10] "La guerre dans le milieu social," *Revue de Défense nationale,* May 1956, p. 606.
[11] *Le Monde,* October 18–19, 1959.

chessplayer, loves the process of the game, not the end of it." Yet aspects of the "intoxication" became a calculating strategy, sustained by personal integrity, and difficult to abolish by the mere literary attack of fashionable left-wing journalists and intellectuals.

If at the turn of 1962 *la guerre révolutionnaire* no longer suited the mission of the French Army, there was no assurance that it would not capture other national armies in the future. There is nothing explicitly French about the theory except for its temporary expediency, discovered as wars of a certain character developed that did not respond to the typical military imagination.

Tomorrow, if the plans and predictions of General de Gaulle and his Minister of the Armed Forces, Pierre Messmer, come to fruition, there is to be a new Army, based in Europe and endowed with nuclear arms.[12] How successfully this new Army can be "Messmerized" is another problem to be dealt with in my conclusion. But what one knows is that if the Army described in these pages belongs to the near past, that past is terribly real and tangible, measured by fifteen years of continuous conflict. An Army that has been at war, and is not merely preparing for war or to deter war, is in a special situation. This is the Army I mean to discuss, an Army with a vivid past, a memory, a martyrology.

Summary

What will be perceived here is a complex chronology out of which specific facts can be established concerning the experience of an army, a pattern of events that might befall other armies. Though this is not an easy chronicle to trace, it is possible to grasp certain threads through a fifteen years' labyrinth. One of these is the global history of decolonization, on which I shall pass no judgment. Another is the ill fortune of national political institutions. A third is the psychology of military alienation from the civilian community. A fourth is the experience of defeat in ambiguous battle and, later, of conquest without victory. A fifth is the larger background of the Cold War. A sixth is the repudiation of military advice within the sacrosanct citadel of civilian government. A seventh is the impulsive preoccupation with doctrine or ideology and the temptation to bring it into the realm of practice. The last is the existence of one man — de Gaulle — without whom all the other things would have been very different.

I must pause for a moment at the last point, if only to distinguish between the Army's attitude toward the Fourth and Fifth Republics. Its

---

[12] See "L'armée de demain," *Revue des deux mondes*, February 15, 1962. There is an English translation in *Orbis*, Summer 1962, pp. 205–216.

responses *have* been very different. In the first case, the regime was broadly accused of endemic weakness and the inability to pull itself out of the morass. But the general reaction to de Gaulle's republic has been quite opposite. At first the Army hoped for understanding of its position from the regime it had helped to bring to power; within a year and a half it was harshly disabused of this notion. It never criticized the Fifth Republic for its lack of strength; rather it challenged the President for using this strength in an arbitrary, duplicitous, and ultimately unsound manner. I shall return at length to this argument in my conclusion.

This is the story of a reluctant groping toward sedition, of the agony of those who took arms against the regime or blackened its name from the witness stand, of the equal agony of those who, if anguished, nevertheless held back at the peril point. The motives of these actions are neither entirely pure nor entirely selfish; they are highly confused. A long and disordered road is traced between the surrender of Cao Bang and the capitulation of General Challe, a road that I attempt to retrace as best I can. First of all, let us glance into the past, to a time when the Army was called *la grande muette,* "the great silent one," abstemious of politics, contemptuous of the governing class, but unprepared to move against it.

II

AGONIES OF THE
GRANDE MUETTE

Nous autres, on ne pense à nous que quand il pleut.
— *Marshal Saxe*

THE PEACETIME role of the military forces has always been somewhat anomalous in the modern democratic state. The complexity of twentieth-century Western society, its pluralism of interests, and its lack of sharp divisions of function and command have prevented the easy absorption or accommodation of a professional element whose rules of life seem medieval, hierarchical, oversimplified by comparison with those of civilians. The regular military society has, most often, lived to itself and by its own peculiar values in enclaves half cut off from the temptations and bewilderments of the wider world. Yet, paradoxically, in time of danger the military has been called upon to lead in the defense of an order which its training has caused it to distrust and to understand very imperfectly.

To be sure, in recent times, armies have found themselves linked with the civilian world by a thousand new bonds; and their leaders have accepted these new relationships with reasonably good grace. In the conditions of modern total war, they have seen the conventional military forces almost swamped or pushed into the background by men who came from civilian pursuits to take a leading part in forging instruments that would have been doomed to defeat by relying exclusively on the old, time-honored skills and crafts. To maintain the vitality of their métier, they have recognized the enormous qualitative changes in the art of war brought about by the scientific revolution. So far as their intellectual training has made possible, they have studied these changes and their effects.

Professional officers have been accustomed to regard the Army as an instrument of force at the service of politics. Since World War I they have gradually grown aware of the dangerous possibility that it might be expected to become a blind and docile instrument, serving not broad national interests that appeal to all patriotic men but the interests of pressure groups or the demands of doctrines that are global in scope rather than expressive of the historical reality of the Nation. To see armies reduced from their proper concerns in this way was very troubling to those whose conception of armed combat was more old-fashioned and removed from ideology. In the twentieth century, when an army has been led to engage in propaganda on its own behalf, this has not been an attempt to reassess its function in the state as an abstract exercise. Rather it has been an attempt to defend itself against the erosion of its traditional place and privilege.

The relationship between military and civilian and the special tensions produced in the military mind when it finds itself in a civilian milieu pose problems in many countries. In some, however — the Anglo-Saxon countries, a half-dozen North European nations, and Switzerland — they rarely provoke debate or deep anxiety. They are more serious, however, along the Mediterranean and wherever Mediterranean civilization has spread, and in the politically unstable center of Europe. France exhibits some of the restraints of the first group (because of her long, if troubled, career as a democratic state) and much of the turbulence of the second group. Much of the sympathetic impulsion behind the recent activities of the French Army has come from a trans-Mediterranean population. Nevertheless, geography here is only a method of description, and the more valid reasons for the contemporary tension between State and Army in France must be sought in historical development and in the complex psychology of the postwar period.

Political-Military Equilibrium in the Third Republic

In a country renowned as the inventor of the "democratic Army," the *levée en masse,* and other military techniques that heralded a new age of surface warfare grounded in new concepts, the Army has never felt entirely comfortable in the service of "radical" democratic institutions. In the past this was a social rather than a political problem; those at the top of the military hierarchy had little but contempt for a bourgeois class that was making a commercial operation out of governing. Still, despite a series of rude shocks in the latter half of the nineteenth century, the Army made its uneasy peace with the state apparatus, on which it came increasingly to depend, and sought nonpolitical outlets for its superfluous energy. Of these, colonial adventure was the most conspicuous and profitable. At the same time, the State recognized the need for maintaining fighting forces adequate not only to defend the national territory and enlarge its interests abroad but even one day to execute the long-awaited *revanche* on Germany. Even among the militant Left of the turn of the century (where deep suspicions of military prerogatives were harbored) there were few thoroughgoing pacifists where the national interest was concerned. Pacifism as such would not flourish until the 1920's.

Jean Jaurès, the pre–World War I Socialist leader, hoped to see the transformation of the Army into a new and revitalized organism that would act in the democratic perspective for "the organization of national defense and the organization of international peace." He may also have been the first to suggest authoritatively that there must be a close correspondence between the technical role and equipment of an army and the international policy that the nation as a whole was prepared to follow.[1] For Jaurès, naturally, there was no doubt that both missions should be construed defensively. Later, Paul Reynaud, as spokesman for the theories of a young Colonel de Gaulle, was to use the same argument in the opposite sense when he claimed that France's active policy of alliances (with Great Britain, Belgium, Poland, Czechoslovakia, Rumania, later Soviet Russia) demanded the construction of an elite motorized striking force to act offensively.[2]

However trenchantly it was argued before 1939 that there was an essential connection between diplomatic action and military preparation, almost no concerted effort was made to act as if they were connected. For this dissociation was itself a consequence of the *dépolitisation* of the Army, its explicit alienation from the productive political energies of the nation and from the governing class. Collaboration in theory between the two jurisdictions was unlikely where the practical divorce was so extreme. This accounts in part for the archaism of military strategy that was to lead to the disaster of June 1940. Cut off from the influence of rapidly changing political and social factors, the

[1] Jean Jaurès, *L'Organisation socialiste en France: l'Armée nouvelle* (Paris, 1915).
[2] Paul Reynaud, *Au coeur de la mêlée* (Paris, 1951), pp. 149–157.

Army high command transformed itself into an impregnable citadel and clung to doctrines that had been serviceable in bygone times. Barred from healthy communications with other national elements, the military leaders asserted their own primacy in a specialized field. Somewhat mystified by military affairs in any case and well content to leave matters as they were, the politicians of the Third Republic hastened to agree with them.

The alternative to this sterile escapism — which the young de Gaulle and others tried to surmount on a purely technical plane — would have been the reinvigoration of strategic thought through immersion in, and comprehension of, the wider complexities of interwar Europe and the challenges of industrialization and invention. This could have taken place only through the development of military cadres whose training would be more spacious and subtle than before and free from obsolete conventions of the past. Jaurès had recommended for his "new Army" an education based on high intellectual values and civic spirit that would transform the military force into an instrument for the propagation of democracy rather than a reflex against it. But if any re-education was going to take place, it was much more likely that it would ignore all appeals to Socialist principles. Although "depolitized," the Army as a whole deeply disapproved of the Left, which it equated with the government itself and held responsible for the weakening of the national sinew and the venality of political life. "Repolitization," if encouraged, would probably come in a form that transgressed against the convictions and inner harmony of the bourgeois Republic. Therefore, there was implicit agreement in political circles that the intellectual modernization of the armed forces was best avoided altogether. The high command was, in a sense, a hostage for the perpetuation of this immobility; for the leading generals recognized that they could be deposed or exalted in the measure that they antagonized or served the government of the day. This is not to say that they abandoned professional principle lightly, but they showed little inclination to venture down new paths, and they imposed sanctions on those of their subordinates who were not so cautious.

The Army, if psychologically hostile to the Third Republic, salved its conscience by the exercise of viceregal prerogatives throughout the French "Empire." It played its role of *grande muette* to perfection. If there was a profound distrust between the politician and the soldier, neither really invaded the other's realm according to the long-established rules of the Third Republic game. In fact, much of the mutual abuse and recrimination was simply *pro forma*.

For a number of very specific reasons the "repolitization" of the

Army, when it finally came, years after an intervening national catastrophe, was to be the work of those most immersed in the colonial experience rather than those whose perspectives were essentially European, like the heroes of 1914–1918. Much of this may be attributed to the fact that the action of the Free French Army in World War II had been from the periphery of the "French Empire" toward the center, from Brazzaville and Diégo-Suarez through Algiers to Paris. But the traditional structural distinction between "metropolitan" and "colonial" branches of the Army will not serve here, and is confusing. In the first place, for reasons of political organization that are well known to all, Algeria, which was later to see the apogee of the Army's political discontent, was included in the "metropolitan" military sphere, as were Tunisia and Morocco. Secondly, by the time a maximum of force levels had been achieved in Algeria in 1957, metropolitan and colonial officers alike had virtually all seen service in peripheral revolutionary war. The image to retain, however, is that both World War II and its protracted aftermath of conflict produced in the military mentality a physical and spiritual alienation from continental France and a disposition to regard the colonial presence as a symbol of national greatness.

The majority of the military leaders reaching stature in the late 1950's had cut their teeth and won their palms, not on the Meuse or the Somme or the Rhine, but rather in the rice paddies of Tonkin and the djebels of Algeria. This was the deeply etched experience they carried with them. It would prove to have little in common with the Carolingian perspective of the one general on the service list — de Gaulle — who, conspicuously, had never served or fought in either Indochina or North Africa. This distinction is by no means trivial, though it bears little resemblance to the prewar military pattern, to which we now return.

Despite the ever-increasing power of disaffected veterans' organizations such as the Croix de Feu, the appearance of the sinister Cagoule,[3] and the penetration of the ranks of the serving Army by swelling antirepublican sentiment during the 1930's, the period actually saw much close, if not devoted, collaboration between leading politicians (mainly the Radicals, who were a part of every combination) and a good many military chiefs. This was done for the self-interest of both groups, as a means of career advancement, and as a part of the complex *quid pro quo* of Third Republic politics. If there was a danger of military discontent, it was not genuinely grave or well articulated. General Gamelin

[3] It appears that there were some connections between the Cagoule, a nationalistic-Sorelian conspiracy of activists, and the aging Marshal Franchet d'Esperey. The retired heroes of France were characteristically more dangerous to the regime than the serving ones. For evidence, see Jean-Raymond Tournoux, *L'Histoire secrète* (Paris, 1962), pp. 376–379.

could write in his memoirs: "I was definitely classed by certain people as the military chief who would never let himself be dragged into an elaborate combination against the legal government: they wanted to bar my access to the supreme post or get rid of me at the earliest occasion."[4] But Gamelin never conjectures how powerful the "certain people" might have been, and his own career and friendly association with Edouard Daladier show that his analysis was on the gloomy side. Even General Weygand, the *alter ego* of the French Army during the period, though obviously out of sympathy with the political institutions of the country, seems never to have had a close relationship with any groups that were inclined toward *coup d'état* and, according to the best evidence, was even unaware of the confused political planning that preceded the right-wing riots of February 6, 1934.[5] Pétain owed much of his political strength and prestige to the mistaken notion that he was a "republican general." And when Colonel de Gaulle and his political ally, Paul Reynaud, as "Young Turks," fought their losing battle for the elite mechanized corps — and the implications of such a step — they were stopped by the combined opposition of Daladier and the General Staff. Politicians of any importance had their collaborators somewhere in the upper military echelons, and the fortunes of the latter followed those of the former with a fairly rigorous consistency. The "outsiders," who shouted vengeance and retribution from the platforms of the ex-servicemen's clubs, did not run the Army.

Defeat and Reconstruction

The stable but stultifying equilibrium was destined to last no longer than any of the other institutionalized forms that came crashing down after the defeat by the Germans and the birth of the Vichy regime. It had done great disservice to France not only by choking off those new and salutary ideas that could have raised the quality of thought among the military leaders, but by obscuring the military catastrophe of 1940 through the excuse of loyalism and the orderly and constitutional transfer of power, which Pierre Laval's rigged assembly was held to have achieved. For some years after June 1940, leading French military figures — perhaps best exemplified by Weygand — shielded themselves casuistically from the effects of the intense injury that their organization had suffered. But neither the causes nor the extent of the wound could

---

[4] Maurice Gamelin, *Servir* (Paris, 1946), Vol. II, p. 109.

[5] See Maxime Weygand, *Mémoires* (Paris, 1957), Vol. II, *Mirages et Réalité*, p. 409. Also, Max Beloff, "The Sixth of February," in *St. Antony's Papers*, No. 5 (New York, 1959), p. 32.

be so lightly overlooked. The Allied landings in North Africa in November 1942 resurrected the question vividly for all those who, loyal to the Marshal in 1940, had sat in numb but guilty meditation during the intervening years. Survivors of the defeat then began to troop back in increasing numbers to the tricolor, on which was now embossed the Cross of Lorraine, some bearing the ghost of the old attitude (of which General Giraud's "Moi, je suis militaire; je ne fais pas de politique" may be considered the classic example); but their shaky preference for the old way of doing business would not ultimately commend itself to a new Army forged piece by piece out of the shattered remnants of the old and wedded to the political consequences of its origin.

This new Army, heroic in its achievements and dear to its creator, General de Gaulle, was nevertheless a crazy, patchwork thing. The prestige of Pétain, Weygand, and others, combined with the unmistakable social and political orientation of the officer caste of the period, had been sufficient to associate the bulk of the leadership with the side of defeat and betrayal. A certain number of these leaders — of whom by no means all were in sympathy with the political initiatives of Vichy, but who in great majority had approved the Marshal's action in taking France out of the war — were rehabilitated by incorporation in the Free French forces after the North African landings. However, many others who waited too long, either through conviction or caution, were quietly retired from service at the close of hostilities. The missing ranks were filled by Gaullist promotions and by the prudent assimilation of elements of the Forces Françaises de l'Intérieur and others of the civilian underground. The latter were first politically weakened by dispersed integration, and later, when the Cold War began, systematically kept out of the higher echelons of the regular forces.[6]

Even before they had had time to consider the position of the new Army in a peacetime situation, military men were gnawed by second thoughts about its legitimacy, its function in the new France, and its relations with Frenchmen at large. Basically colonial rather than metropolitan in experience, the new military leaders reacted uneasily toward the civilian population and occasionally toward the irregular guerrilla forces of the French Underground, which, because of different political orientations, were not themselves especially harmonious. Frequently they misconstrued the aims of the Resistance fighters (who would have preferred to see an Army refashioned along the lines of Jaurès), and, in

[6] Cf. Alexander Werth's résumé of a release by Jules Moch, then Minister of Defense, to the Anglo-American press in early 1951: "Moch . . . again assured his audience that there were only *three* Communist lieutenant-colonels in the French Army, and none above that rank, and that they were being most *carefully* watched." *France, 1940–1955* (New York, 1956), p. 508.

turn, were distrusted and misunderstood by members of the Resistance. The feeling of isolation that the Gaullist Army was already experiencing is nowhere better evoked than in the passage where de Gaulle describes his tour of the front in late 1944 and his communication with General (later Marshal) de Lattre:

> The commander of the 1st Army reported to me that depression was infecting the minds of his subordinates. He attributed this crisis less to losses, fatigue, or the harshness of the winter than to the moral separation from the nation. "From one end of the command to the other," he wrote, "especially among the officers, the general impression is that the nation is ignoring and abandoning them." De Lattre went on: "Certain people even go so far as to imagine that the regular Army from overseas is being expressly sacrificed." He added: "The profound reason for this malaise lies in the failure of the nation to take part in the war." [7]

A prophetic utterance.

The malaise of de Lattre's Army in Alsace in 1944 was a passing mood, soon dissipated by the hysteria of Allied victory. But the mood was destined to return, because the victory was, from France's point of view, somewhat hollow. Nor was the difficulty of assimilating the Resistance fighters the only serious structural problem the postwar Army would have to solve. The simultaneous impact of social and technological renovation, coupled with the lingering atmosphere of guilt and inferiority vis-à-vis the Anglo-Saxons, was to take a fearful psychological toll from an institution that had seen its base all but destroyed and the legend of its heroism besmirched.

As the years passed, the new Army was being increasingly penetrated by new blood; both the experience of the war with its social interpenetration and the lowering of competitive standards for want of applications contributed to the transformation of cadres. The history of this phenomenon has yet to be written, but the tendency is widely acknowledged by numerous commentators.[8] In the Fourth Republic the politicians maintained a surer grip on commissions and promotions

[7] Charles de Gaulle, *Mémoires de Guerre* (Ottawa, 1960), Vol. III, *Le Salut*, pp. 148–149.

[8] See especially, "Essai sur la structure sociale de l'armée française," *La Nouvelle Critique*, No. 107, June 1959, p. 55: "Two facts are . . . characteristic: (1) The constant falling off of the number of candidates at the School of St-Cyr: 2452 candidates in 1939, 587 in 1959, 360 in 1954. At the same time the number of former students of the Ecole Polytechnique tends to become insignificant in the cadres of the so-called 'learned' branches of the Army, where they were formerly the majority: in 1913, the proportion of captains of artillery who were former polytechnicians was 53%, it fell to 11% in 1939, to 5% in 1953, to 1.5% in 1958. (2) The proportion in the cadres of the Army of officers advancing from the ranks, which is incessantly growing: if we take captains, the proportion has progressed from 5.4% in 1949 to 35.8% in 1958."

than before, and they were, by and large, determined that the composition of military hierarchies should in some measure reflect the new political life, of which *tripartisme*[9] was the temporary manifestation. The Minister of the Air Force was, in fact, during this period a Communist.

At the same time that necessity and conviction were producing a lower-echelon democratization of the officer corps (usually through advancement from the noncommissioned ranks), while the Gaullist and pre-Vichy elements of the upper echelons endured rubbing shoulders with difficulty, the majority of old military families came out of the war ruined, decimated, or disgraced. They were unable to maintain traditions that seemed suddenly superfluous. Nor were the scions of the upper bourgeoisie any more anxious to play their role: by this time they had largely renounced the romantic emulation of the *noblesse*, and had, in addition, discovered that war was a highly dangerous, unglamorous, and unremunerative pastime. The Ecole Polytechnique, which regularly before the war supplied at least a hundred officers a year to the services, now furnished three or four.[10] At the same time, deaths in the Indochina hostilities amounted to three fifths of the six classes that graduated from St-Cyr during that war.[11]

Thus, by the end of the Indochina conflict, it may have been correct to label a vocal "activist" segment of the French Army as *ultra*, but the term will need redefining. The new *ultras* were neither wistfully *maurrassien* nor royalist, but disillusioned, technical *ultras*, susceptible to dangerous political intervention but essentially uninterested in the political process as such. Their most extreme utterances were, to be sure, antirepublican. Colonel Lacheroy put it this way in 1954: "One will never insist enough on this point: propaganda directed from the base of a mild-mannered democracy loses nine tenths of its chances, while on the contrary it achieves its maximum efficiency from the base of a clean, hard [*pure et dure*] organization of parallel hierarchies."[12]

[9] The governing coalition of the PCF (Parti Communiste Français), the SFIO (Parti Socialiste-Section Française de l'Internationale Ouvrière), and the MRP (Mouvement Républicain Populaire) that collapsed in May 1947 to make way for the "third force."

[10] See J.-R. Tournoux, "A Proletarian Army," in *The Reporter*, XXII, No. 4 (February 18, 1960), p. 19.

[11] Jean Planchais, *Le malaise de l'armée* (Paris, 1958), p. 10. The official casualty figures for officers furnished to the National Assembly by Jean Letourneau, State Secretary for the Associated States (i.e., Indochina) are as follows: 24 (1945); 208 (1946); 184 (1947); 147 (1948); 137 (1949); 187 (1950); 127 (1951 through December 15). Total: 1014 officers killed in combat for the period. *Journal Officiel. Débats de l'Assemblée Nationale*, December 28, 1951, p. 10081.

[12] *Le Monde*, August 4, 1954.

As Jean Planchais has sagely observed to this author: "The most democratized armies are apt to be the most antidemocratic ones, at least in Europe."

Malaise

In view of the circumstances just described, the heterogeneous French Army was obviously hard-pressed to find motive, mission, or solidarity in the years of its reconstruction. There were now any number of dichotomies operating: old versus new, socially liberal versus socially retrograde, metropolitan versus colonial, total-war versus guerrilla-war strategists, nationalists versus Europeans, Gaullists versus anti-Gaullists, and so on. Undoubtedly it is the memory of this slow and uncertain recovery from major surgery that prompted General Ely, resigning as Chief of Staff in the chaotic days of May 1958 to proclaim to his subordinates: "Feeling as profoundly as I do the anguish which is yours today, I ask you, in the highest interests of France, to maintain, each in his place, the cohesion and unity of the French armed forces that are the supreme warrant of the national unity." [13] Many other commanders stressed the same point. As had been the case in 1942, they failed to tackle the problem of where duty theoretically lay. It was, in fact, no small achievement for the French Army to have discovered some measure of solidarity and a certain, though admittedly pathological, *esprit de corps* in the intervening years, seemingly *envers et contre tout*. But, then, it is said that misery loves company.

The ordeal of root-and-branch reconstruction in the meanest of circumstances would have been enough in itself to leave scars that could be healed only by time, stability, and new generations. But there was still worse, much worse, to come. France had hardly emerged from the most severe psychological strain of her history, a situation that had almost become a civil war disguised by the cloak of foreign occupation, when she was plunged into a series of colonial wars. They plagued her economy, caused the idealism of the Resistance to be offset by the rapacious venality of private interests, sapped her fighting strength in faraway struggles, and widened the grave chasm that already separated the nation and its bewildered Army.

The proof of the Army's ingrained propensity to neutrality is that even these things did not immediately produce the wish among its leaders for a "return to politics." They were, after all, professional career men first; and they had had their fingers burned too often. They

[13] Quoted from Serge and Merry Bromberger, *Les treize complots de 13 mai* (Paris, 1959), p. 247.

confined themselves for the time being to issuing explicit warnings to the government that it would be dangerous to sacrifice loyalty of the Army or to allow it to deteriorate into a second-rate instrument. The following passage may be considered an extreme early warning:

In principle the Army is charged with the external security of the country, and the police with its internal security. According to rule regular troops should not, under any pretext, be used to put down internal troubles. We know of no rule more hypocritical, for in France all regimes, including that of the Fourth Republic, have used the Army to defend themselves on the inside, and it is precisely when they have not had the Army at their disposal or when that Army has grown deficient that they have been beaten or turned out.[14]

The leaders were not in a position to seek the solution of *coup d'état*. If they could but master their military trade and function reasonably as a team, they were doing well. In the upheaval of the remodeling, with innumerable new assignments and promotions being made all the time by rapidly changing Ministers of National Defense, the high-ranking officers were initially shy of joining forces to fight the politicians. Moreover, in many cases, they were fighting each other, each one seeking to hitch his horse to the right wagon, his career to the right minister. Thus there were Catholic generals, Radical generals, even Socialist generals.[15] This situation bears a superficial resemblance to the political-military equilibrium of the 1930's; however, now the politicians were all but supreme, and the military leaders, except for giants like de Lattre, had no charismatic appeal to fall back on as had their semideified predecessors. The politicians took advantage of their opportunity to use the generals as pawns in complicated ministerial games. Thus, the humiliation of the military services was already well under way before the crushing blow of defeat in a strange, new kind of battle sent the more thoughtful of the leaders into deep and unrestrained meditation. Before this had happened, however, the exposure of the Revers-Peyré case[16] in 1950 had aroused enough passion among the military to ensure that henceforward most of the officer corps of the French services would entertain the profoundest distrust of the political mechanism of the Fourth Republic.

There were also many petty grievances contributing to the military malaise. Salaries were abysmally low; privileges of rank vis-à-vis the horde of civil servants of a semi-*dirigiste* state were ludicrous and

[14] Colonels Georges-André Groussard and Georges Loustaunau-Lacau, *Consuls, Prenez garde!* (Paris, 1952), p. 220. Loustaunau-Lacau was former operations chief of the Cagoule as well as a hero of the Resistance.

[15] Planchais, *op. cit.*, p. 34.

[16] See Chapter IV, pp. 65–70.

humiliating.[17] Relations between French soldiers of all ranks and their own civilian population had deteriorated immeasurably. As Raoul Girardet writes: "Less than ten years after the end of the [Second World] war the feeling that seems to dominate with regard [to the Army] in a very large sector of opinion is that of a rarely malevolent but willingly defiant indifference." [18] Then, at the highest echelons, the fight over the merits of the European Army was bitter, divisive, and inconclusive. Frenchmen were just learning that they were expected to be Europeans as well, and they were uncertain and belligerent as to the extent of their commitment. To be sure, there was the "glamorous" occupation of Germany (*la petite revanche*), "where the colonel, with his villa, gave receptions and the second lieutenants danced, as they had in earlier times." [19] Also, French commanders shared the defense of the West with their military allies. But these external contacts were themselves disillusioning. They revealed that the nation had lost much virtue and power compared with the Greats. At home there was the distracting experiment of Gaullism (1947–1952), which won many sympathizers in military circles but repelled others, and was threatening, once it came to power, to reward the faithful and punish the hesitaters.

Finally, there was Indochina and all its consequences that would later find their echo in Algeria.

Stirrings of Protest

Between these wars — or better, as one died away and the other flared up, for they are almost consecutive — the Army strode back into politics. The advance was sounded by the brilliant and dogmatic General Lionel-Max Chassin, a leading strategist and military author, who had commanded the French Air Force in Indochina and observed many specific factors that affected the outcome of that war. In a much-noted article in the *Revue militaire d'Information* published in 1954 he wrote in part: "It is time for the Army to cease being the *grande muette*. The time has come for the free world, unless it wishes to die a violent death, to apply certain of its adversary's methods. And one of these methods — probably the most important — resides in the ideological role which, behind the Iron Curtain, has been assigned to the military forces." [20] Again, two years later, the General enlarged on his thinking: "What can the Western nations do to avoid the accomplishment of

[17] Planchais, *op. cit.*, pp. 17–18.
[18] Raoul Girardet, *La Société militaire dans la France contemporaine, 1815–1939* (Paris, 1953), p. 322.
[19] Planchais, *op. cit.*, p. 25.
[20] *Revue militaire d'Information*, October 10, 1954, p. 13.

Mao's plan for world conquest? We must oppose a struggle based on subversion with the same weapons, oppose faith with faith, propaganda with propaganda, and an insidious and powerful ideology with a superior one capable of winning the hearts of men." [21]

The creation of the *idéologie nationale* proposed by General Chassin required the transformation or overthrow of the Fourth Republic. But this could not be said openly. Therefore, the "defense of the West" was called in as a euphemism. This does not mean that these military ideologists did not believe themselves genuinely attached to "Western values and traditions," but by "Western values" they understood the traditional values of France. Certainly, they did not mean any further extension of European supranationalism, especially if it involved the military forces, because that would have separated them even further from the nation whose essential and distinctive quality they believed themselves to embody as well as to protect.

The French military structure became increasingly prone to regard itself as the psychological homeland of the *pays réel,* from which all the rest was, more or less, a monstrous aberration. More and more, the Army was seen by its leaders, many of whom had once quarreled bitterly with each other, as the core of the renovation, the motive force in the reforging of national unity and purpose. It was not so much a question of the type of government, except among those of the extreme fringe; democracy was, apparently, the form most acceptable to that Occident which the military writers professed was at stake in the jungles of Tonkin, and they were not, after all, constitutional lawyers like Michel Debré. As Planchais has put it: "Republic, then, let it be, since that was apparently the spot situated geometrically between a fascism that had officially disappeared from the planet and communism. . . . But a Republic that knows what it wants. And, according to all appearances, this is precisely what it didn't know." [22]

There were, to be sure, more genuinely "republican" generals than this — a handful of them — who intellectually resisted the consequences of their distress and who would neglect to express their sympathetic solidarity in May 1958.[23] But they were a small minority who commanded little solid admiration in the middle ranks of the officer corps,

[21] "Vers un encerclement de l'Occident," *Revue de Défense nationale,* May 1956, p. 548.

[22] Planchais, *op. cit.,* p. 8.

[23] For example, the Brombergers, *op. cit.,* p. 379, cite General Gilliot, military commander of the district of Marseilles, as one who refused Salan's overtures for "Operation Resurrection" (the projected *coup d'état* in the *métropole*). Other leaders were lukewarm, and certain influential persons were not even sounded out. However, the government doubted the loyalty of even the CRS (Compagnies Républicaines de Sécurité), and the Socialists more than once spoke wistfully of arming the workers.

and it would be no task whatever to neutralize or isolate these convictions when the great ground swell of indignation finally burst forth. It would always be more convenient to be removed from the scene of the battle, and keep one's nose clean. Both those personally involved and those professionally disinterested were to receive promotions, without apparent bias and with a sage concern for unity, when de Gaulle returned to power.

Common goals were accepted by leaders of the three services in the period 1956–1958, though most reluctantly by the Navy, which had been badly singed by its political associations with Vichy. Without venturing toward too specific an analysis of how these goals were to be achieved, if at all, or even whether their realization would require the magical intervention of General de Gaulle (who, contrary to a myth outstanding at one time, has not been loved in military circles), the service leaders were broadly agreed on the following points: (1) that the existing regime needed a radical reshaping and a change of direction bolstered by constitutional guarantees of stability; and (2) that the moral fiber of the nation as a whole was in serious need of reinforcement. The corollary of these arguments was that the military organization seemed the only coherent group fitted to take the lead. Governments seemed condemned to increase in fragility and lack of moral stature, and the spirit of the nation seemed constantly threatened with slow decay, without the real possibility that anything could or would be done about it. It was into this breach that the advocates of new techniques with political implications eventually stepped with both a plan and a method, and this in great measure explains why, contrary to normal experience, the younger officers were temporarily so successful in imposing a number of views on their superiors and elders.

Total War and Total Politics

The supreme irony of the situation described here is perhaps that, regardless of the many particular events of the decade 1945–1955 which impelled the French Army to seek a political orientation, broad circumstances affecting international relationships, the nature of total war, and the evolution of the modern state were pointing in the same direction.[24] Defense policy had become in the fullest sense national policy, and any artificial separation between the two, which was characteristic of "depolitization," could no longer be tolerated. If there had been less unwillingness on the part of self-styled defenders of "liberal in-

---

[24] For an analysis of this problem, see Maurice Mégret, "Fonction politique de l'armée," in La Défense nationale (Paris, 1958), pp. 133–182.

stitutions" in France to make a place for the military in the national society and to recognize that an element of such potential influence can be neither kept from prominence nor ignored, an orderly plan for reintegration might have been achieved. (This plan would have been neither that of Jaurès nor the one that imposed itself so precipitously in 1958, but something both humane and plausible.) Instead of feeding its cadres heavy doses of an indoctrination which, if not seditious, was at least perilously at odds with the ambiguous mystique of the government, the Army might have been willing to co-operate in a genuine national enterprise of renovation, one in which the soldier and the syndicalist, the farmer and the shopkeeper could have rubbed shoulders. Some sort of unity between the intellectuals of France — the group most deeply suspicious of all aspects of the Army — and the most intelligent military leaders, who, no less than the *lycée* and university professors, must today be men of knowledge and vision, might have been forged. Instead, the Army attained real camaraderie only with elements of the population that harmed its real interest and vocation, in particular the settlers of Algeria, who, anxious for their patrimony, willingly ignored all else. The intellectuals, with remarkable lack of foresight, attacked all military prerogatives indiscriminately, proving themselves as guilty of unrationalized passion and traditional prejudice as any other social element.

At moments the Army was seen as the vessel containing the most precious values of the national heritage, the mold in which the nation itself might profitably be pressed. Others denied it the right to speak for the nation at all and heaped callous ignominy on its undeserved anguish. This, one might say, was an inevitable turn of politics, which thrives on disagreements concerning the nature and purpose of man and his group activity and countenances duplicity as easily as honor in the pursuit of goals.

For "apolitism" was dead in a country and a world where politics at every turn transcended the limited range of "liberal" institutionalized forms. A "total" politics had developed as the logical complement of "total war." The curious persistence in ignoring this fact and going on the assumption that things could proceed as they did in less dangerous decades only retarded the development of a new and humane art of politics over which all shoulders should be bent in desperate labor. It resulted in a situation in which a politically conscious and biased group brought forth systems and ideas that were malformed and unstable because they were not the product of co-operative labor. This was the danger in national renovation flowing from a single source, especially one that had no unchallengeable popular credentials.

27

PART TWO

INDOCHINA

III

LA SALE GUERRE:
BACKGROUND

... vraiment ... le Tonkin ... n'a jamais excité l'opinion
que pour se faire maudire. Et pourtant il s'y est dépensé autant
d'héroïsme qu'en Algérie, avec un pays aussi rude, un climat
plus meurtrier. Mais personne ne l'a chanté, illustré, et c'est
une grande injustice.
— *Marshal Lyautey, letter from Tonkin, 1895*

FRANCE HAS many aspects for its idolators. The aspect that is foremost
depends greatly on France's momentary position in history: *la France
conquérante, la France vigilante, la France héroïque, la France
généreuse,* and a multitude of others.

In May 1954 the statesmen of the tottering Laniel cabinet were
striving frantically to communicate the legend of *la France héroïque* to
a stunned population. A by no means obscure battle (since some thought
it had almost precipitated World War III) but one that was little understood had just ended halfway around the world. No one doubted
that the defenders of Dien Bien Phu were heroic, but it took a flexible
imagination to assign heroism to those who had determined that the
battle should take place. If the names of Colonel de Castries (promoted
to General) and Geneviève de Galard ("the angel of Dien Bien Phu")
were on the lips of all, it was clear that Army and Nation had suffered

an unparalleled defeat. Surely the exasperating, grisly war that had been fought since 1947 across the marshes, rice paddies, jungles, and plateaus of Tonkin was approaching its ignoble end, for no government would now be able to support its continuation. The soldiers caught in that isolated valley by the heavy artillery of General Giap and forced back inch by inch into an indefensible perimeter a thousand yards wide were heroes, alive or dead. But the pacification had failed utterly: peace instead would come, a peace without honor.

When Premier Joseph Laniel and his Minister of National Defense, René Pleven, betook themselves to the hallowed arch on April 4, 1954, to propitiate the heroism of the last battle of a lost war, they had their shins kicked piously by some infuriated activists who professed to be "Anciens d'Indochine" (veterans). The honorary president of this organization was, coincidentally, General Raoul Salan, a former Commander in Chief of the theater. Not surprisingly, the police were slow to come to the aid of their hard-pressed chiefs; they were already heavily infiltrated by the antirepublican propaganda of ex-Commissioner Jean Dides. Pleven, who had made a tour of Indochina in February and, it appears, finally perceived the hopelessness of the French position after years of militantly espousing the "pacification," may have been inwardly prepared for the affront.[1] Laniel may not have been surprised, either; he had had his dignity ruffled on other occasions.[2]

The Unknown Indochina

The realities of Indochina, half a world away, had dawned on the French people very gradually.[3] In the early years this had been a terrain for professionals, experts, and opportunists, with even the average politician ignorant of the situation or not much interested — certainly not well-informed. The Army that fought there was a tough, motley group of careerists, Africans, and legionnaires (including ex-SS troops of the Third Reich, as the Communists and men like Claude Bourdet were fond of pointing out). They were officered by the flower of young St-Cyrians and generaled by some of the most impressive heroes of the war: Salan, Valluy, de Lattre, Boyer de Latour, Cogny, Navarre.

[1] But see J.-R. Tournoux's vigorous defense of Pleven, "l'honnête homme du XVIIIe siècle," *Secrets d'Etat* (Paris, 1960), p. 28.

[2] Notably at the Bermuda conference of December 1953, where protocol easily extended to President Eisenhower and Prime Minister Churchill was withheld from Laniel on a number of occasions.

[3] Cf. Jacques Fauvet, *La Quatrième République* (Paris, 1959), p. 55: "Government power was feeble, changing every six months, incapable of defining a policy clearly and overseeing its execution. Opinion was indifferent, more preoccupied with its daily bread than with a distant conflict."

Later, serious attempts would be made to fashion a substantial Viet-namese fighting force led by its own officers — on the model of the Americans in Korea. In part, this war could be ignored, even though it cost 250,000,000,000 francs a year (old-style, 1952 rate of exchange), as long as it remained professionally isolated. But with the increasing threat that soldiers of the *contingent* (draftees) might have to be sent, it became a public affair and entered the domain of national politics with a vengeance. This threat was to linger importantly in the back-ground of Pierre Mendès-France's race against the clock at Geneva in June–July 1954, after he had come to power with the unenviable task of washing the dirty linen of previous governments and concluding the hostilities.

But in 1947, when something could and should have been done about Indochina in the way of political settlement, few knew anything about the circumstances of the region, and fewer cared. Fewer still recognized the incredible difficulties of fighting a war there. The late General Jean Leclerc, who had been sent to negotiate the French out of a per-ilously weak position in Southeast Asia at the close of World War II, had warned strenuously against any action that might prompt the cohorts of Ho Chi Minh (then the *de facto* government in Tonkin) to take to the *maquis*.[4] But his advice had fallen on deaf ears. His mission had furthermore been compromised from the start by the activities of that other eminent Gaullist emissary, Admiral Georges Thierry d'Argenlieu, the High Commissioner of Indochina, who was reli-giously supporting a "tough" policy, seconded in his efforts by the Colonial Office (Ministère de la France d'Outre-Mer).

What was this Indochina where France had determined to fight a war?[5] A country of contrasts, if you considered it from a geographer's point of view, for it incorporated both highlands and lowlands, plain, mountain, marsh, and jungle. But this analysis is, in effect, quite mis-leading, since the soldier does not cover terrain like an eagle: he per-ceives only the small spot where he is rooted. This spot was apt to be marshland or rice paddy, where one sank up to his neck and had to guard besides against minefields and ambushes of a hidden enemy. If

---

[4] Jacques Dinfreville, in *L'Opération Indochine* (Paris, 1952), p. 169, quotes from the Leclerc report (April 1946) as follows: "Given the size of the country and the im-portance of its population, the idea of maneuver has always been to take and hold the necessary, nothing more; otherwise France would be drawn into an adventure exceeding present capabilities. . . . The ambitions of this country in the age in which we live should correspond to available means, or else we will have catastrophe. Better to hold half or a third of it solidly than the whole of it feebly."

[5] A good ethnographic and geographic description of the area called "Indochina" may be found in André Leroi-Gourhan and Jean Poirier, *Ethnologie de l'Union française*, Vol. II (Paris, 1953), pp. 515–678.

not, it was most likely jungle — covering three quarters of the land surface — a jungle such as Malraux describes:

Amid the welter of the leafage heaving with scaly insects only the spiders kept steadfast vigil, yet some vague resemblance linked them, too, with the other insects — the flies and cockroaches, the curious little creatures with heads protruding from their shells crawling upon the moss — with the foul virulence of bacterial life seen on a microscopic slide. . . . Here what act of man had any meaning, what human will but spent its staying power? Here everything frayed out, grew soft and flabby, tended to assimilate itself with its surroundings. . . .[6]

Heroism alone, even combined with great resourcefulness, was not enough to conquer the climate, the pestilence, the turbulent terrain, and the unorthodox tactics of an indigenous enemy. Moreover, by 1951, the border with Communist China assured an inexhaustible supply base from which badly needed motor vehicles — some captured from the Americans in Korea, others produced in Czech factories — and the heavy guns that were to seal the fate of Dien Bien Phu could reach the flexible forces of the Viet Minh.

Postwar Confusion

The confusions of the application of French policy in Indochina went back to the regime of de Gaulle, even though by the time the Far Eastern crisis was festering seriously the General had already retired to his village in stoic discouragement.

On the one hand, France had come out of the disaster of World War II with territorial good fortune. The Free French movement had been peripheral rather than nuclear, rallying to itself numerous dependencies and possessions even before its network in the *métropole* was fully established. Consequently, practically all the prewar colonies rejoined France in 1945. Indochina was a rather special case. Distant from all other French influence, especially from the physical capability of de Gaulle's Army, and subject from 1942 on to the menace of Japanese intervention, it had remained a Vichyite pocket. Admiral Decoux, Pétain's Governor-General in the region, had maneuvered adroitly to preserve all that was possible of the French "presence," flattering the Japanese with enough territorial privileges to make total occupation of the country unnecessary, jollying the settlers with a fluent exploitation of the Pétain myth, initiating certain reforms to placate the natives and mitigate "Co-Prosperity Sphere" propaganda, and generally apply-

[6] André Malraux, *La Voie Royale* (*The Royal Way*), translated by Stuart Gilbert (New York, 1935), pp. 101–102.

ing the axiom *divide et impera*.[7] Against the confused background of Japanese intervention, future Chinese aspirations, and a motley of national groups — not least among them Ho Chi Minh's Communists — Gaullism had little chance to take spontaneous root. Only later would it be imposed by force of arms. But de Gaulle was determined to keep Indochina.[8]

On the other hand, de Gaulle and France were vexed by the abrupt relinquishment of the Levant. The British, who had intruded rather brashly into a sphere that was not felt to be germane to their interests, were branded as culprits. It was feared that they, or the United States, might similarly interfere in Indochina if France did not rush to reassert her claims in the boldest possible manner.[9] Mistrust of her allies undoubtedly launched France into some hasty actions. The American pressure on the Dutch to withdraw from Indonesia, already manifest, gave no reassurance.

Consequently, when the war with Germany ended, a French task force under General Leclerc was sent full steam for the Far East to participate in the operations against the Japanese and establish France's claim to a vigorous voice in Asiatic matters. In the meantime the Potsdam Conference — from which France had been absent[10] — had already settled the temporary military disposition of the Indochinese territory. Since there were no French forces active in the area, the

[7] Admiral Jean Decoux gives at length his version of the Vichy regency in Indochina in *A la barre de l'Indochine: Histoire de mon Gouvernement Général* (Paris, 1949), written from prison. He attributes his policies to farsighted patriotism and maintains that he almost managed to avoid Japanese seizure and the consequent chaos of the last months of the war. He concludes: "The pages that France wrote in Indochina from 1940 to 1945 are worthy of her past and best traditions. This handful of Frenchmen, cut off from the mother country at the other end of the world, did their duty magnificently . . ." (pp. 482–483).

[8] Available facts indicate that de Gaulle's remarks on the possibility of a spontaneous Free French uprising in Indochina in early 1945 under the command of General Mordant are excessively optimistic. What plan there was the Japanese forestalled without great difficulty. But see Charles de Gaulle, *Mémoires de Guerre,* Vol. III, *Le Salut* (Ottawa, 1960), p. 224. If we can credit the contents of the interview of 1953 reported by J.-R. Tournoux, *op. cit.,* pp. 24–26, de Gaulle had done some serious rethinking of the Indochina problem and the colonial situation in general during his retirement.

[9] That the French suspicions were not without foundation is amply illustrated by the following excerpt from a press conference of President Franklin D. Roosevelt on February 23, 1945: "With the Indo-Chinese, there is a feeling they ought to be independent but are not ready for it. I suggested . . . to Chiang that Indo-China be set up under a trusteeship — have a Frenchman, one or two Indo-Chinese, and a Chinese and a Russian because they are on the coast, and maybe a Filipino and an American — to educate them for self-government. . . ." Reproduced in Allan B. Cole (ed.), *Conflict in Indo-China and International Repercussions, 1945–1955* (Ithaca, 1956), p. 48.

[10] Leclerc learned of the Potsdam military settlement regarding Indochina only when he was in Madagascar, on his way to the Far East.

country was to be occupied above the sixteenth parallel by the armies of Chiang Kai-shek, and below that boundary by the British forces coming from Malaya. Both these occupying powers were to undertake the surrender of remaining Japanese troops, the task of disarming them, and the assumption of local authority until a civil settlement could be reached. By this time the Japanese were firmly entrenched in the country with the aid of native auxiliaries; on March 9, 1945, they had presented Admiral Decoux with an unacceptable ultimatum, then proceeded to disarm or massacre the Vichy troops, on whom de Gaulle was also counting. Their choice for puppet ruler was His Majesty, Bao Dai, Emperor of Annam, who was to have many political moods, emerging finally as the Western bellwether against the aspirations of the Viet Minh.

Leclerc arrived in the Far Eastern theater in time to sign the instruments of the Japanese surrender on board the U.S.S. *Missouri* on September 2. He also found help in an unexpected quarter: he captured the sympathies of General Douglas MacArthur, who allegedly advised him to "send troops, more troops, and still more troops" to Indochina.[11] To be sure, this copious supply of manpower was not available, but Leclerc still found it possible to put a certain force ashore in Cochinchina and reclaim the traditional capital of Saigon. As this was in the British occupation zone, Admiral Lord Louis Mountbatten, the commander, assented to the withdrawal of his own troops toward the end of 1945, as soon as it became apparent that the French were in a position to re-establish their authority. In the meantime Thierry d'Argenlieu assumed his office of High Commissioner. Since there was little activity of the Viet Minh in Cochinchina and southern Annam in this period and the zone was effectively removed from the suspicious machinations of the Nationalist Chinese, Leclerc was bold enough to announce on February 5, 1946, that pacification had been achieved below the sixteenth parallel. This assumption was to prove fatuously optimistic in view of later developments, although it is true that the southern regions remained thereafter under nominal French control.

In the North — the provinces of Tonkin and northern Annam — the situation was quite reversed from the French point of view, and extraordinarily confused besides. The French presence was virtually nowhere, unless it was in the detention camps from which the Viet Minh had conveniently neglected to release the half-starved and disease-

[11] Reported by Philippe Devillers, *Histoire du Viet-Nam, 1940–1952* (Paris, 1952), p. 150.

ridden soldiers of Admiral Decoux. Nor were the Chinese occupation troops themselves masters of the situation after they arrived, for they were not joyously received by the local populations, nor were they able to prevail in many regions against the well-organized movement of Ho Chi Minh, which had steadfastly refused all Chinese collaboration from the time of the closing of hostilities.[12] In fact, the Viet Minh had effectively seized power in much of Tonkin before the appearance of the troops of Chiang Kai-shek, since the Japanese, never formally in possession of the hinterlands, had created a vacuum through calculated withdrawals and had scrupulously avoided the transfer of authority to those native groups which were working hand-in-glove with the Kuomintang.

We must briefly examine the history of the Viet Minh.

Vietnamese Communism

At the outset it was not Communist aspirations but rather Chinese Nationalist imperialism that had guaranteed the preservation of the Vietnamese "Reds" and a number of other native revolutionary groups. The French collapse in June 1940 had produced a corresponding enfeeblement of authority in Indochina and a rise in the pressure exerted by the Japanese. This had led to a series of isolated nationalist uprisings in the autumn of the same year, which the French succeeded in suppressing. The frustrated revolutionary elements had then retired to Kwangtung and Kwangsi provinces, where, under the tutelage of the Kuomintang, they prepared for future military action. The Communists fused voluntarily with other nationalist action groups to form the Viet-Nam Doc Lap Dong Minh Hoi, or "Viet Minh" in popular parlance. This action was inspired by the spirit of their leader, Nguyen Ai Quoc (later to become celebrated under his Chinese *nom de plume,* Ho Chi Minh), who had once written: "All races must unite in one movement of revolt against France." [13]

The Chinese were particularly interested in managing this coalition for their own reasons, but the relationship of the groups proved extremely inharmonious, and after a few months, the unity was broken.

---

[12] On this point see Bernard B. Fall, *The Viet Minh Regime* (Ithaca, 1954), p. 3. The statement holds true as a generalization: however, the situation is too complicated to submit to generalizations. At the arrival of the Chinese Nationalist occupying Army in September 1945, Ho Chi Minh was forced to make compromises and concessions. He also dealt on a purely Machiavellian basis with certain "warlord" elements in South China that were playing Chiang off against the Communists.

[13] Quoted from Fall, *op. cit.,* p. 1.

Ho Chi Minh cooled his heels in a Kuomintang jail for eighteen months as a punishment for his breach of discipline. By 1943, however, the Chinese recognized the inefficacy of Ho's opponents and, liberating him, gave him considerable license for reorganizing the Vietnamese revolutionary apparatus.

At a congress held at Liuchow on March 25, 1944, the various dissident elements of the past came together once more to establish the "Provisional Republic of Vietnam," which was to operate continuously on Chinese soil until the surrender of the Japanese. The government pledged itself to the liquidation of both French and Japanese influence in the national territory, and to the achievement of independence with the aid of the Kuomintang. Ho's supporters were in a minority in the new government,[14] but he easily overcame this disadvantage by undertaking the creation and proliferation of revolutionary networks in the back areas of Tonkin while his colleagues rested at their ease on Chinese soil.

In 1944, Ho himself crossed into Vietnam to bring a measure of political organization to the isolated partisan groups formed under the auspices of the Communists from Kwangsi and also by the indigenous Marxist leader Vo Nguyen Giap, a former schoolteacher and later Commander in Chief of the military forces of the Viet Minh. These recruiting campaigns enabled the Viet Minh to emerge from the war with a hard core of trained military cadres and a substantial area of control. Actually, there was almost no combat with the Japanese invaders, who were satisfied to leave the countryside to the native guerrilla groups and concentrate on protecting lines of supply and communications. Following the Japanese capitulation and before the arrival of the Chinese occupying forces, the Viet Minh were able to seize a good deal of military equipment and become the *de facto* rulers of much of Tonkin. Furthermore, they could draw on the enthusiastic support of the population, owing to the "national" character of their revolutionary activity and their abstinence from direct intrigue with any of the potential occupying powers. They entrenched themselves in Hanoi to await the Chinese and nominated a Provisional Government, headed by Ho Chi Minh but moderate enough in composition to conciliate the anticipated demands of their "liberators." The date of the founding was August 29, 1945. Already, a day before the Japanese surrender, Ho had severed all remaining ties between his own political organs and the Provisional Government on Chinese soil.

A further assist was given Ho through the abdication of Bao Dai on

[14] *Ibid.*, p. 2.

August 25.[15] Following the Japanese coup of March 9, which had brought the uneasy viceroyalty of Admiral Decoux to an end, the Emperor had nullified the protectorate treaty with the French and proclaimed the *Doc-Lap* (independence) of the "three *kys*" (Annam, Tonkin, and Cochinchina).

In the meantime, the French diplomatic staff in Chungking had incidentally given a large assist to Ho by negotiating a settlement with the Nationalist Chinese whereby the latter were to evacuate their zone of occupation, restoring French control of the region. Chiang Kai-shek had more urgent needs for his troops elsewhere. The agreement was signed on February 28, 1946, and provided for the Chinese evacuation to take place in the following month.[16] Thus it became imperative to reach a *modus vivendi* with the Viet Minh, who, as we have seen, had formed a government and were themselves the ruling power. This accord was negotiated and signed on March 6 by Jean Sainteny, another Gaullist emissary of liberal leanings.[17] Sainteny and many others were convinced at this time that Ho Chi Minh, if not basically pro-French, was at least amenable to the survival of French influence in the new state. In January 1946, Ho had been quoted as saying: "We have no hatred for France. We want to re-establish contact with her, all the more since others are interfering in our affairs. A settlement is possible. But if we have to, we will fight." [18] At another later, more critical juncture he spoke of his desire to "return to France, speak French." [19] Whatever illusions existed mutually between the French and the Viet

[15] The character of Bao Dai is not easy to penetrate; at various stages in his ambiguous career he played the roles of sycophant, millionaire playboy, regal personage, and opportunistic mediator. He made his peace at different times with the Japanese, the Viet Minh, and the French. At the time of his abdication he stated: ". . . having declared that I would rather be a common citizen in an independent state than be king of a subjugated nation, I decided to abdicate . . ." (quoted from Fall, *op. cit.*, p. 4). He had earlier made a plea to the Viet Minh to respect the feelings of all national groups, "even though they were not following closely in line with the popular masses." And two years later in Hong Kong, where he finally took up neutral residence, he confided: "My hand has not been forced; I abdicated of my own free will. . . . I did not want to oppose myself to the natural evolution of the people; mine wanted to become a democracy, and I yielded." But by August 1947 Bao Dai was in regular contact with French, American, and anti-Communist Vietnamese emissaries. See Devillers, *op. cit.*, pp. 404–412.

[16] The latter did not, however, leave Hanoi until June and in the meantime precipitated some serious incidents with the French troops, for which the Viet Minh were in no way responsible.

[17] Commandant Sainteny (see his account *Histoire d'une paix manquée*, Paris, 1953) had been the Free French assistant military attaché in Chungking. Years later, in 1962, he was elected a Gaullist deputy in the Fifth Republic.

[18] Quoted from Devillers, *op. cit.*, p. 204.

[19] Dinfreville, *op. cit.*, p. 46.

Minh, the French position at this time in North Vietnam was surely anything but secure. Major concessions would have to be granted to satisfy the sensibilities of the Democratic Republic of Vietnam (DRVN). These were duly accorded by Sainteny. Vietnam was to receive independence within the French Union and be permitted to regulate its own political institutions, raise its own Army, and direct its own finances. The incorporation of Cochinchina into the new state was to depend on a popular referendum to be held at a later date. A military convention provided that the French occupying force of 15,000 troops was to be progressively withdrawn over a five-year period.[20] From this point on, the local political situation deteriorated swiftly and drastically.

Colonialism versus Nationalism

It would be too easy to say bluntly that the French in Saigon were aiming as near to the *status quo ante* as they could get. This must clearly have seemed impossible to even the most primitive colonials. The great Lyautey had once written, half a century earlier: ". . . if we are going to have any colonial policy at all, let us have one that brings us in something, not for the purpose of adding one more sub-prefecture to all the vegetating subprefectures of France, but so as to get to the good places first, the places where one will have to be tomor-row, over which, the day after tomorrow, if one has not gone, he will bite his nails." [21] But certainly this mood of restless expansion had long vanished; furthermore, one no longer went to Cambodia to forestall the British or to Morocco to forestall Spain or Germany — one gritted his teeth to hold on against mounting local pressure and tried to adopt a sly gradualism. Financial motives and the lingering conviction of *grandeur*

[20] It is essential to grasp the fact that the Ho-Sainteny accords were received with great misgivings by the rank and file of the Viet Minh militants, who had particularly felt betrayed by the convention allowing the return of French troops. General Vo Nguyen Giap, however, explained in a public address the desirability of signing the agreement, commenting as follows on the troop clause: "Why has the government per-mitted the French troops to come? First of all, because if we had not agreed to it, they would have come anyway. China and France had signed a treaty providing that the troops should come. Otherwise, there would have been no agreement." Giap continued with the following interesting remark: "France has signed a treaty with China: America has chosen the French side. England has been with France for several months. Thus we were practically isolated. If we had resisted, everyone would have been against us." Finally, the classic argument: "Russia, for example, signed the Treaty of Brest-Litovsk in 1918 so as to be able, thanks to the truce, to solidify its army and political power. Is it not owing to that treaty that Russia has become very strong?" Devillers, *op. cit.*, p. 224.

[21] Louis H. G. Lyautey, *Lettres du Tonkin et de Madagascar*, Vol. II (Paris, 1920), p. 137.

française conditioned the reactions of the "Saigon clique," who, in addition, fell prey to false overconfidence and the incessant machinations of the *métropole*. Holding out had its very tawdry as well as stubborn aspects, as the continuous revelations of corruption and, in particular, the "traffic of piasters" [22] were later to show. The real political objective, seconded by the parliamentary power of the MRP and the resurrected Right at home as well as most of the high civil service, became, therefore, the construction of a Vietnam that would closely guarantee French commercial interests and cede its military and diplomatic prerogatives to the former protecting country. The association of the French Union was to be as tight as it could be made. Furthermore, Thierry d'Argenlieu had no intention of promoting the "unity of the three *kys*" by relinquishing Cochinchina to the new state of Ho Chi Minh, and he began almost at once to raise the specter of an autonomous area, which, it was understood, would be bound closely to the established French interests. Cochinchina, though less developed than Tonkin, was, because of its rice production, the breadbasket for the whole area. None of this reasoning was calculated to soothe the Viet Minh.

Ho Chi Minh appears to have fostered certain illusions of his own, which would be revealed as impractical. In the first place, he, no less than any national leader in an equivalent position, failed to foresee the drastic turn of international events that followed so quickly upon the end of World War II. A convinced Communist (incidentally one of the earliest members of the French Communist Party) and an expert practitioner of orthodox political guile, he had nevertheless been effectively isolated for a long while from the grand currents of major Soviet policy. It is altogether probable that he anticipated a much more gradual breakdown of the wartime alliance and a slower evolution in colonial matters than proved to be the case. In short, he was ready to "manage" the bourgeois over a certain period of time while advancing, step by step, toward his fixed objectives. This interpretation is in no way belied by the severe measure of ideological control he imposed on his army and population through the agency of an omnipotent party once the war had broken out.

No agreement that the Viet Minh might finally have struck with the French concerning the sovereignty and political disposition of the territory of Vietnam could have more than retarded the transition of that country to independence with the hierarchies and institutions familiar to a dozen other People's Republics. But there can be no doubt either that Ho bent over backward to practice this gradualism, both in his in-

[22] See Jacques Despuech, *Le Trafic des piastres* (Paris, 1953).

termittent negotiations with Saigon at Dalat and the military command at Hanoi,[23] and in his conciliatory performance at the Fontainebleau Conference of June–July 1946. Among the Communist leaders of the Viet Minh he was easily the most sophisticated and conciliable from the French point of view — as opposed, for example, to Giap, who was demanding intensive military preparations against the eventuality of guerrilla war. Moreover, he was frequently faced with severe crises of opposition among the rank and file, who had no taste for tactical compromise. Yet, persuasive in rhetoric, unchallenged in prestige, he never suffered that loss of confidence which would have placed his leadership in jeopardy. When war finally erupted, his political and administrative mastery over his people was superb.

Politics in France

In metropolitan France there was extreme confusion. Ignorance of the Indochinese situation was general, and there were not even any metropolitan French newspaper reporters in Tonkin during the difficult period of October–December 1946.[24] Moreover, the country was deeply involved in its own political dilemmas at this time: the election of two constituent constitutional assemblies and one parliament, and the adoption of a constitution. The constitution was intended, among other things, to clarify the nature of the French Union, which was critically important so far as the fate of Vietnam was concerned. During the Fontainebleau Conference of June–July 1946,[25] in which French and Vietnamese delegations confronted each other for the purpose of translating the Ho-Sainteny agreement into final treaty form, the French conference negotiators were played off against the constitutional planners regarding the final concept of community to be adopted, and this did not especially favor the solution of any of the immediate issues at hand.

Also, the three national elections that succeeded one another in the space of twelve months were to have a violent effect on the equilibrium in Indochina. The first, in October 1945, which had returned a Constituent Assembly divided fairly evenly along the lines of *tripartisme* (Communist, Socialist, and MRP), had given hope to the Viet Minh that a sympathetic and left-leaning government in Paris would grant the bulk of its demands: independence, military and diplomatic

[23] See, for example, Ho's letter to Sainteny, dated January 24, 1947, cited by Jean Lacouture, *Cinq hommes et la France* (Paris, 1961), p. 89.

[24] Devillers, *op. cit.,* p. 358.

[25] For a description of the atmosphere surrounding the Fontainebleau Conference, see Lacouture, *op. cit.,* pp. 70–76.

autonomy, a seat at the UN. However, simultaneous with the rejection of the first draft of the constitution by the French people, a second Assembly was returned which increased the confidence of the officials in Saigon. In this election, the MRP, styling itself the "Parti de la Fidélité" (that is, fidelity to de Gaulle), was returned as the largest group, whereas the Communists held firm and the SFIO suffered significant losses. The Viet Minh had placed even greater faith in the support of the Socialists than that of the Communists themselves. Georges Bidault was named President of the Provisional Government of the French Republic. This event coincided almost precisely with the arrival in France of the Vietnamese delegation that was to negotiate at Fontainebleau. The delegates were sent to cool their heels at Biarritz while the new government was being formed.

The elections for the first French parliament of the Fourth Republic (the constitution had, at the same time, been adopted by a meager plurality, more than overbalanced by blank ballots) redressed the tendency of the previous Assembly. The Communists continued to gain strength, and the two Marxist parties held, between them, 46.2 per cent of the vote. The MRP receded, losing support to the Radicals and a resuscitated "classical" Right. The vote could be considered fairly decisive, for it would determine the complexion of political events for five years to come. After failures by Marcel Thorez, representing the largest group, and Bidault, Léon Blum finally formed a homogeneous Socialist government, intended to serve until the January 1947 elections for President of the Republic. This caretaker government, in office for scarcely more than a month, had to bear the burden of the outbreak of the Indochina War.[26]

Upon learning the results of the parliamentary election, Admiral Thierry d'Argenlieu and the personnel of the High Commissariat in Saigon undoubtedly took panic, fearing very logically that the new government would fail to sustain their view of the Vietnamese evolution. The High Commissioner left in great haste for Paris, feeling that he could better influence developments at the nerve center of power, and placed General Valluy in charge in his absence. Valluy did not force an immediate military issue, but he prepared to take advantage of any provocation that might arise, thereby presenting Paris with a *fait accompli* from which it could not easily extricate itself. This development was not slow in transpiring.

[26] The Blum government is principally remembered for its temporarily successful attack on inflation. For a résumé of its activities at the outbreak of the Indochina War, see Alexander Werth, *op. cit.*, pp. 344–347.

The Outbreak of the War

As a result of some events relating to Chinese smuggling operations and the right of the French to set up a customs office in Haiphong — which the Vietnamese government held to be within its unique jurisdiction under the terms of the Ho-Sainteny agreement — fighting broke out in this port city on November 20 between French and Vietnamese troops. All efforts of the higher military command in Tonkin on both sides were applied to quell the disturbance and reach a peaceful settlement, and a joint commission was dispatched from Hanoi to investigate. However, the immediate commander of the French garrison in Haiphong, Colonel Debès, was intent on precipitating an issue, and the orders reaching him from General Valluy in Saigon, which did not pass through Hanoi, encouraged him to take full military advantage of the occasion. Debès attacked the Viets with all he had, including his naval batteries, causing indiscriminate carnage to the civilians. After several days of intense fighting, the French had gained effective military control of the surrounding (Delta) area. Valluy now demanded that his liberal-minded deputy General Morlière in Hanoi open negotiations with Ho to legitimize the *fait accompli* and achieve complete Vietnamese evacuation from the region. This ultimatum was, of course, unacceptable to the Viet Minh. Meanwhile, Thierry d'Argenlieu in Paris was busy imposing his interpretation of events on the political milieu and "public opinion." Reports of the true nature of the incident were suppressed or censored in Saigon. When, on December 15, Ho Chi Minh dispatched a telegram of proposals to the new French Premier, Léon Blum, this highly crucial document was itself intentionally delayed in transit and did not reach Paris until December 26, by which time the second and decisive chapter of the tragedy had unfolded.

Sainteny was, at the supplication of the government, back in Hanoi, and he and Morlière tried, to the extent of their authority, to reduce the gravity of the situation in conversations with leaders of the Viet Minh. But they, too, were hamstrung by Saigon. Sainteny went so far as to say: "France remains faithful to the spirit of March 6. I signed that agreement and I intend to have it applied." [27] Ho Chi Minh, on his part, sagely observed: "Neither France nor Vietnam can afford the luxury of a bloody war." [28] In two weeks, however, both countries were to pay the first installment on this luxury. Tensions were rising

---

[27] Devillers, *op. cit.,* p. 348, quoted from an interview with Bernard Dranber, correspondent of *Paris-Saigon.*

[28] *Ibid.,* p. 357.

sharply in Hanoi and provoking daily incidents which neither high command could foresee or control. The French Army, deep in an alien country and eager to strike a first blow for its protection, was jittery. On the opposite side, General Giap was, as all knew, preparing his forces, while the Tu Ve (Vietnamese self-defense fighters) were even more nervous to strike. All the while, the so-called Nationalist Party and other forces subsidized by the Chinese, which had no love for Ho and saw in the peril of the situation a means of recapturing prestige in Vietnam, were practicing a constant blackmail against the DRVN and infiltrating its forces. The best Sainteny could hope for was to engineer a holding action until the Blum government might send conciliatory instructions and proceed with a housecleaning in Saigon. But, as we have already seen, the Ho telegram was destined not to reach Blum until after irrecoverable damage had been done.

The assault by the Viet Minh took place on the night of December 19–20, with both sides in a tense state of readiness. General Giap had, it appears, in the evening, countermanded the order for the attack after noting the preparedness of the French, but this directive failed to govern the actions of the Tu Ve. In any case, all available troops were swiftly committed to the savage battle, whose terror was compounded by the sabotage of all electricity in the city. The following day found the French in control of the center of Hanoi, but in the meantime about forty Europeans had been massacred, and about two hundred had been carried off as hostages. Ho Chi Minh, in the throes of a high fever, had escaped with his government, according to apocrypha, with little more than an hour to spare, and had set up camp temporarily at Hadong, ten kilometers away. On December 21, he launched his appeal to the people:

The French colonial clique is again fulfilling its aim of subjugating the Fatherland. The hour is grave. Arise, unite. No distinction of ideology, race or religion counts any longer. Fight by all means available. Fight with your weapons, your picks, your shovels, your sticks. Save the independence and the territorial integrity of our land. Final victory is certain. Long live Vietnam independent and indivisible. Long live democracy.[29]

Ho's appeal met with a spontaneous and wide response throughout the length of the land. But the first military victories were almost exclusively French; in a swift series of neatly executed operations they managed to expel the Vietnamese from a number of important towns and villages in Tonkin. This perhaps only added fuel to the fire of a war in its initial stages, if indeed there could have been any withdrawing at this point. Marius Moutet, who had been retained in the Blum

[29] *Ibid.*, p. 357n.

45

cabinet, arrived immediately for a tour of inspection in the unhappy country and, with his usual facility, aided by the experts of Saigon, was able, after much soul-searching, to affirm that he had "absolute proof of the premeditation of the Vietnamese in this attack, which was certainly prepared with great diligence." [30] These assertions, though ambiguous in their proof,[31] helped to resolve certain struggles of conscience on the French Left and unite most of the political class for the pursuit of a "national" war.

But the given quantities of that war remained unchanged, despite the apparent ease with which the French had affirmed their hold over the major centers of population in the first week. As Leclerc had feared, the Viet Minh vanished into the *maquis* to fight a vitiating series of guerrilla operations which "would exhaust the French Army, and make its rebuilding in Europe impossible for a long time." [32] It was certain not to emerge until such a moment when it could challenge the French on equal terms. The wise Leclerc had thought pacification might take three years — regarding this length of time as disastrous — but this was to be a war in which even enlightened prediction would fall short.

Operations of the War: 1947–1953

Recognizing belatedly the continuing need for a political solution in Vietnam, the new French government (Ramadier) sought to re-establish contact with Ho Chi Minh in April 1947. Ho engaged in conversations with Paul Mus, a liberal Catholic sociologist and special emissary of the new French High Commissioner, Emile Bollaert,[33] but the conditions for settlement had so far deteriorated that the meeting ended in failure. In their search for a political counterpoise to the Viet Minh the French now turned toward the former Emperor of Annam, still officially a "Supreme Counselor" of the Vietnamese state though in neutral residence in Hong Kong. They finally engaged him in nego-

---

[30] *Ibid.*, p. 362.

[31] Viet Minh military preparations in the vicinity of Hanoi had been visible to all since the month of May. But it is unproved that they were offensive preparations. Also, even Moutet seemed to entertain doubts regarding Ho Chi Minh's involvement in the attack; we cannot be entirely certain that the Viet Minh leader's hand was not forced by his own subordinates.

[32] Dinfreville, *op. cit.*, p. 169.

[33] Bollaert was a capable high functionary with Radical connections, an excellent Resistance record as Jean Moulin's successor as de Gaulle's delegate to the Conseil National de la Résistance, and no particular background for the job in Saigon. His special task became that of clearing the path for the "Bao Dai experiment"; fortune smiled very infrequently on Bollaert despite his excellent qualities.

tiations that were to result in the Auriol–Bao Dai accords of March 8, 1949, followed by the monarch's return to Vietnam. The Bao Dai solution was apparently hastened by American pressure and by intelligence reports affirming the inevitable victory of the Communists in China, which made some political solution in Vietnam a question of the highest urgency.

Effective military control was already problematical throughout the country, except in the large towns, and a familiar pattern emerged: communications and contact were assured to the French by day, to the Viets by night; the French were lords of the town and the main highway, the Viets of the hinterland, the isolated village, and the footpath. Even in Cochinchina, where Ho's auxiliary Nguyen Binh[34] entered the fray with his forces, the situation was not materially different. The French, limited by the ineffective size and insufficient mobility of their forces, were compelled to choose between alternatives: mopping up in Cochinchina or major attack in Tonkin. The latter alternative meant destroying the enemy force by luring it into battle or "pacification" of the vital strategic regions such as the Red River Delta around Haiphong. With probably correct foresight the French chose to force the issue in Tonkin, and assigned a high priority to guarding their security within the Delta area and along the crucial highway to Hanoi. Seven years of war were to see them defeated in both objectives.

In 1950, the Chinese Communist forces of Mao Tse-tung reached the Indochinese border and were busily consolidating their hold over the contiguous areas of Kwangtung and Kwangsi and the island of Hainan. The establishment of the Chinese People's Republic on the borders of Indochina had intense repercussions on the strategy of the war. French relations with Chiang had never been the friendliest owing to Chungking's irredentism and support of various Vietnamese nationalist groups, and, furthermore, sectarian "warlordism" in South China with its encouragement of piracy and smuggling had been real problems. But Mao's arrival in power created for the French forces an undisguised military threat that might overturn all predictions and rational conduct of the campaign. China became a potent supply base and ideological citadel that the Viet Minh could draw on inexhaustibly. The French did not yield to the opening up of the Chinese frontier without a struggle, but the struggle was to prove costly and chastening. In autumn 1950 the Viet Minh fell on Cao Bang and destroyed its garrison together with the troops rushed to the rescue. The other border posts at

[34] A Cochinchinese "warlord" tactically allied with the Viet Minh, who seems to have been ambushed and killed by a patrol of the latter in 1951 because of his anticentrist "deviationism."

Lang Son, Lao Kay, and Hoa Binh, so isolated that ammunition and provisions could be assured only by parachute drops, were reluctantly abandoned at the same time. At this critical moment in the war, General (later Marshal) de Lattre de Tassigny, one of the genuinely prestigious figures of recent French military history, was rushed to Indochina with the dual function of High Commissioner and Commander in Chief.

In this period, Cochinchina, a secondary theater of operations but in itself no quiet backwater, was infested with guerrilla activity, although at no time did it become a real political base for the Viet Minh. Here the political and religious situations were incredibly confused and not entirely susceptible to the rigorous application of Ho's politics. From the start of the war, an "autonomous" native government under French sponsorship had functioned in Saigon, and local elections were held, as indeed they were later (with considerable success) throughout all the area under the control of the Vietnam national (Bao Dai) government. In Cochinchina the pacification proceeded stubbornly and gradually under the successive command of Generals Boyer de Latour and Chanson.

In the north, in 1950–1951, the superior initiative of de Lattre was partially successful in re-establishing the military balance. The General, whose tireless activity and skill as well as personal charm were legendary, endowed the staggering French forces with an *esprit de corps* and sense of mission. He made the first serious attempts toward developing a loyal Vietnamese auxiliary force, recognized the political demands of the nation as a potent factor in the war he was waging ("Je suis venu pour accomplir votre indépendance, non pour la limiter," he had announced), and, while leading his land campaigns prudently, placed great stress on the integration of air warfare in the total operation.

General de Lattre also became a kind of traveling missionary for the French cause in the Indochina War. His journeys took him to New York, London, and Rome, where he succeeded in largely persuading France's Western allies that the situation in Vietnam had worldwide implications. This was the period of the greatest intensification of the Korean War, and American ears were alert to the arguments that de Lattre put forward. United States aid and delivery of war materials to the Franco-Vietnamese forces dated from this time, attaining by the cease-fire of July 1954 a total of over 400,000,000,000 francs in value. But de Lattre's work in Indochina had only commenced when his premature death cost France her greatest serving soldier. In early 1951 he had, in a series of well-executed ripostes, broken the back of the first general offensive the Viet Minh had seen fit to mount, pushing the enemy back from vital territory and assuring, for the time being, the protection of the Delta. General Giap (in a reversion of strategy which was to become much noted when the phases of a "classical" *guerre révolutionnaire* were strictly defined by the French experts)[35] returned to guerrilla tactics. Observers felt that with the increase of American military aid and the superior fighting technique of the French Expeditionary Corps and its Vietnamese auxiliary army Ho Chi Minh had henceforth lost all chance of winning a major military decision,[36] and that a political settlement would have to concede some advantages to both sides.

By 1952 a considerable portion of the Expeditionary Force had been diverted from its primary area of action and would henceforth have to guard against the threat to Laos, which, as the only Indochinese country amenable to the political solution of the French Union, merited protection. The diversion permitted the rapid "pourrissement du delta" — that is, the infiltration of the Delta area by small groups who proceeded to gain the support of the local population. Also, the permanent political phenomenon of the Pathet Lao (Laotian Communists) was hereafter posed within the boundaries of the neighboring state. One commentator on these developments claims that the French were, nevertheless, able to preserve the advantage of interior lines against the peripheral force of the Viet Minh.[37] But this optimism is confounded by a glance at the realities of the situation. French excursions into the Thai country and Laos actually made them the outer force, as they were to be at Dien Bien Phu; also, the interior base (Delta) meant little when it was so systematically infested with hostile elements. The campaign in Laos amply demonstrated that Giap had forged a maneuverable and well-balanced regular force, led by officers of talent and high morale, accustomed to exacting forced marches and exhibiting great logistical ingenuity.

The map of Indochina will reveal the approximate division of control between the French and Viet Minh forces respectively in June 1953, when General Navarre, the former Chief of Staff of Marshal Juin at Headquarters, Allied Land Forces, Central Europe, arrived to

---

[35] Since, in *la guerre révolutionnaire,* a political terminology often invades military definition, the failure of Giap's "regular" campaign of 1951 also exposed him to charges of "leftist opportunism."

[36] See, for example, Devillers, *op. cit.,* p. 458, who, though no proponent of the pacification, writes: "The reinforcement of the Expeditionary Force, particularly its aviation, thanks to American aid, no longer leaves any hope to the Viet Minh for a decisive victory."

[37] Dinfreville, *op. cit.,* p. 35.

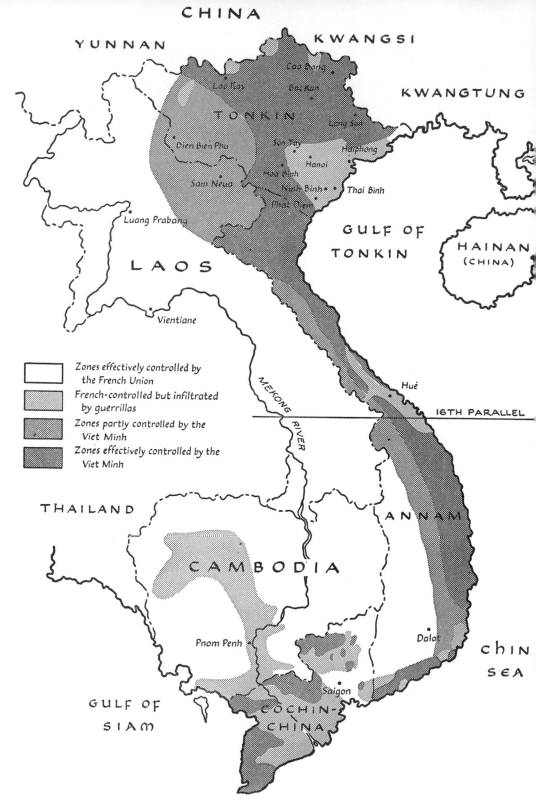

Figure 1. The Situation in Indochina, October 1, 1953. (The map is from Jacques Dinfreville, *L'Opération Indochine, op. cit.,* pp. 40–41, slightly simplified.)

take command. Actually, however, no diagrammatic scheme can more than partially indicate the fluid conditions of this particular war, in which the occurrence of night and day sufficed to produce sharply contradictory impressions. It has been estimated that with the forces they had available the French could probably only have protected a continuous front of 150–200 kilometers.[38] One can readily see that the whole of upper Tonkin and practically all Chinese border posts were within the grip of the Viet Minh, as well as the coasts of Annam and major enclaves in all areas of the country. The neighboring states of Laos and Cambodia had been significantly infiltrated, and the situation in the crucial Delta was, as we have seen, far from reassuring from the French point of view. Land communications between Tonkin and Cochinchina were extremely unreliable. Thus, far from being stabilized, the French position could be described as precarious.

Skilled metropolitan observers had not failed to divine that the situation called for measures of urgency. General Catroux, writing in *Le Figaro* on July 21, demanded that the government place 20,000 additional troops at the disposal of General Navarre before the advent of the next rainy season. Of course, the universal question of the time was: could additional forces be afforded without the resort of sending conscripts to the Far East? The problem was far from simple, not only touching public opinion at a point of extreme sensitivity, but relating also to the length of compulsory military service, which was held to be inadequate for training a soldier in this highly specialized kind of warfare. General Catroux played coy, declaring: "Without having available the precise information that the government possesses, I do not think I am wrong in answering that reinforcements can be sent without calling upon the conscripts." [39] Others were not so sanguine.

Closing Down

In March 1954 the "Big Four" foreign ministers had met in Berlin — for the first time since 1949 — and agreed to promote a Geneva conference in April which would attempt to tidy up some of the loose ends left by the Korean War and deal incidentally with Indochina.[40] The French position at Geneva demanded a possibility of "bargaining from strength," and the Navarre Plan had been set in motion in Indochina to create military conditions favorable for this line of action. The occu-

[38] Admiral Castex, "Les enseignements de la guerre d'Indochine," *Revue de Défense nationale,* December 1955, p. 527.

[39] *Le Figaro,* July 21, 1953.

[40] It is highly significant that the military commander, General Navarre, was not consulted on the decision to hold the Geneva conference.

pation by air and subsequent heavy reinforcement of the isolated bastion of Dien Bien Phu, at the gateway to the Thai country, was designed to lure General Giap into an eventual and, hopefully, decisive battle. In this respect, the strategy must be described as flawless.

Giap, however, was in no hurry to attack. Slowly and methodically he brought up his regular forces and heavy artillery (including 105's), dug in on all sides of the valley from which the French had chosen to challenge him, and waited for a propitious moment to strike. "Our job is to get the Viet to come down," Colonel de Castries, the French commander, explained to Robert Guillain, correspondent for *Le Monde*. "Once he comes down, we'll catch him." [41] On March 13, Giap came down, after unleashing a fearful artillery barrage on the installation. The fortress fell after fifty-six days of murderous attack, in circumstances with which all are familiar, but not until after Georges Bidault, the French Foreign Minister, had virtually persuaded the United States to intervene with its air force in the hope of relieving the pressure on the doomed garrison.[42]

One readily imagines that Dien Bien Phu brought the Indochina War to a grinding halt; actually the combat was to die down imperceptibly over the course of the following month. In Paris the "diehard" Laniel government was still holding on by steadily reduced majorities, attacked by the Socialists, the Gaullists, the Mendès Radicals, and, of course, the Communists. Bidault was still in Geneva biding time, hoping perhaps for the miracle of American intervention, assisted by the *ultra* Minister for Indochina, Frédéric-Dupont (Marc Jacquet having previously resigned). Generals Ely and Salan were rushed to the scene to make on-the-spot judgments; they dismally reported that, as a result of Dien Bien Phu, the French no longer had a prayer of holding on unless the draftees were sent. And this was, of course, politically impossible. The immediate evacuation of the southern part of the Delta was recommended so that available forces could concentrate their energies on protecting the vital Haiphong-Hanoi lifeline.

June 21, 1954, therefore saw the beginning of the last phase of the Indochina War — "Operation Auvergne" — a systematic evacuation of the area where the "pourrissement" had wrought its worst effects. This meant the abandonment of the Catholic bishoprics, which was morally distasteful. But, in fact, the flight of the refugees had started spontaneously well in advance of the military decision to evacuate.

Meanwhile, on June 17, in the wake of the crash of the Laniel gov-

[41] *Le Monde,* February 14, 1954.
[42] See J.-R. Tournoux, *op. cit.,* pp. 48–58.

ernment, Pierre Mendès-France, who had done so much to bring it down, was invested as Premier by the National Assembly. He immediately announced his famous "deadline" for the negotiation of a cease-fire in Indochina, and replaced Bidault at Geneva. Military operations were halted on July 20.

The conditions of the Geneva cease-fire were moderate, considering that the French Army's position had been judged untenable by General Ely. Must we attribute extraordinary negotiating skill to Mendès-France, or seek other explanations? While Mendès undoubtedly conducted his business with skill, it seems unquestionable that he received a decisive assist from the major Communist powers themselves, which scarcely concealed their desire to liquidate the war so as to concentrate their finite economies on domestic retrenchment. At the same time he ably prevented die-hard elements in France from sabotaging the negotiations by threatening them with the burden of political guilt attached to sending the draftees, which all knew would have to be done if the war were to continue.

The local aftermath of the Geneva agreement ceases, for the most part, to belong to French history. Mendès had proclaimed on June 17: "We shall stay in the Far East; let our allies and our opponents make no mistake about it." But the French "presence" was to recede gradually from South Vietnam, as the new government directed by Ngo Dinh Diem, an Annamese Catholic, saw greater advantages in encouraging the lucrative patronage of Uncle Sam. French relations in the adjacent states of Laos and Cambodia are outside the scope of our present discussion.

If the circumstances surrounding the Indochina War were confusing, its lessons and results seemed bathed in almost excessive clarity for those who hoped that the past, in coughing up some of its experience, might guarantee against the commission of old errors. While suffering a crushing military defeat, the French Army had gained the benefit of a cruel lesson which, if properly analyzed, could enable it to fight against other revolutionary armies. But the conclusions did not blossom forth spontaneously in the brains of the upper military echelons simply as a consequence of Indochina. They evolved after a hard struggle of conviction waged internally in the Army in the years 1954–1956. The Algerian War assured their adoption.

IV

LA SALE GUERRE:
POLITICS

J'estime qu'il n'y a plus, désormais, de problème militaire en Indochine. Le succès de nos armes est complet.
— *Paul Coste-Floret, May 14, 1947*

Je suis heureux de constater que nous sommes enfin sortis du tunnel.
— *Paul Coste-Floret, August 7, 1949*

Je crains réellement que le sacrifice de nos hommes n'apparaisse un jour comme inutile. Voilà le cas de conscience du chef militaire que je suis.
— *General Georges-Marie-Joseph Revers, letter of October 6, 1949*

Le sacrifice est-il toujours utile, simplement parce qu'il est un sacrifice?
— *Letter of an anonymous officer, cited by André-François Monteil, October 27, 1953*

In March 1957, nearly three years after the fact, General Henri de Navarre, on whom had fallen much of the odium for the catastrophe at Dien Bien Phu, delivered up his feelings in a public comment:

We had no policy at all. . . . At the end of seven years of war we had come to a complete imbroglio, and no one, from the common soldier to the commander in chief, knew exactly why the war was being fought.

Was it to hold on to French positions? If so, which ones? Was it simply to participate, under American aegis, in the containment of Communism in Southeast Asia? Why then should we have kept applying so much effort, since our interests had practically disappeared?

This uncertainty over political goals is the real reason why we were prevented from a continuous and coherent military policy in Indochina. . . . The divorce between policy and strategy dominated the whole Indochina War.[1]

General Navarre might have had premonitions of trouble long before, had he reflected on the circumstances that brought him to Indochina in 1953 to succeed Raoul Salan as Commander of the Expeditionary Force. Plucked from the staff of Marshal Juin at Fontainebleau (Allied Land Forces, Central Europe) by René Mayer, the fleeting occupant of the premiership, this reserved Norman professional had never seen Tonkin or been obliged to consider the kind of war being waged there. Thus he would "begin with a clean slate," burdened by none of the errors of his predecessors, as Mayer intimated during their walk in the Matignon garden.[2]

Navarre was not so green as to fail to pose the essential questions. Reinforcements? Perhaps the draftees? These were ideas to give French premiers delirious nightmares. All substantial increase of aid is out of the question, he was told; the essential is to do the best with what you have. In other words, win without winning: achieve those elusive "positions of strength" from which negotiation is possible, that siren slogan of Western diplomacy since the end of World War II. Much troubled, Navarre consulted his superior Juin, who had enough political power to demand his retention in Europe. "Somebody's got to do the job" ("Il faut que quelqu'un s'y dévoue"), the Marshal observed. And so Navarre went to Saigon, free from old errors but deprived of new resources. The errors would be more easily requisitioned.

The dreary succession of fourteen tottering governments of the Fourth Republic had perhaps done well to give the Indochina War as much consistency of direction as it possessed. But there were several fatal institutional flaws in the arrangement. The filtrations of vast distance made the problems of the war look very different to Paris than to those on the spot. The French responsibility for the direction of the war was diffuse, negligent, and contradictory. And the political solutions critical to the proper conduct of the war were indifferently

---

[1] Cited by Jean Lacouture and Philippe Devillers, *La fin d'une guerre, Indochine 1954* (Paris, 1960), p. 12n.

[2] The episode is recounted by Jules Roy, *La bataille de Dien Bien Phu* (Paris, 1963), pp. 17–18.

pursued and ambiguously perceived, partly because of the French un-
familiarity with confederal forms of association.

Political Confusions of the French Union

The French, stung by their bittersweet role in World War II, were
slow in recognizing that the epoch of pacification had ended and the
age of decolonization begun. Moreover, French centralism, with its
string of prefectures and subprefectures all over the globe cast in the
image of the political system of the mother country, was singularly un-
fitted to mediate the modification and withdrawal of imperial sovereignty. A new institution known as the French Union, hinted at by
de Gaulle's Provisional Government in the Brazzaville declarations of
1944 and authenticated by the Constitution of the Fourth Republic
(Title Eight, Articles 60–104), had been brought into being and offered
to the Indochinese states. But what this amounted to really was an
extension of certain privileges of local self-determination. The President
of France was *eo ipso* the President of the French Union; its parliamentary body was merely a consultative appendage of the National
Assembly; and all diplomatic, military, and currency arrangements
were reserved to the exclusive decision of the metropolitan power.[3] In
Indochina these general principles were already much mitigated by the
unique conventions which France had been forced to sign with the
Viet Minh in the Ho-Sainteny agreements and in the negotiations undertaken at Fontainebleau.

Reversion to the rather strict spirit of Title Eight would be difficult
for the French even when the arrangements with Ho Chi Minh were
declared dead letter and the negotiating partner became Bao Dai. And
this in turn would create irresistible pressures elsewhere for the
loosening of the metropolitan bonds. By the time of the coming to
power of the first Pleven government (July 12, 1950), and with the implementation of Bao Dai's sovereignty in Saigon, the status of "Associated State" had to be created within the French Union to accommodate the Indochinese components. This was duly formalized in Paris
by the invention of the portfolio of the Ministry (or State Secretariat)
of Associated States and its detachment from the Ministry of Overseas
France.

Neither Bao Dai's Vietnam nor Cambodia would finally ratify the

[3] For a comprehensive discussion of these relations, see Roger Pinto, "La France et les
états d'Indochine devant les accords de Genève," *Revue française de Science politique,*
January–March 1955, pp. 63–91.

instruments of membership in the French Union as Associated States. In Cambodia, King Norodom Sihanouk went into voluntary exile and refused to return until his country had been granted full independence. In the case of Vietnam the scenario was somewhat different.[4] Collaboration with Bao Dai (who spent much of his time away from his troubled kingdom, enjoying himself on the French Riviera) had never been popular with the Socialists and other Left-Center members of the French Assembly. Consequently, the instruments of "association" with France had included guarantees about popular sovereignty and the free expression of will by the people of Vietnam. Bao Dai now cleverly turned these tools on his French partners by summoning a national congress in Saigon in September 1953. Resolutions were passed declaring that Vietnam was not part of the French Union, pointedly neglecting to specify homage to the French Army and French efforts in particular. This prompted a bitter exchange of notes and a full-dress debate on Indochina policy in the French Chamber of Deputies on October 27, 1953. Laniel, the Premier, was hard-pressed to mitigate the anger of the Right and the jeers of the Left. "Yes or no — does our Vietnamese partner maintain a loyal attitude?" he asked. "Yes or no — does he keep the language of sincerity? Yes or no — were we in the process of playing a game of fools?"[5] Many, in a swell of outrage, did indeed think they had been taken for fools by the portly Emperor. The government had to fight a combined opposition of the Left, who now wished for nothing more than negotiation and liquidation of the enterprise, and a nationalist Right, who wished the pursuit of the war, but only to secure "French interests." Laniel survived the occasion, but in weakened shape. "France will never abandon her friends, but she would have no reason to prolong her sacrifices if . . . the significance of these sacrifices were misunderstood or betrayed,"[6] the government leader declared.

This episode did not advance the morale of an Army that was already weary and warsick and, since the time of de Lattre, in expectation of a more devoted co-operation from its Vietnamese national partner. Military tastes did not run much to the person of Bao Dai, in any case. As early as the spring of 1949, General Revers, sent by the government to

[4] A development that angered Vietnamese sensibilities and was undoubtedly unprofitable to some of the leading citizens of the country was France's unilateral devaluation of the Vietnamese piaster in the first week of May 1953.

[5] *Journal Officiel: Débats de l'Assemblée Nationale*, October 27, 1953, p. 4602. All future references to the *Journal* will be indicated by the abbreviation *J.O.* and will refer to the National Assembly (Chamber of Deputies) unless otherwise specified.

[6] *Ibid.*, p. 4603.

Saigon to map revisions for its Indochina policy, had not minced words about the fragility of this "third solution." The famous leakage of his classified report attributed to him the following position:

General Revers is not an enthusiastic partisan of the Bao Dai solution, but since he is obliged to adopt it, he thinks it is worth no more or less than our determination to stay in Indochina and the effort we exert to that end.[7]

Later, Colonel Jean Leroy, one of the most effective pacificators of Cochinchina, would deliver an attack on the sybaritic corruption of the Court and the inefficacy of the nationalist government. He would raise the argument, so frequently to be heard later in Algeria, that only root-and-branch social reform was capable of producing victory and preserving the French influence:

Victory *is* possible, certain, and almost immediate if, right away, becoming thoroughly aware of the moral crisis that is tormenting many minds, the French and Vietnamese officials will resolutely launch into the necessary political and social reforms and correct their mistakes.[8]

Paradoxically, it was the Laotian willingness to join the French Union as an Associated State that set the political background for the last, catastrophic battle of the war. At the origin of the planning leading to the collapse of Dien Bien Phu and the liquidation of the French effort, both Marshal Juin and General Navarre argued against giving the Army a mission of defense in the upper Thai region. But the line of thinking was unmistakable in the National Defense Committee: Laos must be protected; it is our best ally. This judgment became almost poignant after the altercation with Bao Dai. The acute and impartial Far Eastern correspondent Robert Guillain was led to declare: "Dien Bien Phu was not born in Indochina, but in Paris." [9]

The Political Conduct of the War

Perhaps the most curious consequence of France's tardy and reluctant federal arrangements was the placement of inordinate influence over the conduct of the war in the hands of a single official, Jean Letourneau, the Secretary of State for the Associated States. Letourneau, a member of the Mouvement Républicain Populaire, occupied this position through seven successive governments, from October 28, 1949, to June 28, 1953;

[7] *La bulletin de la nuit,* June 21–22, 1949.

[8] In *Revue française,* quoted by the deputy René Kuehn, *J.O.,* October 27, 1953, p. 4561. See, also, Leroy's account of the war, *Un homme dans la rizière* (Paris, 1955).

[9] Robert Guillain, *La fin des illusions, Notes d'Indochine: février–juillet 1954* (Paris, 1954), p. 69. This is a collection of his *Le Monde* dispatches.

moreover, his predecessor as Minister of Overseas France, Paul Coste-Floret, had been a close associate and party colleague.

This situation created its own paradox. Whereas, in the words of J.-R. Tournoux, "over-all views and perspectives were absent, no government was of sufficient duration to trace them out," [10] a political vested interest was maintained in the Indochina post with a continuity that was all too inflexible. The MRP leaders wanted peace in Indochina, to be sure — they had said it a score of times in the Assembly[11] — but the conditions for that peace were never satisfied. It was clearly impossible to negotiate with Ho Chi Minh, the argument ran; after all, had not Paul Mus tried in 1947 and failed, and had not the Socialist minister Marius Moutet himself called the Viet Minh leader a "war criminal"? [12] In other words, negotiated peace was a utopian prospect for the governments in which the MRP played a leading role. Debates on the subject could accomplish nothing but damage to the morale of the armed forces. Let peace come, as long as the settlement conceded the integrity of the French presence. "May my voice," exclaimed Paul Coste-Floret,

carry from this tribune to [our Army] the hope that their sacrifice will finally determine peace in Vietnam, a true peace that leaves no envenomed sores. . . . But, to be precise, the Government intends to place this solution of peace within the context of the French Union.[13]

Letourneau's control over the conduct of the war requires some explanation. Normally, high policy for military decisions was determined by the Council of Ministers and by the National Defense Committee, which included relevant members of the Cabinet, the President of the Republic, and Marshal Juin. But their decisions were in turn filtered through the office of the State Secretary for the Associated States and thence to the French High Commissioner in Saigon, who transmitted them to the military Commander in Chief of the Expeditionary Force.[14] Furthermore, Indochina appears not to have been a frequent subject of discussion in the full cabinet meetings. "Indochina?" Edgar Faure, the State Secretary for Finance, is alleged to have commented. "I practically never hear it spoken of in the Council." [15]

[10] J.-R. Tournoux, *Secrets d'Etat* (Paris, 1960), p. 19.

[11] For example, Paul Coste Floret declared in the National Assembly, on March 10, 1949: "The government . . . has but one supreme goal which it has always pursued indefatigably since the beginning of the conflict: to restore peace." *J.O.,* p. 1525.

[12] Moutet made this statement in May 1947. It was recalled to the Socialists on March 10, 1949, by André Mutter, a conservative. *J.O.,* p. 1564.

[13] *J.O.,* March 10, 1949, p. 1572.

[14] See Tournoux, *op. cit.,* p. 28n.

[15] *Ibid.,* p. 19.

The Minister of National Defense had correspondingly less control over the Indochina operations through regular channels of military command. By Decree 50-1506 of December 4, 1950, he was made "nothing but the furnisher of arms and troops for a policy over which he had a supervision equal to that of his colleagues of the Comité de la Défense Nationale." [16] When, after the departure of Letourneau, René Pleven became Laniel's Minister of National Defense, he simplified and improved the proceedings through the creation of a "Restricted War Committee" made up of the President of the Council, the Minister of Foreign Affairs, the Minister of Defense, and the State Secretaries for Military Affairs.[17] Orders continued to pass to Saigon through the State Secretary for the Associated States, who was now Marc Jacquet. But by this time the fateful decision to defend Laos from an entrenched position in Upper Tonkin had been implicitly made.[18]

Things looked very different from the perspective of Robert Guillain in Hanoi, who watched the fatal issue of Dien Bien Phu being prepared, and deplored the insouciance of the political elite class:

Incredible fact . . . the Council of Ministers itself is very often kept in the dark about intelligence received and decisions taken. The attitude of our ministers is on many occasions an "I don't want to know," which persuades them to leave Indochina to a "restricted ministerial council."[19]

In the curious way we have described, many of these failings can be traced to the inadequacy of the concepts and institutions of Overseas France and to the consequences that followed. The maverick MRP deputy André Denis was perhaps not far from the truth when he declared in a debate:

A precise and bold conception of the French Union — if we had had that at the start, we might have been guided toward the orientation of independence; if it had been granted in these circumstances we might have avoided war and, ultimately, hatred.[20]

Parliament, War, and Army

The Army was not geared to protest. It felt these consequences obliquely and at a distance. In contrast to the labyrinthine meanderings of politics, it had received the simple mission to pacify and prevail, and

[16] Lacouture and Devillers, op. cit., p. 24n.

[17] Ibid., p. 67.

[18] Cf. Joseph Laniel, Le drame indochinois (Paris, 1954), p. 38. General Navarre's order to implement the build-up of Dien Bien Phu was issued on December 3, 1953. But see ahead, p. 72.

[19] Guillain, op. cit., pp. 87–88.

[20] J.O., January 28, 1950, p. 677.

these orders were not altered up to the very end. Though one of its own leaders, General Leclerc, had warned at a very early date that "anticommunism will remain a lever without force as long as the national problem is unresolved," [21] no government had ever really heeded the advice.

The Army, swollen already to the total of 153,000 men by mid-1949,[22] locked in vague combat 12,000 kilometers away, was not as yet "feared" by anyone. On the contrary, Communists, democrats, and reactionaries alike mounted to the tribune to pay homage to the French soldier — the former, albeit, to accuse the government of the carnage and demand that "la sale guerre" be stopped and the Expeditionary Force withdrawn. There was no more certain way to draw applause from all sectors of the Chamber than to pay lavish compliment to the Army, no surer means of curtailing an embarrassing debate than to invoke the need for supporting military morale. To speak of negotiations, said Raymond Dronne, "is the surest means of raising the morale of the adversary and of demoralizing our own troops." [23] In the same debate, Laniel warned the Chamber: "If imprudent words come to be pronounced, [the government] is perfectly conscious of the damage which might be caused our troops who are fighting over there so valiantly and to whom I want, in my turn, to pay homage." [24] Joseph-Pierre Lanet suggested timidly: "A debate like the one today will not demoralize the Expeditionary Force if we have the courage to speak the truth," [25] but Henri Laforest, from the Right, dramatically voiced the opposite view:

I have shared the existence of those fighters 12,000 kilometers away. Often they have questions over the national interest of their sacrifice, and I am thinking today of the harm we may be doing to their morale.

May they know, those glorious fighting troops of the French Union, that the National Assembly, with the entire nation, salutes with emotion their courage and sacrifices! [26]

In this debate, Alain Savary, speaking for the Socialists, evoked a dark shadow whose outlines had not crossed the minds of most politicians: "Some day the French Army will demand a reckoning for the blood it has shed." [27] But the Socialists themselves were not pure. However

[21] Quoted by Lacouture and Devillers, *op. cit.*, p. 20.
[22] Statement by Max Lejeune, the Secretary of State for War, June 10, 1949, *J.O.*, p. 3293.
[23] *J.O.*, October 23, 1953, p. 4547.
[24] *Ibid.*, p. 4539.
[25] *Ibid.*, p. 4562.
[26] *Ibid.*, p. 4564.
[27] *Ibid.*, p. 4562.

much they might criticize the war — Guy Mollet had done so as early as March 9, 1949, in a letter published in the newspaper *Franc-Tireur*[28] — they continued to vote the military credits and had no very plausible solutions to offer. Furthermore, a homogeneous Socialist government (of Léon Blum) had been responsible at the time of the outbreak of hostilities. As the unpopularity of the war grew, the Socialists found themselves battling the Communists on their left for schematic ways of halting the operation, while trying to show that they were not deserting the national effort. Gaston Defferre, who was often the major speaker for the SFIO, wanted the government to spare no efforts to reach a settlement with Ho Chi Minh before Red China could intervene actively to "internationalize" the war. For if this happened, "it is certain that all Southeast Asia would be open to the forces of invasion." [29]

Edouard Daladier, at whom the Communists delighted to cry "man of Munich," wanted the war internationalized, but "politically" internationalized, by UN discussion, a formal cease-fire line, and truce talks.[30] He deplored especially the vitiating effect of the Indochina War on French military preparations in Europe and the inevitable consequence of German rearmament, which he opposed. The French military preparedness in Europe was a recurrent worry of other speakers of varying shades of opinion. Thus, François Quilici, the Algerian Radical deputy asked this question:

Hasn't it always seemed paradoxical that we went to fight Communism 12,000 kilometers from our doors when a powerful Communist Party camps on our soil and Soviet tanks are two days away from Strasbourg?[31]

Savary and Defferre echoed the same preoccupation, Savary concluding notably: "The soldiers know that there will be no French Army as long as the war lasts in Indochina, for it absorbs a third of our officers and half our NCO's." [32]

Finally, there was the "Cassandra of the Fourth Republic," Pierre Mendès-France, waiting in the wings with his motto "to govern is to choose." Mendès warned the Chamber on November 22, 1950: "We must choose . . . outside of the military solution [requiring three times as many troops], outside of the solution of force, there is but one possibility: negotiation. . . . Have we the means to avoid this outcome after

---

[28] He wrote notably: "No military solution has been gained; Bao Dai enjoys no authority in Vietnam. Vietnam is behind Ho Chi Minh. We have to negotiate, in the first place, with Ho Chi Minh."

[29] *J.O.*, December 28, 1951, p. 10079.

[30] *Ibid.*, p. 10054.

[31] *J.O.*, October 27, 1953, p. 4597.

[32] *J.O.*, October 23, 1953, p. 4562.

having made it inevitable by our errors and mistakes?" [33] He would be the solitary deputy to abstain voluntarily from voting the military credits for the Associated States and Overseas France on December 28, 1951.[34]

Professions of French war aims were as oblique and hesitant as attacks on existing policy. Too inflexible with regard to associational forms, as we have seen, they were vague and shifting in terms of French world strategy. Savary cited and dissected some of the principal arguments in his speech of October 23, 1953: "defense of the French Union, struggle against subversion, strategic necessity . . . of defending Southeast Asia against the Chinese peril, finally the struggle against communism." [35] Each of these arguments had its exponents, but the principal leaders involved in the conduct of the war usually introduced a sequence of indiscriminate reasons, willy-nilly, as it suited their purpose.

A number of themes were heard which would later be commonly employed during the Algerian fighting. Paul Coste-Floret declared on December 28, 1951: "For more than five years France alone has been pursuing the defense of the free world in Indochina." [36] André Mutter, on June 10, 1949, contributed the following apostrophe: "Our soldiers fighting over there have the intention and impression of also defending civilization, cultural interest, and the glory of France." [37] "Either the French and their allies of Vietnam will maintain in the Far East one of the frontiers of human and spiritual civilization," said Louis Terrenoire, later a Gaullist minister, on January 28, 1950, "or else we shall be submerged by a despotism and an imperialism that will smash them both." [38] The secret but widely divulged Revers Report of 1949 saw the conflict as one of national interest and great-power politics:

> France has an obligation to succeed, especially since any defeat or withdrawal in this Asian region would mean the signal of the dislocation of the French Union. In our present world this dislocation would have as vast an effect, in space and time, as the loss of the French colonies in the eighteenth century.[39]

General Paul Ely agreed, in an article written shortly before the final disaster: "In the Far East, like it or not, our position as a great power is definitely at stake." [40] For him the distant struggle was not isolated

[33] Cited by Lacouture and Devillers, *op. cit.*, p. 30.

[34] *J.O.*, December 28, 1951, p. 10117.

[35] *J.O.*, October 23, 1953, p. 4562.

[36] *J.O.*, December 28, 1951, p. 10056.

[37] *J.O.*, June 10, 1949, p. 3298.

[38] *J.O.*, January 28, 1950, p. 688.

[39] Quoted by Tournoux, *op. cit.*, p. 13.

[40] General Ely in "Pourquoi l'Indochine?", included in his *L'armée dans la nation* (Paris, 1961), p. 159.

but rather part of a "sane global strategy that agrees with the higher interests of the nation." [41] France's sacrifices in Asia, Ely continued, might have delayed or prevented the outbreak of war in Europe.

As the final eclipse of the French power approached, numerous spokesmen emphasized, as some would later in the case of Algeria, that abandonment of the loyal Vietnamese associates would constitute unpardonable duplicity and damage to the credit of French promises and strength in all the colonies.[42]

From the Right came the Gaullist attack. Senator Michel Debré framed this sentiment in one of his periodic assaults on the government in the Conseil de la République: "The French people have the feeling of a war that escapes them, and a fate they do not command. . . . They have the impression . . . that France herself doesn't know what she wants, that she is fighting without any exalted or clear objective." [43] Christian Fouchet, a Gaullist deputy who was later to figure so prominently in the last days of French Algeria, was one of the first to voice a suggestion which would later lead a part of the Army down narrow and troubled paths: "In the face of adversaries who have a mystique — good or bad — you [he was addressing the government benches] have not been able to convince our allies and partners that they, too, should have a mystique." [44] Fouchet did not specify the nature of the mystique he wanted; the France of this time spoke with a confused voice. But the de Gaulle of the RPF (Rassemblement du Peuple Français) was not yet the knowing liquidator of the burdens of the colonial enterprise; his mystique was presumably nationalism and honor — and victory, pure and simple. As Edmond Michelet recalled:

> Another voice has been raised [de Gaulle's, in early February 1950] to remind us that in the face of the new imperialism that seeks to overwhelm the world a single army is fighting, and fighting well, in the Red River delta — the French Army of Indochina.[45]

The Far Left chanted the bankruptcy of the national effort. As Robert Chambeiron, a *progressiste* fellow-traveler once taunted: "You

[41] *Ibid.*, p. 151.

[42] For example, see André Denis: "I think that [the simple withdrawal of the French Expeditionary Force] . . . would be more criminal than the war itself . . . because the Vietnamese soldiers allied to France would be exposed to a massacre. . . . These people have placed confidence in us. We want to return their freedom to them." *J.O.,* January 28, 1950, pp. 677, 688.

[43] *J.O., Conseil de la République,* 1953, p. 1741. Cited by Lacouture and Devillers, *op. cit.,* p. 24n.

[44] *J.O.,* October 23, 1953, p. 4574.

[45] *J.O.,* February 7, 1950, p. 1033.

have gotten yourself into an adventure and you don't know how to get out." [46] Unwittingly, the extreme right-wing deputy Frédéric-Dupont probably summed the case up best of all when he said that "distant expeditions are enormous trials for democracies." [47]

The "Affaire des Généraux"

There was a trial within the trial of Indochina, which passed and was forgotten, but left its persistent scar on the bitter history of French civil-military relations. This was the *affaire des généraux*.

In May 1949, the French Army Chief of Staff, General Georges-Marie-Joseph Revers, had been dispatched by the government to Indochina to make political and military recommendations *sur place*. A man of intelligence and professional acumen but short on political sense, Revers reviewed the Indochina dilemma after consultations with persons of divergent views and a series of trips through the field. Chiefly, his report recommended intensified defense of the Delta region in Tonkin and the pursuit of the pacification in the South. It expressed extreme skepticism about the effectiveness of Bao Dai — a view which Revers was already known to hold — and implied criticism of the policies of the French High Commission under Léon Pignon. By June 21, General Revers was back in Paris; his report, according to his own testimony, was signed on June 29 and had been reproduced for limited classified circulation by July 4.[48]

However, as early as June 21, 1949, the scandal sheet *Bulletin de la nuit* had already published what later proved to be the major outlines of the Revers Report. This was not to be the extent of the damage. It soon became apparent that copies of the completed document had found their way into the hands of both the Viet Minh and the nationalist Vietnam government and were being widely disseminated. When High Commissioner Pignon arrived in Paris on July 11, he heard immediate talk of the contents of the document "as soon as I had stepped out on the airstrip."

Before long, official Paris was alerted to the buzzings occasioned by the leaked report. No official government mention of the incident was, however, made until January 11, 1950. By this time, Henri Queuille's cabinet had fallen and Georges Bidault had been invested as Premier. Bidault, no longer able to hold his silence, finally arose in the Assembly

[46] *J.O.*, January 27, 1950, p. 632.
[47] *Ibid.*, p. 608.
[48] *J.O.*, testimony of Pierre July, May 4, 1950, p. 3271.

to deliver a government communication on the *affaire des généraux,* of which numerous interpretations had already appeared in the public press.

Bidault appeared anything but anxious to communicate more information than had already become public knowledge. After a brief summary of the dossier, he declared: "Such is the information, the only information which this government possesses. If others know more, as the rumor is, let them say so." [49] At the same time, he counseled discretion: "Behind [certain] men, persons are taking aim at France and her army, at the French Union and its cohesion." [50] Although the disclosures of the *affaire des généraux* gravely compromised a number of Bidault's political rivals of the Socialist Party, he knew that the total effects of the scandal would hardly benefit his own MRP, which, more than any other group, was implicated in the conduct of policy for Indochina. He asked that the debate be recessed.

The Assembly would have none of it. Not only were the Communists and Gaullists bristling with fury and determined to make a case, but numerous speakers arose from the Center to disclaim their part in any whitewash. A parliamentary Committee of Inquiry was demanded. Maurice Viollette, the aging Radical with a long-standing interest in colonial problems, said notably:

We have a duty . . . to see that this affair does not harm the morale of our armies fighting in Indochina. We have the duty to give the French Army the witness of our impartiality.[51]

Eventually, after a competition of motions and some maneuvering — Bidault having ceded — the Assembly created a Committee of Inquiry under a Center deputy, Eugène Delahoutre, to make a full and impartial report on the *affaire des généraux.* The body did not function without impediment — two of its twelve members resigned — but it did succeed in completing its findings and in laying the groundwork for the debate of May 4, 1950. Maurice Kriegel-Valrimont, the Communist member, managed to keep the issue prominent through daily leaks of committee proceedings to his party newspaper, *l'Humanité.*

It had become obvious that the leakage of the Revers Report involved much more than a case of simple espionage. It concerned military-political collusion for favor, and the obscure rivalries of internal politics in Vietnam. Above all, it concerned intimate contact between high French military chiefs and a civilian opportunist named Roger Peyré.

[49] *J.O.,* January 11, 1950, p. 282.
[50] *Ibid.,* pp. 280–281.
[51] *Ibid.,* p. 291.

Beneath their "third force" amenities, the Socialist and Popular Republican parties had been struggling for primacy in the French government coalition. Not only did the Socialists wish to alter the "hard" Indochina policy pursued by the MRP Minister of Overseas France, Paul Coste-Floret, and his surrogate in Saigon, Pignon, but it appears that certain of them wished to capture the profits flowing from that war as well. To this end they had a candidate for High Commissioner to succeed Pignon, General Mast, a military expert in oriental affairs. General Mast and General Revers were friendly, and they had, moreover, a valued mutual acquaintance in Peyré. Revers had forwarded and secured Peyré's nomination as Chevalier of the Legion of Honor, even though the latter proved, on investigation, to have been a Fascist double-agent and former militant of Jacques Doriot's Parti Populaire Français. Peyré had assets and excellent connections in Indochina; these were placed at the service of General Revers during his visit.

Revers's connections with Peyré had been more than casual; he had written to him from Washington on April 2, 1949:

Bravelet [Revers's aide de camp, Lieutenant Colonel Bravelet] must have told you that, as much for local reasons as, with greater justification, if I have to go to the Far East, we have to settle the question of the fifth star [rank of *général d'armée*] and the presidency of the Committee of the Chiefs of Staff.[52]

In short, Peyré was interested in profit and political influence; the General was interested in advancement; and certain others were interested in venal political infighting. General Mast, too, was anxious to secure his High Commission; he had been studying Vietnamese for months with this hope in mind.

In Saigon, a second intrigue was simultaneously transpiring: that of General Xuan to become the power behind the throne in Vietnam or even to supplant the Emperor Bao Dai. Roger Peyré was the link between these two operations.[53]

The Revers Report was therefore delivered or disclosed to unauthorized sources through the connivance of Peyré and with the authorization of Generals Revers and Mast, the latter of whom was privy to the classified distribution. It went, in the first instance, to Van Co, an agent of the nationalist government, and then to Vinh Xa, a relative of Bao Dai, considered a "national Communist" by General Mast, but apparently a bona fide agent of Ho Chi Minh. General Mast lent himself to the Vinh Xa maneuver, it appears, in the hope of conciliating

---

[52] *J.O.*, May 4, 1950, p. 3269. Cited in a speech by Maurice Kriegel-Valrimont.

[53] See the testimony of Pierre July, rapporteur (but who resigned) of the Parliamentary Committee of Inquiry that researched the *affaire des généraux. J.O.*, May 4, 1950, p. 3271.

various kinds of political support prior to his expected nomination as High Commissioner.[54]

When these events were brought to the attention of the government early on the morning of September 20, 1949, three ministers became immediately involved. The counter-espionage branch of the Sûreté, which had picked up and questioned Peyré, reported to its chief, Bertaux, who took the liberty of awakening his superior, Jules Moch, the Minister of the Interior, at six o'clock. Queuille, the Premier, was next informed, and it was decided to put Paul Ramadier, the Minister of Defense, in touch with the situation. The three men, two of them Socialists and one a Radical, held several tense conferences over the affair. Finally, it was agreed that Ramadier would examine the documents seized to determine whether breaches of national security were involved. On September 23, Ramadier returned his judgment that there had been no betrayal of military secrets. The charges against Peyré were dropped on the following day, many of his papers were returned, and there is every evidence that alerted French officials aided his subsequent flight to Brazil. Of this act, the Parliamentary Commission of Inquiry under the chairmanship of Eugène Delahoutre later stated: "It appears . . . that the verdict given by the competent minister which led to the dropping of charges was not dictated by the absence of national security secrets as claimed." [55] It was, in fact, dictated by *raison d'Etat*. Ramadier's indiscretion rebounded on Queuille, his knowing superior. However, both would be cleared by the committee of criminal culpability, albeit under a heavy cloud.

Jules Moch, the Minister of the Interior, received a stiff reprimand for his part in the operation. His services had conducted the Peyré interrogation with many irregularities and had caused certain critical documents to disappear, be destroyed, or be returned to the opportunist at his release. Even Ramadier's office had felt it necessary to chide the Minister of the Interior in a letter dated October 13, 1949, which stated in part: "Such irregularities could lead to the gravest consequences. . . ." [56]

Moch — who retained the office, though there had been an intervening change of government — replied to the charge on December 29:

This affair had to be conducted with extreme haste. . . . In such precipitation, the services in question lacked the material time to achieve their mission in perfect formality and within the prescribed time-limits. . . .
This is why, in the narrow limits of time which they were allowed, cer-

[54] *Ibid.*, p. 3277.
[55] Testimony of Eugène Delahoutre, *ibid.*, p. 3255.
[56] Letter from Ramadier to Moch, cited by Kriegel-Valrimont, *ibid.*, p. 3261.

tain documents seized between the 21st and 24th of September, but which, after examination, could shed no light on judicial matters, were returned to the interested parties.[57]

The committee repeated the Ramadier criticism of Moch's procedures: they had "led to grave consequences."

Probably no procedural gravity matched the blow to the Army, and to the morale of its officers and troops. Within a short time the Viet Minh had managed to reproduce 2000 copies of the military portions of the Revers Report, diffusing them in Vietnam to show both the French Army and its partners that national secrets were not secure. Bulletin No. 45 of the General Staff of the Expeditionary Force, issued on November 15, 1949, revealed that the acquisition of the report had led to hasty revisions of Viet Minh strategy, with counterdeployments for the now-anticipated Franco-Vietnamese attacks on Phat Diem and on Nam Dinh and Ninh Binh.[58]

Léon Pignon testified before the Delahoutre Committee:

The harm to the soldiers' morale was considerable. This fact can be checked. The fact that the Viet Minh were acquainted with the report caused the French soldiers an undoubted indignation and loss of morale.[59]

The version of the Revers Report broadcast by the Viet Minh radio-telegraph stations VNA-2 (serving Rangoon, Burma) and KSA (serving Tonkin) and intercepted by the French communications service in Saigon was rigorously identical to the text of the actual document, according to the sworn affidavit of the French radio intercept chief for the Far East. These broadcasts were made between August 26 and September 9, 1949.[60]

Various annexes of the Revers Report had adverted unfavorably to the Army's discipline,[61] although the General himself had stated that "on the whole, the Army is solid and disciplined." These innuendoes of estimating the Army's morale and solidarity for purposes of political warfare could not help but disturb the troops when revealed by the enemy.

Finally, the explanations given in the debate by Queuille and Ramadier of their part in the miserable series of events reinforced the conclusion that they had acted in part from fear of the damage to French power and morale, the same forces the Communists were trying to sap

[57] *Ibid.*, Moch to Pleven.
[58] Delahoutre testimony, *ibid.*, p. 3255.
[59] *Ibid.*
[60] *Ibid.*, testimony of July, p. 3274.
[61] Notably that of Valéry, a Socialist lawyer of the Saigon court of appeal. See the quotation by July, *ibid.*, p. 3285.

through persistent efforts at sensation and exposure. In reaching their questionable decisions, explained Queuille, "we took the political arguments fully into account." At the moment of crisis, discussions over the structure of NATO were in progress in Washington, and the United States Congress was about to debate its foreign aid appropriations. Amid the laughter of the Communists, he concluded: "The appreciation of our decision belongs to the National Assembly." [62]

Ramadier was still more vociferous in his insistence that the Army — which now knew — should have been spared the pain of knowing about such things:

The scandal! We had to weigh the consequences for the Army. . . . Yes, for the Army, for don't you see . . . in that sort of pillory where two generals of the Army are fastened, there is something which touches the most pure and noble soldiers in the deepest part of their heart? [63]

It was scarcely the fault of Queuille's government that two of its leading generals had defected to baser pursuits and managed thereby to deal a blow to their own officers and men. It was rather the fault of a whole system which rewarded military leaders for political chicanery and played them off against each other. De Lattre would soon arrive to smooth the surface and assert the authority his predecessors had lacked. But the Army had been both hurt and ashamed. If it was, in the words of Pierre Montel, "an institution good in itself, which, throughout the centuries has always shown that it was good," [64] it had traveled one step of the way toward its alienation from the civilian power. Grudgingly — since it had satisfied no one's political killer instinct or wish of oblivion — the Assembly adopted the Delahoutre Report, by 335 to 201, officially closing the *affaire des généraux*.[65] René Capitant, the vigorous and able Gaullist law professor, exaggerated somewhat when he labeled it "a scandal of State, the scandal of the regime." [66] In truth, the ultimate scandal was yet to come.

Dien Bien Phu: The Ultimate Scandal

It took its name from an obscure valley settlement submerged in the Thai country of Upper Tonkin: Dien Bien Phu, a word which General

---

[62] *Ibid.*, p. 3256.

[63] *Ibid.*, p. 3293.

[64] *Ibid.*, p. 3288.

[65] However, see its evocation in the special number of *Les Temps modernes* (August–September 1953) devoted to Indochina, especially Claude Bourdet, "Les hommes de la guerre," pp. 419–421.

[66] *J.O.*, May 5, 1950, p. 3309.

Navarre had perhaps never heard when he arrived to take command of the forces in Indochina in early May 1953.

In the four years intervening between the Revers-Mast scandal and the stage-setting for the final blow to French fortunes in the Orient, nothing and everything had changed. The political dilemma of maintaining national positions in collaboration with the sovereign but dependent "Associated States" had come no nearer to solution. But in the meantime two events of capital importance had occurred: a militant Communist China had arrived on the periphery of the fighting zone and cast its shadow over it, and the armistice in Korea had been concluded by the new American administration. The threat of Chinese intervention was now more squarely posed, and the Indochinese opponents were visibly transformed into the shadow-surrogates of Chinese and American power.

The political issue for the French, reeling from internal political weakness, became the hope of limited victory, stalemate, and negotiation. Marshal de Lattre is said to have perceived this before he died. This and the Laotian motive, cited earlier, are the background of Dien Bien Phu, a battle about which much has been and remains to be written.

General Georges Catroux has effectively described a main issue:

Dien Bien Phu was incontestably the bitter fruit of a strategic error of General Navarre. But it was also a fulfillment. It was the harsh penalization of the defects of a military policy undertaken long before the advent of the Laniel government and of methods ill-adapted to their purpose and furthermore imprecise. It was also the penalization of a defense organization of little coherence, which failed to define neatly the respective prerogatives of political power and military command.[67]

No sooner had General Navarre accepted his Indochina command than the René Mayer government fell, leaving a political void. The new Commander in Chief had not only to brief himself swiftly on an entirely new set of military problems, but to depend on a new array of civilian superiors and military subalterns. During the campaign season of 1952–1953, despite local successes by Generals Salan and Linarès, the Viet Minh had carried through a series of cleverly plotted raids across the Laotian border, which widened the strategic area of the war and dispersed French offensive capacity. Prospects for victory looked dim. General Navarre was therefore committed to the achievement of the "positions of strength" needed for a negotiating stance.

Additionally, the French government had had serious altercations with the Vietnamese national regime of Bao Dai and had fallen into a

[67] Georges Catroux, *Deux actes du drame indochinois* (Paris, 1959), p. 120.

position of extreme dependence on American military and financial aid. The augmentation of defending forces undertaken by Marshal de Lattre through the creation of a Vietnamese national army ("jaunissement") had been a signal failure.

Nevertheless, the form of strategy eventually adopted by General Navarre was of almost Cartesian clarity, avoiding many of the empirical mistakes of the past. The idea was to take the strategic defensive in 1953–1954 in preparation for a rational offensive in the following year. Major pressure was to be exerted on the enemy in the critical Delta region by General Cogny's troops, and the highlands of Annam were to be cleaned out in an operation christened "Atlante." Unfortunately, the political and strategic temptations of barring the enemy's path to Luang Prabang, the capital of Laos, denying him a part of his rice crop, and conceivably luring him into battle where his lines of supply were insecure were too overpowering. Already General Salan had daringly placed an air-dropped garrison at Na San in the upper Thai country, which had caused embarrassment to Vo Nguyen Giap.

The key to the Dien Bien Phu catastrophe was undoubtedly twofold: the temptation of attracting the Viet divisions to a place where the French anticipated logistical supremacy, and the obligation of ensuring the defense of Laos, which the French government had hinted at in its accords but never explicitly stated in military orders. As Jules Roy has put it, in his exhaustive treatment of the episode: "Il faut le défendre sans le défendre tout en le défendant" ("Laos had to be defended without being defended and all the while being defended").[68] General Navarre, as he wet his feet in the "merdier" (General Linarès's expression) of Indochina, became progressively intrigued with the temptation and bound by the obligation.

General Catroux has maintained that the meeting of the National Defense Committee that General Navarre attended on July 24, 1953, left the maximum of strategic flexibility in his hands, although it implied a political obligation to the kingdom of Laos. Consequently, the conclusion is that General Navarre "undertook on his own initiative an enterprise that he judged politically necessary." [69] The situation was not, however, without its nuances. The order defining General Navarre's mission in the general terms of "convincing the enemy of his impotence to achieve a military victory" and omitting any positive mention of Laos did not follow the July meeting. It arrived only after the repeated inquiries of the commander of the Expeditionary Force, dated November 13, 1953, and was not revealed until December 4,

[68] Jules Roy, *op. cit.,* p. 31.
[69] Catroux, *op. cit.,* pp. 148–149.

exactly the day after he had issued his own orders "to accept battle in the Northwest," centering the defense on Dien Bien Phu, a base "to be conserved at all cost." [70] Navarre, Roy says, hid the order.[71]

Robert Guillain, the newspaper correspondent who left such a memorable account of this episode, had seen things differently. Not only was the "general conduct of the most difficult of wars in the hands of civilian ministers who have no thorough acquaintance with the military aspects of their decisions," but "[the mission of defending Laos] was maintained without giving General Navarre the means he judged indispensable. He needed fifty thousand men . . . and they gave him less than twenty thousand. . . ." [72] By someone's mistake or by some series of mistakes, the defense of Upper Tonkin was determined in the winter of 1953. Impeccable as a strong point in "classical" terms, it was, as General Catroux pointed out, a deceptive position in the context of Asian strategy, in a locale where Western military textbooks are not generally in use.

"Dien Bien Phu — " wrote Guillain, "it is the fate of the whole Indochina War that is being settled there. . . ." He added:

If we lose, we won't be militarily out of action or out of Indochina, but politically the Indochina problem will no longer admit any variety of solutions. If the Viet Minh lose at Dien Bien Phu, they will not be militarily eliminated and we will not grasp victory . . . but their political downfall will be enormous.[73]

In succumbing to this temptation to battle, which his original plan said should be avoided before 1954, it seems certain that, with or without positive political direction, General Navarre was implementing a strategy whose dangers had been only too apparent to him earlier. A parliamentary committee investigating the background of the decision, in the wake of the catastrophe, dwelt on the fact that General Navarre had stepped outside the precise boundaries of civilian control in deciding to occupy and fortify Dien Bien Phu.[74] In the absence of further evidence, however, the fault would seem to lie in the system itself — a system that Pleven finally tried to rationalize with his "restricted committee," a system that Robert Guillain criticized also for not being broader and better informed. It was a system, too, for which the whole French legislature was at fault; in the words of the deputy Charles Serre:

[70] *Ibid.,* pp. 147, 155.

[71] If Roy (*op. cit.,* pp. 86–88) is right, Navarre's guilt is heavy.

[72] Guillain, *op. cit.,* p. 68.

[73] *Ibid.,* p. 32.

[74] J.-R. Tournoux, *op. cit.,* p. 460.

You often hear about the crisis of the State. If that crisis is often the fault of the administration, too often also it has its origin in our own faltering, the reflection of certain troubles of conscience which prevent us from assuming our responsibilities clearly.[75]

If we judge correctly, General Navarre had seen the outlines of his strategy accepted and the means to effect that strategy denied. He had demanded orders from the government and attempted to transact its implicit policy in the absence of direction (committing several military errors of his own), then had been censured in the aftermath not only for losing but for exceeding his prerogatives. But Navarre was a disciplined soldier; he later wrote in response to a critic:

Admiral Castex thinks . . . that "military strategy has the right to rebel, if necessary, to retire rather than submit," when "political bondage" leads it "along a path with risk of catastrophe at the end." This point of view — which I share entirely — ceases to be valid when the "political bondage" is such that to fail to conform would change the purpose of the war. Then, after demonstrating the risks to the political authority which, in the last resort, has the power to decide, the man responsible for "military strategy" can do nothing but "submit." To "retire" would be, in this case, a desertion.[76]

The history of the Indochina experience would not read as a valorous episode to the Army. In it they would see the magnified rigors of their own experience, records of political duplicity and ineptitude which had perhaps not fully reached them on the scene, a heightened consciousness of their alienation from civilian concerns (the Bourse, the rhetoric of the Palais Bourbon, the political dinners of the Brasserie Lipp on the Boulevard St-Germain). They would, in their intellectual vanguard, achieve a full meditation of these things, together with the horrible futility of their late mission. As Robert Guillain wrote of this "decimated, exhausted army" even before Dien Bien Phu: "When an army has a mission beyond its means, the only thing to do, unless you want the army to destroy itself, is to reduce the mission to the realm of the possible." [77] A report delivered by the General Staff to the Laniel government at about this time stated that "a cease-fire . . . would be greeted favorably by the Expeditionary Force. However, the greatest concern about the integrity of morale would have to be entertained if hostilities were then to be resumed." [78]

Instead, Dien Bien Phu and the horrifying constabulary tasks of the

---

[75] *J.O.*, January 28, 1950, p. 684.

[76] General Henri de Navarre, "Les données de la défense de l'Indochine," *Revue de Défense nationale*, March 1956, p. 273.

[77] Guillain, *op. cit.*, p. 62.

[78] Tournoux, *op. cit.*, p. 460.

evacuation followed, with hundreds of thousands of Western wards fleeing southward. As Colonel Jean Thomazo was later to testify, at the trial of General Salan: "When you have lived through these things and seen them, how can you avoid bearing in your heart a feeling of reprobation for the powers that tolerated them?" [79] This was the cancer that took root and grew, until it would shock the world. [80]

[79] *Le Procès de Raoul Salan* (stenographic reprint; Paris, 1962), p. 372.

[80] From the vantage point of March 1965, as I review this text for the last time, I cannot help being struck by the poignant parallels between the current American involvement in South Vietnam and many of the events I describe here. The arguments adduced both for and against a negotiated settlement and the dangers and virtues ascribed to each position have not changed greatly in the interval. The words are simply in the mouth of Secretary McNamara instead of Pleven, or of Senator Church instead of Daladier. The course of the war is not dissimilar; the centers of greatest guerrilla activity are strikingly reproduced. The French had the advantage of a relatively stable nationalist government; the Americans have finally discerned the value of having a buffer area (North Vietnam) between them and the great-power protagonist (China). Colonialism is a more oblique issue today. And, at this writing, America has gone to the air to win her "positions of strength," rather than seeking them in a Dien Bien Phu. For all that, most of the problems remain as obdurate as ever, and the Yankee solutions have been no more gifted than the French.

V

LA SALE GUERRE:
THE ENEMY

Depuis dix-sept mois je me battais contre ce peuple que je ne connaissais même pas. Si on me demandait pourquoi je suis venu en Indochine et pourquoi la France menait la guerre en ce pays, j'aurais honte . . . de ne pas savoir que répondre.
— *"Vietnam Information, No. 3/54," January 21, 1954, broadcast by a French aviation NCO, a prisoner of the DRVN*

IF THE pivot of the French Army's return to politics was Indochina, its spur was that enemy which it cajoled, threatened, fought, detested, and later grudgingly admired — the Democratic Republic of Vietnam, or, for short, the Viet Minh.[1] The Viet Minh was far from owing its chief success to highly individualistic groups of marauders and the miraculous initiative of local tactics. From the first days of the war thoroughly developed hierarchies were established in many places, and

[1] The terms Viet Minh or DRVN (Democratic Republic of Vietnam) are used interchangeably throughout this chapter to denote the Ho Chi Minh regime. An excellent study of the military organization of the Viet Minh will be found in Colonel Nemo's article "La guerre dans le milieu social," *Revue de Défense nationale*, May 1956, pp. 605–623. The structure of the state has been admirably covered by Bernard B. Fall in his voluminous *Le Viet-Minh, 1945–1960* (Paris, 1961). Much of this material may be found in the same author's *The Viet-Minh Regime* (Ithaca, 1954). For the benefit of those who read no French, I have referred exclusively to the latter work.

the network grew rapidly.[2] Vertical echelons of command extending from the highest headquarters to the remotest village came to be efficiently articulated. This is demonstrated not only by the Cromwellian discipline of the small groups but also by the ease with which regular troops could join the population to avoid capture, as well as the mobility between the various levels of troop command, the success of the recruitment agency, and the absorption of the dissident national elements into the war effort with a minimum of disruption. Throughout the war the DRVN remained a flesh-and-blood state on its own soil, observing — albeit under revolutionary conditions — the normal functions of a state. This clearly distinguishes it from the Algerian revolutionaries, who had to build on sand.

Viet Minh Administration

The general administrative apparatus of Ho's government was simply removed from Hanoi to the *maquis* at the outbreak of hostilities. The strict control he had already established in much of Tonkin permitted him to rally troops, command harvesting operations and food supply, issue money, control finance, and bargain in the international market for weapons and ammunition in a way that would have been precluded if he had started from scratch. Thus, in a certain sense, Indochina defied many of the later French models of revolutionary war: the actual conflict began in the mid-course of revolutionary articulation.

The requirements of this government-to-village hierarchy, if extraordinarily exacting, were often brilliantly fulfilled.[3] Liaison agents traveled widely, co-ordinating plans and actions and assuring integration of the national effort, or serving the French and spying on them.[4] Military units made exacting and seemingly impossible forced marches to reach objectives or escape pursuit, helped by their knowledge of the terrain and Spartan food requirements, and sustained by "the veritable mysticism of 'the road at any price' which had been instilled in both the troops and population," according to a publication of the French Information Services.[5] Logistical demands were exceedingly burden-

[2] See Fall, *op. cit.*, p. 24ff.

[3] Vietnamese society had had a millennial preconditioning for the type of stratification that was to be imposed so unrestrainedly by Ho Chi Minh. Strict hierarchies were observed in family, village, and state. Cf. André Leroi-Gourhan and Jean Poirier, *Ethnologie de l'Union française,* Vol. II (Paris, 1953), pp. 558–561.

[4] These agents, called Can Bo, were members of the party specializing in sabotage, antireligious struggle, propaganda, public education, assassinations, and co-ordination of the various networks. See Yvonne Pagniez, *Le Viet-minh et la Guerre psychologique* (Paris, 1955), pp. 15–16, also pp. 38–43.

[5] Fall, *op. cit.*, p. 85, quoting Claude Guiges, "Logistique viet-minh," in *Indochine-Sudest-Asiatique* (Saigon, March 1954).

some. It has been estimated that the two Viet Minh divisions operating in the Laotian offensive of 1953 used the services of a supply column of 95,000 porters.[6] But the fact remains that these things were accomplished. Clearly, too, it was a well-articulated government that went into hiding in December 1946 and a no less structurally complete one that returned triumphantly to Hanoi in October 1954. For the purposes of the Indochina War the DRVN was a vastly more efficient organization than the French Republic itself.

To be sure, Ho's administration was not a monolithic success. He was forced in many cases to use radical and violent methods to persuade the indifferent or subject the unsympathetic. The classical Oriental phenomenon of "warlordism" was never entirely absent from the common effort against the French. The areas of southern Annam and Cochinchina, which had always escaped Ho's administrative grasp, were torn by obscure sectarian factionalism. But, on the whole, the Viet Minh imposed its law with awesome discipline.

If, however, the Viet Minh entered the war enormously strengthened by a pre-existing network of administration, it did not as yet dispose of a particularly imposing military instrument. Its forces lent themselves to wide-ranging guerrilla activity, but it would take years to build the kind of army that could hope to fight major military engagements. Thus the burden of early resistance fell on the local village irregulars (Du-Kich), while, removed to the sanctuary of the high plateaus, General Giap began his systematic training of cadres for the regular forces (Chu-luc), which were formed first into autonomous battle groups, later into regiments and divisions. By the end of the war it was estimated that the DRVN possessed the equivalent of fourteen fully armed divisions and was augmenting its forces at the rate which weapons supply would permit.[7] Furthermore, military aid from the Communist bloc was arriving in significant quantity.[8] It was certainly not the impending threat of military attrition but rather diplomatic considerations that led the Viet Minh to acquiesce in the Geneva ceasefire.

The forces of the Chu-luc were unceasingly restored hierarchically from former fighters of the Tien Doan Tap Trung Tinh (territorial units) in sufficient number to compensate for the high casualty rate. This promotion was of great advantage to the soldier, both in social dignity and material standard of living.

[6] *Ibid.*, p. 86.

[7] *Ibid.*, p. 81.

[8] Bernard B. Fall, "Indochina — the Last Year of the War," *Military Review*, October 1956, pp. 3–11.

Before the Hanoi incident Ho had exhibited a certain doctrinal prudence toward his conduct of affairs and the balance sheet of national objectives. Now he proceeded to tighten his ideological grip over a nation at war. The Army, in particular, received the most thorough-going kind of political indoctrination and was conditioned to respond not only to patriotic pressures but to the imperative of class struggle. The political hierarchies typical of the structure of the state as a whole were duplicated in the Army, down to and including village level — a more stringent extension of the commissar system than the Soviet Army itself had ever known. As General Giap proclaimed: "The military force is the Party's essential arm for any political aim." Since the entire nation was on a war footing, this influence systematically penetrated all other social elements, including the humblest and most traditional.

The attack on illiteracy — always a concomitant of aggressive nationalism in Southeast Asia — melted imperceptibly into the teaching of elementary Marxist materials. The village schools were filled by government specialists who had at least a passing acquaintance with those aspects of "scientific socialism" that could strike a chord in the mind of the peasant; this campaign was feverishly extended to all territories won from the French or, through infiltration, often preceded military and administrative control. Meanwhile, savage reprisals against "Europeanized" Viets who served the French or collaborating village "notables" cautioned the waverers and the indifferent. The ritual Marxist emphasis on crop and production planning, the "Stakhanovite" mentality of overfulfillment of quotas, and the intrinsic connection between collective agriculture and collective political action played a role in accommodating the population to the regime's principles of organization.

Contrary-minded national elements were ruthlessly eliminated under the guise of wartime emergency, and the Communists succeeded in capturing the higher posts of the Army and bureaucracy.[9] In the days when negotiation with the French had seemed possible, Ho found it advisable to preserve the pretense of a coalition cabinet and a docile opposition. Still, it proved comparatively easy to shunt the liberals and non-Party men into innocuous positions or, better, appoint them to various negotiating teams and send them abroad while the loyal Communist hard core cemented its grip on the state apparatus. After the war broke out, it would be a simple matter to isolate and discredit these elements. The competing nationalist parties, though tactical allies of the Viet Minh in the legislative elections of January 6, 1946, would be ripe for suppression once they had been sundered from effective

[9] Fall, *The Viet-Minh Regime,* pp. 11–13.

contact with their sponsors, the Kuomintang. They had, moreover, never enjoyed great support in the countryside but had centered their activity mainly in the cities and the areas contiguous to the Chinese border; it was precisely these regions over which the French asserted control in the early stages of the war.[10]

French Tactical Errors: The Catholics and Other Sects

The French themselves, though not unaware of the need for a political alternative to the Viet Minh, lost two years before they finally achieved an inadequate equipoise in the person of Bao Dai. Meanwhile, many hesitant members of the Vietnamese intelligentsia, the "notables," and the numerically small bourgeois class, though fearing a Marxist Vietnam, nonetheless threw their support to Ho on patriotic grounds. The leader of the Viet Minh, in turn, used them until they ceased to be of value or, in some cases, converted them into passionate Communists. A few returned to the banner of Bao Dai, but without the impact their action would have made in 1947.

Certain national groups, because of their potency, had to be managed autonomously by Ho within the framework of his revolutionary state, even after the fighting had started. This was particularly true of the religious groups, the Catholics of Tonkin, the Cao Dai[11] and Hoa Hao of the South, and the widely scattered Buddhists. The sects of the South competed with the Viet Minh on a political plane. In the case of the Buddhists (nominally 80 per cent of the population)[12] it was feasible to promote a kind of "national Buddhism" linked to the aspirations of the Marxist state by intermediary committees and "hierarchies."

French policy stumbled badly in the case of the Catholics, a natural ally. Vietnamese Catholicism, claiming 10 per cent of the population and especially strong in part of Tonkin, had been long established and had taken a particularly vigorous lead in the independence movement, moreover with the active support of the French Catholic hierarchy. Sharing with the West a common treasury of spiritual values, it was nevertheless not to be deterred from national aspiration by any form

[10] *Ibid.*, map on p. 7.

[11] Leroi-Gourhan and Poirier, *op. cit.*, p. 578: "Finally in 1926 there appeared a new religion: Caodai-ism, which sought to create a synthesis of all the others: Confucianism, Buddhism, Christianity, and even Islam. Victor Hugo rubbed shoulders with Confucius, Buddha, Christ, Mohammed, Joan of Arc, and others." Hoa Hao, more aggressive, was less eclectic.

[12] *Ibid.*, p. 571. "In reality the religious life of the Vietnamese is rather shallow. . . . It consists especially of executing a great number of practices of diverse origins, varying with the nature of the accompanying acts . . . whence proceeds the great tolerance of the Vietnamese toward all religious systems without exception." See also p. 576.

of ulterior pressure. This is well illustrated by the appeal sent to Pope Pius XII by the four Vietnamese bishops on September 23, 1945, in support of the Provisional Government of Ho Chi Minh: "We Annamite Bishops beg Your Holiness, the Court of Rome, their Eminences the Cardinals, their Excellencies the Archbishops, the Bishops and all Catholics of the whole Universe and especially those of France, to support the decision of our dear Fatherland. . . ." [13]

The vacillating political intentions of the French substantially forfeited the support of the local Church hierarchy and, needless to say, the congregations in their charge. On the other hand, the Viet Minh, practicing a flexible policy toward the Catholics in the early days of the war, rallied many sympathies. Catholics fought in Giap's army, and, at best, the ecclesiastical authorities remained neutral, despite continual and severe pressure on them by the French to support the "forces of order."

As late as August 1953, the Viet Minh was able to attract a satisfactory modicum of Catholic support for its "National Congress of Religions," which concluded its deliberations by issuing a report calling for allegiance to the national effort of the Viet Minh and observing that "freedom of religion is inscribed in our Constitution and expressly recognized by the statutes of the National Front." [14] Even Yvonne Pagniez, the Swiss journalist, whose convictions were strongly in favor of the pacification and of the emergence of the Bao Dai state, admits in a description of her visit to the Tonkinese bishoprics in 1953 that a good deal of the old rancor remained: "To touch on a delicate subject — but we are anxious that this study . . . should leave nothing in shade — we can say that the famous Tonkinese bishoprics caused us more than one disappointment. It is not so long ago that, in the fief of Msgr. Le Hun Tu, the schoolteachers dictated this lesson to the pupils: 'We have two enemies, the Communists and the French.' " [15] But subsequent repressive activities of the Viet Minh were to lead to the voluntary migration of 500,000 Catholics into South Vietnam when the division of the country was formalized in 1954. [16]

Whereas both the Viet Minh and the French made continuous overtures for Catholic support, the former was able to touch the allegiance of these people at a time when national cohesiveness was imperative

[13] Fall, *The Viet-Minh Regime*, p. 70, quoting *Bulletin des Missions*, Vol. XX, Abbey of St-André-les-Bruges, "Un appel des évêques vietnamiens en faveur de l'indépendance de leur pays," 1946, pp. 38–40.

[14] *Ibid.*, p. 71.

[15] Yvonne Pagniez, *Choses vues au Viet-nam* (Paris, 1953), p. 83.

[16] See Dominique Tréanna, "Les évadés du paradis viet-minh," *Hommes et Mondes*, April 1955, pp. 78–87.

and then discard them at will. On the other hand, the French, if the ultimate beneficiaries of Catholic support, had been initially unable to exploit such an obvious fund of mutual interest. The unhappy fate of the Catholics themselves reveals the serious predicament of any moderate faction caught in the maelstrom of extremes.

Subversive Capacity of the Viet Minh

Numerous factors gave the Viet Minh an aptitude for subversive warfare. The first advantage was the political character of the apparatus. One cannot insist enough on the importance of the "civilian party control," which commanded a hierarchy as complete as that which can be found in any Communist country in time of peace. The Vietnamese Workers' Party concentrated both on doctrinal "guidance" and on practical matters, such as fulfillment of quotas, with vengeful exactitude. Its members were organized into cells and village committees, thence into three regional structures of graduated importance, and finally co-ordinated by a supreme central committee. From top to bottom the administrative responsibilities were well defined. The flow of information upward and orders downward was regular and uninterrupted. Political indiscipline was swiftly punished by appropriate sanctions, and autocriticism became a regular practice for preserving the spiritual cohesion of the enterprise and eliminating heresy at the root. Commandant Jacques Hogard, a contemporary expert in *la guerre révolutionnaire,* described the effects of this procedure: "Autocriticism, a confession made orally or in writing to a specialist, a sort of 'engineer of the soul,' is sometimes public, often private, always frequent. He who experiences it knows that it will be noted down and clipped together with all the other information the Party possesses with regard to his activities. Mature revolutionaries therefore have no need to generalize terror." [17] Because of its incessant and complex demands on the whole being of the individual, the party network, or the "parallel hierarchy," was often more fully articulated than its administrative counterpart.

In the case of the Army, an especially tight co-ordination was assured between the political and military hierarchies from General Staff level on down. Political indoctrination was provided at all times for the troops, even when on the march, and a well-organized short-wave radio network carried out psychological tasks as well as relaying orders and military information. In addition to the regular organic grip of the

[17] "Guerre révolutionnaire et pacification," *Revue militaire d'Information,* January 1957, p. 8.

Party on the troops, an Army-constituted corps of political commissars was established.[18]

As if this were not sufficient political control over a wartime nation with a primitive communications system, an extensive state police organization reached into the tiniest villages of the least accessible areas. Its primary concern was with internal subversion, and in fulfilling its mission it freely encouraged all loyal citizens to inform against "counterrevolutionaries." The police were closely connected with the Party hierarchy and administered by trusted Communists of long standing.

The picture is completed by a host of seemingly redundant administrative organs, even at the lowest echelons of the state. These were not exclusively concerned with executive activity, but might include paramilitary organizations, Chinese and Russian friendship societies, wounded veterans' groups, etc. These complicated vertical lines of force were crossed incessantly by lateral ones that bound each individual by even tighter ligatures to the state: leagues of mothers, of the youth, of the peasants, etc.[19] In short, there was no corner of the state into which the tentacles of the hierarchical apparatus did not reach. From this point of view, no modern people on earth — with the possible exception of the Chinese — has experienced less of individual liberty than the Vietnamese of the zones held by the government of Ho Chi Minh. But there appear to have been other compensatory exaltations, and this point was not lost on the later French proponents of *l'action psychologique*.

Propaganda Techniques of the Viet Minh

Propaganda was inseparable from the political techniques of the Marxist state. In discriminating among propaganda themes, it is useful to note the audiences to which the Viet Minh addressed itself.

Propaganda for the national Army was largely undertaken by the political commissars serving with the troops,[20] and in the case of the regular forces, it was generally less elementary than that served up to the civilian population. It stressed the elements of patriotic discipline

---

[18] It is estimated that the political commissars numbered as much as one sixth of the total officer corps.

[19] Again, the novelty of these corporative ligatures of the state can be overstressed. "Honorary associations" of veterans, the aged, etc., existed in pre-Communist times in the Vietnamese village and were instrumental in its direction. Cf. Leroi-Gourhan and Poirier, *op. cit.*, p. 568.

[20] Commandant Hogard states in "Le soldat dans la Guerre révolutionnaire," *Revue de Défense nationale*, February 1957, p. 212: "The Viet Minh devoted almost half its time to directing the 'political formation' of its troops."

and struck a careful balance between the themes of independence and class struggle. The extraordinary efficacy of the single phrase *Doc-Lap* (independence) was enough to impress many French officers with the salvations of sloganry, and it is on this analogy that the psychological warfare bureaus of the French Army concocted and prepared to launch the slogan "integration" in the days prior to May 13, 1958.

With regard to propaganda for the people, the principal themes and the results hoped for are summarized in a directive of June 1952: "To propagandize is to mobilize and to educate the population so as to make it hate the enemy; so that it shows ardor in national reconstruction and is fully confident of the final victory . . . the people have in their hearts love for the fatherland, hatred for the enemy, and the will to win." [21] The most emotional, immediate, and frenzied type of propaganda was given general dissemination, while the more sophisticated types, which stressed Marxist themes, were reserved for those groups that were politically and intellectually more advanced. Slogans for the accomplishment of specific tasks were also widely propagated, often accompanied by the dreary statistics of work quotas fulfilled in other parts of the country that are so typical of Communist exhortation and so frequently spurious. Basically, two other themes predominated: the *Doc-Lap* (independence) theme, and the *hate* theme. The latter underwent the usual metamorphoses: hatred of the French enemy, hatred of the imperialists, hatred of the whites, hatred of the rich. To it was joined the corollary of enemy atrocities, so familiar to American audiences after the Chinese germ-warfare campaigns. Far from confining themselves to reporting the many violations of human dignity (a stain upon both armies) that flowed from this exasperatingly cruel war, the Viet Minh invented accounts of Herculean rapes and, as Professor Fall informs us, of a barbaric scientific process whereby the French were able to convert puny Vietnamese into powerful Senegalese troops.[22]

Propaganda was carried on continuously within the neighboring states of Laos and Cambodia by special agitators and agents or beamed in by radio. Efforts, often quite transparent, were made to reach the many ethnic groups — Laotians, Khmers, Thais, Muongs, Meos — who lived within the boundaries of the polyglot former French protectorate. In general, these other peoples often entertained just suspicions concerning the petty imperialism of their aggressive neighbors. It is in Cambodia that the most critical agitation was waged by the Viet Minh, in collaboration with the Khmer Workers' Party, and not with-

[21] Quoted from Fall, *The Viet-Minh Regime*, p. 42.
[22] *Ibid.*, p. 44.

out some success. Their propaganda units infiltrated deeply into this country and took the lead in promoting a Khmer uprising, which became a serious side issue to the major war. The Cambodian state, while not enjoying especially cordial relations with its former protectors,[23] employed initiative in coping with these problems, aided by French military units, and the danger was checked if not totally eliminated.

In dealing with the large Chinese minority within their territory the Viet Minh exercised a nervous prudence which, after the victory of Mao Tse-tung, tended to go to rather unctuous extremes of flattery. The important revolutionary holidays of the huge neighbor were celebrated joyously, and the brotherhood of the two peoples was continually being stressed. Representatives of the People's Republic of China and local Chinese customarily played a welcome part in these ceremonies.

The propaganda effects wrought on the French forces were qualitatively more serious; the subsequent heavy emphasis which the French Army placed on troop information tells us as much. Here we have a situation where fewer of the effective fighting forces (excluding officers) were French nationals.[24] The propagandists of Ho Chi Minh swiftly recognized this and achieved a discrimination between French-directed and other-directed psychological warfare. The latter was further shaded to aim at North Africans, Black Africans, Germans, and other groups. The "captive colonial peoples" were, of course, enjoined to revolt against their imperialist masters and form a solid bloc with other oppressed nations. Later, a number of those Muslims who had fought in Indochina were to become cadres of the Algerian National Liberation Army. On the other hand, the Germans of the Legion were promised safe conduct back to East Germany, guaranteed full amnesty and professional training. Some seem to have deserted, but the surrounding circumstances are obscure, since it was a matter of prisoners of war who might have been involuntarily transported.

The propaganda themes used against the French very much followed the characteristic line of the Communist Party at home: questioning of the justice and legality of the war, imputations against the politicians

[23] The Khmers have never enjoyed friendly relations with the Vietnamese. In the critical period of Vietnamese expansion (eighteenth century) the Khmers were systematically evicted from Cochinchina, leaving, however, a substantial minority, which today is numbered at about 350,000. There is likewise a considerable Vietnamese population within the borders of Cambodia. It is justly estimated that Cambodia would sooner or later have been overrun by its more numerous neighbors, had it not been for the French intrusion in the nineteenth century.

[24] General Navarre, in "Les données de la défense de l'Indochine," Revue de Défense nationale, March 1956, p. 277, cites the following figures: 54,000 French, 20,000 North Africans, 18,000 Black Africans, 20,000 Légionnaires (mostly German).

and high command, stories to the effect that civilian France had forgotten them. Finally, the Viet Minh took full advantage of radio broadcasts in which "brainwashed" prisoners of war recounted their own doubts about Western democracy and their joy in discovering the remarkable clarity of the dialectic. If *Doc-Lap* became the recurrent internal motif of the Viet Minh propaganda machine, externally it was *la sale guerre*. The blood of many thousands of upright but misguided young Frenchmen was being spilled for John Foster Dulles and for Wall Street. Notwithstanding the many acts of heroism in combat by French soldiers and the unwavering will of that hard core found in any army, for whom the battle is its own compensation, many regular troops were, at bottom, politically naïve and needlessly responsive to the themes of a carefully controlled propaganda. This could not be expressed numerically, even if figures were available; it affected the vague domains of stamina and resolution in the constitutions of otherwise loyal soldiers.

When the Viet Minh moved into a newly conquered area, it brought its vast and flexible political network in its wake. This made reconquest harder and re-education sometimes impossible. The village schoolhouse became the center of powerful efforts of agitation and indoctrination from the time it fell into revolutionary hands; exemplary reprisals, deportations, and executions completed the picture.

The stationary condition of the Vietnamese village population was distinctly favorable to the Viet Minh's conduct of the war.[25] As the aggressive force, they were thus provided with a series of static targets which could be attacked in the desired order either by force of arms or propagandistic infiltration. The French forfeited the advantage they might have gained from being able to dislocate hostile populations from critical areas where guerrilla tactics were having a disruptive effect. Neither could they rescue friendly elements through displacement in situations that counseled military withdrawal. Gradually, some realized that this procedure could have materially aided the war effort.[26]

The famous "*pourrissement* of the Delta" illustrates better than any other example the methods employed by the Viet Minh in advancing

---

[25] Material advantages often accrued to the villagers if they resisted the temptation to emigrate. Aside from the strong traditional ties of the community, they might expect to benefit periodically from the redistribution of communal lands. Leroi-Gourhan and Poirier, *op. cit.*, p. 566.

[26] Jacques Dinfreville, *L'Operation Indochine* (Paris, 1952), p. 149, complains: "Why wasn't the system of resettlement of populations that had been practiced by the British in Malaya used in Indochina?"

its hold over populations and territory. In many cases its success in this area long preceded its extension of administrative control. Yvonne Pagniez describes the evolution of the situation:

Entire regiments infiltrate into the very interior of the protected zone. . . . Cleverly dispersed, these "regulars," according to the consecrated expression, "encyst" themselves in small groups, in underground posts hidden from the air and in reconnaissance patrols, establishing arms and ammunition depots, supply dumps, stations for the wounded. . . . The population, feeling no longer safely protected by the Franco-Vietnamese army, falls to the mercy of the rebels, who know how to exploit both persuasion and terror. . . . The village chief and the "notables" faithful to the Bao Dai government are assassinated. Viet Minh functionaries are substituted to surround and keep careful watch over the citizens. A schoolteacher instructs the children in Marxist doctrines. The young men are raked over in the search for soldiers. And Communist cells partition each little citadel, imprisoning it in their espionage net.[27]

The lessons of Vietnam seemed to indicate that in the future the "forces of order" would be obliged to reach the indigenous populations ahead of the rebels with an effective, if simple, social doctrine that could offset the magic of the word "independence." Furthermore, the natives would have to be trained in effective methods of self-defense or, failing that, would have to be relocated and protected in another area, while awaiting pacification of their own region.

Prison Camps of the Viet Minh

Under the influence of the techniques of the Chinese Communists, the Viet Minh began to allow themselves extensively the luxury of taking prisoners, especially after the appearance of their northern comrades at the border in 1949. No longer were the captured French, African, or "loyalist" Vietnamese regarded as a disagreeable burden — and frequently shot — but as raw material for repentance and conversion. An intercepted Chinese directive of 1952 points out very clearly the doctrine regarding prisoners in the People's Republic:

When our volunteers capture enemy soldiers on the battlefield [French or puppet soldiers], they should immediately send the captives through their respective units to our General Headquarters for questioning. Afterward they should be delivered to the General Headquarters of the Vietnamese People's Army. No unit is to mistreat prisoners of war. . . . Our comrade political workers must also use every means to gain the support of the captives with propaganda, utilizing them to do anti-French work such as

[27] Pagniez, *Choses,* pp. 64–65.

broadcasting, writing letters, and exposing the weak points of their troops, and the violent conduct of the French forces.[28]

The experiences of some of the prisoners have become next to legendary, for this is the context in which certain French officers received the full brunt of the *action psychologique* that was to leave an undying impression on their concept of warfare. All prisoners were given political indoctrination, were kept alive by a bare minimum of daily rations (which, however, might vary according to their political potential) once they had reached the staging area, and in addition were subjected to manual labor as coolies in the Viet Minh supply trains.[29] On January 15, 1954, the French government officially protested against the "inadmissible political indoctrination of the prisoners," but quite obviously without result.

Camps of prisoners were formed indiscriminately — the officers being mixed with the NCO's and the latter compelled to address their superiors by their last name — and an intensive, carefully prepared program of ideological training was followed. The indoctrination included compulsory readings and lectures on Marxists texts, study groups, and the enforced practice of autocriticism. As the process began to take effect, discrimination in duties and rations was introduced, and obvious efforts were made by the captors to create doubt and apprehension among the prisoners as to the intentions of one another. The extreme procedures of the Viet Minh obtained results in numerous cases. Some soldiers — many of whom later renounced their action — were persuaded to make ideological broadcasts which were beamed to the French Expeditionary Force. Incessantly, petitions of the germ-warfare variety were circulated, and often signed collectively in despair, ironically, or under menace.

In a noteworthy article, constructed as a dialogue by two French field-grade officers, which appeared in 1956 in the *Revue des Forces terrestres,* many of these events and methods are discussed. One conclusion reached is the following:

Insufficiently prepared, many officers, if not all, believed that Communism could be known by studying its slogans closely. A number of them were diffusely conscious that this was a dead-end street, but without having clearly reasoned why; and it is not very remarkable that after five years of this regimen some liberated prisoners should have pounced on the funda-

[28] *Far Eastern Notes, No. 8* (May 7, 1954), p. 11. Political Department of the General Headquarters of the Chinese People's Volunteers to Help Vietnam. Printed and issued on December 15, 1952. Reproduced in Allan B. Cole (ed.), *Conflict in Indo-China and International Repercussions: A Documentary History, 1945–1955* (Ithaca, 1956), p. 130.

[29] Conditions were, of course, brutal and subhuman on the march. See testimony in *Les Réscapés de l'enfer* (Paris, 1954), *passim.*

mental works of the Marxist doctrine so as to understand finally the nature of Communism.[30]

This was to be the spontaneous reaction of a small but influential group often identified collectively under the name of "Milites," who ultimately succeeded in drawing the attention of their chiefs to the full ideological aspect of *la guerre révolutionnaire*.[31]

The prisoners were treated according to nationality; for this, too, was a cardinal point of Ho's psychological action. Basically, the same principles that applied to propaganda production were in force in the prison camps. Europeans were sequestered together and received the same treatment, although special themes were employed where applicable. We know, in fact, of the liaison existing between the Viet Minh propaganda and that of the French Communist Party. An anomalous legal situation actually permitted a Viet Minh mission, under the supervision of Tran Ngoc Danh, to operate in Paris during the early years of the war, even while French troops were dying in combat; it is one of the agents of this mission that received the highly confidential Revers Report. After the war had ended, a newspaper entitled *La Voix du Rapatrié* sponsored by the French Communist Party kept the ex-prisoners informed about conditions in the DRVN.[32] Because of these links with the metropolitan Communists the Viet Minh had no difficulty in casting their indoctrination in terms most familar to French ears.

In the case of the non-Caucasian races, the approach was much more friendly. If the captured Algerians or Senegalese were not exactly killed with kindness, they were granted more sympathetic attention than the Europeans. An Italian legionnaire reports as follows:

. . . if the Viets treated the legionnaires badly, knowing well that Communist propaganda would not affect them, they acted otherwise with the North Africans, fed them a bit better, though distributing to them along with cigarettes a fiercely anti-French propaganda. "The French," they said, "are your enemies, just as they are ours. They seek only to enslave you. Only communism can liberate you. Go and rebel, and teach your racial brothers." [33]

Summary

The significance of Ho's doctrine of war was not as yet entirely grasped by the French. To them a "pacification" was still predomi-

[30] "L'endoctrinement des prisonniers de guerre dans les camps du Viet-minh": a dialogue between Battalion Chief Grand d'Esnon and Captain Prestat, *Revue des Forces terrestres*, October 1956, pp. 31–46.

[31] See Chapter VII, pp. 110–124, and Chapter VIII, p. 130.

[32] Fall, *The Viet-Minh Regime*, p. 56.

[33] *Les Réscapés*, p. 97.

nantly military, and insofar as the tactics of regular armies could not be employed, the principle was *divide et impera*. There was still little thought of using doctrine to fight doctrine. Of course, it was essential in a territorial war to gain the sympathies of the regional chiefs or "notables" and to work through them wherever possible to eradicate trouble, but the Viet Minh effectively forestalled this technique by terror and reprisal.

For Ho, on the other hand, the war was, first of all, political, and consequently *total*. All available resources were carefully manipulated and applied toward a unified end. The economic, social, and ideological terrains were major battlefields in their own right. The rumor became no less a weapon than the bullet; the propaganda tract might be worth a number of artillery shells. Soldier melted into civilian imperceptibly and re-emerged just as stealthily. Women carried messages along jungle trails; small boys pasturing their buffaloes counted French ammunition trucks moving up and down the roads. Viet Minh currency appeared mysteriously in the market place of a "protected" town without a hint of military operations in the neighborhood. Such tactics were unnerving and difficult to challenge.

An army could withdraw, bide its time, avoid the necessity of a major battle which might have risked disaster; the trophy of war became the population itself. Thus the conduct of a regular campaign might be meaningless and futile. On the other hand, it would be dangerous if the "forces of order" merely lent themselves to a servile imitation of enemy tactics. When defeat finally came to the French, it was stunning, and the torpor of embarrassment descended. Gradually, the bits and pieces of the experience were picked up and reglued with the mortar of theory into the new military doctrine in which *la guerre révolutionnaire* and some of its psychological corollaries were to play so large a role.

VI

LA SALE GUERRE:
PACIFICATION AND EMPIRICAL
RESPONSE

Pour amener progressivement les populations à vouloir la
pacification, à 's'engager' à nos côtés et à combattre s'il le faut,
une seule méthode est possible: l'intégration ou au moins la
combinaison étroite des efforts de tous, civils et militaires.
— *Jacques Hogard, "Le Soldat
dans la Guerre Révolutionnaire"*

As THE French gained experience in Indochina, the stodgy immobility of classical warfare was challenged. If the high command was late
to draw conclusions about refashioning its techniques of combat, junior
commanders in the field (often at company or battalion level) perceived through bitter circumstance that the traditional manual of tactics
had to be thrown away. But these responses were largely isolated and
empirical, spread out over a vast territory where the conditions of the
battle fluctuated. They implemented no single viable strategy of countersubversive warfare.

The political and propaganda measures were equally reactive. At
no time during the Indochina War did the French Army really assign
a paramount urgency to these tasks or pursue them as an inseparable
part of the military problem. Still, many could not help but observe

91

that this was precisely one of the foundations for the enemy's persistency and success. Yet the new strivings after a combined political-military doctrine were not born exclusively in reaction to the methods of the enemy. For there were similarities as well as distinctions to be observed between the new techniques of subversive war and the time-honored principles of *pacification*.

Pacification

Pacification in contemporary terms still bears the meaning of the over-all pursuit of action tending to re-establish peaceful conditions in an overseas territory. But the time span between the period of first colonization and the present led necessarily to radical changes in the method and context of the action. Marshals Galliéni and Lyautey, France's unremitting colonizers, had based their notions on a sense of mission that is now as obsolete as the military tactics of the turn of the century. Lyautey had had a broad vision of a stern but benign imperialism in which the French race exchanged the courtesy of its superior civilization for the acquisition of territories that could enhance France's strategic and commercial place in the world. The native peoples were to be treated humanely; allowed to develop politically, but not too much; educated, but scarcely beyond literacy and the essential vocational tasks required of them.[1] Evolution toward independence was only barely conceivable; the relation was fundamentally one of mutual interest between a highly developed race and a backward one.[2]

The presence of the superior power could assure conditions of tranquillity in which the native population — usually divided among unfriendly tribes — could achieve the maximum advantages of its regressive stage of civilization. Campaigns of pacification were therefore usually waged: (1) to assert control over hitherto unoccupied territory;

[1] Cf. Louis H. G. Lyautey, *Lettres du Sud de Madagascar, 1900–1902* (Paris, 1935), p. 290: "Primary education . . . with less ambitious objectives than today would avoid a grave peril that is already threatening to form a population of outcasts to whom no employment can be given, fully prepared to make up a class of discontented and needy. In the same order of ideas we have been able in the South [of Madagascar] to remark how important it is to exercise prudence in sending natives to French schools. Neither the speeches made by those who have come back nor the letters they write from France to their friends in Madagascar favor our authority."

[2] In its most liberal form, this attitude was touched with a lively realization of social justice. Cf., for example, the speech of Albert Sarraut on July 19, 1930, before the Comité National d'Etudes Sociales et Politiques: "In the name of humanity and its right to live, colonization, the agent of civilization, will administer those riches which the weak possessed without profit for themselves. But as a trustee of civilization, whose strength is in human solidarity, the colonizer falsifies his mission and destroys his authority if he seeks to escape the moral obligations that inhere in everything he does."

(2) to protect commercial interests; (3) to assist native elements friendly to the imperial power and drive off their enemies; (4) to keep order as evidence of efficiency, responsibility, and the advantages of colonial rule. Nationalist uprisings on the scale of today were impossible; either the national sense of the people was not highly developed or difficulties of communication over any appreciable distance precluded concerted action. Plentiful armament was not available nor the knowledge of its use widespread, and "spheres of influence" agreements among the colonial powers tended to keep gunrunning within manageable limits. Pacifications of seventy years ago were most frequently undertaken against warring tribes, pirates, or similar elements.

It was clear by the 1940's and 1950's that these old circumstances no longer applied. But both the old doctrines of *pacification* and the new theories of social action recognized that a favorable situation between colonial rulers and colonized peoples could best be achieved by a judicious measure of fraternization. Metropolitan soldiers and functionaries were to establish fruitful contacts with the indigenous populations, going among them to perform educational services, distribute aid in time of catastrophe, train their soldiers, care for the sick. Thus Lyautey had written, in his essay "Du Rôle Colonial de l'Armée":

In brief, the goal pursued by General Galliéni is the use of each man of the occupation army according to his talents for the good of the colony. What he cannot abide is that the lively force which a Frenchman in the colonies represents would remain unemployed. . . . Ah, that audacious idea of spreading our men throughout the native population, tolerated, as I say, planned, ordered by General Galliéni — what have we not heard said about it by the guardians of the Holy Writ? But the facts are there. . . .[3]

This idea, as much as any of the novel conceptions of modern war, was to inform the creation of the Specialized Administrative Sections (SAS) in Algeria in 1955.[4]

At the turn of the present century, Galliéni and Lyautey had introduced striking new concepts of strategy and combat into a military organization imbued with the Continental experience and the Napoleonic reflex. Many of these innovations not only were radical in their time but would continue to prove their effectiveness long after. Between the Lyauteyan pacifications and the French colonial experience of the 1950's there is an undisguised doctrinal continuum; the earlier theory, as it were, created a habit of mind in which acceptance of new

[3] Lyautey, *op. cit.,* pp. 284–285.
[4] Governor-General Jacques Soustelle signed the decree creating these entities on September 26, 1955, thereby reanimating the old idea of "Arab bureaus," which had been started by Marshal Bugeaud over a hundred years earlier. See Chapter X, p. 175.

departures could come about more quickly. Nothing illustrates this continuum more succinctly than a quotation from one of Galliéni's directives, written on May 22, 1898, in Madagascar:

The best means for achieving pacification in our new colony is provided by combined application of force and politics. It should be remembered that, in the course of colonial struggles, we should turn to destruction only as a last resort and only as a preliminary to better reconstruction. We must always treat the country and its inhabitants with consideration, since the former is destined to receive our future colonial enterprises and the latter will be our main agents and collaborators in the development of our enterprises. Every time that the necessities of war force one of our colonial officers to take action against a village or an inhabited center, his first concern, once submission of the inhabitants has been achieved, should be reconstruction of the village, creation of a market, and establishment of a school. It is by combined use of politics and force that pacification of a country and its future organization will be achieved. *Political action is by far the more important.* It derives its greatest power from the organization of the country and its inhabitants.[5]

In the absence of a concrete political mission for much of the war, this is precisely what the French Army was unable to do with any consistency in Indochina. Internationalized in essence, politics had overgrown the skills and competences of military force. In Algeria the Army would come closer to success and inevitably closer to the chronic bitterness born of failure.

The Growth of Countersubversive Theory

Countersubversion was not, however, a realm of activity for which any previous pacifications (including the Rif War of 1931–1934 or the more recent bloody events of Madagascar in 1947) had prepared the French Army. The initial reaction to the success of the Viet Minh's program of subversion was the wish to emulate the tactics of the enemy, on the assumption that subversive war and countersubversive war are analogous. An article by Colonel Schmuckel in the *Revue des Forces terrestres* recommends this.[6] Here the issue is not one of employing totalitarian practices but the simpler problem of copying the enemy's military operations. A vigorous answer by Colonel Trinquier, an Indochina veteran and expert at the Geneva Conference in 1954,

---

[5] Cited in Marshal Lyautey's article, "Du rôle colonial de l'Armée," *Revue des deux mondes,* CLVII (1900), p. 316. Quoted by Jean Gottmann, "Bugeaud, Galliéni, Lyautey: The Development of French Colonial Warfare," in Edward Meade Earle (ed.), *Makers of Modern Strategy* (Princeton, 1941), p. 243.

[6] Colonel Schmuckel, "Contre-guérilla," *Revue des Forces terrestres,* April 1956, pp. 5–24.

attacks this point.[7] On the contrary, says Trinquier, no method that depends on servile imitation is apt to bring success; we must improve on the enemy's revolutionary tactics and oppose him where he is weakest. This can be accomplished by denying him the support of the surrounding population and by depriving him, by whatever means possible, of his food supply, on which the strength of his army depends. Trinquier goes on to cite an operation conducted in Cochinchina in 1949 along these lines, which resulted in an unquestioned success.

Finally, in the sphere of psychological warfare itself the French Army had no doctrine and little experience. It is significant that the primary impetus for a special branch came not from the armchair planners, as one would ordinarily expect, but from the intelligence staffs and the officers in the field. The nominal independence of Bao Dai's "Associated State of Vietnam" demanded that this operation be undertaken under the auspices of both the government of Saigon and the French Expeditionary Force command, which was at this time led by General Salan. Thus a "Direction Générale de la Guerre Psychologique" was duly created in October 1952 under joint civil-military direction, with a Vietnamese official, Nguyen Huu Long, as its head. He was assisted by French and Vietnamese advisors, Commandant Fossey-François and Colonel Don, respectively. The official text set forth a mission "of proposing, carrying out, and integrating all activities judged necessary for the waging of psychological war throughout the national territory."[8] Basically the mission divided itself into two components: improvement of the morale of the national army, and agitation in the fence-sitting villages and among certain of the prisoners of war, in all places where the roots of Ho's ideology had not as yet sunk too deep for the "demonstration effect" to promise a fair measure of success.

The absence of ideological propaganda in the initial French efforts is not strange. In the first place, it was hard to determine exactly what type of ideology could effectively challenge Ho's Marxism, which, below the surface of the dialectic, combined quasi-religious fervor with a sort of Asian Robin-hoodery. Lacking a positive message, Franco-Vietnamese offerings tended to become counterpropaganda. They dealt with practical matters: how to cultivate a better crop, how to improve harvesting operations, how to take advantage of educational opportunities, and the like. "What doctrine do you oppose to the Marxist teaching which has so often been given these peasants?" asked Yvonne

[7] Roger Trinquier, "Contre-guérilla," *Revue des Forces terrestres*, July 1956, pp. 128–134.

[8] Yvonne Pagniez, *Choses vues au Viet-nam* (Paris, 1954), p. 116.

Pagniez of a psychological warfare officer in Hanoi. " 'None,' he replied, with a shadow of regret too timid for my satisfaction. 'We still don't have any. We have to be happy for the time being with issuing anti-Communist propaganda. We turn all the theories, all the claims of the enemy, upside down to show how they have been lying. That's the main thing.' " [9]

Also, one had to take into account the temperamental qualities of the Vietnamese themselves. Traditionally an industrious, self-effacing people who attached little importance and considerable embarrassment to shows of emotion, they were basically loath to overdramatize issues in the way that successful propaganda must do. Ho's vigorous campaign, based on a skillful blend of contagious enthusiasm and terror, had miraculously managed to awaken fanaticism in his followers. Nonetheless, it was difficult to see how reform, as opposed to revolution, could achieve as impressive a result. The themes most capable of arousing passion in this phlegmatic population were *atrocity* and *deceit*. Each side tried feverishly to attack whatever confidence the other enjoyed. "The reactionary imperialists have betrayed you, and continue to enrich themselves at your expense," thundered the Viet Minh apparatus. Now the Franco-Vietnamese teams railed against the duplicity of the Viet Minh:

He comes to you talking about independence; but it's your rice he's after, your corn, your potatoes. . . . How many times have you seen the village chief forced by the enemy, under threats, to make a tithe of your harvests, so as to build up, they tell you, a reserve in case of famine, sheltered from the danger of fire at some distance from the huts. A good long distance, in fact, because it's the reserve of the Viet. He'll "eat" your health with it; and you are no better off than rats.[10]

This counterpropaganda had a certain success, because it could be verified by experience and observation. Still, the Viet Minh continued to have the best of the "duplicity" theme; and they had made *Doc-Lap* their word.

A low literacy rate in Vietnam (which Ho was straining every nerve to overcome in the sections that he controlled)[11] made the written word, even when accompanied by photographs or drawings, of limited value. Literate persons in the Bao Dai territories had, for more sophisticated reasons, already turned their back on intransigent Marxism; those in the Viet Minh areas were likely to be convinced Communists

[9] *Ibid.*, p. 127.

[10] *Ibid.*, p. 151.

[11] Stories are told of cases where peasants were forcibly prevented from buying and selling goods in market until they had learned their daily lesson. An effective language reform was also speedily undertaken by the Viet Minh, which had a majority of the country's educators and linguists.

whom even the most effective propaganda had little chance of touching. Therefore, great reliance had to be placed on the spoken word and its dissemination. Whispering campaigns (*la propagande chuchotée*) were resorted to in many instances. The radio could generally be employed only to reach the military units and some of the urban population that owned receiving sets. Elsewhere, use was made of portable loudspeakers, mounted either in trucks or low-flying aircraft. This technique betrays the influence of the Americans, who had already an established military doctrine for psychological war and had practiced the art tactically in Korea.[12] The electric loudspeaker equipment was, in fact, of American issue, and American psychological warfare personnel advised and instructed the French from their own knowledge of "psywar" tactics: themes to be employed, methods of propaganda production, techniques of communication. Basically, the type of audio propaganda practiced by the French in Vietnam belonged to the category that the United States Army calls "consolidation propaganda."[13] The doctrines of consolidation propaganda were orginally developed for either mopping-up operations or control of civilian populations in occupied territory.

A characteristic example might find a Franco-Vietnamese propaganda team taking a loudspeaker truck to some small village recently recovered from the grip of the Viet Minh, where the people would still fear to collaborate with the French, thinking that their oppressors might return. A band of native musicians might be on the truck, for the effectiveness of musical accompaniment in an *action psychologique* was well recognized. The truck would stop in the middle of the village; the band, its volume magnified by the loudspeakers, would strike up, sometimes with traditional music, sometimes with a military march. Their curiosity aroused, the peasants would come running. Comments Yvonne Pagniez:

Their attitude, to be sure, is at first timid and suspicious. Who was after them now? What unpleasantness might happen after this spontaneous little show? To reassure these simple people, to prepare the terrain for the cultivation of the soul [*sic*] is quite an art. A thousand little ruses are needed, also intelligence and sympathy. The children are given candy. Then the announcers address the public, try to open up a general conversation, talking

---

[12] It has unfortunately been impossible to establish the earliest use of these techniques in Indochina by the French. The meager accounts of such operations seem to relate uniquely to the Psychological Warfare Services. However, Jean-Marie Domenach, in *La propagande politique* (Paris, 1950), alludes — without reference — to such cases, and Domenach's book was published before the formation of the "Direction Générale de la Guerre Psychologique."

[13] See Extension Course of the Psychological Warfare School, U.S. Army Subcourse 12, "Consolidation Propaganda Operations" (Fort Bragg, N.C., June 2, 1954).

the language of the peasants, showing interest in their work and their worries. "It seems you had a good harvest this year?" Objections. A farmer is never satisfied with his harvest. And now the contact is made, the bond is tied. . . .[14]

This scenario, simple in itself, became the prototype of a certain mode of psychological action, even though the methods were refined through experience. The novelty of the loudspeaker device contributed to its effectiveness. Superiority and flexibility of transmission could be obtained from the electric loudspeaker mounted in a low-flying airplane or helicopter, even though the advantages of direct contact were sacrificed. As a United States Army document somewhat magisterially remarks: "Among many primitive peoples a supernatural importance is attached to the voice from the sky." [15]

Re-education and Reform

An exceptional and (if we are to believe Yvonne Pagniez) profitable excursion into the more rarefied reaches of psychological action — directly inspired by the practices of Ho Chi Minh — was the "rehabilitation camp" (*Le Camp de la Liberté*) established in 1953 twenty kilometers from Hanoi by the Psychological Warfare Office of Tonkin. This was a "school" for the re-education of Viet Minh prisoners, carefully selected for their special aptitude. An atmosphere of "voluntary constraint" surrounded its operations. The intention was not only to turn the soldiers of the Viet Minh away from Marxism but to make of them effective and skillful propagandists for the Bao Dai government and the French Union.

Miss Pagniez comments that it was not difficult to turn the Communist ardor of the Viet Minh prisoners in other directions. But it is reported from other sources that the most thoroughly indoctrinated fighters of Ho proved generally unshakable regardless of the skill employed in their "re-education." In fact, the journalist herself notes: "The soldiers of the regular army, especially the officers, have more stubborn convictions. Some are impossible to shake, including the political commissars and, generally speaking, those who are members of the Communist Party." [16] She goes on to say that the majority of persons chosen for the sojourn in the Camp de la Liberté were civilians, guerrilla fighters, or village irregulars, "prisonniers susceptibles de donner satisfaction."

[14] Pagniez, *Choses*, p. 126.
[15] Extension Course, Lesson 11, "Psychological Warfare Operations," *op. cit.*, p. 42.
[16] Pagniez, *Choses*, p. 120.

The camp could hold three hundred men at one time, although the "graduating classes" were staggered in thirds. Three large barracks accommodated a hundred men apiece, who were divided according to their "political permeability." Neatness, simplicity of style, and fresh paint were the order of the day. However, public rooms were allotted to recreation or the exercise of manual skills; here the internees could give vent to their decorative impulses on traditional holidays. The day commenced at 6 A.M. with a patriotic ceremony during which the Vietnamese (Bao Dai) national flag was hoisted and the national anthem sung. Then there followed a physical exercise period. From 7:30 to 11:30 A.M., the prisoners were employed in manual labor; those with a useful skill were allowed to practice it. With the exception of sleep, meals, and a limited amount of leisure, the rest of the day was devoted to pedagogical training — that is to say, counterpropaganda and "citizenship." In each dormitory, moreover, there was the inevitable loudspeaker, which transmitted news, songs, and political instruction at random to the internees. The prisoners were encouraged to edit their own newspaper, in which they could make public record of their political reconsiderations or give their literary talents a chance for expression. There was an orchestra and a theatrical group. As certain inmates grew politically reliable, they were permitted to accompany the sound truck to the countryside and make broadcasts to their fellow citizens.

The psychological war had also to be fought on the fronts of educational, social, and agricultural reform. In all these cases Ho Chi Minh had made a considerable head start — in the recruitment of teachers, establishment of schools (and even universities), as well as land seizure and redistribution, confiscation of goods, and indemnificatory taxation; furthermore, he had the advantage of his proletarian doctrine. The Vietnamese national government of Bao Dai had neither the ability nor the desire to resort to these lengths of totalitarian surgery on the body social; it is probable that its efforts erred on the side of modesty. However, an extensive agricultural ordinance of June 9, 1953, attempted to rectify the worst abuses by redistributing abandoned land, setting limits on the terrain a single proprietor might cultivate, and accommodating the needs of some of the landless peasantry.[17] It came too late to be significant in the outcome of the war.

[17] *Ibid.*, pp. 200–203.

Resettlement Experiments in Cambodia

Mass resettlement was not widely practiced in Vietnam for a number of reasons:[18] strong traditions of village solidarity, scarcity of new areas because of the extreme demographic density of the more habitable parts of the country, and desirability of not interrupting the intensive forms of agriculture practiced by the Vietnamese. However, these same factors militated in favor of village or communal self-defense structures.[19] It was the Viet Minh that took particular advantage of this state of affairs, both within its own zone and in the Franco-Vietnamese areas through the clandestine imposition of "parallel hierarchies" on the normal political arrangement. When the Vietnamese National Army of Bao Dai came to be formed, it possessed no such formidable network of irregulars. Still, there was occasion, particularly in Cochinchina, for the instruction of whole villages in the effective means of self-protection. This involved not only training in methods of local and especially nocturnal combat, but also means of passive defense, such as concealment of the harvest, warning systems, and, of course, education of the village population about the issues at stake. Counterespionage and propaganda against the covert Viet Minh agents, the Can Bo, were also a part of the picture.

By contrast to Vietnam, different procedures were applied in the neighboring state of Cambodia. An article by Captain André Souyris, a frequent analyst of *la guerre révolutionnaire,* described these measures in detail.[20] His study had a considerable influence on the later pursuit of pacification operations in Algeria.

"Counterguerrilla" tactics in Cambodia were to be anchored to the technique of resettling large portions of the population.[21] There are a number of reasons why resettlement should have been viable in Cambodia, and not in Vietnam. In the first place, Cambodia was not so densely populated as Vietnam, thus providing greater opportunities for

[18] But see *The New York Times* dispatch filed by Tillman Durdin, April 29, 1960, describing government-sponsored relocations in South Vietnam as a passive defense measure against Communist operations. These "agrovilles" did not prove wholly successful.

[19] André Leroi-Gourhan and Jean Poirier, *Ethnologie de l'Union français,* Vol. II (Paris, 1953), p. 569: "Mutual aid may be shared among several villages, thus forming intercommunal alliances (Giao-hieu) with the aim of the widest possible protection against brigands, who formerly constituted a real danger."

[20] André Souyris, "Un procédé éfficace de contre-guérilla," *Revue de Défense national,* June 1956, pp. 686–699.

[21] Resettlement of populations was extensively practiced against the Communist terrorists in Malaya under the administration of General Sir Gerald Templar in 1951, accounting for the involuntary displacement of about half a million persons, most of them Chinese farmers and part-time laborers.

demographic mobility. The village structure was not so severely hierarchical, nor were the traditions binding the peasant to the exact confines of his community so strongly felt. The Cambodian, more-over, has been temperamentally softened over a period of many centuries by his contact with the gracious winds of Buddhist and Hindu culture blowing from the West; he has not the assiduous and stern character of his neighbor beyond the Mekong. He is more flexible, pliable, given to leisure and the pastimes of song and dance, and he exhibits in his social customs and mores a becoming lack of tenacity which, however, often degenerates into laxity. Finally, the revolutionary Viet was regarded as an invader. Some two hundred years ago the sovereignty of the Khmer state had been extinguished in Cochinchina by the constant and aggressive pressure of the more numerous Viet-namese spreading down from the north, and there was little historical affection between the two peoples.

A considerable Vietnamese minority was living within the frontiers of Cambodia. These people often fulfilled the same role as the Chinese in Vietnam, being artisans and shopkeepers, while the vast majority of Khmers remained peasants or fishermen. A substantial proportion of this minority acted as Ho's "fifth column" in the country, assisted by the activities of regular Viet Minh troops, the Can Bo, and propaganda agitators who incessantly crossed the border, and they found a natural ideological ally in the Marxist Khmer Workers' Party. The method of operation was basically the same as that practiced in Vietnam: the object at stake was the control of the population, accompanied by in-filtration, instruction, the proliferation of political cells, and a judicious measure of terror and reprisal. "Parallel hierarchies" were constructed, and a regular police apparatus took root in the Viet Minh–controlled zones. By extremely methodical operations before 1952, vast areas of the country were snatched from the jurisdiction of the government, and there was every danger that the rest of Cambodia would follow os-motically.

The goal of the *riposte* became: "Take away from the rebels the sup-port of the population, and in order to do it, shield the people, scat-tered over quite wide distances, from enemy reprisal." [22] A solution, already adopted with success as early as 1946 in the frontier province of Svay-Rieng, was accepted. It consisted of two general principles: "(1) At the onslaught of the rebels, to organize the people so as to oblige them to take sides with the legal government, thereby assuring their self-defense; (2) consequently, to regroup the population into signifi-cant clusters, placed in locations where surveillance by the government

[22] Souyris, *op. cit.,* p. 688.

forces will be easy." [23] This plan was put into practice in 1951 in the province of Kompong Cham, which had previously been a major base of the Viet Minh. Here, several points of relocation were chosen, subdivided, made habitable, and organized into a complex of self-defense. As soon as they had been constructed, the population was invited to come and occupy them. Over half accepted immediately, and in the following months the laggards gradually arrived to join their kinsmen.

From this and other examples, Captain Souyris concluded: "The regrouping of populations therefore seems to be the only method capable, at the same time, of dislodging the Viet Minh, *without leaving them the chance to return,* and of shielding the inhabitants from their influence." [24]

In 1952, these early attempts at defensive resettlement, undertaken through private military and civilian initiative, were officially noted by the Cambodian government, and the political resources of the state were placed behind the pursuit of the operation. A "Direction for the Self-Defense of the Populations" was created in the Ministry of the Interior and charged with elaborating a national plan. The provincial governors assisted in defining the procedures of regrouping to be followed.

The program, as developed by the Cambodians, recognized the following necessities: (1) The resettled peoples must be able, without great difficulty, to continue to cultivate their plots; (2) the situation of the new villages must take account of the demands of collective life: water points, health, cleanliness, and town services — and the towns must be large enough for the anticipated number of inhabitants; (3) the new villages must help to meet the needs of the self-defense of the *canton,* the *arrondissement,* and the *province.* Consequently, towns were constructed so that, as a general rule, they would not be more than three kilometers distant from the fields of their inhabitants. In some cases, where peasants had been collected from isolated localities, this was impossible, and equivalent lands had to be awarded. Essentially, the procedure was an experiment in village redevelopment, and the new towns were constructed in such a way as to answer to the problems of effective defense. All were laid out close to existing roads. The planning of the village was rectangular; and the market, school, infirmary, etc., were advantageously located — not only so they would be relatively impermeable to enemy attack but so that village activity could not be easily concealed from the "forces of order." Strict responsibility for local defense at all echelons was easily imposed by the rectangular form of the town.

[23] *Ibid.,* pp. 689ff.
[24] *Ibid.,* p. 698.

Each town, moreover, was artifically fortified through the construction of ditches, blockhouses, barricades, and other defensive positions. The village was responsible for assuring its own defense and was also required to contribute a *commando de contre-guérilla* for the protection of the surrounding area.

Populations were normally resettled during the four or five months between the harvesting of the rice crop and the onset of the rainy season. In the preceding period they received indoctrination designed to enlist their enthusiasm for the new venture. Meanwhile, the model village was being put up, usually by military labor. Those peasants who had been chosen as leaders of the new enterprises were taken to the village early and given military and administrative instruction. Finally, units of the Cambodian Army supervised the migration of the bulk of the civilians from their former dwellings.

Because of the vast numbers involved in this resettlement, the program had genuinely revolutionary consequences for the Cambodian society. In one season, close to half a million people's traditional lives were thus disturbed, out of a total population of 3,748,000 (1948 census). On the military plane, the successful conduct of local defense promoted optimism and confidence in the national forces. The Viet Minh, deprived of its stable source of food levies, was forced to fall back on its own bases, leaving previously infiltrated areas to the authority of the national government. The contagious publicity of the victories of local defense cost the Viet Minh the support of numbers of intimidated or opportunistic waverers, who now refused to meet its demands or undertake its missions. Captain Souyris concluded:

This Cambodian example can furnish us with precious information, which would merit a special study. . . . Even if one considers an Asian country with its individual characteristics, we find in North Africa the application of similar techniques of *la guerre révolutionnaire*. . . . Such an experiment, accomplished on such a large scale, teaches us that a modest country, disposing of slender material resources, was able to resolve its particular problem of security. Furthermore, it provides both general and particular intelligence about a system which, it seems, represents an effective procedure for counterguerrilla warfare: as such, the elements of this method deserve to be meditated on.[25]

Lessons and Paradoxes

In Indochina a war was lost; but certain lessons were won. Not all of these lessons would be salutary once they exceeded their military boundaries and were applied in the sphere of politics. The point of con-

[25] *Ibid.*, p. 699.

vergence was social and psychological: the principle that revolutionary wars are fought for the allegiance of a people. This could, *in extenso,* justify many contradictory practices: fraternization, social aid, increased educational and hygienic facilities, on the one hand; on the other, the "black arts" of propaganda, psychological manipulation, involuntary re-settlement, and political "re-education." Transferred to the political plane, this contradiction would contribute to tearing the Army apart, in body and in spirit. It led, in the first instance, to the frantic search for a counter-ideology to this potent Marxism, some doctrine of noble and all-encompassing purpose that could resolve and justify hesitations of technique by the dialectical process.

Such a solution was never found in the Western treasury of values, but from 1954 on this search drove an influential group of French officers, fresh from the fighting or prison camps of Indochina, to the libraries of sociology and politics in their dogmatic quest. In October 1954, General Cogny saluted the colors for the last time in Haiphong;[26] thereupon a bitter and self-critical Army embarked for the shores of the *métropole,*[27] little aware that the next, and greatest, war would germinate within a month's time. The years of meditation had set in.

[26] For a French view on the developments in the Indochinese states following the cease-fire and partition of 1954, see Jean Lacouture's articles, "L'Indochine cinq ans après," in *Le Monde,* December 27–28, 1959, and dates immediately after.

[27] The best available description of the French departure and the attendant bitterness of the troops will be found in Jean Lartéguy's novel *Les Centurions* (Paris, 1958). This book enjoys a high degree of endorsement in the Army itself as an accurate representation of military feelings.

PART THREE

MEDITATION

VII

RECIPE FOR ACTION:
LA GUERRE RÉVOLUTIONNAIRE

> L'esprit militaire français repugne à reconnaître à l'action de
> guerre le caractère essentiellement empirique qu'elle doit
> revêtir. Il s'efforce sans cesse de construire une doctrine qui lui
> permette a priori d'orienter l'action.
> — *Charles de Gaulle,* Le Fil de l'épée

EVENTS SINCE 1945 have transformed our way of looking at war,
throwing extreme emphasis upon its technological aspects, suggesting
that it may be a frustration rather than an extension of politics. But
even had nuclear weapons never been invented, the present era of
ideological upheaval and anticolonial revolution would have caused
many new wrinkles in the face of Mars. Deficiencies in military strength
seem able, time and again, to be offset by a saving collaboration with
the "wave of history." In the past fifteen years imperial nations have
waged small wars with an abundance of military zeal but a definite
political shamefulness. On the other hand, states struggling to be born
have subordinated all rules of conduct to that single end without too
many moral second thoughts.

But the nature of the wars of national uprising in Asia and Africa
has been complicated by the East-West conflict and the existence of
nuclear weapons. The achievement of a condition known loosely as
"mutual deterrence" or the "balance of terror" probably increased the

volatility of low-threshold or subversive wars by making the great powers much more reluctant to intervene in them directly for fear of escalating them. These wars continued to be an extension of politics; the question was — whose politics? For, in the broader continuum of the Cold War, the frequent ambiguity of these wars made their political consequences hard to read.

Few would claim that the dangers of nuclear war are sufficiently remote to be assuaged by faith in the rational conduct of states alone. But the obsession with utopian solutions to prevent nuclear apocalypse is equally fatuous. War exists, even if the nuclear recourse is not reached; and there remain political criteria that determine whether or not war will be the resort. If nuclear war cannot safely accommodate those goals to which nations are bound, then other doctrines of war have to be sought, unless, of course, war ceases to serve as an instrument for the pursuit of coherent aims and becomes nothing more than the killer instinct writ large.

The kind of war that would seem to be the logical result of these considerations has been recorded about twenty times (the catalogue will vary according to the prejudice of the analyst) in the past decade and a half. The misleading treatment, particularly in America, of peripheral "revolutionary" conflicts as "brushfire wars" (implying their lack of importance),[1] the vast ambiguity of moral feeling surrounding colonial relationships, and the fact that the principal member of the Atlantic alliance had until recently to commit its own troops to a genuine "revolutionary" war are among the reasons for neglect of this type of conflict. Great Britain, while fighting "revolutionary" wars to successful conclusions in Kenya and Malaya and an unsuccessful one in Cyprus, and often innovating cleverly in the field of tactics, scarcely improved on the United States in doctrinal assessment of *la guerre révolutionnaire*. Her island defense remained paramount, and it belonged to another spectrum, another category of war.

French Assessment of Revolutionary War

The French, whose armies in the field knew no repose from the end of World War II, were led to some very different conclusions. The consecutive rigor of ideological battle, combined with an unstable search

---

[1] There had been occasional recognition, however, of the mode of revolutionary war. Cf., for example, James E. King, Jr., *Limited War in an Age of Nuclear Plenty*, L57-154, Industrial College of the Armed Forces, 1956–1957, p. 15: "In combatting guerrilla actions against us, our aim should be primarily at the population, and only secondarily at the guerrillas, as Magsaysay so brilliantly demonstrated in the Philippines."

for political values at home, made the concept of *la guerre révolution-naire* vivid and potent. For it was the cardinal fact of the French military experience after 1945.

Colonel Charles Lacheroy expressed his feelings in the bitter anecdote that follows:

Very swiftly the conversation among the seventeen participating nations turned into a dialogue between the two lone possessors of the atomic bomb, the English and the Americans. The French representative tapped idly on the table in a somewhat absent frame of mind. When his turn came to say what he thought of the decisions that had been made, he answered: "Nothing." The brilliant areopagus was stupefied. "Really, General, you don't think anything, when all the nations of Central Europe are under your command?" "No," he replied, "but I did not say that I had nothing to say; I said that the subject you have just been treating did not interest me. However, having something to say, I shall say it in the form of a sketch, which is traditional in Anglo-Saxon circles when a serious problem is being discussed. I shall give you then a sketch of Bulganin and Khrushchev, who have just learned of the conference we are holding here. Bulganin says to Khrushchev: "That's a nice little Kriegspiel they've put together over there; only we can afford to laugh at the atom bomb: no one will ever use it." "Yes," says Khrushchev, "that's right, no one will ever resort to the atom bomb, but they've made a very serious decision — they've decided to use the bomb first if they are attacked." "That's a good one," says Bulganin. "They won't be attacked." "What?" says Khrushchev. "Won't be attacked? Betrayal, is it? Shall we betray Lenin? Shall we betray the spread of communism in the world?" "No, don't worry; nothing will be betrayed. There will always be war. But since we are communists, since we are used to this regime and its ways of doing business, since we are well ahead in this field, we know how to wage a war that will always be below the level of general war, below the level of the atom bomb. We'll get what we want; we know how to get along. We'll do it through intermediaries. There's no point in having our flag flying in the middle of this escapade. And naturally we'll attack the links that seem weakest, first and foremost the links in the chains of the French and English colonial empires." And he added in conclusion: "In the field of so-called colonial wars we have some incredible good fortune. Our most powerful opponents, the Americans, will be our allies." [2]

One of the enemy's advantages, then, in waging *la guerre révolution-naire* was that the motives of the war itself would be misconstrued and would help to divide the Western alliance.

Deeply imbedded in French thought, and with a history whose major manifestations are well known to all students of politics and sociology, is the penchant for creating self-enclosed universes of ideas, for translating insights into mystiques, for acting under the banner of theory.

[2] In Charles Lacheroy, "La guerre révolutionnaire," contained in the anthology *La Défense Nationale* (Paris, 1958), pp. 308–309.

However, when we return to the particular and the time-bound, it is difficult to anatomize *la guerre révolutionnaire* as an abstract intellectual idea, if only because it was closely implicated in the institutional pains of the French services and the political crises of the regime. Discontent with liberal democratic formulas pervaded the thinking of many officers returning from Indochina. Political judgments were undisguisedly voiced in the official and semiofficial publications of the French services. The enemy mobilizes his resources totally for the pursuit of *la guerre révolutionnaire,* the argument ran; how much less a mobilization can we afford? By the beginning of 1958 a field-grade officer was able to write in one of the service journals: "To obtain these means [of combat] and adapt the present institutions for subversive war, a vast effort of national retrenchment is needed. The Nation must not tolerate the fact that the generosity and liberalism of its laws permit subversiveness to exploit its antinational activities." [3] The proximity of this remark to McCarthyism is striking. Let us remember, however, that the French political picture has been much more complicated than the American, the atmosphere of institutional crisis infinitely more intense, the scars much deeper. Not least of all, the idea of Communist conspiracy underlying the premises of *la guerre révolutionnaire* was much more sophisticated than the disordered jargon of the American reactionaries of the early fifties.

To much of the military command, however, the shaded distinctions of parliamentary politics were academic. Politics was frequently seen as a confrontation of *le Bien* and *le Mal,* with Thorez making room in the latter camp for Mendès-France, Mauriac, Servan-Schreiber, Duverger, P.-H. Simon, Mitterrand, and many others. The Manichaean formula of *la guerre révolutionnaire* made it possible to extend the category of treachery to absurd extremes, into the very Council of Ministers itself.

The cause-effect relationship between the formulation of *la guerre révolutionnaire* and the Army's re-entry to politics was ambivalent. On the one hand, there was the internalization of the experiences of combat; on the other, the notion of the inseparability of politics and war. The doctrine as a whole spurred the Army toward its political vocation, because it implied that the regime did not understand the ideological facts of the twentieth century. But the doctrine was more than a mere rationalization of discontent; it was an elaborate essay in creative history.

[3] Commandant Mairal-Bernard, "Cinquièmes bureaux et septième arme," *Revue des Forces terrestres,* January 1958, p. 78.

Revolutionary War: The Scheme

The context of *la guerre révolutionnaire* was the unlimited aspiration of the Marxist ideology, its inexorable designs on the entire world. By attributing not only tenacity but undeviating skill to the strategy of international communism and by virtually eliminating the independent seriousness of the anticolonial struggles of Africa and Asia,[4] the theories of *la guerre révolutionnaire* arrived at a unitary doctrine of subversion with little local variation. Thus the strength of the doctrine — its simplicity — was also its greatest logical fallacy. *La guerre révolutionnaire* was essentially a combination of two ingredients: (1) a large and ever-growing catalogue of guerrilla and other tactics combed from past and contemporary experiences and going at least as far back in time as the Peninsular War of 1808–1814; and (2) the universal revolutionary ideology. Without the latter there could be no revolutionary war, only a series of isolated skirmishes such as those that have embellished classical warfare in other times.

In *la guerre révolutionnaire* the ex-colonial nations or those dependencies presently striving for national existence were either agents of communism or dupes. If they had not sold body and soul to the Kremlin before the launching of their struggle, they would infallibly do so during the course of it. Believing occasionally that they were acting independently, they would actually be at the mercy of their Soviet and Chinese manipulators. Communism recognized that direct intervention was not necessary in most cases; the action of the nationalists themselves would be enough to weaken the West. However, Moscow and Peking would maintain close liaison with these movements, bring them gradually to heel through financing, arms supply, and infiltration, and turn them in a Marxist direction at the right moment. It made little difference whether the revolutionaries were purely nationalist at the outset or at what speed they were being transformed into an advance guard of the Communist movement:

The enemy is in the last analysis always the same. The Marxist-Leninist doctrine of revolutionary war has, in the past few years, shown itself to be sufficiently effective to impel subversive movements of all types, whatever their mystique, to borrow it henceforth. Persuaded that they are ultimately working for its own ends, the party of the Cominform aids and advises them with the best of good will.[5]

---

[4] For an interpretation of relations between the Algerian nationalists and international communism, see Chapter IX, *passim*.

[5] Jacques Hogard, "Guerre révolutionnaire et pacification," *Revue militaire d'Information,* January 1957, p. 7.

There has been general agreement among the analysts of *la guerre révolutionnaire* that the Marxist ideology strengthens the moral fiber of the revolutionary combatant and is thereby a much more potent force, both materially and psychologically, than mere nationalism alone.[6] Autocriticism, "parallel hierarchies," and all the rest of the revolutionary machinery are at the base of this inculcation. Colonel Lacheroy quotes the story of a dying Viet Minh soldier (from the book *Journal d'un combattant vietminh*) in which a priest asks the young man if he is a Communist. "No, Father, not yet," replies the hero. "Because I am not yet worthy to be one." [7] In effect, it is believed that Marxism has shown an uncanny ability to substitute itself for traditional religion. Therefore, the type of war which *la guerre révolutionnaire* is held to approximate most closely is the "holy war," or jihad, and, according to Claude Delmas, "one can say that revolutionary war is a secularization of the wars of religion." [8]

The reasons for this similitude have, of course, been carefully analyzed — and not by military experts alone. The earthly eschatology of the Communist society, achieving perfection in "future generations" (*les lendemains qui chantent*), is compared with the Christian revelation of immortality in paradise. Whatever hastens the day of the establishment of the Communist order is axiomatically good; it is the only Good. Conveniently, there is no appeal from this dictum, because it can never be tested in advance but only interpreted by the omniscient prophets of the movement. *La guerre révolutionnaire,* constantly magnetized toward simplicity, demands a universal and total commitment from the janissaries of communism. As Commandant Hogard writes:

Impossible to ruse with communism. One can be its accomplice; but either one becomes a Communist through "engagement in action" or else he is sooner or later cast off, condemned, "physically liquidated." There is no "peaceful coexistence" possible. . . . Communism pursues the destruction of all that is not itself. . . . If it were otherwise, it would no longer be communism.[9]

Dominated by a resourceful ideology, one powerful enough to suppress and master its internal contradictions, the Communist nations are understood as a single entity which is threatening to storm the ramparts of the West. Traditional measures will, in this instance, be unavailing. *La guerre révolutionnaire* demands an antithesis that will in many respects resemble rather than differ from it, a *guerre contre-révolution-*

[6] But see the "Simplet" letter, Chapter XIV, p. 304.

[7] Lacheroy, *op. cit.,* p. 319.

[8] Claude Delmas, *La Guerre Révolutionnaire* (Paris, 1960), p. 31.

[9] Jacques Hogard, "La Tentation du Communisme," *Revue des Forces terrestres,* January 1959, p. 26.

naire. It can be found only in the intensive study and critique of revolutionary tactics, and in the fastidious preparation of proper countermeasures, *la parade* and *la riposte* (that is, the "parry" and the "thrust").

Without the universal appeal of the Marxist ideology there could be no revolutionary war. Whether fought in the jungles of Malaya or the hills of Macedonia, revolutionary war exhibits certain essentials that can be modified by local factors but never dispensed with. Great flexibility in the realm of tactics is balanced against supreme rigidity of purpose and over-all strategy. *La guerre révolutionnaire* requires that every "nationalist" conflict be analyzed from the perspective of international ideological struggle. The case of a "half-revolutionary war" has never been posed; the doctrine is pure, or it is nothing.

In the global scheme the true base of *la guerre révolutionnaire* can never be attacked; all eruptions must be combated piecemeal. Soviet Russia could not be obliterated by the SAC, even if the United States were able and willing, simply because fifteen throat-cutters had terrorized a village in the Algerian Constantinois. This is a matter of political realism and also a function of the "balance of terror." The French have theorized that the incidence of *la guerre révolutionnaire* will be in some kind of proportion to the minatory power of the deterrent, the vaunted but uncertain "pouvoir de dissuasion." This principle is necessarily somewhat modified by factors of opportunity. If the tactics of *la parade* are niggardly in the germinating period of a revolutionary war, this will obviously encourage the universal enemy to take advantage of the deficiency. But the paradox of modern war remains and can be thus stated: as military power approaches the conceivable limits of destructiveness, there is correspondingly less chance that the weapons threatening this cataclysm will ever be unleashed. Wars of the future will be, therefore, "revolutionary." They will be no less *total* than general war in the sense that they will require the constant application of all relevant economic, social, and political levers, but they will reject as inappropriate the resort to weapons of mass destruction.

Another consequence of revolutionary war is that the conflict will almost inevitably be much more total from the point of view of the revolution than from that of the defenders. While Ho Chi Minh strained every resource to put his whole population on a war footing, the fleshpots of Saigon went uncurtailed, not to mention those of Paris or New York. This imbalance of commitment, if not disastrous to the posture of the "forces of order" in the field, will nevertheless give the revolution a keen psychological advantage in the spheres of morale, propaganda, and unity of political design. The rebel agents of the Communist bloc will be self-sacrificing, objectively admirable; but fifty miles away from the fighting the "forces of order" will seem, on the contrary, soft and decadent.

If revolutionary war is one and indivisible, it is potentially capable of breaking out anywhere, so long as the conditions are ripe. If its timing is occasionally haphazard and if it has, in fact, been prepared for decades by a local evolution that is a side issue of communism, it will sooner or later be adjusted to the Marxist global timetable. The possibilities of success interest the manipulators most; premature action that ends in defeat and the disruption of the revolutionary network is roundly condemned as "leftist opportunism." When the Markos rebellion in Greece (1945–1949) gave all signs of aborting, Moscow quietly and brutally dropped the case and failed to assure the resupply of the guerrilla army.[10] A revolutionary must know how to wait, like Lenin, for decades if necessary, and then seize his chance.

Recognizing its most favorable terrain, *la guerre révolutionnaire* will be generally restricted to the underdeveloped, and particularly the colonial, world. In this sense, it contradicts the premises of orthodox Marxism. Here the situation is organic and promising: the traditional West is in retreat, embarrassed, beset by a conflicting conscience; nationalist movements of quite long standing are already in place or are being born through diffusion and example. Therefore the scenario of *la guerre révolutionnaire* will customarily concern a hypothetical country of this character. But the techniques will still relate to those aimed at the seizure of power in a more modern state such as Greece or Czechoslovakia.

Contemporary Masters of Revolutionary War

If there is, properly speaking, no revolutionary war without the Marxist-Leninist ideology, there is no revolutionary strategy that does not derive from the same source. Communism is the catalyst for both the military and political disciplines of revolutionary struggle; it combines them in a single instrument, a single reflection of the same goal: the seizure of power. Consequently — ignoring the fact that Russian national engagement in partisan or subversive war, especially during World War II, was not always an efficient or characteristic model of Leninist theory[11] — those who paint the canvas of *la guerre révolution-*

---

[10] The Titoist schism likewise had a profound influence on the ill fortunes of the Greek Communists.

[11] See N. Galay, "Partisan Warfare," in Basil Liddell Hart (ed.), *The Red Army* (New York, 1955), pp. 153–171.

naire usually credit its primary inspiration to the Soviets and cite their pioneer work of indoctrination among the peasantry in the Civil War of 1917–1921. The masters of revolutionary war are not, however, uniquely on the Communist side. Clausewitz is recognized as the spiritual father. And together with Lenin, Trotsky, Frunze, Tukhachevsky, Mao, and General Giap, one finds the illustrious Western names of T. E. Lawrence and Basil Liddell Hart. These men had the merit of recognizing the limitations of "classical" war.

To Mao Tse-tung the theorists of *la guerre révolutionnaire* have owed the recognition that control of the masses is the rational aim of the conflict. This is not just a matter of economy; it is one of necessity. If the criterion of a base of popular support could not be met in a country such as Algeria, the numerical balance of the regular fighting forces, although in some measure contingent on the tactics employed and the terrain of combat, would be of little relevance, particularly if the spirit of the revolutionary forces remained undaunted. This point can be illustrated by noting that in Indochina, a war that the French lost after seven years, the ratio of fighting effectives was, at its height, 6:4, in favor of the "forces of order." This meant, however, many instances of local superiority for the Viet Minh. In Greece, where the "forces of order" were victorious, they enjoyed an advantage over the rebels of approximately 8:1. In Algeria, on the other hand, where the estimated ratio was 16:1, the elusive pacification continued to escape the French.[12] The balance of the armies is a subsidiary feature of *la guerre révolutionnaire,* although local initiative and enterprises of attrition may count very heavily in the military operations. What we have here, whether in a rural or urban situation, is, as Colonel Nemo aptly expresses it, "a war in the crowd," "a war in the social milieu."

Leon Trotsky provided the skeleton of operational theory to the French strategists of revolutionary war through his description of the procedure by which small, well-drilled revolutionary cadres, the "vanguard of the proletariat," capturing the allegiance of the masses, could achieve the seizure of power.[13] In contemporary times, however, it has been widely conceded, following Mao, that the primary impetus will

---

[12] See the chart of force totals presented to the United States Senate Armed Services Committee on January 22, 1959, by Secretary of the Army Wilber M. Brucker, quoted in Ivo D. Duchaček and Kenneth W. Thompson, *Conflict and Co-operation Among Nations* (New York, 1960), p. 451:

Indochina: "forces of order" — 500,000, "Revolution" — 350,000
Greece: "forces of order" — 210,000, "Revolution" — 25,000
Algeria: "forces of order" — 490,000, "Revolution" — 30,000

[13] Leon Trotsky, *The History of the Russian Revolution,* translated by Max Eastman (New York, 1932), esp. Vol. III, pp. 167–192.

come through action among the rural masses, since these represent the constant numerical element of strength in most countries ripe for the revolution.

Later, we paraphrase two of the most characteristic descriptions of revolutionary tactics. The first is a "scenario-type" of revolutionary war, proposed by Colonel Lacheroy in 1956,[14] which places particularly detailed emphasis on the methodology of the five stages (the "sacred pentad"); the second is by Commandant Hogard, more precise and framed more in terms of the combat itself.[15] Both writers, despite certain differences of approach, insist on the desirability of squelching the revolutionary threat in its early stages; otherwise the task assumes immense proportions.

Two Scenarios

Colonel Lacheroy begins his exposé by sketching the conditions of the modern world which, in his opinion, make both the classical military *riposte* and the traditional conduct of *pacification* operations insufficient in a revolutionary situation. He foresees that the vigor of the Revolution may easily lead the civil authorities in a "spoiled" (*pourri*) territory to demand that the military forces assume their functions. Therefore he recommends that the military command devote serious study to this likely phase of its mission. Finally, he rejects Indochina as a model example of revolutionary war for reasons that are not spelled out but may be surmised: the peculiarities of the terrain, the inescapable link with the unsettled conditions left in the wake of World War II, the effective numerical strength of the enemy, the desire not to suggest a lost war as the prototype of future engagement.

Lacheroy then proceeds to describe the five stages. *Surprise* will be the typical element of the first stage. The revolutionary storm will at first be heralded by signs so vague and oblique that only specialists can be expected to discover their true meaning. Then, suddenly, aimless terror will burst forth "in a spectacular fashion." Bombs will go off, assassinations will be attempted, slogans will be spread. The objects of attack will not be especially notable or distinguished persons, but will rather be chosen with the end of creating an air of randomization, bewilderment, and suspense. A climate of insecurity will reign; the public press will react with huge black headlines, and international opinion

---

[14] Charles Lacheroy, "Scenario-type de Guerre révolutionnaire," *Revue des Forces terrestres,* October 1956, pp. 25–29.

[15] Hogard, "Guerre révolutionnaire et pacification," *op. cit.,* pp. 11–13.

will begin to take notice. This is described as the *publicizing phase* of *la guerre révolutionnaire*.

The second phase will be more discreetly demonstrative. Besieged by the consequences of the terror, the public "forces of order" will be led to react with unpopular measures such as police control and curfews to ensure a proper degree of security. These measures, combined with the incipient fear created by the terror, will promote a psychological state of discontent in the population. Exemplary reprisals will now be carried out by the rebels, always with emphasis on the slogan: "Here is the destiny reserved for traitors." The victims again will be chosen not for their prestige but for their attachment and loyalty to France. Disturbed and terrorized, the bulk of the population will now enter the "complicity of silence," refusing the least collaboration with the "forces of order," suppressing all testimony they might give against the terrorists.

The scene is prepared for the third phase, in which political and military activities will begin to be distinguished. It is at this point that the first elements of the rebel armed forces will appear. However, they will still operate according to the formulas of guerrilla warfare, in small groups and usually at night, by day disguising themselves among the civilian population. At the same time, careful indoctrination will commence among the active elements of the civilian mass. The mission of these first cadres will be to "transform the passive complicity of silence into an active complicity, the spectators into actors, the neutrals into sympathizers, then into fanatics." This will be achieved both through the authority of threats and through blackmail.

The fourth phase is qualified as being one of transition. Semiregular forces are now differentiated from the guerrilla fighters. The quality and extent of the infiltration are constantly improved, and the formation of hierarchies commences. Some agents of the revolution specialize in agrarian questions, others in justice, still others in youth organizations, and so forth.

Finally, in the fifth and final phase, a regular army emerges. A unity of command over the entire rebellion will have been achieved through the ruthless elimination of all but the most reliable elements. An independent territory — snatched from the jurisdiction of the "forces of order" — is created, either in isolation or contiguous to some friendly state, whose resources or control of supply can support the campaign. "Parallel hierarchies" now envelop the entire territory and permit indoctrination to proceed under the most favorable conditions. The legal authorities, as well, are progressively duplicated by the organs of rebel government in all communities, so that from the point of view of the population the distinctions of administrative command are thoroughly nebulous.

"In practice," concludes Colonel Lacheroy, "legality and force have both changed camps."

Commandant Hogard, in his probably more "classical" interpretation of the five phases of revolutionary war, sees a similar procedure of expansion, but one that is distinctly attached to the creation and organic multiplication of bases of support. At the same time he recognizes the psychological factor, and insists on the parallel development of the "intoxication and demoralization" of the enemy, the famous *pourrissement* experienced in the Indochina War.

Hogard does not speak of terror or overt acts in his first phase but rather of the "constitution of clandestine nuclei of agitation and propaganda . . . which diffuse the chosen ideology" and take advantage of the internal contradictions that are present in any society. He removes the initiation of acts of revolutionary violence to the second phase, including among them strikes, sabotage, demonstrations, riots — a more traditional, and incidentally more Communist, interpretation than that of Colonel Lacheroy. At the same time, the primitive "kernels" (*noyaux*) are expanded steadily into intelligence networks.

In the third phase, in accord with Lacheroy, the revolutionary enemy passes to the offensive with guerrilla operations, while propaganda and psychological action achieve a greater density. The fourth phase anticipates Lacheroy's "creation of a liberated zone," as well as the formation of a revolutionary provisional government or government-in-exile (such as the Algerian Provisional Government, the GPRA). At this juncture it is presumed that the People's Democracies will extend diplomatic recognition. Finally, in the closing phase, the battle is massively joined between the two forces through a skillful mixture of "neoclassic" and revolutionary operations.

Hogard concludes his definition by describing what he sees as the peculiar features of *la guerre révolutionnaire* as contrasted with ordinary conflict. "Revolutionary war . . . is very different from classical war: beginning 'in dispersion' it little by little draws its strength and resources from the enemy, does not seek the conquest of military or geographical objectives, but of the population, in order to conclude, when the situation has ripened and if there is still need, with a single great battle where it concentrates all its means. This final battle is generally already won before being fought, for the enemy, intoxicated, demoralized, and subverted, is morally ready for defeat."

All commentators agree that, under ordinary circumstances, direct military defeat of the revolutionary forces will not suffice to stifle them.

If their activity has progressed as far as Hogard's fifth phase, they will only have to fall back on the tactics of the preceding one while regrouping their forces.

Elaborations: The "Parry" and the "Thrust"

Still another author (actually a group of officers writing collectively under the name of "Ximenes") [16] provides a summary of the "constructive" and "destructive" techniques of the revolution as they exist without direct reference to the five phases of operations. The "destructive" category includes: (1) dislocation of the former body social through riots, terrorist acts, and so on; (2) intimidation of populations, or what Lacheroy has called the "complicity of silence"; (3) demoralization of the adversary and intoxication of the neutrals through propaganda that places in doubt the good faith of the existing order; and (4) elimination through execution and reprisal of those whom it is impossible to convince or intimidate. The "constructive" techniques as listed by "Ximenes" are five: (1) selection and training of a base of activists; (2) propagation of bases and infiltration activities; (3) psychological indoctrination; (4) *encadrement* through the Party organization, "parallel hierarchies," and vertical and horizontal organizations; and (5) "edification" of the struggle through creation of a "liberated territory" and a "national government."

Finally, "Ximenes" insists on the necessity of three categories of "process crucial to the successful waging of revolutionary war." The first of these is "crystallization," which implies the ability to rally mass support and to manipulate it through periods of changing political tactics. Secondly, there is "organization," which is principally fulfilled through the construction of "parallel hierarchies." Thirdly, there is "militarization," which means simply that the whole apparatus is put on a total war footing, and that the actual fighting forces are properly and clearly distinguished as local forces, territorial guerrillas, or "units of intervention" capable of fighting a major battle.

Schematically, we might summarize all these descriptions by noting the following points about *la guerre révolutionnaire*: (1) Its conduct is distinguished from that of classical war by the fact that even though there may be units fitted to fight more-or-less classical battles, the bulk of the war effort is thrown back on smaller groups operating according to the tactics of guerrilla warfare. (2) It is ideologically motivated, ultimately by the Marxist doctrine. (3) It is a war, not for the control of

[16] "Ximenès," "Essai sur la guerre révolutionnaire," *Revue militaire d'Information*, February–March 1957, pp. 11–14. This is the famous "special number."

territory or military objectives, nor even so much for the destruction of the opposing force, but for the conquest of the population. (4) It is a war waged with all relevant means within a restricted space. In this context the pursuit of the classical *ripostes* of *repression, pacification* by administrative reform, traditional *surface warfare,* or *war of total annihilation* will be generally inappropriate and self-defeating.

The question then becomes one of approaching a new methodology of "counter-revolutionary" war replying directly to the analysis of the weaknesses inherent in the procedures of the enemy. Experts of *la guerre révolutionnaire* generally summarize these strategies under the classical headings of *la parade* and *la riposte,* which may in some senses be said to correspond to the "constructive" and "destructive" techniques of the revolutionaries. It is worth while recalling Colonel Trinquier's article "Contre-guérilla" in this regard, where he urges measures to deprive the enemy of his food and arms supply through destruction of his local security. Commandant Hogard provides us in the same connection with a very instructive series of "do's" and "don't's" of this type of conflict, under the title "The Ten Rules of Anti-revolutionary Tactics." [17] His catalogue is as follows:

1. Negotiations on equal terms with a revolutionary enterprise could not be more dangerous; this will facilitate its success.

2. All rebel territory should, as quickly as possible, be isolated from the exterior, materially and morally.

3. Revolutionary war must be checked in its early stages.

4. Both strategy and tactics of counter-revolutionary war depend on the close linkage of all civil, military, social, cultural, and economic resources, with the view of holding or recapturing popular support and attacking the enemy apparatus from all angles.

5. Final victory over revolutionary forces can be achieved only through the destruction of the apparatus.

6. The conquest of popular support must be the main objective of the legitimate authority. This depends on the promotion of a vigorous *action psychologique* among the people that will stress the universal values of the "forces of order" and reveal the duplicity and contradictions of the enemy. At the same time, the hopes of the people must be fulfilled by continuous progress toward a better social order. The population itself must be trained in self-defense.

7. The destruction of the forces of the revolution should be regarded not as an end but as a means of securing popular support.

[17] Jacques Hogard, "Stratégie et tactique dans la Guerre révolutionnaire," *Revue militaire d'Information,* June 1958.

8. The irregular forces of the revolution need not be defeated in battle but can be suffocated if deprived of material and moral support in the previously friendly zones.

9. The single way of reducing the guerrillas is to wear them down morally and physically by tracking them with units suited to the purpose, operating always in familiar zones.

10. The safety of arteries and vital points depends, not on static defense, but on the ability to create conditions of constant insecurity for the guerrilla forces operating in these areas.

All of Hogard's injunctions, properly speaking, belong to the phase called *la riposte* or are at least prohibitions of false *riposte,* because it is this side of tactics that pertains once the insurrection has broken out. In the eyes of Captain André Souyris, a close student of revolutionary organizations in both Indochina and Tunisia, an effective *parade* (the term given to preinsurrectional measures) is no less vital.[18] *La parade* is perhaps the more difficult phase of the counter-revolutionary operation, for its technicians must read and interpret the frequently ambiguous signs of which Colonel Lacheroy has spoken in his "scenario-type." Two other factors contribute to the problem of *la parade,* in the opinion of Captain Souyris. In the first place, the military command, which most fully understands the techniques of revolutionary war, will not normally be in place in the pre-insurrectional period, nor qualified to undertake the activation of *la parade.* Secondly, during the germinal period of revolutionary struggle the task is often made easier for the subversive forces owing to the tendency of the legal authority to interpret the disturbance in the "classical" manner and act accordingly. These defects are apt either to stifle the inception of proper measures of *parade* or raise contradictions that will limit its effectiveness.

A resourceful *parade* in the face of mounting revolutionary activity will depend on the avoidance of these "errors of appreciation" and on the utilization of qualified area specialists and a well-developed intelligence service. The legal authorities should be always abreast of the situation they are facing and will be strongly advised to cultivate numerous and fruitful contacts with the population.

Once this situation has been achieved, the technique of *la parade* is twofold. It will depend in the first place on the existence of a forceful, progressive, and humane administration of the territory. Social reforms cannot be allowed to fall behind the needs of the time or the legitimate demands of the people. Reforms must work not only toward the satis-

[18] André Souyris, "Les conditions de la parade et de la riposte," *Revue militaire d'Information,* February–March 1957, pp. 91–111.

faction of popular aspirations but also with the view of suppressing those "internal contradictions" of the society which would otherwise give fuel to the propaganda of the revolutionary forces. Administrative contact with the population must avoid the impersonal and the austere.

Secondly, a vigorous *action psychologique* must be waged among the masses, designed both to promenade the virtue of Western values and to protect the subject from the revolutionary indoctrination. Souyris suggests that there is a conflict here between the end and the means, and concedes that the traditional democratic methods are not entirely compatible with this type of campaign. Therefore, citing the psychologist Serge Tchakhotine,[19] he dismisses the question of the means for the desirability of the end: "The author of the *Viol des foules* specifies . . . that a fundamental doctrine [i.e., democracy] can be independent of the methods of action." This, in effect, was the traditional justification employed by the "African school" of psychological action for techniques that others have thought excessive — when indeed a justification seemed necessary to them. But it was a suspicious procedure for making perfect democrats, "individuals safeguarded against the snares of the State."

Between *la parade* and *la riposte* there is, in Souyris's analysis, an intermediary phase, the pre-insurrectional preparation for the *riposte*. Its specifications resemble those of *la parade,* with the exception that they are oriented toward the establishment of favorable conditions for the real *riposte,* once the revolution has broken out in earnest; it is recognized that a perfect *parade* could stifle revolutionary activity and thus obviate the need for more direct measures. The preparation of the *riposte,* then, demands effective intelligence and civic indoctrination as well as the prior establishment of a counter-revolutionary military infrastructure, of which a part, under optimum conditions, will be clandestine. In any case, the forces must be properly located, dispersed, and mobilized so as best to combat the expected revolutionary activity, the type anticipated by the Lacheroy and Hogard models.

Once the revolution bursts forth and assumes a military character, the resort is to the *riposte* proper. If its preparations have been sufficient and skillful, it will go into immediate operation. As opposed to the "classical" *riposte* or surface warfare, the counter-revolutionary *riposte* will be swiftly and totally directed toward the surrounding population. Since *la guerre révolutionnaire* is essentially a "war in the crowd" and "a war for the crowd," the object of the *riposte* will be to mobilize the crowd for military and patriotic actions in defense of the legal order. The people will be immediately organized into groups for self-defense,

[19] See Chapter VIII, p. 135.

and their leaders will be given indoctrination in village and local war-fare. The aim will be to isolate the bases of rebel support and reduce them systematically without giving the contagion a chance to spread. "Moral mobilization" through an effective program of *action psychologique* will accompany this effort. Where the re-education of populations becomes necessary after they have been recovered from the grip of the enemy, camps for "disindoctrination" will be set up to facilitate the conversion by "persuasive and humane" means.

The technical conclusion that Captain Souyris reaches as a result of his examination of the conditions of *la parade* and *la riposte* in revolutionary war is that the Army must assume responsibility for the mobilization and organization of populations living in the danger zone. The implication is clearly that the administrative civil services of a modern democracy are ill equipped to perform this task with appropriate comprehensiveness, timing, and results. *La guerre révolutionnaire* is singular. It goes on in the Chamber of Deputies as well as in the combat zone. Consequently, the role of the Army that Souyris proposes, although seemingly confined to battle areas, is, in fact, indefinitely expansible. Again we have verged on politics in a way that is perhaps unavoidable. Doctrines, however, live on permissive license, the promise not to push their premises too far. By no means the greater part of the Army command was favorable to direct political involvement according to these premises. Nevertheless, latitude in defining the enemy and the limits of the battlefield became, and would continue to be, a useful tool.

The Appeal of the "Revolutionary War" Interpretation

The more extreme propositions of *la guerre révolutionnaire* invited skepticism and distaste. When, for example, Commandant Hogard assailed a book such as Duverger's *Les Partis Politiques* as a subversive Marxist tract,[20] one could only react with astonishment. Since the prophets of revolutionary war showed their political bias so often, one may ask why this theory, which other nations have been reluctant to endorse, took such a firm hold in French military circles. For its popularity was not restricted to that portion of the officer corps that believed in a "political mission," but extended to many loyalists. There were a number of reasons for the vogue.

In the first place, *la guerre révolutionnaire* was the French Army's answer, its defensive *riposte,* to the nuclear preoccupation of its Anglo-Saxon allies. Where military commentators did not go to the extremes

[20] Jacques Hogard, "Stratégie et Tactique du Communisme," *Revue des Forces terrestres,* October 1959, p. 53.

of Colonel Lacheroy in proclaiming the inviolability of the "balance of terror" and the unlikelihood of limited nuclear war, they forged a dichotomy of "nuclear" and "revolutionary" war, making them both aspects of a new "total" war doctrine. The intellectual impulse was strong to insist on the importance of subversive as opposed to classical conflict, both for reasons of considered judgment and for requirements of national prestige.

Secondly, there was the matter of experience. A nuclear war has never been waged, except in *Kriegspiel,* whereas conflicts answering to the major characteristics of *la guerre révolutionnaire* are costing lives at this very moment. This fact, which is without real political significance to many, was nevertheless powerful persuasion to the French Army.

The third factor counseling the acceptance of the doctrine of *la guerre révolutionnaire* was of an unquestionably higher order: the intellectual satisfaction provided by a monistic interpretation of the world crisis. If a Colonel Trinquier could stake his conviction on the basis of combat experience and a rudimentary glimpse of the social forces at play in the world, others had broader perspectives. They felt that history, in its grand outlines, would infallibly connect the surge of communism with the displacement of Western influence in the former colonial territories. According to their view, a "third way" was impossible. The underdeveloped countries were intellectually and economically incapable of supporting a real independence in the ideological competition and, sooner or later, would have to succumb to the persuasions of the stronger camp.

Once accepted as a cosmic theory, *la guerre révolutionnaire* drew its lines harshly. Gray was scarcely admitted to its bicolored palette. *Le Bien* and *le Mal* confronted each other, not simply across national boundaries, but throughout all nature; if the white had been dirtied through shabby upkeep, it must be purged and purified. Since the enemy played incessantly on the ambiguity of Western pluralism, manipulating the contradictions of the richer civilization, some of this richness would have to be curtailed in the interests of solidarity and survival.

If there was Good and Evil, and Evil possessed an effective operating doctrine, then Good had to be no less well equipped. It was not enough for Good to be the absence of Evil; no negative definition could secure anyone's faith or enthusiasm. As Claude Delmas wrote: "It is easier to rally crowds in the name of a false idea, as long as it seems seductive, than in the name of multiple ideas, true but prosaic." [21] The "counter-revolution" therefore attacked pluralism with might and main, for in pluralism there was no truth — only, at best, many competing

[21] Delmas, *op. cit.,* p. 108.

half-truths. Consensus, when achieved, was philosophically impure and simply a type of tactical compromise. "The apparent weakness of the West is its inability to provide a total Truth in the fact of an ideology which itself claims sufficient means to be the incarnation of such a Truth." But the formation of a synthetic "counter-ideology" would prove to be a particularly trying problem. Different cliques were to put forth the ideas of corporatism, Church-State fusion, "national socialism," and even "national communism," [22] without discovering either the intellectual cause or the enthusiasm needed for a Western "single solution." Beside some of these formulas the regal personalism of Charles de Gaulle seemed centuries more modern.

To see the earth with one sweep of the naked eye was to miss the particularity of its atoms. The atoms were, to be sure, joined to a nucleus but only inferentially to each other. The rabid nationalism of the theorists themselves fitted rather badly with their interpretation of a Manichaean world. There was a fundamental illogic in feeling France so intestinally, while denying that Arab or Maghrebian nationalism was anything more than a kind of Communist measles.

Many proponents of *la guerre révolutionnaire* felt these reservations very keenly. As Delmas writes: "Is it possible to elaborate recipes of counter-revolutionary war with which to oppose revolutionary war, to build 'parallel hierarchies' to combat identical 'parallel hierarchies,' to 'organize' populations to disorganize the opponent's systems? These recipes will always remain conjectural, and it is not with counter-terrorism that one can lastingly oppose terrorism." [23] But, as the same author reminds us, "the Revolution fascinates."

Some were later to carry this fascination to the pitch of "intoxication." But these actions should not blind us to the things that were of real merit in the pioneer analysis of revolutionary war, tactical truths that Western military forces needed to learn. As for the "intoxicated" officers, their later acts could not be excused by the bitter circumstances that engendered their protest. Still, the profuse and often deep thinking that went into the elaboration of the doctrine of *la guerre révolutionnaire* established a rationale for what would follow. It suggested an antagonism that was more than peevish, a malaise more than transitory.

[22] See Chapter XII, p. 247.
[23] Delmas, *op. cit.*, p. 122.

VIII

PSYCHOLOGICAL ACTION:
THE "SEVENTH ARM"

It was the game, the game, that fascinated me.
—*Fyodor Dostoevsky,* Notes from Underground

THE PRECEPTS of psychological war as they were codified for the Algerian situation departed at many points from those techniques customary in democratic armies and betrayed an indebtedness to the methods of the enemy that is beyond question. Moreover, they exerted an unmeasurable but significant influence upon the attitudes toward politics within the French Army as they filtered through the military situation. They created the rationale and the agents of a core of sedition which, at moments of crisis, would draw more orthodox souls to it. If the main component of the anguish in the Army was a rather basic perception of civilian vacillation and betrayal, it was the propaganda artists — often nebulously allied with civilian anti-regime groups — that incessantly channeled the inchoate sentiments of grievance into their most potent and concentrated form. One did not have to be a disciple of the Psychological Action Services to be affected by their backlash of anti-metropolitan and anti-republican feeling.

The Indochina conflict cast up a certain number of strategically placed individuals of field-grade rank, most of them former prisoners of the Viet Minh. For a period of about three years these officers gained a virtual stranglehold on the Army's semiofficial organs of information and access to a great deal of publicity. They circulated a large number of papers internally. Consequently they had a forum which exaggerated their influence. They found willing pupils among the younger officers, and they acted with the knowledge and consent of their superiors, both military and civilian. Their road to success was paved by acquiescence of many more temperate persons including General Ely and the (then) Minister of Defense, Maurice Bourgès-Maunoury.

The regular Army in the field, despite its own brand of malaise, had relatively little respect for the "psychologues" and the *cinquièmes bureaux* (Psychological Action) staffs which they were permitted to establish throughout the Algerian territory. The strength of the novelty-seekers was most pronounced among the officers of the 10th Military District in Algiers and in the Réserve Générale, an elite body of about thirty thousand troops not committed to the territorial *quadrillage* that included a high proportion of Foreign Legion and colonial paratroop units. It was precisely these organs and units that were found at the nerve center of Algerian operations and in most direct contact with the urban Europeans. As we shall see, it is the Réserve Générale that was most specifically involved in the Algerian political crises of May 13, 1958, January 24, 1960, and April 22, 1961.

War by Persuasion

Psychological war, however, dawned gradually and fitfully on the French Army.

An army that is prepared to fulfill its mission must periodically re-examine its arsenal. The French Army was caught notoriously short in this regard in 1940; the colonial wars of the 1950's convinced many Army men that repetition of the error might again lead to catastrophe. A field army can be, and sometimes is, decimated in combat, rendered incapable of pursuit of the conflict; a whole people cannot be so summarily liquidated if the stages of the struggle are to be honored by the exercise of equivalent means. What can be done instead is to mute or subvert the hostility of the adverse masses or, better, to convert them, at least in part, to one's own vision of events. At the same time one is obliged to keep one's own civilian support in a state of high morale, to "protect one's base."

Because these things can be and have been done on numerous occasions, it is essential to examine the techniques, which some would go so far as to call laws, appropriate to mass indoctrination and control that have heretofore lain outside the province of traditional warfare. As the French psychologist Paul Reiwald puts it:

The events we have just witnessed in these latter years, this explosion of dementedness, can only support our conviction that we are dealing with an ineluctable process whose mechanism still escapes us. Its irrational character proves in no way that we should refrain from affecting its course once we discover its origin, although it is hard to imagine at the present time that man will ever master psychic forces as he has mastered natural ones. But do not these former, as well, not participate in what we call "nature"? Are they not attached to rules which, however different, are nonetheless equivalent to laws?[1]

We find here, above all, a situation far exceeding the significance of this or that school of politics. At the same time that the changing face of the world makes the seizure or retention of power incumbent on the effective control of the masses, the science of psychology is leading an assault on some of the most formidable barriers of hidden wisdom. The dementedness is a fact. Social psychology seeks a cure through an understanding of the phenomena that produce mass hysteria or hypnosis. But in so doing, it makes its discoveries available to the tyrant and demagogue, who will assuredly use them abusively. Perhaps the latter are even on firmer ground than the experimental psychologists, since they know a priori the particular brand of "normality" that they want to impose by manipulation, the particular mass consent that they desire to create. "Intoxication" with technique must not be confused with detached experiment. Some of the most ardent dabblers in *action psychologique* had little interest in psychology as a science, but they saw beyond it the availability of new methods of control that promised success for their own, often confused, goals of political action.

There is, of course, nothing new about the use of the psychological weapon in war or totalitarian politics.[2] Variations were in systematic application. For example, the crowd doctrines of Hitler and Goebbels had been relatively pragmatic, because the Nazi premises of the leader-mass relationship were based on the transmission of irrational charisma. However close the techniques of Nazism came to touching behavioral "laws," they were, in basic tendency, mystical, romantic, and "volkisch." Circumstances led the "colonels" in France to adopt a different view. In

---

[1] Paul Reiwald, *De l'Esprit des masses* (Paris, 1949), p. 3.

[2] Cf., for example, Urban G. Whitaker, Jr., *Propaganda and International Relations* (San Francisco, 1960), p. 3: "In the Book of Judges it is recorded that in the thirteenth century B.C. Gideon used a form of propaganda to confuse and panic the Midianites. In *The Book of War* (a Chinese classic) Sun Tsu advises the use of beacons and drums at night, banners and flags during the day to deceive the enemy regarding the size of the forces facing him. Herodotus described how Themistocles engraved inscriptions on stones in the path of the Ionians, direly threatening them if they continued to advance."

the first place, justification by the systematic language of science counts for much in a democracy; it can give even a subversive a rather legitimate, experimental allure. Secondly, although the French admire certain types of despots, they detest Führerism. Finally, there was no available or willing leader to whom to attach the potential of *action psychologique*. General de Gaulle was neither privy nor sympathetic to these nascent methods; they ran directly counter to his traditionalistic view of leadership and annoyed his historical sense. Moreover, in 1956, when the various conspiratorial camarillas were forming,[3] *action psychologique* was in its infancy and still a predominantly military field of speculation.

So, if the uses of psychology in war and politics are old, there were certain obvious qualitative differences from the past. The current availability to an army of the means of communication and dissemination was assuredly one. Because propaganda warfare has been resolutely championed over a period of time, modern armies now go into battle with fixed radio installations, loudspeakers, printing presses, elaborate photographic equipment, and considerable spares and supplies. Additionally, if a campaign is being waged in an area like Algeria, where, to a large extent, the normal civilian activities and services were placed under military control, these diverse facilities may be joined to the organic equipment of the military forces. If such a situation achieves a measure of permanence, the effect will be to regularize the military grasp over the organs of information and channels of communication, or to allow military ventures an unlicensed predominance. For example, the Army's regular Algerian weekly publication *Le Bled,* whose columns were readily available to proponents of *action psychologique* as well as to espousers of other novel doctrines, enjoyed once a circulation of 350,000 copies — in other words, almost as many as *Le Figaro,* almost twice as many as *Le Monde,* and more than any weekly in metropolitan France.[4]

Incentive for Psychological Action

The supreme assurance that France must learn how to fight a new kind of war was perhaps nothing more than a provisional probing in 1954. The "colonels" were not at first such resolute theorists as they

---

[3] This aspect is thoroughly reported in Serge and Merry Bromberger, *Les treize complots du treize mai* (Paris, 1959). Useful substantiation (or contradiction) is provided in J.-R. Tournoux's *Secrets d'Etat* (Paris, 1960).

[4] According to Colonel Charles Lacheroy in "La guerre révolutionnaire," *La Défense Nationale* (Paris, 1958). Another writer cites the figure of 280,000. Cf. Commandant Mairal-Bernard, "Cinquièmes bureaux et septième arme," *Revue des Forces terrestres,* No. 11 (January 1958), p. 88.

later became. But the clarion of the new doctrine was sounded at this time by General Lionel-Max Chassin, a military writer who had been de Lattre's air deputy in Indochina, in an article in a leading military journal.[5] In effect, Chassin urged the Army to return to politics and assume an ideological posture. The ferment grew especially among the younger officers.

The first step was to convince the higher staffs that a colonial war could be nothing but a meaningless carnage unless ultimate political aims were firmly fixed. Then the methods of the enemy had, at very least, to be carefully studied so that he might be attacked at his weakest points.

These reflections did not all dawn at once. It took time to share and compare common experiences. Furthermore, a serving officer with the germ of an idea is not automatically thrown into wide contact with kindred spirits. Yet there was an unhappy fraternity that existed from the start among these men, strengthened by organizations such as the Anciens d'Indochine (war veterans) and by the fact that, as participants in the most recent war, many were called to the faculties of the war colleges or to the higher staffs. Undoubtedly, the Chassin article helped to rally opinion. Gradually, as Jean Planchais explains,

. . . small groups of officers, some taking as their point of departure techniques and others ideology, exchanged the results of their studies. Some went to sit on the benches of the faculties, prepared certificates in psychology and sociology. The Marxist classics became familiar to them. . . . They discovered the analysis made by Lenin in the 1920's: "In fifty years armies will not make much sense. We shall have so well eaten away at our enemies before the conflict breaks out that the military apparatus will fail in the hour of need." [6]

It must be said that the technicians had the easier time of it; one does not stumble over an ideology by accident. If the techniques of the enemy could be duplicated to some degree, the ideological need was for a counterdoctrine as dynamic as that of the enemy and yet designed to oppose it effectively point by point. Though Lenin, Trotsky, and Mao Tse-tung were assiduously studied as strategists for whatever light they could shed on the waging of *la guerre révolutionnaire,* they obviously could not provide an ideology for the West.

With regard to military use of the psychological arm, there was a twofold discrimination which, though often abused in practice, was clearly specified in a directive of the Minister of the Armies signed on

[5] General Lionel-Max Chassin, "Du rôle idéologique de l'armée," *Revue militaire d'Information,* October 10, 1954, p. 13.
[6] Jean Planchais, "L'Armée et l'action psychologique, II," *Le Monde,* June 26, 1958.

July 28, 1959. *Guerre psychologique* pertained to those techniques of propaganda war directed toward the enemy, such as loudspeaker and leaflet campaigns, radio broadcasting, and other means that modern conflict have made familiar. *Action psychologique,* on the contrary, was designed to support and animate the friendly forces or expressly contribute to "winning the souls" of the population in the battle zone. Thus, in the Algerian setting, it was directed toward natives and French troops alike, even if the methods used in each instance were notoriously dissimilar. Moreover, it was expanded to apply to the entire French metropolitan population, by extension, since *la guerre révolutionnaire* was unbounded and indivisible.

The "Rapprochement Armée-Nation"

The latter concern related the new idea of *action psychologique* directly to the traditional problem of the *rapprochement armée-nation* ("the drawing together of army and nation"). This facet of the problem, decades old, would summon forth wide interest in the latter half of the 1950's without, for that matter, ever achieving a satisfactory solution.

Even in the days of Lyautey the Army had always felt more or less prevented from its mystical communion with *le pays réel,* but after the evacuation of Indochina the problem became much more acute than before. The Army was now thrust back on the *métropole,* with little room for maneuver that could provide a sop for its high and nervous spirits. Even the "Viceroyalty" of Morocco — the sacred Lyauteyan mecca[7] — was gone. Even Algeria, critical appendage — some would say the heart — of the Nation was in dire jeopardy. These moods that exist today in blackest intensity have their origin in what we may call the "years of meditation."

A study written by the team "Milites," which first appeared in the review *Hommes et Mondes* in 1955,[8] was the first concrete plan of operations made available to the general public. The essay as a whole is of vast interest, but only parts of it are germane to the Army-Nation problem.

The public, says "Milites," is indifferent to questions of national defense. Ignorance is therefore the first condition of the gap which sepa-

---

[7] Even as the insurrection of April 22, 1961, was breaking out, the ashes of Marshal Lyautey were being prepared for transit from Rabat to a more permanent home in the Invalides. This is not the only irony of France's colonial wars of the past decade.

[8] "Milites," "Enquête sur la Défense nationale," *Hommes et Mondes,* April–May 1955.

rates Army and Nation. The high command of services is important in the present political system:

The morale of the Army depends effectively on the support it senses in the Nation. Morally isolated from its chiefs, from policy and opinion, the Army lives more and more in a stopped-up jar. . . . In an age when war drags in its wake all the living strength of a nation — civilian populations, industries, scientific facilities, fearful weapons of propaganda — the intellectual isolation of the Army would not be less dangerous than its moral isolation. . . . By virtue of the misunderstandings of military problems, opinion fails to visualize the disproportion which exists and grows each day between national responsibilities . . . and the precise possibilities of our armed forces. This is how, little by little, the disaster of Indochina was forged, in the silence of our rulers and military leaders. . . .[9]

The study proceeds to an examination of the nature of modern war, the possibilities for the defense of the (then) French Union, and the reorganization of the Defense Ministry — matters that need not occupy us here. In Section Five of their essay, however, extended observations are made on the moral preparedness of the nation. The authors call for a reinvigoration of the traditional values of the nation, the conviction of a faith or cult. The concepts of the French Union and of "Europe" are explicitly rejected: they are too artificial or amorphous. Some foundations of an *idéologie nationale* are specifically laid: restoration of traditional patriotism and national pride; exaltation of human dignity, justice, generosity, liberty and individuality of thought and expression; will to fight for "Christian and Mediterranean" values; projection of a goal for which the consent of all may be obtained. The virtue and piety of these declarations are evident; the stumbling block has always been the means for putting them into practice.

An obvious, though not immediate, way is to give the youth a new kind of education; this is what the "Milites" authors specifically recommend. With a quite transparent reluctance to endorse the activities of the Ministry of National Education, they nevertheless suggest that consistent ideological training (but "without political engagement") be given the young people through a co-ordination of the latter ministry with the Ministry of National Defense through the Presidency of the Council. This new type of training would not necessarily invade the classroom but might operate through sports clubs and youth associations. It is just to remark that the authors conscientiously avoid any kind of authoritarian inflection. Their goal is, nonetheless, abundantly and clearly to entrust the task of civic formation to the Army.

It is proposed that the Army itself is admirably suited to fulfill this

[9] *Ibid.*, pp. 4–5 (April).

function of national education, inasmuch as practically every male citizen of France passes through its portals. The Army would be prepared to "give the citizen a 'moral armature' against aggression that would be not only material but also psychological, make him feel the *reasons* for which he fights, strengthen his will to fight, show him how to fight effectively on both the material and psychological planes." [10] This would involve a fortification of the role of *information* in the training program and an "active immunization" against propaganda proceeding from hostile quarters. Few armies today, it is true, refrain from the precaution of indoctrination. But the political implications of this step on such a wide scale are obvious, especially if carried out in the white heat that surrounded the thinking of the "Milites" officers and many others in 1955.

Many of the reforms suggested by the "Milites" article were implemented by the government and armed services, particularly as the situation in Algeria worsened. Maurice Bourgès-Maunoury, no friend of *ultras* but a believer in "modern" methods of combat, was especially influential in these developments during his long tour of duty in the Rue St-Dominique under the presidency of Guy Mollet. An Army-Youth Committee, established in 1953 while René Pleven held the portfolio of National Defense, was reanimated with the end of achieving some of the conditions sought by "Milites"; General Jacques Faure[11] was made its chief. Troop information was also pushed forward at this time. More importantly, for a while,[12] a new unity in the Army, extending down to the level of the rawest proletarian conscripts from Roubaix or St-Denis, was forged beneath the merciless Algerian sun.

From the conclusions of "Milites" it was but a small leap forward to the kind of doctrine that girds itself in the cloak of *race*, in short, the antithesis to supranationalism. We should not be misled into thinking that any Hitlerian concept of blood and soil was involved; on the contrary, the French have traditionally given this word a measured and well-balanced interpretation. *Race* ("breeding") in this sense is something that develops out of a community of ideas and customs and

---

[10] *Ibid.*, p. 163 (May).

[11] Aide to General Larminat (himself a "European") in the pre-EDC discussions. Posted to Algeria in 1955, he was a year later involved in an abortive Poujadist plan for *coup d'état*, returned to the *métropole*, and sentenced to ninety days' fortress confinement. After a subsequently *nuancé* career he was indicted in 1961 for metropolitan involvement in the April putsch and convicted and sentenced to ten years' imprisonment in September 1961.

[12] The *contingent* in Algeria balked at supporting the "putsch of the generals" in April 1961 and resorted to sit-downs and the sabotage of orders. A number of the leaders of this resistance came from the Catholic industrial or agricultural unions.

not a fixed potpourri of physical characteristics. Despite these just boundaries, the question of *race* was nevertheless posed.

One of the pioneer crowd psychologists, Gustave Le Bon, had given *race* a prominent position in his analysis. When the sociologically minded officers of 1955 ferreted through their own national treasury of behavioral science for theories to substantiate the measures they were about to propose, Le Bon was of eminent use. He had written in his central work, *The Psychology of Crowds* (*La Psychologie des foules*):

Invariable and dominant at the base of the race are superimposed certain novel and special characteristics, and there is produced the orientation of all feeling and thoughts of the collectivity in a single direction. Only then can what I have called earlier the "psychological law of the mental unity of crowds" express itself.[13]

Inspired by Le Bon and other sociologists as well as by the needs of the occasion, certain officers began to propose the systematic exploitation of the national mentality, hoping to find there clues to the emotional trip wires which, if triggered, could set the French people along the path of renovation.

General Faure himself, addressing a congress of representatives of the youth movements attached to his Army-Youth Committee at Chamonix in February 1956, warmly recommended to his listeners the "Milites" article and brought forth another document entitled "Note au sujet de la reconstruction des valeurs nationales." This unsigned paper was known to reflect his personal views. It recommended to psychologists and teachers the task of accumulating a "precise inventory" of national myths and "the definition of the myths accompanied by an appreciation of their emotional depth and the most favorable conditions for their propagation." [14] The case is indicative; the results obtained from this proposal are unfortunately unknown.

The "Rape of Crowds"

By the theory of the "psychologues" people were seen as a mass. "That mass is for the taking," declared Colonel Lacheroy, rhetorically. "How do you take it?" Not everything, he reminds us, is ideological; the approach will be necessarily varied.[15] But there are certain mechan-

---

[13] Gustave Le Bon, *La Psychologie des foules* (Paris, 1895), p. 14.

[14] Jean Planchais, "L'Armée s'inquiète," *Le Monde,* January 19, 1957.

[15] Lacheroy, *op. cit.,* p. 312. Colonel Lacheroy was the head of the Psychological Warfare Section of the Ministry of Defense under André Morice; later he was chief of the Section d'Action Psychologique et d'Information in Algiers immediately following the *coup d'état* of May 13, 1958. Subsequently, he taught at the Ecole Supérieure de Guerre, was implicated in the plot of April 22, 1961, and sentenced to death *in absentia*

ical and scientific aids that will render a mass more susceptible to conversion, and it is here that some much-disputed points of psychology arise.

In 1939, in the shadow of advancing world conflict, a Russian émigré experimental psychologist, Serge Tchakhotine, produced an amazing study entitled *The Rape of Crowds by Political Propaganda*.[16] This book, despite its extraordinary interest, might be slumbering today in comparative obscurity if the "colonels" had not rediscovered it in 1954–1955. On the evidence available no one can doubt that it had a telling influence on psychological war operations in Algeria.

The conjuncture is a fairly strange one. Tchakhotine was a disciple of the great Pavlov, and a Marxist himself, if unorthodox in several respects. The dual impact of Pavlov's experiments on dogs (and, according to Tchakhotine, on human beings before he died) and the milieu of Germany, where the author was living in the early 1930's, gave rise to a series of very doctrinaire observations about controlling crowds according to strict psychological principle. This was naturally destined to appeal to the proponents of *action psychologique,* since it not only bolstered their experiences in Indochina but promised drastic improvements and refinements in the art of psychological war.[17]

Tchakhotine believed, with Pavlov, that reflexes could be conditioned in the human organism by the gradual substitution of an abnormal for a normal excitant, if both stimuli were presented in conjunction over a period of time. Thus, if the offering of meat to a dog is associated a sufficient number of times with the ringing of a bell, a point will finally be reached where the bell alone will produce the reaction normally connected with the meat (that is, salivation). The "artificial" or "temporary" reflex will have been substituted for the "innate or absolute" one. The bell will have become an "adequate excitant."

On the other hand, the characteristic play of the nervous system will continue: "relative inhibitions" can be introduced. If, for example, a cat appears at the same time that the dog perceives the sound of the bell, the salivation will not occur. It is possible to manipulate the subject between a series of inhibitions and excitants. The essence of the theory for Tchakhotine is this possibility of control and manipulation. The

---

by a military tribunal on June 1, 1961. A fugitive in Spain, he was deported by General Franco to the Canary Islands in the fall of 1961 at the instances of both the French government and General Salan's OAS, with which he had broken over issues of strategy.

[16] Serge Tchakhotine, *Le viol des foules par la propagande politique* (Paris, 1939).

[17] Lacheroy, *op. cit.,* p. 317: "The best-known book is Tchakhotine's *Le viol des foules:* it gives a certain number of recipes. . . . Without going as far as that rape of souls which I detest, which is bad, the Service Psychologique . . . has thought of a certain number of formulas."

important link with human behavior is supplied by Pavlov himself, who, again according to Tchakhotine, made experiments demonstrating how speech could easily be substituted for sound as an "adequate excitant." "Speech enters into conjunction with all external and internal excitation that reaches the cerebral hemispheres, conveys it all, replaces it, and thereby can provoke the same reactions as those aroused by these same excitants." [18] The interplay of stimulus and inhibition could induce bewilderment and a corresponding breakdown in the individual of the will to resist: "If in these conditions the subject is struck by imperative speech, by an order, that order becomes irresistible, thanks to the irradiation along the entire surface of the inhibition caused by that order." [19] Finally, the possibilities for individual resistance to such a technique are in direct proportion to the degree of culture that the subject has attained, in other words, his richness in systems of conditioned reflexes before the experimentation. "Ignorance is thus the best environment for forming masses who lend themselves easily to suggestion." [20] One readily divines the congenital sympathy between these propositions and the goals that the French military "psychologues" were trying to achieve.

Tchakhotine goes on to postulate four basic absolute reflexes upon which all human reaction is normally founded (the instincts of struggle, nutrition, sex, and maternity). As he particularizes his armory of propaganda techniques, it is evident that their efficacy relates to their power to activate one of these four instincts. He joins Hitler more closely than Marx in averring that the combative instinct takes precedence over its more materialist counterpart, the nutritive.

Another Hitlerian characteristic is Tchakhotine's conception of the role of the mass, which runs counter to the orthodox theory of the Communists. For example, according to Trotsky, "one commits a gross fault in thinking that the mass is blind and credulous. . . . Where different versions that circulate concerning the movements of the mass are contradictory, we must consider as closest to the truth that interpretation which the mass has made its own." [21] But, for Tchakhotine, the mass is inert; in the words of Lacheroy, "elle est à prendre." From time to time, says Tchakhotine, it is necessary to "refresh" the mass by means of an elaborate auditory and visual spectacle. This is consonant with the Pavlovian observation that a "conditioned reflex" may over a period of time wear out and need reinvigoration. In between demon-

[18] Tchakhotine (quoting Pavlov), *op. cit.*, p. 25.
[19] *Ibid.*, p. 26.
[20] *Ibid.*
[21] Trotsky, *History of the Revolution,* quoted by Reiwald, *op. cit.*, p. 233.

strations the conditioning is most easily reinforced through the sagacious use of symbols (such as the swastika, Cross of Lorraine, "V" for
Victory). Thus:

. . . The art of government by dictatorship always proceeds in the following order: (1) bring the mass together in a crowd and call it to attention
with a psychic whiplash while haranguing it violently and presenting it at
the same time with certain symbols, reviving its faith in these symbols; (2)
dispersing this "crowd" once more into a "mass"; and surrounding it on all
sides with the revitalized symbols.[22]

Again, the distinction of "mass" and "crowd" recalls Hitler. It was the
great caution of the latter when staging his monster rallies that all
sense of individuality or class consciousness should be lost in the midst
of the demonstration. The puritan attitude of the Communists toward
class was abandoned, because any insistence on this distinction would
interfere psychically with the reception of the harangue from the platform and some of the communion between leader and crowd would be
lost in the process.

Even a layman can find legitimate room to criticize Tchakhotine's
theories. His postulation of mass action upon the scanty results of individual experiments is shaky. The examples he educes a posteriori to
bolster his system were obviously affected by many elements other than
the ones Pavlov describes. Historical and sociological factors of the
most diverse sorts predispose crowds in different directions, which may
or may not correspond with what the demagogue is trying to achieve.
Nor is the demagogue himself so all-powerful as Tchakhotine suggests;
he may depend inwardly on the flattery of the mob as much as it depends on the force of his harangue, and this will substantially modify
his relation to it. Thus Tchakhotine approaches a uniform, "classical"
view of man when there is no evidence to suggest that the racial and
geographical milieu is not of high importance in discrimination. It
would probably be more correct to affirm with Colonel (now General)
Nemo, one of the best-balanced commentators on psychological war
and former commander of a section in Indochina:

This mobilization of the crowd cannot follow uniform rules. If the objective
is the same everywhere, one cannot universally apply like techniques. For
the system to be adopted depends on very disparate and different factors
according to the country, composition of the body social, state of opinion,
individual and collective psychological reactions to events, ways of life depending on the average level of material existence.[23]

[22] Tchakhotine, op. cit., p. 46.
[23] Colonel Nemo, "La guerre dans la foule," Revue de Défense nationale, June 1956,
p. 728.

Nemo's criticism suggests that even in its most advanced spearheads the French Army was by no means united in its endorsement of "conditioned" crowd psychology. However, there were enough recorded instances of operational techniques similar to the ones Tchakhotine proposes (such as controlled discussion, meetings, films, and spectacles for the Muslims) to demonstrate that these modes of action found considerable favor. Insofar as the events subsequent to May 13, 1958, on the Algiers "Forum" were not spontaneous or accidental, they were essentially Tchakhotinian.

As the enthusiasm of the "colonels" mounted in the wake of the events of May 13, their obsession with crowd control was made evident in a series of immoderate remarks. "Call me a fascist if you like," said Lieutenant Coloniel Trinquier in a newspaper interview, "but we must make the population docile and manageable; everybody's acts must be controlled." And Colonel Goussault, Lacheroy's adjutant in the Psychological Action Services at Algiers, wrote in the review *Atlantique Nord* in the middle of 1958, "Revolutionary war is total war and the different activities at stake in it must be employed in the unique perspective of the psychological conquest of populations."[24]

Other Guidelines

Tchakhotine's *Le viol des foules* was, of course, not the only book that found its way to the shelves in the "colonels' library." There were the works by Le Bon and other social psychologists (particularly esteemed if they were French);[25] there were the Communist classics, and miscellaneous books of value such as Curzio Malaparte's *Coup d'Etat, the Technique of Revolution* and the very useful summary text *La propagande politique* by Jean-Marie Domenach.

Mao Tse-tung, as the most voluminous and important writer on the subject of *la guerre révolutionnaire,* a topic in which he considerably outdistanced the Soviets,[26] was bound to occupy a particular place at the core of the new doctrine. Not one of the least attractive features about the work of the ruler of Red China was its extraordinary clarity. The "colonels" widely regarded Mao as the teacher of the Viet Minh, and perceived that the war in Indochina had followed a course rigorously consistent with the revolutionary schema of the great strategist.

[24] "Les principes de l'action psychologique et de la guerre subversive décrits par deux de leurs practiciens," *Le Monde,* July 10, 1958.

[25] Especially, Philippe de Félice, *Foules en délire: Extases collectives* (Paris, 1947).

[26] Although a classic example of Communist brainwashing seems to have occurred with Japanese prisoners of war returning from the U.S.S.R. in 1949. See Jean-Marie Domenach, *La propagande politique* (Paris, 1950), p. 6.

This interpretation is arguable in the sense that most of Mao's observations are occasional and concerned with purely Chinese phenomena. But the "colonels" regarded the line of influence as direct and decisive, and were quick to throw themselves into an intense study (which for some had already begun in Viet Minh stockades) of the genius of this novel form of war.

Mao taught especially that the role of the masses was paramount in revolutionary war ("Revolutionary war is the war of the popular masses; it cannot be waged except by mobilizing the popular masses and enlisting their support").[27] The cause of revolutionary war was just because it was "progressive." The spectrum of warfare was not confined to the traditional range: "Military questions are only one of the instruments permitting the fulfillment of political tasks." Mao insisted on the necessity for the political education of every soldier,[28] and affirmed his famous formula according to which the Army should be in the midst of the people "like the fish in water." Critics of the French use of psychological action were not long in pointing out that a "French fish in Algerian water" was scarcely analogous to the "Chinese fish in Chinese water."

The very concise book on propaganda, by Jean-Marie Domenach, the liberal Catholic editor of *Esprit*, which appeared in 1950, was intended to summarize one of the worst curses of our totalitarian twentieth century. Out of his investigations of advertising, sloganry, psychology, and Hitlerian and Stalinist propaganda, Domenach refined certain laws of manipulation (law of simplification and the "unique enemy"; law of enlargement and disfigurement; law of orchestration; law of transfusion; law of unanimity and contagion — as well as techniques of counterpropaganda) and documented their effectiveness with liberal historical examples. Later the Psychological Warfare Services would avail themselves gratefully of this scholarship, while Domenach (who, in his book, had given careful consideration and respect to the theories of Tchakhotine) could only complain: "Aided by curious 'university students,'[29] enterprising colonels mount the mechanics of mass management which is based on the crudest sort of Pavlovism and which gives those in control the exalted illusion of having complete power over men."[30]

---

[27] Mao Tse-tung, "Let's Be More Concerned About the Life of the People" (January 27, 1934).

[28] "Thanks to the political education work that has been accomplished, all the soldiers of the Red Army have a class consciousness." Mao Tse-tung, "Struggle in the Tsing-Kang-Chu" (November 25, 1928).

[29] Domenach here is referring to the followers of Pierre Lagaillarde.

[30] Jean-Marie Domenach, "L'armée en République," *Esprit*, November 1958, p. 638.

Psychological War and the Resistance

A final point should be clarified in connection with the origins of *action psychologique*. This concerns the problem of linking the doctrine with the experiences of the French Resistance. It would appear that the Resistance, with its *maquis,* its sabotage, its *noyautage,* and its uses of propaganda should be recognized as a precursor of the awareness of *la guerre révolutionnaire* and its ancillary techniques.[31] Yet there is little evidence that the "colonels" accepted the legitimacy of this lineage. For them, their doctrines either were novel or at least owed their inspiration to the Communist rather than the Western world. This was not so much because of the leftist orientation of the Resistance and the distaste for many of its personnel; instead it seems to have derived from the conviction that the Resistance (which most of the "colonels" understood little because they participated in the regular fighting forces) was a kind of child's play, an adventurous interlude beside which *la guerre révolutionnaire* was deadly serious, massive, and total. Subversive war in the Resistance was simply not regarded as sufficiently technical or astute according to the new principles;[32] it was merely an impressive application of guerrilla tactics, without sound ideological basis or meticulous conception.

In the years following its codification, the practice of *action psychologique* in Algeria was modish and arrogant, often stupidly dogmatic or unreasonably brutal. With some officers it became a true "intoxication"; with others it became at least a plausible military technique. Many shunned it or heaped it with ridicule. The most we can say of it from short perspective is that it failed to prove its mettle and became part and parcel of the maelstrom of military insurrection. There were many more honorable and palpable reasons for mutiny in April 1961 than the defense of this theory.

[31] For a description of Resistance-style *noyautage,* which may be interestingly compared with the "scientific" style of "parallel hierarchies," see especially René Hostache, *Le Conseil nationale de la Résistance* (Paris, 1958), Chapter VIII, pp. 236–254.

[32] See, for example, André Souyris, "Un procédé efficace de contre-guérilla," *Revue de Défense nationale,* June 1956, p. 698: "This ideological character gives to a revolutionary struggle an aspect of total war to which we are not accustomed in France despite our trial of national resistance from 1940 to 1944."

PART FOUR

ALGERIA

IX

THE WAR THAT COULD NOT BE LOST: BACKGROUND

Nous avons promis aux Arabes de les traiter comme s'ils étaient enfants de la France. . . . Ainsi, nous pourrons espérer de leur faire supporter tout d'abord notre domination, de les y accoutumer plus tard, et à la longue de les identifier avec nous, de manière à ne former qu'un seul et même peuple.
— *Marshal Bugeaud, in 1844*

C'est, en effet, le sort de l'Occident et celui de la Chrétienté qui se joue actuellement en Algérie.
— *"Message des Forces Armées,"*
No. 12, February 1956

On November 1, 1954, following a haphazard plan developed by the nationalist Comité Révolutionnaire d'Unité et d'Action (CRUA), the first shots of what was to become the Algerian War resounded in the forbidding fastnesses of the Aurès Mountains, a landlocked area in Eastern Algeria, some one hundred miles south of the city of Constantine. This was only four months after the cease-fire in Indochina; the preparatory touches were being added as the last remnants of the French Expeditionary Force withdrew from that country.

Some feel that the timing of the rebellion was directly connected with the struggle for power among the nationalists. Serge Bromberger, for example, writes: "It was an idea of very brief content that inspired

this handful of men, but one which, because of its brevity and simplicity, would spread over the central Maghreb with astonishing ease:
the national party is torn by factions; by unleashing [revolutionary]
action we will reforge its unity."[1] The point is not proved; but there
were, clearly, at that time, a "handful of men" engaged in an inevitable
revolution.[2]

At the time of the 1954 outbreak the French garrison forces in Algeria
numbered no more than 50,000. Their countermeasures were therefore
severely restricted in a territory four times the size of France. During
the coming years their number would grow ninefold, without, for that
matter, permitting them to achieve the pacification. Their adversaries
would never muster more than 40,000 fighting men at one time.

The "Passion" of Algeria

Algeria became a tragedy of much passion on both sides, a spectacle
which, more than any other contemporary event, is ill fitted for academic or routine interpretations. Facts here meant little and meant
much; absolute right did not exist, and relative right was an evanescent,
shifting quality. Passion could not fail to spin the plot in Algeria; for
here was a land in which two incompatible peoples felt at home, a geographical surface that both called home. This simple fact lay at the core
of the Algerian tragedy. For more than seven years there was no
power competent to make peace between warring ideals and cultures
that gradually lost the gift for speaking the same language.

Many Western commentators glibly discussed Algeria as an Arab
state passing through an especially violent stage in its evolution toward
independence, the stage reached by Egypt in 1922, Syria in 1945, Morocco and Tunisia in 1955. Others in France argued with great conviction that Algeria was the measure of France's noble experiment of

[1] Serge Bromberger, *Les rebelles algériens* (Paris, 1958), p. 21. Of course, the germ
of the CRUA, called the Organisation Spéciale and dedicated to revolutionary action,
had existed in the bosom of the MTLD since 1948. Its first chief was Hocine Ait Ahmed;
its second, Ahmed Ben Bella, who controlled the CRUA at the outbreak of the rebellion.

[2] One of the *chefs historiques* of the Algerian revolution, Mohammed Boudiaf, would
later in an interview deny that Egypt had granted important aid — an assertion running
contrary to known facts — and would continue thus to describe the origins of the
rebellion: "[We had no precise conceptions] other than national independence and the
desire to make the masses take part in the insurrection. The word revolution . . .
pointed especially to the way in which we intended to conquer our independence,
against the colonial apparatus, on the one hand, by violence; against the reformist and
bureaucratic methods of the pre-existing nationalist movement, on the other, by exploding the old structures of the movement." *Le Monde*, November 7, 1962.

economic generosity and cultural assimilation. Both of these interpretations were partly true, but neither was the truth. Both sides staked too much sticky honor on the outcome, too many bullets and impassioned political words on the principle of final solution. For the nationalists, the Algerian War was, officially, a "war of reconquest" against the colonialists. More privately, it was a precious war in which the real cement of nationhood was being molded together. For the French Army, reeling from Indochina, it was the war that, even against the will of God or man, could not be lost.

Algeria exerted an undoubted fascination on diverse temperaments. Hardened military officers, civil servants, even intellectuals from the *métropole,* after they had spent months in this country that gleams in the naked beauty of Mediterranean poverty, became its sons and lovers. They found Auvergne in its twisting valleys and goat paths, Languedoc in its flat, sunny vineyards, the Massif des Maures in the Cézannesque geometry of its hills. Above all, they discovered a curious wonderland of its own dimensions that seemed strangely suited to be called "France." This "Algerian intoxication" struck people on the Left and people on the Right, and was far from being an artificial excuse.

If the land was capable of affecting transients so profoundly, what could have been the feelings of the descendants of the hardy pioneers of 1848 or 1852 or 1871 who were the substratum of the French population? What of the mood of the Spanish and Italian "petits blancs" who had escaped the economic uncertainty and political rigor of their native countries to find relative comfort under the law of republican France? Unlike the French residents of Morocco, for example, this population was simply under no circumstances prepared to leave; it had literally nowhere to go, no other place where it could feel at home.

In time there arose a parallel between the feelings of the settlers toward their country and those of the professional Army toward the terrain it was fighting over; to bleed on such magnetic soil was somehow to possess it by right. Algeria had never been especially favored in military annals until the war against the FLN (Front de Libération Nationale) brewed up in earnest. It had been a sheltered preserve of businessmen, large agriculturalists, and functionaries, a permissively lucrative extension of metropolitan France. Morocco, the sacred Lyauteyan fief, was the favored haven for the professional officer. The loss of the Protectorate in March 1956 was a heavy blow to the traditional mentality of the overseas Army. Since it came at a time when the Algerian revolution had already assumed grave proportions, the Maghreb seemed seized by a concerted revolutionary earthquake that not only threatened the national honor and patrimony but jeopardized the

Army's overseas sphere of action. If Algeria, too, were to be lost through blunder or bargained away by a "gutless" government like those of Mendès-France and Faure, the Army, through no fault of its own, would be thrust back on that *métropole* where it no longer had the sense of belonging and where its spirit and particularity would be snuffed out. Hell would open, and the soldier would be drowned in the aimless, godless, and self-seeking national life, the life of "la bagnole et le métro à six heures."

The "Moroccan Reflex"

Though the shock of abandoning Morocco was very great, a certain number of French troops and technicians remained in the former protectorate. The barbaric vigor of the Casablanca riots of December 1952 (which prophesied the cruelties of Algeria and gave the lie to professions of Franco-Arab harmony), the spectacular mishandling of the deportation of Sultan Mohammed Ben Youssef (King Mohammed V) to Madagascar and his triumphant return two years later, the speedy transfer of sovereignty by the Treaty of Saint-Cloud — all these shook the Army's faith in the government to the very roots. The Army in Morocco, loyal to the letter if not the spirit of the Lyauteyan ideal of proconsulship, had cast itself in an administrative, benignly imperial role, inspiring the initiatives of the *maghzen* (Court). This implied a solidarity of interest with the "big business" and "big finance" that commanded the economy of the country and exerted extraordinary pressure in favor of the *status quo*. The Moroccan habit would have an oblique but significant bearing on Algeria. As the French Army was compelled more and more to assume all administrative functions in Algeria in the years 1956–1958, it did so under the influence of the Moroccan reflex, in a highly tenacious and deliberate manner.

The transfer of sovereignty to the two independent states of Tunisia and Morocco in 1956 radically altered the course of the Algerian War. The rebels now enjoyed the advantage of two contiguous supply and staging bases and the psychological encouragement of friendly frontiers — a condition of revolutionary war against which Commandant Hogard and others had specifically warned. But the Moroccan situation had other effects on Algeria. As Jacques Soustelle was later to write:

There was not one Algerian in a thousand who knew that August 20 [1955] was the [second] anniversary of the deposition of Sultan Mohammed V. But on the outside, others knew. The decision to unleash serious trouble in Algeria [the "Constantinois massacres"] on that date was taken, far away from Algiers, on the territory of a neutral country, during a meeting where a representative of Colonel Nasser was present; I have received the proof since that time.[3]

Soustelle was correct in perceiving that the deep involvement of Egypt in the early stages of the Algerian revolution had been a decisive factor. This conflict, which the antagonists made every effort to limit superficially, actually became "internationalized" from the moment of its outbreak.

Loyalty and Loyalism

Throughout the war the Army occupied an ambiguous and evolving position vis-à-vis the settler population. On the one hand, there was camaraderie with a people that drew the fighters to it, in the same measure that the civilian metropolitans tended to repulse them. Many elements of the Army, especially its elite — the paratroops and the Legion — actively sympathized with the main body of Europeans — workers, shopkeepers, small functionaries, café owners — who formed the vanguard of opposition to any negotiated settlement with the FLN. On the other hand, the Army had other motives for the pursuit of the conflict than the restoration of the *status quo ante*. Predominantly anti-capitalist in spirit, it distrusted the prerogatives of the *gros colons,* and wished, in majority, for the emergence of a more socially equitable Algeria that would integrate the Muslims into the European sphere of life.

But, above all, a civilian-military link was forged over the matter of loyalty. The Army felt its honor to be committed in the preservation of French Algeria; it was obligated to the European settlers who placed such consummate trust in its regency and to the many Muslims who, often putting themselves and their families in great jeopardy of reprisal, fought with it or assisted it in administrative tasks. As Raoul Girardet somewhat poetically put it, Algeria had become a part of the "sentimental geography of the French Army." Finally, over the course of the Algerian rebellion, the Army tended to become a substitute for the State; there are few *de facto* states that willingly transfer their authority to a competing power.

Many officers, as late as 1960, were still infected with the proposition "better death than dishonor," and announced their readiness to fight the pacification for twenty years, if necessary. This was the legacy of Indochina. As Jean-Yves Alquier narrated, "I knew a captain . . . who was obsessed with the thought that he had lost his honor in Indochina in persuading hundreds of young Vietnamese Catholics to stay with

[3] Jaques Soustelle, *Aimée et souffrante Algérie* (Paris, 1956), p. 113.

his auxiliaries by repeating to them, because he believed it himself, 'We won't ever let you down.' And when we pulled out, the Viets shot them for having believed his promise." [4] The obsession with honor was no novelty; neither was it merely a noble anachronism or an unreflective excuse. It was reason and passion mingled, the ultimate reflex of a profession which can look to neither material reward nor comfortable security for its wages. As a distinguished American general has written: "Professional soldiers are sentimental men, for all the harsh realities of their calling. In their wallets and in their memories they carry bits of philosophy, fragments of poetry, quotations from the Scriptures, which, in times of stress and danger, speak to them with great meaning." [5] Indochina, too, was portable, a fragment of bitter poetry.

Shortly after General Jacques Massu, commander of the Algiers army corps and superprefect (*igame*) of the region, had given the explosive interview to the German journalist Hans Kempski that merited his withdrawal in January 1960, he is supposed to have confided to Pierre Guillaumat, the Minister of the Armies: "Je me suis fait pigeonner." [6] *Se faire pigeonner* — this was not an uncommon fate. Much of the structure of Algerian intrigue depended on the complicity of the thoughtless handshake or a few words uttered without sober reflection. Casual loyalties could become suddenly binding obligations in this weird, out-of-focus situation; the assertion "il marchera avec nous" could be the guarantee of practically anything. Algiers, with its seven hundred thousand inhabitants, was basically a small town. In many curious ways, the ideological rivalry with Paris would reveal the unconscious, volatile suspicion and resentment inspired by the Big City.

Almost without any conscious planning the whole geographical and emotional milieu of Algeria became one huge *action psychologique,* a bottomless well of illusion and delusion drugging the creatures that drank of it. The scene of a cruel war, it was also an Arcadia where normal logic was curiously suspended. One must not forget that this is and was, long before the coming of the loudspeakers and the colonels with their theories, the land of desert and mirage, of hills that change shape as the eye fastens on them, of clouds no bigger than a man's hand suggesting the outlines of familiar objects in the real world. It was, par excellence, a setting for mass hypnosis.

The European population of Algeria, as Maurice Mégret points out,

---

[4] Jean-Yves Alquier, *Nous avons pacifié Tazalt* (Paris, 1958), p. 231.

[5] General Matthew A. Ridgway, "My Battles in Peace and War," *Saturday Evening Post,* January 21, 1956.

[6] See André Euloge and Antoine Moulinier, *L'Envers des barricades* (Paris, 1960), pp. 73–74, for a partial text of the Massu interview.

did not need ulterior persuasion; it was already "heated white hot."[7]
When concerted psychological action came on the scene, it could only
channel this frantic energy, attack fear, and possibly restore some equilibrium. It also helped to expand the myth — or truth — of this people's
individuality, of its heroic situation on the border marches, of its
spiritual isolation from that other France anesthetized with liberal
torpor. Solidarity muted class antagonisms. As a necessary consequence,
local leadership passed from the hands of the *gros colons,* the Borgeauds
and the Quilicis, who now rendered silent approbation to a genuinely
mass movement shaped by the *petit peuple.*

The Settler Population

The composition of the European population must be understood.[8]
By 1872 it included 130,000 Frenchmen, 71,000 Spaniards (mostly in
the Oranie), 18,000 Italians, 12,000 Maltese, and 14,000 others. These
proportions are hard to trace forward because of European intermar-
riages — the kind of alliances that produced offspring like Albert
Camus (and Joseph Ortiz). However, by the turn of the century, there
were 633,850 Europeans, and 800,000 by 1922. By 1960 the number was
about 1,200,000, including the Jewish community of 140,000, of which
a part was indigenous but almost totally assimilated to European habits.

We pass to the urban-rural ratio. Urbanization was such a constantly
accelerating feature among the Europeans that by 1957 there were only
19,400 inhabitants who could be called *colons* (landed proprietors) in
the strict sense. Of these, 7432 possessed holdings of less than ten
hectares (about twenty-five acres); they were, in other words, little
more than subsistence farmers. Of the remaining 12,000, according to
Germaine Tillion's estimate, only "three hundred are rich and about
a dozen excessively rich (perhaps richer collectively than all the others
put together").[9] Jacques Soustelle has presented us with slightly different figures, listing 32,000 Europeans living by the soil, who either cultivated or owned about 22,000 plots of land.[10] The average plot was
about 17.5 hectares but tended to diminish near the coast and increase
in the infertile hinterlands. According to his analysis, the majority of
cultivators could be classified as "small peasants." Soustelle claimed
that the average per capita wage of the European in Algeria was 20
per cent lower than that of his compatriot in metropolitan France. For

[7] Maurice Mégret, *L'action psychologique* (Paris, 1960), p. 163.
[8] See Albert Mousset, in *Le Monde,* May 22, 1956.
[9] Germaine Tillion, *L'Afrique bascule vers l'avenir* (Paris, 1960), p. 32.
[10] Soustelle, *op. cit.,* p. 56.

the more than a million urban dwellers, representing more than three quarters of the vital economic activity of the country, one could identify the normal scale of occupational activity from business executive to manual laborer, although most of the unskilled jobs were performed by Muslims.

The myth of a ruling class of landed exploiters (though the rich were very rich indeed) is quickly shattered. European Algeria is seen in true perspective as an approximate extension of Southern France, with its people engaged in much the same activities and in roughly the same proportion. It is impossible to escape the conclusion that the Europeans of Algeria were well settled and deeply attached by every conceivable economic as well as emotional tie to the land in which they were dwelling. As one observer wrote: "A people has more dead souls than live ones: the European Algerians are at home in Algeria and not in Europe not only because there are 1,200,000 of them living there, but because there are several million buried there." [11]

The notable militancy and "mobocracy" of the Europeans, seemingly antithetical to their "Southern" temperament, was in part due to the fact that, faced with an emergency that transcended economic, class, or occupational lines, they made common cause and allowed themselves to follow the intransigent leaders, of whatever stripe, who seemed most resolute in defending the threatened patrimony.

This aggressive spirit also resulted from the autonomism of the paramilitary habit. In the early days of the rebellion the Governor-General showed extreme reluctance to make arms available to the civilians for the defense of their homesteads against terrorist attack. Mobile military security was also lacking. The Cairo-inspired massacres of August 20, 1955 (the anniversary of the exile of the Sultan of Morocco), which accounted for over a hundred grisly deaths throughout the Constantinois, were held to be a direct result of this refusal. Governor-General Soustelle had announced the previous April: "Nobody denies that certain centers must be protected from danger. But to achieve this end, the only lawful solution is to call upon guards who shall be recruited and directed within the scope of the law by the *communes* and who shall act as *gardes champêtres* . . . under the prefectorial authority." [12]

Many Muslims also perished in the surprise assault; the rebel plan seems to have been to terrorize both communities. Orders issued by Ahmed Ben Bella, the FLN chief, and later captured by the French

[11] Alain Peyrefitte, "Pour sortir de l'Impasse algérienne, I," *Le Monde,* September 28, 1961.

[12] Cited from Michael K. Clark, *Algeria in Turmoil* (New York, 1959), p. 178. Despite its controversial aspect, the Clark book is a mine of reliable and significant information for the early years of the Algerian crisis.

confirmed this hypothesis. They read in part: "Liquidate all personalities who might act as valid intermediaries [that is, between the two communities]."[13] Soustelle made a tour of the ravaged areas the next day, inspecting the dead and wounded in the hospitals. His book recounting his tour of duty in Algeria includes pictures of the atrocities, and we may surmise, despite his denial, that the ghastly event gave his personal conviction a few sharp twists.

After the massacres of the Constantinois there was no holding back on the issue of self-defense. Small, maneuverable units — Mobile Rural Protection Groups — were quickly formed and equipped, assisted by native *harkas*,[14] and by the end of September 1955 the French Army in Algeria totaled 120,000 men. It was chiefly a case of too little and too late, for by now the terror had become frequent and general, breaking out in the west of the Oranie, near Tlemcen, and especially in Kabylie, east of Algiers. Inadequately protected by territorial authority, the homesteaders either abandoned their lands reluctantly or took matters into their own hands. As incidents spread to the major cities in 1956, particularly Algiers, the French would have recourse to a whole motley of ancillary forces, civilian and military gendarmes, the *harkas,* the mobile groups, groups of self-defense, and the Unités Territoriales recruited from the civilian population (at first European, later Muslim as well), persons who gave one day of service out of each ten to tasks of patrolling and surveillance and drew rifles and submachine guns from the police caserns.[15]

From 1956 on, normal politics in Algeria were suspended. Representative institutions were adjourned until 1958, and if there still existed rudimentary branches of the metropolitan parties, the SFIO, the MRP, the Radicals, and the Indépendants, they were organized as pressure groups for urging a commitment to *Algérie française* from their parent formations in the *métropole*. Their local power was nil, and they tended to become replicas of each other. Basically, the European in Algiers felt politically uncommitted; he would easily lend his vote and active support to that group or action movement which defended his interests most vigorously. De Gaulle was never revered, and it was certainly not the wish of the European settlers to see him come to power in 1958. To many of them he was the man who had taken Thorez into his government in 1945. For many families that had long harbored pictures of Marshal Pétain or "Moustachu" Giraud in their homes, de Gaulle, back in power, was to seem like a reprehensible compromiser

---

[13] Soustelle, *op. cit.*, p. 119.
[14] A *harka* is a native auxiliary force of group strength composed of *harkis*.
[15] See Chapter XIII, pp. 257 ff.

who had strangled the national counter-revolution in its cradle. He had come to terms with the *gens du système:* the unctuous Guy Mollet, the jackal Antoine Pinay (who, as Minister of Foreign Affairs in the Edgar Faure government of 1955, had signed the Treaty of Saint-Cloud with the Sultan of Morocco), and, above all, the antichrist Pierre Pflimlin, who had sought power proclaiming the politics of the cease-fire.

The leaders of the Algerian rebellion correctly predicated a part of their success on the intransigence of the Europeans.[16] When the revolution was weak in effectives and badly supplied, its strategists resorted to barbarous and demonstrative acts of terror calculated to destroy the chances for any Franco-Muslim reconciliation. It was felt that the small sparks of revolt could be continuously fanned by transverse gusts of hatred, that atrocity would lead to retaliation, and that social intercourse would cease between the two races. This, in effect, had almost happened by 1956. From that point on, the Army sought to take the situation back in hand — aided by the directives of Robert Lacoste, the Resident Minister — by extending protection and encouraging fraternization. In 1961 General Salan's Secret Army Organization would resort to the same tactic, hoping to lure the Muslims into mass violence and thus place the Army decisively in the same camp as the settlers.

The Muslims

In eight years the agitation and militancy of the FLN succeeded in creating emotional conditions for Algerian nationalism where few had previously existed. This was done chiefly by making city and country aware of common goals and a common interest, enforced by "oil-spot" tactics, continuous indoctrination, menaces, and the mixed euphoria of sacrifice and success. But the revolution was not born in the hearts of the peasantry and proletariat, nor was its ideology directly derived from their deepest concerns. However, as continuous war often leads to technological advance in all spheres, this one inspired extreme social and psychological change among the people at large and, necessarily, a vastly increased political consciousness.[17] The growth of Algerian nationhood was osmotic, compulsory, and subterranean.

Largely owing to a reduction of the death rate in the twentieth century, a characteristically high natality, and a dramatic assault on infant mortality, the Muslim population had come to number some nine

[16] European intransigence also produced corresponding intransigence in the ranks of the revolutionary directorate. See, for example, the account of the FLN meeting in Tunis by Max Clos, "Les extrémistes algériens ont fait échouer les tentatives de conciliation de Bourguiba," *Le Figaro,* March 23, 1957.

[17] See Germaine Tillion, *Les ennemis complémentaires* (Paris, 1960), p. 16.

millions, of whom more than half were under twenty-one years of age. This drastic pressure compelled the dismantling of once-productive terrains into next-to-useless small plots, the exodus of the agricultural populations to the cities or to France itself, and the growing pauperization of the people as a whole. Westernization, meanwhile, had both its economic and social impacts. Approximately two million out of the nine had achieved habits and standards of living which would be recognizable in Southern Europe; another half-million perhaps lived in a dangerous transitional state where new values and consumption habits clashed hard against the hereditary culture.

For the remaining six million the mounting sacrifice of certain traditional reassurances and controls was in no sense balanced by any amenities of the modern world. In fact, the disappearance of older spiritual values went hand in hand with the loss of land and material goods. The disruptions of a revolutionary war sank these people deeper and deeper into a bottomless misery from which there was no escape except death by starvation or disease, or by a bullet in combat.[18] It is these Algerians who were the real victims of, and silent witnesses to, a violence that threatened their marginal subsistence for over seven years.

When the rebellion broke out in November 1954, the Algerian countryside was still, by and large, a territory of petty particularisms, of clans and vendettas, and of insubmissiveness to a single source of authority. There was also the tension of the two racial communities within the Muslim spectrum, the Arabs and the Kabylians, the people of the plains and the people of the hills. The early history of the revolution was plagued by these types of factionalism.

Specific areas of Berber particularism survived in the tortuous mountain region of Kabylie (east of Algiers), in the Aurès region, and in scattered spots elsewhere. From Kabylie would come some of the most notable leaders of the rebellion, such as Hocine Lahouel, who would force the break with Messali Hajd's Mouvement pour le Triomphe des Libertés Démocratiques (MTLD) in 1954 and Belkacem Krim, formerly the military commander of the Kabylian *willaya* and later Vice-President of the Algerian Provisional Government. The Kabylians were strong in the "internal organization" of the revolution (Armée de Liberation Nationale) and even, in its mid-course, made attempts to capture authority in the Algérois.[19] Their resourcefulness and individualism did not contribute particularly to the inner harmony of the movement; in the formative years of the political apparatus of the

---

[18] See Germaine Tillion, *L'Afrique bascule vers l'avenir, op. cit.*, pp. 47–48.
[19] Bromberger, *op. cit.*, "L'heure des Kabyles," pp. 74–118.

revolution, such amusing epithets as "berbéro-materialiste" occasionally crept into the ideologically tortured vocabulary of the FLN. Perhaps the difference in mood between the two peoples is best summarized by the ethnologist Eugène Guernier: "The Berbers are Western rationalists in formal contradiction with the Arabs, who are, above all, imaginative Orientals."[20]

One should not be too far misled by these differences, which by 1957 had been largely resolved in the political sense, at least for the duration of the war.[21] There is no doubt that they have been real and vexing to the Algerian nationalists and will be destabilizing in the future Algerian state; but their centrifugal effect was grossly overexaggerated by French propaganda, and not surprisingly by many of the same sources that were to play on the idea of Franco-Muslim integration. The chief fact is that Arab and Berber share a common religion, a mostly parallel way of life, and a common occupancy of the territory that dates back almost a millennium.

The FLN's "mobilization of the masses" did not come easily. A peasant population, necessarily engaged in the daily dawn-to-dusk drudgery of winning enough from the soil to keep body and spirit alive, cannot suddenly launch itself into political adventure, especially if its political consciousness remains basically undeveloped. Beyond a probable militant 20 per cent who had discovered their "Algerianness," the great majority leaned in the direction where real power seemed to exist at the moment. This substantiated a certain premise of *la guerre révolutionnaire;* what the French theorists were incorrect in appraising, however, was that there was surely an innate proclivity in the Muslims to want independence that was destined to grow as the idea became more familiar and the revolution appeared more insuperable.

In late 1955, at the height of indiscriminate terror, when French military resources were still very inadequate, the FLN was undoubtedly approaching its primary objective of controlling the population. But it had not yet created a politically aroused national consciousness. Then the French began to win notable — and often brutal — victories (such as Massu's *nettoyage de la Casbah* in early 1957), and counterforce elicited respect. The much-stigmatized success of the French Army in organizing the referendum of 1958 and marshaling 60 per cent of the

---

[20] Eugène Guernier, *La Berbérie, l'Islam, la France,* Vol. II (Paris, 1950), p. 173 and *passim.*

[21] Another interesting sect, more difficult to assimilate for the FLN, was the Mzabite people, a Berber group that had originated in the North Sahara and for generations had monopolized the grocery trade in the coastal cities. In June 1955, in attempting to enforce a commercial boycott, the FLN practiced a systematic terror against this community. Mzabites were prominent in the "fraternization" of May 16, 1958.

population to the polls, despite FLN orders for a boycott, merely demonstrated that the principle of force could work both ways. From September 1959 on, with the promise of self-determination announced by the President of France, the fence-sitters grew gradually anti-French, either through reanimated conviction in the Revolution or through fear of reprisal from their nationalist rulers-to-be.

Many of the traditional *caïds* (as long as they remained alive) supported the French, and about 150,000 Muslims served with the French forces as *harkis* or other auxiliary troops. Within Muslim families there were innumerable instances of divided convictions or, what was probably worse, convictions swayed by opposing menaces. To a high degree, the Islamic family structure was strained to the breaking point both by the problem of allegiance and by enforced separation and dislocation. An interrogation conducted by Jean-Yves Alquier, when he was a lieutenant of the Sections Administratives Spécialisées (SAS), may well be typical of thousands of others:

"Lieutenant, my cousin Boutaleb is in the convoy, you know, the one that was caught the other day at Tichkaia. He hid in the bottom of a truck. You've got to take him with you. He hasn't done anything." I looked at the so-called cousin's information slip. "Charge: collector of funds. Value of the information: certain. Source: informer." "You don't think he's done anything! He put the bite on people." "Yes, that's right — like everybody else, earlier. But I swear to you that he refused two months ago and hasn't lifted a finger since. He runs away because he's afraid, that's all. Sarine [the rebel chief] even tore up all his papers as a sanction, gave him a hiding, and told him he'd get his throat cut if he didn't collect the money next month. He still refused, so he runs away when the *fellagha* arrive at the *mechta* [hamlet]."

"But you left the *mechta* a long while back. How do you know all this? Sure, he's your cousin; but if he's a *fellagha,* too bad for him. All he had to do was come and request pardon if he's on the outs with Sarine."

"I swear it's true. . . . Leave him to me. I'll keep him here, and if he runs away you can do what you want with me." [22]

In a struggle whose premises were for a long time ambiguous to the people and whose outcome was in doubt, the natural reactions were bound to be hesitancy, watchfulness, opportunism. Circumstances lent themselves easily to the idea of a *guerre révolutionnaire* in which the sympathies of the population were at stake.

Somewhat paradoxically, the so-called "moderate" solution of the *troisième force* was prevented from coming into being by the same factors. The polarities of France and independent Algeria were explicit enough and had attracted their cohorts irrevocably by 1956, long

---

[22] Alquier, *op. cit.,* pp. 62–63.

before the French had become susceptible to compromise solutions. Neutralism or opportunism in Algeria meant reluctance to take sides, not eagerness for some third solution that might eventually win acceptance from both parties. There was no literal power in the center of the argument that could supply mediation and reason. De Gaulle toyed briefly with the idea of creating a "third force" through the unquestioned caliber of his reputation among the Muslims, after he had come to power in 1958.[23] But the polarities were much too strong, and the Algerian parliamentary elections of the fall of that year must have convinced the General that all moderation was destined to fail. The "law of the excluded middle" had operated with a vengeance.

The Revolution: Historical Background

What was the revolution, its historical origins, its ideology, aims, and methods?

The past history of Algerian nationalism is a long and complicated narrative that has been well described elsewhere.[24] If we pick up the story in 1954, it is fair to say that the outbreak of the revolutionary war caught the nationalist movement at sixes and sevens. Its avowed messianic leader, Messali Hajd, through whose perseverance and dogmatism the spark of independence had been kept alive since the mid-1920's, was losing his grip. As the result of a revolutionary sortie of speechmaking he had conducted in Algeria, he was consigned to forced residence in the *métropole* by the French authorities on May 14, 1952. This had effectively cut him off from the internal leadership of the movement.

Messali had been the most inflammatory of the nationalist chiefs, and the central figure in the brief but bloody insurrection of 1945, whose motives had been primarily local and economic. He attempted to impose an iron discipline on his followers, much akin to the "cult of personality" that the FLN was later to denounce. His major dictum was: "If I were a teacher and the Algerian people my pupil, I would have him conjugate the verb 'to organize' every day." Messali had flirted narrowly with communism in the 1930's, but his formation of the MTLD in 1937 reflected a rupture with doctrinaire Marxism for the more promising spaciousness of an unmitigated nationalism. Scarcely

[23] A positive indication of this thesis, which is questioned by Jacques Soustelle, in *L'espérance trahie* (Paris, 1962), Claude Paillat, in *Le dossier secret de l'Algérie* (Paris, 1961), and others, may be found in General de Gaulle's interview with Pierre Laffont, publisher of the *Echo d'Oran*, on May 1, 1959.

[24] The best recapitulation in English will be found in Clark, *op. cit.*, to whom the author is indebted.

had he been restricted to his sanctuary in the department of Deux-Sèvres when an outburst of popular indignation in Algeria threatened to turn his sequestration into a *casus belli*. Even the circumspect Ferhat Abbas, leader of the Union Démocratique du Manifeste Algérien (UDMA), who was recommending patience and nonviolence in the pursuit of increased political liberty, expressed indignation at the French action. Nevertheless, within two years Messali Hajd, divorced from the internal leadership, was to lose effective control of the movement.

His primary antagonist for power was a Kabylian named Hocine Lahouel, at the time assistant mayor of Algiers under Jacques Chevallier. Despite urgent warnings from the Messalist camp that Lahouel was a cat's-paw betraying the party into the hands of the French, scission developed in early 1954. Messali, seething with impotent rage at Niort, saw the Central Committee of the MTLD leave the exercise of authority on native ground ambiguous, though it granted him power and funds to operate in France. He issued a violent denunciation of the "party bureaucracy" on April 3, and threatened reprisal. Meanwhile, the mysterious Comité Révolutionnaire d'Unité et d'Action (born out of the expatriate Organisation Spéciale, formed in 1948), which now represented an activist fusion from among both Messalist and Lahouelist elements but was basically contemptuous of both, made its appearance by calling on the feuding parties to mend their differences. Among the original members of the CRUA was Ahmed Ben Bella, later to assume leadership of the FLN. The CRUA contemplated withdrawal from the MTLD and seizure of its smaller clandestine remnant, the Parti Populaire Algérien (PPA). Most of these leaders had spent time in Cairo and were acquainted with the new revolutionary chiefs that the antimonarchical *coup d'état* had swept to power in Egypt.

In the meantime the Lahouelist group of the MTLD was not idle. In early September it issued a manifesto calling for immediate demands upon the French and betraying traces of Kabylian particularism. But it had already fallen behind in events. The CRUA, pressed by its Cairo friends to embark on revolutionary action, tried unsuccessfully to mediate between the factions of the MTLD in Switzerland. Failing this, and with the financial support of the Arab League's "Maghreb fund" and other contributions, it prepared for action. The internal military commands (*willayas*) were parceled out at a meeting in Algiers on July 10, 1954. The war began on November 1, and would be halted only by the concession of Algerian independence in the agreements reached at Evian, on March 19, 1962.

Many intrigues and changes affected the balance of the rebel leadership during the course of the war. The atmosphere of Cairo, where the FLN directorate under Ben Bella stationed itself, was rife with the pretensions of conflicting personalities. Fortune, prestige, and ideology were all at stake in the dynamics of revolutionary leadership.

More serious challenges to the central authority of the rebellion were posed by the military chiefs in Algeria and their supply auxiliaries, who operated mostly on Libyan and, later, Moroccan and Tunisian soil. Geographical autonomy, racial particularism, personal clashes, and other factors made control of the rebellion from abroad difficult. Policy trips were wearisome and dangerous for the central leaders, and considerable scope for action had to be left to the local commanders, whose own relations were sometimes unharmonious. Moreover, as the French *riposte* stiffened, attrition among the military leaders was high; replacements had to be furnished on the spot without elaborate attention to political nuance. A certain degree of contention between the military organization (ALN), whose sphere of action was Algeria, and the political directorate (FLN), centered in Cairo, was unavoidable. The availability of Tunisia and Morocco as neighboring bases and the removal of the FLN to Tunis in 1957 eased this situation somewhat, even though the French interposed troops and miles of floodlighted, electrified wire (the famous "Morice Line") to cut off contact.

Sometimes the internal disputes in the FLN were used by the nationalists themselves as an excuse for the inconsistencies of their own policy. In an exhibition of either frankness or tortuous duplicity, Ferhat Abbas stated to an Austrian newspaper in 1957: "Perhaps the emigrees would willingly have negotiated with Gul Mollet [whose government had made quiet overtures in Belgrade in 1956], but it is itself divided and, above all, it is by no means sure of its power over the activists. It has very few illusions about its influence." [25]

Finally, there was the matter of the politicians who remained behind in Algiers, some of them co-operating with the French until the cloture of the territorial parliament in 1955, others living in mute but watchful retirement. Much of this "swing group" had joined the revolution in Tunis by 1957 and adhered to the formation of the Algerian Provisional Government (GPRA) a year later. They unquestionably brought a moderating influence to bear on the collective leadership that, for a time, fitted well with Tunisian President Habib Bourguiba's sponsorship of the provisional government.

Of course, the most noted case of a politician that joined the rebellion late was Ferhat Abbas himself, the leader of the provisional govern-

[25] *Die Presse* (Vienna), June 1957.

ment until midsummer 1961. Abbas, whose moderation as late as 1955 had cost him the life of his nephew at the hands of FLN terrorists, could still state in August of that year: "However great the misfortunes that assail it, the UDMA will not allow itself to be distracted from the objectives and from the ideal for which it means always to conduct the same fight." [26] But by the following year he was denying that his political party continued to serve any function. In an interview with the Tunisian publication *Action,* he declared: "I am in no way qualified to negotiate with France. The men who lead the action are alone entitled to do so. My party and I myself have thrown our entire support to the cause defended by the National Liberation Front. My office, today, is to stand aside for the chiefs of the armed resistance." [27]

In April 1957, Abbas was in Cairo; by September 5, he was able to announce the formation of a new executive committee of the FLN with himself at the head. Included in his honor roll of thirty-four members were the five chiefs *in absentia,* most notable among them Ben Bella, who had been conveniently plucked from the sky by the French on October 22, 1956, while en route from Rabat to Tunis, and sent to cool their tempers in prison.[28] It was into this gaping vacuum created by the unexpected capture of the primary leadership that Abbas moved, though not without some modification of the command structure.

On April 17, 1957, the "external organization" of the FLN transferred its headquarters from Cairo to Tunis. This was a response to tactical requirements and also an indication that Nasserism was no longer such a direct influence on the evolution of the Algerian rebellion. A more moderate, Bourguibalike approach seemed to be germinating in the FLN in 1957, as the independent Maghreb began to assert itself as a center of power, with more lines thrown open for a negotiated settlement with the French. Though this mood was rudely shaken by the Tunisian border incident of early 1958 and by the coup of May 13, it was reasserted with the arrival of General de Gaulle in power. The General was thought by the rebels to be more "realistic" and better able to impose his judgments on the recalcitrant French Army. The latter, as we shall see, would prove a long and anguished process.

From 1958 on, the FLN reforged its committee into a provisional government, waged strenuous and highly remunerative diplomatic warfare abroad, and prepared cautiously — after 1959 — to come into its

---

[26] Quoted from Clark, *op. cit.,* p. 183.
[27] *Ibid.*
[28] The incident is well described in J.-R. Tournoux, *Secrets d'Etat* (Paris, 1960), pp. 127–136.

kingdom. It played cleverly on the themes of Maghrebian solidarity, pan-Arabism, Nasserite egotism, Soviet calculation, Chinese opportunism, American strategic misapprehension, anticolonialism, Western capitalist profiteering, and a number of other devices. Not least, it sought the moral support of the neutralist "third force," in whose ranks it particularly admired the militancy and much of the doctrine of Marshal Tito's Yugoslavia.

When Benyoussef Ben Khedda succeeded to the presidency of the GPRA in August 1961 in replacement of Abbas, observers surmised that the Left Wing had gained control of the organization in preparation for a "tough" policy. Abbas was known as a reasonable bourgeois, a shrewd and garrulous Mediterranean politician whose tastes "ran French." On the other hand, his successor owed nothing to France, had a full career as a militant revolutionary and well-known Marxist, and had been one of the first to make the pilgrimage to Peking, earning him the sobriquet of "le chinois" (curiously enough, also General Salan's nickname). However, it was Ben Khedda's government that led the negotiations to their successful conclusion at Evian.

The Revolution: Ideological Background

The foregoing historical sketch of the FLN leads unremittingly to the question: what was the ideological center of the revolution and who, besides the Algerians, were likely to benefit from it? The French Army fought this war seven years, more or less convinced that Algerian nationalism was directly or obscurely linked to the worldwide Communist movement of expansion; this, as we have seen, was one of the primal tenets of the doctrine of *la guerre révolutionnaire*. It is therefore relevant to consider communism in the first priority.

As indicated, Messali Hajd had flirted intermittently with the Comintern in the 1930's, but never in a highly orthodox way. The Communist Party in Algeria was an adjunct of the Parti Communiste Français and not directly involved with Algerian nationalism. However, it did make certain obeisances to the incipient revolutionary movement. The Communists had campaigned shoulder to shoulder with the Messalists on combined election lists and lent organizers and agitators to Messali Hajd for his triumphal tour of 1952. At the outbreak of armed conflict the Communists willingly opposed French authority. Their involvement is suggested by a mysterious trip to the Aurès region made in October 1954 by Benoît Frachon, chief of the Communist labor union, the Confédération Générale du Travail (CGT). At first, the Communists misjudged the real center of gravity and cast their lot with the Lahouelists; Ben Bella and his companions seemed to be in Nasser's pocket.

The Communists had several trumps to play at the beginning of the rebellion that were extremely attractive to the nationalists. In addition to their extensive international network and command of vital funds, they possessed a daily newspaper, the *Alger républicain,* which would serve as a major outlet of FLN expression until shut down by the authorities in 1955. Joint action was also undertaken by Communist and nationalist terrorist cells; at the height of the terror it was not uncommon for the Sûreté to uncover FLN bombs with timing mechanisms coming from Communist sources of manufacture.

However, the PCA made its inevitable attempts to dogmatize and direct the revolution; the FLN grew wary and resisted this pressure. The Algerian Communist Party, never more than 12,000 strong, was soon engulfed in the generalized nationalist feeling. At first, like Messali's Mouvement Nationaliste Algérien, it attempted to retain its particularity by establishing a unique guerrilla zone; but by June 1, 1956, in the more promising interests of infiltration, this idea was abandoned, and the Communist "Freedom Fighters" (*sic*) were directed to integrate with the Army of National Liberation.

The PCA was predestined to vanish among the cohorts of the FLN — what was left of it. A majority of its 80 per cent European clientele refused to support the terrorists; as polarization of the war increased, they perceived that their interests lay more closely with the "forces of order." Communist railway workers, for instance, did not particularly enjoy seeing their comrades blown to pieces by FLN bombs. Thus, as Eugène Mannoni later reported: "Prominent among those who booed M. Mollet when he came to Algeria on February 6, 1956 [provisionally with General Catroux and a "liberal" policy] were organized workers just as convulsed as the rightist veterans. . . . The ethnic reflex took precedence over the former class solidarity." [29]

By 1956 the Communists had succeeded in going underground in the Algerian liberation movement. When apprehended, they could still be identified because of their past associations. As fighters and terrorists they were welcomed by the FLN; as agitators they were muted, because the Algerians promoted their own, not dissimilar, forms of agitation and propaganda. Several cases of terrorism are fully documented where known Communists were in the forefront of the action. Still, it is clear that the Communists never came close to capturing either the leadership or the ideological direction of the movement.

A report made by the Socialist International in July 1957 had the fol-

[29] *Le Monde,* March 23, 1957.

lowing to say: "There is no doubt that the Russians are present in the corridors of the rebellion, but they do not direct it. If the FLN were to win, then the Communist elements would show their face. Their presence would be influential since the present rulers of the FLN have no political experience." [30] Times and the caliber of experience have changed since 1957. However, let Robert Lacoste, who directed the French efforts for two years, reply: ". . . contrary to what might have gone on in other places and even if, in the background, disquieting Communist propaganda and the Islamic passion for conquest are mutually insinuated, our adversaries of today, the terrorists, the rebels, have no other ideology than that of evicting France from Algeria." [31]

This was not precisely true, as will be shown; but the allegation of orthodox communism by inspiration or by proxy does not square with the evidence.

Pan-Arabism is an influence that is outside the scope of this study to measure. Clearly, it was present, especially in the early phases of the rebellion, when the FLN was weak and Nasser's Egypt seemed all-powerful by comparison. As Maghrebian solidarity grew and took shape, Arab universalism tended to wane in direct proportion, becoming more a cultural than a political impetus. The current of pan-Arabism had at least two prevailing ideologies: one, modern and secularizing, easily susceptible to Marxist accommodation; the other, traditionalist and anti-materialist, which could still rally to the call of jihad (holy war). The former ideal was manifestly predominant in the formula of the Algerian revolution, although certain symbolic obeisances (such as ritual terrorism) were made in the direction of the latter in order to impress rural populations.

Nasser's new Egyptian state played a major role in instigating the Algerian revolt. It assiduously cultivated Ben Bella and his clique until shortly before their untimely kidnaping. It poured funds, arms (sometimes transshipped from Yugoslavia), and trained technicians and saboteurs into the caldron of revolution.[32] It sponsored "Maghreb bureaus" in the Arab League at a time when none of these countries was independent. Finally, it smoothed the path for the practice of East-West blackmail throughout all Islam by its pioneer example of 1956.

[30] Quoted from Jacques Hogard, "Stratégie et tactique du Communisme," *Revue des Forces terrestres,* October 1959, p. 51.

[31] Quoted in *Revue militaire d'Information,* June 25, 1956, p. 15.

[32] There is the well-known example of the ship *Athos II* (intercepted and searched by the French on October 29, 1956). See also, Tournoux, *op. cit.,* p. 468, for the interrogation of the captured leaders of the FLN (Ben Bella, etc.) by French Intelligence: "Ben Bella, Khider, and their assistants . . . agree that Egypt has furnished them with very important material and moral assistance. . . ."

Still, after the rebellion was on sure footing, the Algerian nationalist leaders began to keep their brotherly distances from Egypt and to cultivate their Maghrebian neighbors instead.

Was the Algerian revolution ever inspired by any ideology other than "nationalism," a term that explains little? The Club Jean Moulin, in a recent study, has answered: "it is much more of Jacobin than of Marxist inspiration." [33] Many of the available FLN documents bear out this point. But it is probably more correct to assign a trinity of inspiration: Marxist, Jacobin, and opportunist.

The Algerian revolution has been Marxist because its premises of revolutionary war derived chiefly from this context, as many French officers were correct in perceiving. Moreover, Marxism-Leninism was the dynamic in which global changes seemed most precipitous and favorable, and the Algerian leaders were aware of this. They identified Marxism as the doctrine that most clearly defined the vicious and immutable nature of that imperialism against which they were struggling. As one of their declarations argues:

The historical importance of armed struggle resides not only in the possibility for the people to undertake military combat against the colonial forces . . . [but also] in the ability to aggravate the contradictions of colonial society and hasten its progressive collapse.[34]

The "Jacobinism" of the Algerian revolutionaries was principally evident in their penchant for a strong, centralized "social-democratic" state and in their political ethos as a whole. "What is needed," says an FLN document, "is the revolution, a great revolution like that of 1789." [35] Further, they have been preoccupied, at least abstractly, by the metaphysic of liberty and its implications:

It is not true that liberty for the Algerians limits and, in its turn, denies liberty for the French [settlers]; for liberty is indivisible, it is not a factor of opposition, a force of destruction. Real liberty draws liberty in its wake. Liberty for others does not limit my liberty; on the contrary, it is the condition for it.[36]

Again, we read numerous passages in the FLN's scattered professions of doctrine concerning "power to the people," "equality," "destruction of the survivals of medievalism and feudalism," belief in a secular state, and the eradication of privilege. The revolution is inevitably

[33] "L'avenir de l'Algérie," *Le Monde*, November 26–27, 1961.
[34] *El Moudjahid* (official newspaper of the FLN), November 1, 1959. Text reproduced by André Mandouze (ed.), *La révolution algérienne par les textes* (2nd edition; Paris, 1961), p. 33.
[35] *Résistance Algérienne*, May 20–31, 1957. Quoted in Mandouze, *op. cit.*, p. 43.
[36] *Résistance Algérienne*, February 1–10, 1957. Quoted in Mandouze, *op. cit.*, p. 50.

qualified as "democratic." And there has been a strain of Jacobin nationalism as well: strictures against both capitalism and communism are found, if not in the same bitter intensity.

Finally, the Algerian revolution was in large measure opportunist and pragmatic, for obvious reasons. Harsh doctrine and marginal struggle — despite Ho's success — are not always the most comfortable bedfellows, even if Eastern-bloc blandishments tempted the nationalists to accept their congruity. Somehow, for seven years the Algerian revolution — severely contained on the battlefield — managed to stay in business by the skillful playing of disharmonious diplomatic chords and the extraordinary accomplishment of building a subterranean nation. But the sum of these efforts did not make a squad of Communist robots out of the primary leadership. Rather, their interests would lie in "discovering" and cementing the foundations of a nation they thought they had created but were not entirely sure of. After that, the entire Maghreb might be a source of maneuver and profit.

A "Revolutionary War"

Interpreters of *la guerre révolutionnaire* insisted that the Algerian revolution played into the hands of international communism. They held, moreover, that the rebellion was plotted, channeled, controlled to a very high degree. Much of the professional French Army came to take these hypotheses for granted. Actually, this war was much more confused and spontaneous than the war in Indochina. Nevertheless, many of its aspects fitted the categories of the theoreticians. This was not surprising, for it was during the early stages of the Algerian conflict that the doctrine of *la guerre révolutionnaire* was being elaborated and distinguished from mere guerrilla action and even from the more general *guerre subversive*. These analyses owed a great deal to the empirical observation of events in Algeria. Algeria was, so to speak, the model into which Indochina, and even Greece, Iran, and the Philippines, were made to fit with a shoehorn. Still, the correspondences deserve to be noted.

In the first place, the Algerian conflict was, to a great degree, a war for the control of civilian allegiance and support. Classical warfare, however successful, did not seem to be the key to the puzzle.

Secondly, it was a struggle of propaganda and psychological persuasion, with both sides resorting to a wide range of manipulatory techniques that went far beyond the character of traditional war.

Thirdly, it was a war fought with a quite total allocation of resources within a confined area.

Fourthly, it resembled closely, although not precisely, the models of Commandant Hogard, Colonel Lacheroy, and others. There were distinct phases of agitation and propaganda, indiscriminate terror, directed assassination, irregular and semiregular warfare. Also, we can note the operation of the establishment of bases or "kernels," infiltration, demoralization, psychological action, "parallel hierarchies," and other revolutionary phenomena. Eventually the rebellion established a provisional government on alien soil.

Fifthly, despite legitimate dispute over its importance, the ideological factor was thrust forward. Political officers occupied positions of prestige in the rebellion; more surreptitiously, they were created in the French Army.

Finally, the struggle was always implicitly internationalized, whatever the immediate goals of the combatants, thereby thrusting it against the global background of the Cold War.

But the tragedy of Algeria was deeper and more complex than any dualistic theory of war or politics. It was the tragedy of two distinct peoples, united by their love for a single soil, sundered by a fatal suspicion of each other. Into this dilemma was interposed a bitter and ill-used Army, with consequences that would shake the foundations of France itself.

X

THE WAR THAT COULD
NOT BE LOST: OPERATIONS

> When men are subdued by force, they do not submit in their
> minds, but only because their strength is inadequate. When
> men are subdued by power in personality, they are pleased to
> their very heart's core and do really submit.
>
> — *Mencius*

"I see no prospect of a government strong enough to get out of Algeria, even if such a step were indicated by the trend of events there," Marshal Bugeaud told the French Chamber of Deputies a century and a quarter ago. "Since withdrawal is impossible," he concluded, "the only remaining alternative is total domination."[1] Dispatched by the July Monarchy to Algeria with an army of 40,000, Bugeaud proceeded to do precisely this — dominate.

The words have a somewhat ghostly and prophetic ring in modern times. The Fourth Republic was, indeed, too weak to disengage from Algeria, "even if such a step were indicated." As much was proved by Guy Mollet's experience in Algiers on February 6, 1956, when, though armed with a fresh electoral mandate from the French people, he reined in his liberalism before the vegetables and hoots of the citizens,

[1] General Paul Azan (ed.), *Par l'Epée et par la Charrue: Ecrits et Discours de Bugeaud* (Paris, 1948), pp. 64–65. Quoted by Melvin Richter, "Tocqueville on Algeria," *The Review of Politics*, July 1963, p. 369.

withdrew the nomination of General Georges Catroux as Resident Minister, and steeled himself to the "hard line" pursuit of the war. Eventually the Fifth Republic of Charles de Gaulle would prove "strong enough" after three years of interrupted initiatives and at the expense of broken ideals, hearts, and careers.

Let us return to Bugeaud's conclusion: "the only remaining alternative is total domination." The echo of these words did not direct the French Army's efforts in Algeria in the years 1954–1962, but gave it a bad conscience. It had to conquer and justify, but it could not dominate just in the name of the flag and the French Union. If Indochina had proved too distant for France to maintain, Algeria was too close to maintain in a form that suited the logic of the situation, and certainly too close to surrender. Since it could not be surrendered or drastically modified according to law, since it was *France* and not a colony, no politician of either Right or Left perceived at the outset that radically new arrangements might be needed.[2] As soon as this error had taken its toll, Algeria was probably, in potential, lost to France by the route of a war that would be desperately hard to stop. By the time Paris was ready with its timid *lois-cadre,* its modifications and reforms, they had lost their usefulness. For by now the battle lines were squarely drawn: the Europeans of Algeria were approaching a hysterical militancy, the FLN had spread its network everywhere, the middle ground of compromise had collapsed, metropolitan France was more aggressively nationalistic, and the Army had been given its mission and had formed its mystique.

The novel nature of "revolutionary war" itself meant that the Army was committed to pursuing the goal of controlling the population. Consequently, it became involved, by order and by choice, in a host of activities that fall normally within the civil administrative domain. This extended the Army's potential for political pressure, teaching military men new skills and making them aware of new potentialities at a time when the normal administration was abandoning its prerogatives by weakness and default. By contrast, when the military leaders tried to approach problems in the official style of the government, they were often put off by vacillations. They grasped desperately for a role in the decision-making process.

[2] Muslim Algerians were permitted to opt either for full French citizenship (status of *droit commun*) or to retain the antecedent protection of Koranic customary law. Algeria had, since World War II, been endowed with a special parliament chosen with double electoral lists. In electing the first of two equivalent "colleges," the Europeans and about 50,000 "assimilated" Muslims participated; the remaining population chose the "second college."

The Spread of the Rebellion

Even though the rebel uprising of November 1, 1954, was a somewhat dislocated plot that did not enjoy the advantage of meticulous organization, the FLN still swiftly developed the talent for establishing a close network of insurrection and for spreading it to most parts of the territory. In Mao's phrase, slightly altered, this was the "Algerian fish in Algerian water," and it soon developed the skill of swimming with dexterity. From the inaugural outbreak of violence in the Aurès-Nementchas, the rebellion spread inexorably to the Nord-Constantinois, to Kabylie, to western Oranie, to the Ouarsenis, and finally to Greater Algiers. By early 1956, the battle was squarely locked in all quarters, and certain tracts of rebel territory — especially the mountainous ones — could not be reduced by available French military power. More importantly, the Armée de Libération Nationale (the military arm of the rebellion) had succeeded in imposing its sway over large segments of the Muslim population by inducing fear and respect and by demonstrating the impotence of the French in their efforts to protect the weak or retaliate against the strong.

Merchants and shopkeepers — even in the large urban centers — paid protection money to the silent FLN collector who visited them periodically; servants spied on their French military masters and reported to the rebels; adolescent striplings cast their surveillance over French troop displacements; Muslim functionaries practiced infiltration in the communes and other areas of administrative activity; ardent "detribalized" young women distributed propaganda leaflets or planted plastic bombs in cars or cafés; whole communities obeyed orders to strike or observe boycotts on certain commodities, such as tobacco. By the end of 1956 the rebel authority ruled more effectively than the French in many localities, albeit more surreptitiously. By this date the implantation of "parallel hierarchies" had proceeded to such a degree that a subterranean Algerian nation with widespread if inexpert administrative services had precipitously come to birth.

The ethnologist Germaine Tillion, an acute and experienced observer of the Algerian scene, has written in corroboration of the growth of Algeria's secret government:

In a second phase — beginning in December 1955 — the masses allowed themselves to be organized by the nationalist networks, and from February 1956 on, the movement spread with incredible speed. At the end of that same year [December 1956] the work was finished. . . .

The responsible French politicians then committed the fault — perhaps an irreparable one — of failing to understand the irreversible character of a movement that was fulfilled in the silent depths of a people that no longer had any newspapers or political representation.[3]

By 1956 it had become the urgent and primary task of the French Army, now swelling from its original 50,000 to over 450,000 effectives, to combat the FLN for control of the population, the milieu of the conflict. In some cases, this meant the encouragement of intimidated but willing loyalists; in others, the reconversion of temporarily alienated persons; in still others, the persuasion of the recalcitrant through demonstration and force. The *guerre révolutionnaire* beginning to be described by the experts had reached its apogee. From unpredicted small assault, sabotage, and indiscriminate terrorism, it had proceeded through the stages of cautionary assassination, zones of control (even the Communists and Messali Hajd's MNA aspired to set up their own *maquis*), administrative infiltration, and "parallel hierarchies." Robert Lacoste, the Resident Minister, recognized the character of the situation in a directive of August 21, 1956. He wrote: "We wage a very special combat. It is modern revolutionary war, above all psychological, with the adherence of the population at stake."[4]

Military Hierarchy of the Rebellion

At the outset of the rebellion the territory of Algeria was divided into seven military zones (*willayas*), approximating but not precisely paralleling the ethnic, geographic, or economic regions of the country: Oranie, Algérois, Aumale-Sud, Kabylie, Nord-Constantinois, and Aurès-Nementchas, plus an additional coastal zone close to the Tunisian border. The latter zone, after the independence of Tunisia and the resettlement of the FLN directorate in Tunis in 1957, was expanded under the title of "Base de l'Est" (see the map of Algeria, p. 170).[5]

[3] Germaine Tillion, *Les ennemis complémentaires* (Paris, 1960), pp. 17–18.

[4] The complete texts of Robert Lacoste's directives to the armed forces can be found as an appendix to Michel Déon's *L'Armée d'Algérie* (Paris, 1959).

[5] In 1957, when the ALN may well have reached its greatest strength of military effectives in Algeria, the Tunisian newspaper *Petit Matin* (organ of the Néo-Destour) gave the troop total as 42,000. Recomposed by Serge Bromberger, *Les rebelles algériens* (Paris, 1958), p. 249, into a breakdown by *willayas,* the picture was as follows:

Tunisia and the Base de l'Est	8000
Willaya 1 — Aurès-Nementchas	5000
Willaya 2 — Nord-Constantinois	5000
Willaya 3 — Kabylie	8000
Willaya 4 — Algérois	7500
Willaya 5 — Oranie	8500
	42,000 total

Willaya 6 (Aumale-Sud) had by this time been suppressed and divided between the Algérois and Kabylian commands. It reappeared as an entity later in the war.

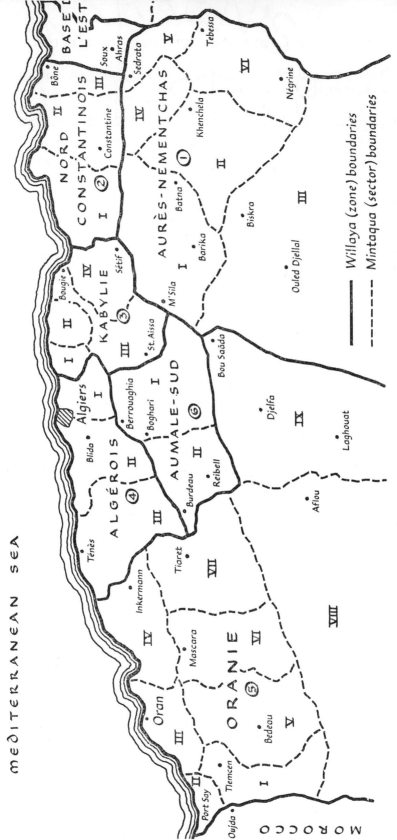

Figure 2. Organization of the Rebel Command in Algeria. (From Serge Bromberger, *Les rebelles algériens, op. cit.,* pp. 16–17.)

In practice, because of the difficulties of communication with the outside, many tactical decisions had to be made by the "internal" military commanders on the spot, often through the initiative of the individual *willaya* commands. These arrangements, moreover, often bordered on the chaotic, because of contending factional rivalries and because of the success of the French Army, after 1957, in disrupting the internal military networks. Correct relations did not always exist between the military and political arms of the rebellion, which, perforce, viewed the conflict from very different angles. Three facts, nevertheless, combined to reinforce the authority of the political directorate: (1) the Algerian War was being won by political and diplomatic initiatives from the exterior, and not by strict military pressure; (2) disputes among the internal commanders weakened their position in the power equation; (3) the attrition rate of Algerian military leaders was extremely high.

On paper, each *willaya* of Algeria was commanded by a colonel (the highest regular rank in the ALN); the *willaya,* in turn, was broken down into *mintaquas* (zones), *nahias* (regions), and *kasmas* (sectors), somewhat in the same manner as the French Army's territorial *quadrillage*. The *willaya* (territorial unit) was construed as comparable to a regiment (unit of a fighting force). Below regiment level, the following organic units were postulated, although continual harassment by the forces of the pacification ensured that they would usually be well below strength:

1. Battalion (4 companies, 600 men each, 25 officers), commanded by a captain or major.

2. Company (2 sections, 150 men each, 5 officers), commanded by a lieutenant.

3. Section (3 groups, 25 men each), led by a master sergeant.

4. Group (11 men), led by a sergeant.

5. Fire team (half-group of 5 men), led by a corporal.[6]

At each level under command of an officer a political commissar directly responsible to the FLN was attached. This "political-military representative" had a staff of officers or NCO deputies responsible for military operations, political propaganda, intelligence, and liaison — a situation reminiscent of the Viet Minh and, indeed, of any Marxist combat organization. In addition to being able to intervene in military

[6] Much of this information is gathered from an unpublished paper written by the *New York Times* correspondent Peter Braestrup while he was a Niemann Fellow at Harvard University in 1958–1959. Braestrup passed some time with the ALN and accompanied them on operations.

decisions, the political officers intensified the "politization" of the operations through their direct link with the external organization.

The entire military organization of the ALN was seconded by a subversive agency, the widespread OPA (Organisation Politique et Administrative), through whose activities entire "parallel hierarchies" of both vertical and lateral types came to be implanted throughout Algeria — in administration, labor, commerce, education, and other vital categories of enterprise. The OPA operatives levied funds and food supplies from the local populations and carried out reprisals when necessary.

By the spring of 1958 the Algerian forces sequestered on the soil of the neighboring Maghrebian countries had been efficiently cut off from direct intervention in the rebellion by the costly and complex system of barrages the French had erected behind the frontier to prevent line-crossing. A final battle fought on the barbed wire and barricades of the famous "Morice Line" [7] in May 1958, just before the *coup d'état,* authenticated the ability of the French Army to thwart the significant resupply of the ALN from the outside. The rebels were forced in the following year to revert to diversionary, ambush, and terrorist tactics, and had to bury quantities of their automatic weapons for lack of ammunition. The strength of the regular rebel army in Algeria probably never exceeded 35,000–50,000 men engaged in combat, a figure far short of the 200,000 that the FLN was optimistically predicting in 1956.[8] They were supplemented by probably 20,000 reserves encamped beyond the Moroccan and Tunisian frontiers, a force that represented a more powerful element than Bourguiba's own army.

The ebb and flow of the revolutionary war, because of its nature, can scarcely be summarized in any type of generalization. Militarily recuperable, certain areas would prove to be politically intractable. Loyalties wavered with the diverse applications of force and political initiatives that were undertaken locally and throughout the territory.[9] One constant, however, was the increasing polarization of the forces of the revolution and the forces of order alluded to earlier. European moderates like Jacques Chevallier, the mayor of Algiers, were neutralized by the contempt of their fellow "pieds noirs." And by 1957

[7] Barrages constructed by the French engineer corps along a large part of the Algero-Tunisian and Algero-Moroccan frontiers during the incumbency of André Morice in the Ministry of Defense proved to be effective means of depriving the rebels of outside supply. These were fixed fortifications of electrified wire and high walls interspersed with mine fields, the complex being several hundred yards in depth, continuously patrolled and lighted at night by searchlights and flares.

[8] See *La NEF,* October 1962–January 1963, p. 9.

[9] See, for example, Jules Roy, *The War in Algeria* (English translation; New York, 1961), p. 75, concerning blackmail paid to the FLN by the settlers.

most of the Muslim Fabians, such as Mohammed Bendjelloul (who, strangely enough, retained his title as Councilor of the French Union) and Ferhat Abbas, a former advocate of "Franco-Muslim integration," had gone over to the rebellion. A few others, like Abderrahmane Farès, who later became the President of the Provisional Executive, announced their nationalist feelings without actively joining the FLN.

French Organization and Countermeasures

The first French response to the menace of the Algerian uprising had been characteristically indecisive. After all, a bloody insurgency had taken place at Sétif in 1945 and had been squelched without great difficulty. The situation in the protectorates had not yet exploded. The astute Sultan of Morocco, Mohammed Ben Youssef (Mohammed V), had been exiled to Madagascar and replaced by a cat's-paw, and Bourguiba had just returned from a long incarceration in Southern Tunisia. There was no air of urgency about a situation that had not yet disclosed its true nature to the political class.[10] Nearly five months after the outbreak of hostilities the government tabled a bill before the National Assembly to meet the situation. It read in part:

> To avoid having recourse to [an] extreme solution, which the present situation in no way justifies, it seemed necessary to bring into existence judicial arrangements which, while leaving the exercise of traditional powers to the civil authorities, reinforces and concentrates these powers in such a way as to make them better adapted to events having the nature of a public calamity likely to endanger public order or to violate national sovereignty. These arrangements are called a "state of emergency." [11]

Submitted on March 22, 1955, the "emergency powers" bill ran immediately into a storm of protest on the part of those Communists and democrats who argued that the security measures implicit in it would endanger personal and civil liberties. After a hectic session on April 1, it passed the Assembly by a vote of 379 to 219. Governor-General Jacques Soustelle quickly undertook to implement the "pacification" as far as the law would allow by declaring "emergency zones," restricting travel, and taking steps against physical and administrative sabotage.

But the *riposte* gained momentum slowly and was essentially a

---

[10] If anything, the politicians were piously dedicated to pursuit of the war. Mendès-France had told the National Assembly on November 12, 1954: "You can't give an inch when it's a matter of defending the internal peace of the nation, and the unity and integrity of the Republic. The Algerian departments constitute a part of the French Republic. They have been French irrevocably for a very long time."

[11] *Le Monde*, March 20, 1955.

civilian responsibility until the rebellion had spread far and wide in Algeria. Only gradually were the regular forces augmented by reinforcements from the *métropole* and finally by the dispatch of conscripts; for the first two years of the war they were never numerically equal to the task of extended offensive operation. As with the judicial machinery, military operations in Algeria were governed principally by the desires of the National Assembly, since the resources at hand depended directly on the legislation concerning involuntary military service and the yearly budget appropriations.

In the rural *communes mixtes* the only symbol of French authority was, very often, the *garde champêtre* with his "ancient pistol" inscribed with the device *La Loi*. When, for example, the rebel apparatus came to the Aurès-Nementchas or to Kabylie, it often filled a need for administrative services that did not exist there. Far from sowing disorder in a centralized French network, the FLN often gathered together the loose ends of tribal anarchy left by colonial default and provided order and legal recourse to the inhabitants. There were few French settlers in the Aurès Mountains, where the insurrection first broke out, and the FLN was able to argue that it was restoring justice and giving protection against the gross malpractices and venality of the *caïds*.[12]

Not until the major tasks of administration in Algeria fell to the French Army in the regime of Lacoste did the colonial power have the semblance of a working system of government in some parts of the country. In the meantime the rebellion had moved into the tempting hiatus, from which it could be dislodged only by superior force.

Failure of means cannot alone justify the French administrative deficiency, whatever the government may have protested after the fact of its poverty of control had become evident. A press release of 1957 states the following:

> In administrative circumscriptions — that were much too large, and had an ever-increasing population, and that were difficult to penetrate and lacked the means of communication — the administrators of the civil services, too few for the crushing task that devolved on them, found themselves, in spite of their devotion and their activity, cut off from the Moslem population, to whom they acted as guides and supervisors.
>
> In 1955, because the administrative corps could not be enlarged overnight, certain army cadres were called on, which possessed all the necessary qualifications for performing this function successfully.[13]

This analysis is not scrupulously accurate. The point is that French civil administration had been not only sparse but lax. Prescient indi-

---

[12] See Bromberger, *op. cit.*, p. 32.
[13] "Building the New Algeria: Role of the Specialized Administrative Sections," Ambassade de France, Service de Presse et d'Information, September 1957, p. i.

viduals, such as Soustelle, recognized as early as 1955 that the administration of Algeria had become a fundamentally military problem. This led to the promulgation of a decree by the Governor-General on September 26, 1955, establishing a "Service of Algerian Affairs," incorporating officer cadres that came from the "Bureau of Native Affairs" in Morocco and the "Bureau of Saharan Affairs." This group was soon to be christened the Sections Administratives Spécialisées (SAS). Reserve officers with technical knowledge of the Algerian situation and ability in Arabic were activated to swell the new service. The over-all mission of the SAS was to re-establish contact with the population — contact that had been abruptly sundered by the activities of the FLN — or to forge a new kind of rapport that had never really existed between Frenchmen and Muslims. Precedent for the operations of the SAS existed in the conception of "Arab Bureaus" formally established by Marshal Bugeaud in Algeria on February 1, 1844; these bureaus had continued to function administratively among the natives until replaced by civilian control in 1922.

The Army in Algeria was contained in a normal peacetime organizational compartment known as the 10th Military District. This entity was further subdivided into three corps d'armée areas, those of Oran, Algiers, and Constantine, respectively, and included also commands for the Sahara and for the air and naval forces. The major areas were broken down into zones, sectors, and subsectors, nominally corresponding to the size of the unit stationed within their boundaries, and either criss-crossing or roughly paralleling the normal administrative atoms of department, arrondissement, prefecture, subprefecture, and commune mixte. The latter were reorganized several times during the course of the Algerian fighting, and, as we shall see, much of the civil administration devolved upon the armed forces, by the de facto conditions of the emergency in 1956 and by governmental decree in June 1958.

At the top of this territorial pyramid sat the military commander, who was, however, always subordinate to the civilian authority in Algiers. In all but two cases (General Challe in 1959 and General Fourquet in 1962), he was a general of the armée de terre. From June 1958 (tenure of General Salan) to the departure of General Crépin in March 1961, he wore the title of "Commander in Chief." Otherwise he was the "Superior Commander." In all cases his jurisdiction was over the combined forces of land, sea, and air (forces interarmées). He possessed his appropriate joint staffs.

At the apex of the strictly military hierarchy in Paris was the inter-force Chief of Staff. During most of the period critical to our concern this post was occupied by General Paul Ely, a man who, as Paul-Marie de la Gorce sensitively puts it, "personified all the stages and all the conflicts of French military society since World War II." [14] Ely was both the Army's conscience and its litmus paper. He shared the concerns of Communist encroachment and *guerre révolutionnaire* with his subordinates, but in a broader and more geopolitical context.[15] His function was to warn and mediate, to mollify and represent — to reconcile. But even Ely was not equal to this task; retained three times in service beyond the date of normal retirement, he would leave the Army for good with a heavy heart just as the "putsch of the generals" was being prepared in early 1961.

The French Army in Algeria: Divisions and Functions

At the height of the war, at least three fifths of France's active military forces, augmented by special troops of order like the *gendarmerie,* by a variety of civilian self-defense groups, and by the Muslim auxiliary *harkas,* were committed in Algeria. Their task was to fight wherever the *fellagha* could be brought to bay, but, above all, to administer, to control, and to convert.

The utter preponderance of French forces meant that from 1957 on the military pacification proceeded apace until the rebel *katibas* (companies) were reduced and isolated and the rebel resistance was cut back to terrorism and small skirmishes. Once the pattern of the territorial *quadrillage* for internal security had been achieved under General Salan, this development was secured by the systematic roll-back and *bouclage* campaigns led in 1959 and 1960 by Generals Challe and Crépin, in one area after another. But this superior force did not, for all its skill, crush the rebellion or demoralize it beyond repair, for as the latter was losing on the battlefield, its political credit was soaring in the chancelleries of the world aided by Western hesitations and by the skill of the external leadership.

The French Army in Algeria itself suffered a common malaise owing to this paradox, but was divided along a number of lines of internal tension and as a result of civilian political pressures. The regular territorial forces, spread out over the Algerian landscape with each unit responsible for the security and order of a particular area of the *quadrillage,* accounted for at least 300,000 officers and men, of whom about 80 per cent were conscripts. The reactions of these forces tended

[14] Paul-Marie de la Gorce, *The French Army* (New York, 1963), pp. 506–507.
[15] See especially General Paul Ely's own work, *L'armée dans la nation* (Paris, 1961), pp. 83–104, 163–176.

to follow the exigencies of the battle and the local situation, and they were reasonably removed from the hotbed of European activism in Algiers. Quite naturally, they felt intensely the drift concealed in ambiguous orders and lines of policy, but they were not generally prepared to make or lead a political protest against the state. They had other, less glamorous tasks at hand.

The Army of the field was subject to the inescapable atomism of command that drew in its wake a cautious political empiricism beneath the shroud of bitterness. Since Algeria was, in a very exact sense, a nexus of local wars dealing with regional guerrilla bands and highly varying degrees of rebel implantation and *pourrissement,* the responses of the French military chiefs charged with zonal and sectoral *quadrillage* had to be pragmatic and particular. For example, as the pacification was progressively achieved, wide areas of the Oranie were rendered almost impermeable to rebel terrorism, while much of the mountainous and densely populated region of the Kabylie still harbored irreducible pockets of ALN resistance that continued to threaten the villages. Consequently, the local responses tended to be very different. This in part contributed to the very lack of official doctrinal definition of countersubversive procedures that so many officers were to deplore and identify with government vacillation.

The intervention of civilians or outside sources (such as the Ministry of Education with its *centres sociaux,* the SAS, the psychological action officers in many cases, and later the functionaries of the "Constantine Plan") in the affairs of a region often gave the local military commanders a heavy bias against upper-echelon intrusion. The several revisions of the units of Algerian civil administration, which often cut across the boundaries of the military districts, extenuated the problem of effective authority. Finally, the decision to promote the Muslims to self-government, taken in connection with the Constantine Plan, often worked admirably in the pacified territories but became simply an additional weapon in the hands of the FLN's Organisation Politique et Administrative in *arrondissements* where rebel activity remained strong.

Opposed in mission to the territorial units, though perhaps only one tenth the size, were the troops of the Réserve Générale. This was a flexible collection of units, consisting principally of the paratroops, the infantry regiments of the Foreign Legion, and the marine commandos; it was based on Algiers and dispatched periodically to various parts of the territory for special missions or to reinforce the other troops in *bouclage* operations. The regular parachute regiments included a fairly high proportion of draftees, although the Legion was composed strictly of professional soldiers; this meant that perhaps 60 per cent of the Réserve Générale was composed of regulars, in quite direct contrast to the "other Army." Furthermore, it vaunted itself as the elite — which annoyed the other troops — and many stories, pro and con, were written in the public press about the "myth of the *paras*," with either General Massu or the "outrecuidant" (de Gaulle's expression) Colonel Marcel Bigeard as the *para* par excellence. The Left Wing stigmatized them as a Fascist praetorian guard; the Right Wing inflated them as model heroes of patriotic strength and steel-hard physical culture. Whatever they were, the *paras* and their officers were close to the political milieu of Algiers, susceptible to making common cause with civilian activism, and less reticent about endorsement of the psychological weapon. A higher proportion of these troops were themselves "pieds noirs," just as the Legionnaire comrades were, of course, chiefly foreigners under contract.[16]

For the *paras* and the Legion there was the precise mission, then the return to the heated climate of Algiers for restaging; for the troops of the *quadrillage* there was the daily drudgery of an intricate and elusive pacification and a million small tasks of administration. Although the fundamental analysis of the character of the war did not differ notably between the two groups — or, let us say, differed generally according to the individual officer's interpretation — the latter group was particularly exposed to the ingenious multiplicity of the war, to its arduous prolongation in space and time, and to the desirability of co-ordinated action and the difficulty of trying to achieve it. As one officer was to write:

> The integration of missions is the new and essential fact of the war. . . . Every "maneuver" in subversive war is immediately punished by the adversary and this leads to a deterioration of our position across the board. The single truth is that we have to attack the whole enemy apparatus at once. Everything else is literature. . . . [17]

If one paid full attention to the pursuit of the *fellagha,* the OPA would surreptitiously implant itself behind the backs of the Army; or if the soldiers of the *quadrillage* were to be given over too exclusively to tasks of countersubversion and civil order, the ALN would use the opportunity to increase its operations: this is the kind of dilemma to which

---

[16] The impending relinquishment of Algeria in 1962 gave rise to the speculation that the Foreign Legion, excluded by law from the *métropole,* might be entirely disbanded following withdrawal from its traditional base of Sidi-bel-Abbès in Oranie. In the summer of 1962 what remained of the Legion had been shifted to Corsica; there bad morale and a high desertion rate were recorded.

[17] Battalion Chief Etcheverry, "Réflexions sur la guerre subversive d'Algérie," *Revue des Forces terrestres,* July 1959, pp. 43–44.

Battalion Chief Etcheverry was referring. But the *para* was more accustomed to the quick strike and the brilliant action — less so to the drawn-out effort of pacification. Consequently, he, as well as some of the military chiefs in Algiers, possessed a greater optimism about eliminating the rebellion quickly than did the officer in Blida or Saïda or Tizi-Ouzou.

Just as the demands of *la guerre révolutionnaire* led the Army, at the behest of Robert Lacoste and later in a government directive of June 1958, to assume many of the responsibilities and prerogatives of civil administration in Algeria, so the same conditions thrust it into the position of fulfilling certain police functions. The nature of the counter-subversive battle in the urban zones made this development inevitable; elsewhere, the deficiency of local police functionaries produced the same result.

A fighting force is never particularly content with the police role; the French Army was no exception. In fact, the mixture of the functions of combat and civil order led to some very unhappy consequences. Normally, the latter mission had been entrusted to troops of the second category, the Défense Intérieure du Territoire (*gendarmerie*), which were, in Algeria, under the orders of the Minister of National Defense but placed at the disposal of other interested agencies — Justice, Interior, Finance. Bourgès-Maunoury acknowledged the importance of these groups of the DIT to the National Assembly in his statement of December 6, 1956:

In the sphere of counterguerrilla, the experience gained in North Africa — and I emphasize that of the *gendarmerie,* which is the basic element of any interior defense deployment — will permit us . . . to put effective structures into operation. . . .[18]

However, in the course of the Algerian events the DIT was frequently insufficient for its assigned tasks or else had to be augmented with regular (third-category) troops for psychological reasons. The reputedly brutal operations of the Dispositif Opérationnel de Protection (DOP) were performed by a composite of regular troops, gendarmes, and members of the civilian Sûreté. And on January 24, 1960, it was a mixed operational group of second- and third-category troops which, ordered to clear the streets of Algiers, led to the first significant civil bloodshed among Europeans in the agonized territory.[19]

[18] *Le Monde,* December 7, 1956.
[19] See Chapter XIII, pp. 270–272.

The SAS and SAU

In the bewildering array of pseudo-civil functions assumed by the Army in the course of the Algerian conflict, the opposite side of the coin is surely the work of the Sections Administratives Spécialisées, previously alluded to briefly. This group of officers, acting in the rural areas, and the Sections Administratives Urbaines (created for urban action on somewhat the same model in 1957) had the flexible mission of re-establishing contact with the Muslim population on a sounder basis of fraternity. Clearly, French links with the Muslims were severely jeopardized by the end of 1956; the FLN had almost succeeded in creating lasting racial hostility through techniques described earlier in this chapter.

Detachments (in total, about 1200 officers) of the SAS were fluid with regard to number and mission. In addition to co-opted native personnel (*moghazni*), the customary table of organization called for an officer (the chief), an NCO (the assistant), and three civilians on contract (a secretary-accountant, a secretary-interpreter, and a radio operator). On these five individuals fell the brunt of the task of "rallying" an area after the combat units had succeeded in pacifying it. The region might extend for several square kilometers and unfortunately was not always congruent with the regular military command.[20]

The SAS officer was hierarchically linked to the civilian command structure and to his particular military chain of authority, which was independent of the operational commander. The pattern may be illustrated as follows:

Civilian	*Military*
SAS Chief	SAS Chief
Subprefect	Subprefect's senior officer
Prefect (chief departmental officer)	Prefect's senior officer
Resident Minister of Algeria (formerly Governor-General)	Commander of the Officer Corps of the Service of Algerian Affairs
	Superior Military Commander (later, in 1958, Commander in Chief)

Ideally, the SAS operations were intended to dovetail with the progress of the military pacification. But, as we have seen, the Algerian

---

[20] The Army was frequently troubled by changes in the administrative circumscriptions in Algeria. Conversely, sometimes an SAS officer would have to deal with two military commanders who had very different ideas on how to pursue the *pacification*.

War was largely one of local recriminatory persuasion waged by small elements of concentrated force (through terror, political action, and ambush). Most of the ALN units were local and tended to move and operate within the sector, which was a subdivision of a *willaya*. As usual, the advantage of surprise and initiative rested with the attacking force, which meant that the bivouacked defenders were compelled to maintain a strength many times that of their opponents in order to deter assault or crush it when it came. Helicopter patrols were highly useful for daytime reconnaissance, but it became habitual for the rebel forces to sequester themselves in friendly villages during the day and move either at night or, if in daylight, to use the effective concealment of the canyons of dried-up watercourses.

Under such circumstances, in an immense territory between three and four times the size of France (though actually the Sahara area saw little activity), even the large defending Army was hard-pressed to cover the terrain effectively. Small detachments had to develop the talent of retaining organic effectiveness in spite of isolation. The task of the SAS was supplementary: to re-create a maximum of self-sufficiency in the villages.

In the early phases of the pacification (1956–1957) very special conditions greeted the SAS lieutenant, who was normally fresh from Algiers or the *métropole* or neighboring Morocco. Sometimes the heavy hand of the FLN ruled by night, terrorizing the people to prevent them from making any contacts with the French. In other instances, whole villages had fled and had to be enticed back to their domiciles by painstaking persuasion. To obtain any degree of success, meticulous local military operations demonstrating that the French could effectively control a given area by night or day, combined with a multitude of practical and humanitarian gestures toward the villagers by the SAS officer and his small staff, were needed.[21]

In the second phase, once the pacification of the region had been effectively achieved, the SAS had to supervise the reorganization of the normal life of the community, develop work projects for the people, and see to the distribution of food and medical aid. Construction of the regrouped villages in the intensive campaign of resettlement that the Army practiced from 1957 to 1961 was also a labor to which the SAS contributed.

The SAS depended entirely on the regular Army for its operational and logistical support, and frequently for manual labor in connection with its construction projects. As one officer of the service describes it,

[21] Notably reported in Jean-Yves Alquier, *Nous avons pacifié Tazalt* (Paris, 1958). Alquier covers only the phase of operations in which the *quadrillage* was being imposed.

"Nothing could have been done without the Army . . . without those young masons of the *contingent,* who, between two nerve-wracking patrols, would wield the spade and advise the workers, helping them to put up their own housing." [22]

But the autonomy of the SAS, the inadequacy of some of its officers, and the nonmilitary character of its mission were bound to create a certain amount of contempt in the regular Army and local attempts to assert command jurisdiction. As the writer just quoted acknowledges,

> The Army gives the indication that it would like to dominate the *Affaires Algériennes* [i.e., SAS] and for a year has wanted to make the service into a cadre of specialists who would relieve the local commands of paper work and be placed under their orders. So you hear it in all the mess halls, a contempt for these soldiers in bedroom slippers who complicate the job of the real troops and make France look ridiculous by its policy of "weakness." [23]

The SAU groups, formed in the wake of the French triumph in the "battle of Algiers" in 1957, paralleled the activity of the SAS in an urban milieu, but necessarily played a somewhat different, more political role. Again, the primary mission was to gain the confidence of the local population and rally it to the French standard. But such responsibilities as education and food distribution were irrelevant in places where they were the normal task of the civilian administrative structure. Basically, the jobs of the SAU were those of control, protection, and counterpropaganda in the dense *medinas* of Algiers, Oran, and Constantine, where FLN agents concealed themselves easily and worked diligently to capture the support of the population. Another important enterprise was the "liberation" of the Muslim woman and her psychological integration into the normal social activities of the community.

Deconversion and Reassessment

Administrative shortcomings were not the only thing that plagued the French in Algeria as they entertained the growing realization that nothing short of winning back the allegiances of the people could check the uprising. Sacrosanct military doctrines had to be tumbled and tables of organization and equipment radically altered to meet the new contingencies. Unfortunately, this shock of recognition came in the middle of a period when France was seriously modernizing its European Army in conjunction with NATO plans.[24] Now this rapid

---

[22] Lieutenant Lion, "Témoignage d'un officier S.A.S.," *l'Armée,* August 1960, p. 39.

[23] *Ibid.,* July 1960, p. 29.

[24] See Jean Planchais, *Le malaise de l'armée* (Paris, 1958), pp. 28–32.

conversion of machines and armament had to be mitigated or halted in the immediate interests of fighting an irregular war. As time passed, practice won out over theory, and the exigencies of the Algerian fighting came increasingly to regulate the form of the French division and retard its projected modernization. One model division was, in fact, "de-adapted," and the slowing of the reconversion itself involved great cost.

The school of thought — born out of the experiences of Indochina — that was proclaiming the primacy of *la guerre révolutionnaire* and codifying its doctrines now moved to take charge of the strategy of the Algerian War — clearly another case in that large catalogue of revolutionary conflict that they had been compiling. The "psychological" role of the Army — frequently held to be second only to its "social" role — was recognized and confirmed by ministerial orders. Beginning in May 1956, a significant series of directives issued to the Army in Algeria by Robert Lacoste, the Resident Minister, emphasized the expanded jurisdiction of the military, its duty to re-establish contact with the population and to agitate openly for a renewed Franco-Muslim community.

The primacy of the "war in the crowd" and the "war for the crowd" became unchallengeable in Algerian military thinking, and the conception was strongly endorsed by noted military writers who set up a monthly barrage of persuasion in the three leading military reviews and elsewhere. In Algeria, *Le Bled,* the semi-restricted *Message des Forces Armées,* and other anonymous and transient documents multiplied to enforce the pressure for the new doctrines and their political implications.

The theory of *la guerre révolutionnaire* divided the fighting in Algeria into two essential categories: rural and urban warfare.[25] Terrorism was at the base of both of these types. In the first case, the necessities for the rebel organization were to upset the population by instances of indiscriminate violence, to disorient its existing administrative and hierarchical structures, and finally to conquer it by imposing its own services and law on the mutilated remnants of the previous order. The essential problem in the cities was similar in conception, but the milieu and, consequently, the manner of operation would be different. Here, anonymous terror, the strike weapon, or the sabotage or interruption of vital services would be paramount. Thus, the *riposte* of the "forces of order" had to be prepared differently in the two in-

---

[25] Later refinements of guerrilla warfare would introduce such concepts as "suburban warfare." See, for example, Ernesto ("Che") Guevara, *Guerrilla Warfare (La Guerra de Guerrillas),* (New York: Monthly Review Press, 1961), pp. 37–39.

stances for maximum efficacy. The urban "war in the crowd," into which many civilians were drawn in a preliminary capacity, became a breeding ground for *coup d'état*. In the extraordinarily tense urban atmosphere of Algeria in 1957 the civilians began to acquire the doctrinal military vocabulary and turn it to frankly political uses.

The Psychological Action Services

As early as March 1955 — before the creation of the SAS — the command of the 10th Military District set up *bureaux psychologiques* at the staff levels of regions, divisions, and subdivisions. These agencies were formed for the joint purpose of making French troops impervious to the propaganda assaults of the enemy and aiding the civil authorities in their campaign of persuading the indigenous peoples. To prepare cadres for this novel mission a Centre d'Instruction de la Guerre Psychologique had been opened in Paris in the preceding month. What had previously been the Section Moral-Information of central Army staff headquarters was rechristened the Section Psychologique et du Moral to reflect the changing emphasis. These revisions were to bear their fruit gradually. At the same time, chairs of psychological warfare were created in the service schools, such as the Ecole Supérieure de Guerre, and it was henceforth assured that the graduates of both the higher and cadet institutions would not enter or return to their active careers without positive conceptions of the new mode of warfare.

In April 1956 a newly formed Service d'Action Psychologique et d'Information (SAPI) in the Ministry of National Defense was placed directly under the authority of the Minister, who was at the time Bourgès-Maunoury. July saw the formation of the first four operational units of Loudspeaker and Leaflet Companies (*Compagnies de haut-parleurs et de tracts*), three of which were assigned to the three Army corps that served the 10th Military District. In the same month the official Army pamphlet for the use of psychological warfare was published, and the service proceeded to the creation of the *cinquièmes bureaux,* which would furnish staff officers to the major Army commands.

By November 1957, *cinquièmes bureaux*[26] were attached to: (1) supreme Army headquarters and the headquarters of the military regions; (2) headquarters of the French Forces in Germany; (3) head-

---

[26] This and much of the previous information is derived from the article by Commandant Mairal-Bernard, "Cinquièmes bureaux et septième arme," *Revue des Forces terrestres,* January 1958, pp. 77ff.

quarters of the superior commanders in Morocco and Tunisia (where the French still retained rights to station troops); (4) headquarters of the Algerian Army Corps of Oran, Algiers, and Constantine, as well as the headquarters in all operational zones and sectors. The psychological weapon was baptized *la septième arme*.

By November 1955 a rudimentary organization consisting of a regional office in Algiers and staff offices in the three Army corps commands had been created. Psychological warfare personnel had taken to the field in the Aurès area under the command of General Parlange. Officers posted to the lesser units supplemented the work of the AMM (Affaires Militaires Musulmanes). Gradually the structure took form and shape, with an important enough volume of cadres proceeding from the Paris school and an increasing inventory of materials for psychological action.

But these efforts were still judged inadequate:

> That didn't seem to be enough; so it was rapidly decided that, within the armed forces, from the headquarters of the large unit down to the battalion, an officer would be specially assigned to the psychological sector: around the skeleton a complete nervous system grew up throughout the pyramid of command.[27]

Quantities of brochures, placards, newspapers in French and Arabic were distributed. The Army's regular weekly *Le Bled* commenced publication, soon attaining a combined Algerian-metropolitan circulation of 230,000–350,000 copies. Finally the three Loudspeaker and Leaflet Companies, now operationally ready, went into action across the Algerian countryside in what would be called in American military terminology a vast "consolidation operation."

General Tabouis paints a rather idyllic picture of these early *actions psychologiques* — presentation of films, playing of records, informal *causeries*. But another officer, writing on the subject in the same magazine, betrays a much more obvious debt to Tchakhotine's methodology and language.[28] In fact, he indicates the length to which he thinks the psychological branch should go, not only in dealing with factors of troop morale and operations among the natives but in the very control of information itself:

> The psychological warfare officer will be the official representative of the commander accredited to the war correspondents and to the organs charged

[27] General Tabouis, "La lutte psychologique en Algérie," *Revue des Forces terrestres*, April 1957, p. 32. In command structure the SAPI and the *cinquièmes bureaux* were integrated in Algeria under General Tabouis in 1956, later separated, then reintegrated by order of General Salan in the wake of the events of May 13, 1958.

[28] See Lieutenant-Colonel de Beaufond, "L'opération de guerre psychologique," *Revue de Forces terrestres*, July 1957, p. 137.

with informing the country or capable of influencing its morale. He will have his say in drawing up the communiqué. He will assure liaison between the command and the national, allied, or even enemy populations of the zone where his superior unit is stationed.[29]

The mutual preoccupation of civilian and military leaders with the possibilities of the psychological weapon led finally to the creation of a joint "Comité Restreint d'Action Psychologique," which brought together high functionaries from the Resident Minister's cabinet and the chief of the interservice Psychological Action branch, representing the Superior Commander. The alleged intention of this group was to translate the government's policy into a broad program of psychological action in Algeria; as might have been foreseen, the committee allowed itself considerable autonomy in interpreting the government's ambiguous directives and applied a good deal of pressure on the government to define its policy in the desired way. Functionally, the committee undertook to sketch out general objectives for the psychological campaign and to allot the various tasks to the appropriate parts of the civilian administration and the military command.

In the strictly military hierarchy, psychological warfare personnel were distributed down to battalion level and sometimes below it. Other *cinquième bureau* troops, not attached to organic units, conducted urban campaigns of psychological action and maintained close contact with civilian activism. And the Loudspeaker and Leaflet Companies, each attached to an Army corps, toured the countryside with their prepared entertainment, records, films, and *causeries*. On page 187 is a schematic diagram of the SAPI hierarchy as it existed in Algeria in 1957.

An example of psychological persuasion, in its crudest form, is the following document, which seems to have been widely used, with variations, in Algeria as a warrant for perpetuating the obligation of a "recaptured" or "rallied" soul. It is, in fact, a virtual pastiche of similar certificates used from a very early date in the conflict by the FLN, which were given extreme solemnity by the signatory's knowledge that any rupture of the contract meant assassination:

Act of engagement: I, the undersigned .... of the village of .... of .... douar, who have accomplished a tour of civic re-education at the Re-education Center of Tigzirt-sur-Mer, freely engage myself to:

1. Work with FRANCE for the return of PEACE.
2. Fight with the French Army against the fellagha and all those who aid the rebellion.

[29] De Beaufond, "L'officier de guerre psychologique," *Revue de Forces terrestres,* October 1957, p. 102.

SCHEME OF ORGANIZATION OF MILITARY PSYCHOLOGICAL ACTION IN ALGERIA

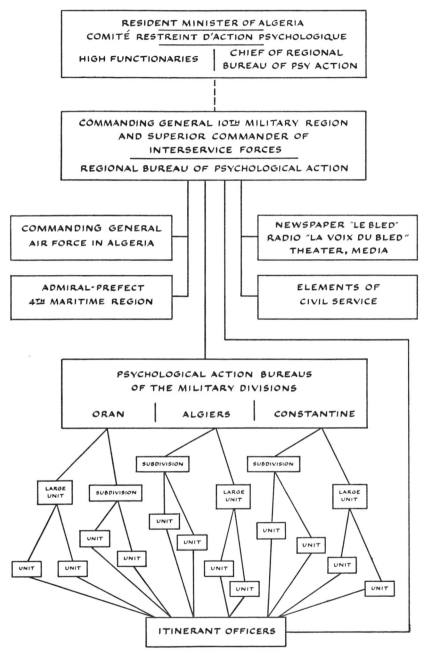

Table of Organization of the Psychological Action Services in Algeria in 1957 (from General Tabouis, "La lutte psychologique en Algérie," *Revue des Forces terrestres,* April 1957, p. 33).

3. Inform the military or civilian authorities of all acts committed by the rebels.

4. Give no assistance to the fellagha.

This is a free and solemn engagement. Any failure to meet the subscribed obligations engages the life of the signatory without prejudice of sanctions that might be applied to his close family.

Read and understood.   At Tigzirt, (date) [30]

Resettlement and "Re-education"

The military effort was supplemented by the policy of mass political reorientation, regrouping, and sequestration that became a cornerstone of psychological action in Algeria. As we saw earlier, these ideas had had a limited application in the closing phases of the Indochina War, where, however, the wholesale transplantation of persons had been neither practiced nor envisaged.

In Algeria, from mid-1957 on, the movement of persons became a gigantic operation. The country became studded with abandoned villages and ruined small plots, while in areas that were more accessible and easier for the Army to protect and control large numbers of quadrilateral, barracks-style centers of habitation were constructed. Resettlement was continuously carried out until the government abruptly reversed its policy in connection with the twenty-eight-day unilateral truce it declared on June 17, 1961. In previous years, according to the declaration of Jean Morin, some 2,075,000 persons had been moved or regrouped by the French Army — between one fifth and one quarter of the Muslim population of Algeria.[31] By physically denying the population to the enemy, the Army had hoped to settle the problem of allegiances once and for all on a massive scale. But in practice it often turned out that the omnipresent rebel OPA was able to stretch its tentacles into the new stockaded villages, as well as into other places such as the *camps d'hébergement* and the *centres sociaux*[32] — locations believed to be invulnerable.

Regrouping was intended to serve a dual purpose: (1) to make the resettled populations "secure," that is, in little danger from rebel assault, and as little as possible susceptible to giving material or moral aid to the FLN; (2) to achieve the "civic re-education" of the individuals thus controlled. An article in the *Revue des Forces terrestres*[33] minutely

---

[30] Quoted in *Express,* January 29, 1959.

[31] *Le Monde,* June 18–19, 1961.

[32] See Chapter XIII, p. 283n.

[33] General Desjours, "La pacification dans le secteur de Blida," *Revue de Forces terrestres,* October 1959, pp. 29–44.

describes one of these giant operations carried out in the Blida area of the Mitidja plain, a short distance southwest of the city of Algiers. Here alone more than 300,000 persons were resettled. Blida had, to that date, been the scene of intense terrorism. The regrouping, undertaken after special security measures and close control over all access to the sector had been achieved, was the pivot for the successful "pacification" of the area. The operations were supervised by the SAS, which instructed the transplanted people in the economic, administrative, and defensive organization of their new villages. Itinerant officers of the *cinquièmes bureaux* then provided obligatory "civic re-education" with the *leitmotif* of Franco-Algerian partnership. From each village the most reliable and able-bodied men were formed into self-defense groups or recruited into the native *harkas,* which served as auxiliaries to the regular French forces.[34]

The standard of living of the regrouped people was universally improved, and in some cases the new villages could be adapted to normal administration and the return of civilian government. But, in general, the results were artificial and distressing in a country that was already suffering upheaval touching on all aspects of traditional life and fixed values.

The practice also dangerously accelerated an already rapid trend toward urbanization. By mid-1959, probably a million Muslims had been resettled in model villages with "self-defense." But several hundred thousand others had been uprooted without provisions and had flowed in a constant stream to the cities, where they endured the anarchy of unemployment and tin-can villages (*bidonvilles*). Meanwhile, the birth rate was skyrocketing. In five years (1954–1959) the population of Constantine doubled. Médéa grew from 28,000 to 40,000; Mascara and Palikao increased from 80,000 to 170,000. Some of the new arrivals were regrouped; others were not. But the effect of the shift was always to place more persons, provided for or not, "within arm's reach of the authorities." [35]

More specialized than the general regroupings were the camps of sequestration and re-education, which formed a cardinal component of psychological action. Detention camps in Algeria were of three sorts. First of all, there were the regular prisoner-of-war camps, concerning which nothing more need be added, since their function was quite orthodox. Also, there were the so-called *camps de triage et de transit* and the *camps d'hébergement.*

---

[34] *Harkas* sometimes represented as much as one fifth of the forces of a sector. The men were paid about 1000 francs (old-style) a day.

[35] *Le Monde,* June 10, 1959.

189

The first sort of center handled a very temporary clientele, consisting of suspects usually rounded up after the encirclement of a region. The detained persons would be closely screened and interrogated, after which (at the end of a month's time) they would be sorted into categories of "reducibles," "irreducibles," and "innocents." The latter would be freed without further ado. The "irreducibles" would be placed under heavy surveillance and restricted in their movements or, if circumstances permitted, tried before military tribunals. The "reducibles," on the other hand, would be assigned to residence in a *camp d'hébergement*.

By 1959 there were ten such centers in Algeria. Collectively, they were directed by civilian authority, a *préfet hors classe* stationed in Algiers. Each camp, however, was under the command of a superior military officer, assisted by an administrative director, a licensed psychologist, and psychologically trained overseers and monitors, each responsible for supervising approximately one hundred individuals. At each of these centers the "carrot and stick" techniques of *l'action psychologique* were employed,[36] with a success that is difficult to evaluate. In his description of the camp at Mazagran, Michel Déon — who was a favorable witness — claims that 50 per cent of the prisoners rallied to the French cause, 10 per cent returned to the FLN, and 40 per cent adopted an attitude of neutrality.[37] In the light of what is known about the fluid optimism among the Muslims in Algeria, one may doubt the reliability of this estimate or at least must take into serious account the factor of least resistance and the possible lure of money that a "converted" rebel might be able to command from the French for his services in an irregular group.

At Tefeschoun the emphasis was on civic re-education. Visits from relatives were permitted, vocational training was encouraged, and considerable time was spent in political classes. Reading matter was censored (*Le Monde* sold on the black market), and great pomp and circumstance were attached to patriotic ceremony and the unpredictable assault of loudspeaker transmission, which followed the internees about like a companion. The results here were apparently indifferent, according to Déon, based on the vote in the September 28, 1958, referendum.[38]

[36] Déon, *op. cit.,* p. 111. Mazagran was a camp especially designed for the "re-education" of ex-cadres of the ALN and the OPA. See also "Notice sur l'action psychologique dans les camps d'hébergement," *Le Monde,* January 23, 1958.

[37] Déon, *op. cit.,* pp. 112–116.

[38] The policy of *camps d'hébergement,* like that of resettlement, came to an official end on June 13, 1961, simultaneous with the announcement of the twenty-eight-day unilateral truce by Jean Morin, the Delegate-General for Algeria.

At Tigzirt better results seem to have been achieved, owing, according to Déon, to superior classification of inmates. Proper assortment was crucial, since one "irreducible" in the midst of a hundred waverers might frustrate the best efforts of the French psychological warfare officers to rally the involuntary guests to the banner of *Algérie fran-çaise*.

No one is in a position to judge the lasting effects of the re-education camps. Much false information was given concerning their humane efficacy, on the one hand, and their barbarian brutality, on the other. It is likely, however, that they did not sink psychologically deep roots. The sojourn in a *camp d'hébergement* probably represented for the majority of tenants another disorienting experience in a life already studded with war, hunger, personal tragedy, and dislocation.

Though the more fanatic officers of the *cinquièmes bureaux* became a kind of laughingstock in the territorial Army, much of the Army shared with the proponents of psychological action a common interpretation of the war that was being fought. Outside the disputed realm of technique the formulations of the SAPI retained considerable influence over the field and staff officers. This was particularly true in Algiers, where each successive crisis was born. The link with extreme civilian activism was promoted through the operations of the "septième arme," and a habit of thinking was created that would have severe political consequences. Soldier and civilian came to share a common jargon with which to describe the multiplex events through which they were passing.

The "Battle of Algiers"

Nowhere is the civilian tension more evident than in that classic of irregular urban warfare, the grim "battle of Algiers," fought between the troops of General Massu and the local FLN network in 1957. It is perhaps the one action — albeit extended in time — of the Algerian fighting that deserves the name of battle. Among other things, the victory of Algiers was an undisputed success of *guerre révolutionnaire* and *action psychologique*.

The FLN was not unaware of the critical importance of sowing terror and disorder at the very nerve center of the French military and administrative network. The creation of panic in Algiers was obviously worth a score of victories elsewhere. To this end, an autonomous zone was carved out of Willaya 4 and handed over in mid-1955 to a young militant of the ALN named Yacef Saadi, of whom a substantial amount has been written.[39] This zone corresponded roughly to the metropolitan zone of Greater Algiers, with its impregnable base, the Casbah, where over 100,000 Muslims lived. This tactic of detaching Algiers from the regular *willaya* command is elsewhere represented as a feature of internal FLN politics, whereby the Kabylian element under Belkacem Krim was seeking to extend its influence, and all factions were trying to thwart the fading Messalists.[40]

By the spring of 1956 a powerful and concentrated terrorist organization was afoot. It had wrested control of the Casbah from the "forces of order." Not only did this demonstrable strength permit Saadi's network to collect important sums of money through intimidation of the local population, but it led to intensive propaganda and terrorist activity which, by early 1957, had brought both European and Muslim Algiers to an almost intolerable state of nervous tension and seemed to have irretrievably alienated the two communities. The extensive and complex structure of the Zone Autonome Algéroise (ZAA), as it came to be called, touched all areas of metropolitan activity — fund collection, clandestine shock groups, bomb networks, propaganda, espionage, administrative *noyautage,* etc. The hard core of this organization probably never numbered more than 1500 individuals; nevertheless, it was able to panic a city of 700,000. This experience inspired Colonel Trinquier's celebrated *boutade:* "Donnez-moi cent bons égorgeurs et je terroriserai la ville de Paris."

The battle of Algiers was almost lost to the French before it was won. But a circumstance with international repercussions extending far beyond Algeria influenced the outcome.

On November 5, 1956, French and British forces went ashore at the north end of the Suez Canal, allegedly to restore order in the canal and Sinai areas following Israel's precautionary attack on Egypt. In undertaking this action — which was inspired and sold to the British by Mollet, Pineau, and Bourgès-Maunoury after solemn conversations with Premier David Ben-Gurion — France had three main goals: (1) the assurance of normal sources of petroleum, which would be jeopardized if the oil-exporting states came under Nasser's domination or if he closed the canal to traffic; (2) the protection of the friendly state

---

[39] See, notably, the chapter "Les Batailles d'Alger," in Bromberger, *op. cit.,* pp. 139–209. This account is partly indebted to that work, as well as to the descriptions by Germaine Tillion of her private conversations with Yacef Saadi, in *Les ennemis complémentaires,* pp. 31–65, and to the criticism thereof in Déon, *op. cit.,* pp. 59–64. Yacef Saadi, released by the French after the Evian agreements, became military leader of the Ben Bella forces in Algiers.

[40] Bromberger, *op. cit.,* pp. 139–142.

of Israel; and (3) the possibility of striking at the heart of the Algerian rebellion's major supply base. Robert Lacoste, for one, had lain particular stress on the third reason during the previous summer, and Suez had been accepted as a desirable operation by the armed forces.

The fate of the Suez expedition is well known to all.[41] After the anticipation of an enormous strategic success, the abandonment of the operation under great-power pressure was more than bitter. It shook the regime, and made the Army resolutely suspicious of its Anglo-Saxon allies, not to mention the United Nations.

Among those forced to retire in disgrace with victory almost in sight was General Jacques Massu's 10th Parachute Division. It was this highly frustrated unit which, a few months later, would turn the tide of the terrorist battle in Algiers through recourse to various methods that were not an accredited part of regular warfare. Massu and his troops arrived in Algiers to take charge of the situation on January 27, 1957, at a time when the frenzy of rebel bombings was at its height, with cafés, dance halls, and trolley buses blowing up willy-nilly. The attitudes of both communities were tensely inimical: there was the danger that the Casbah might explode in revolution to be joined by the *fellagha* forces from Willaya 4, or the equal possibility that the European civilians, blind with fear and fury, might take matters into their own hands.

Other events were rushing to their climax. Later in the year the Algerian issue would be debated before the UN General Assembly, and the FLN was desperately anxious to make a powerful impression on the delegates through the quality of its show of force in Algiers. It was in this desperate atmosphere that Massu's men swung willfully into action. Control was tightened; there was little debate over methods, and the *nettoyage* began systematically. Intelligence-gathering was improved: sudden arrests and confiscations of stocks of bombs (whose manufacture revealed close collaboration between the FLN and Communist sources) began to shake the morale of the rebels. The resourceful Colonel Yves Godard[42] was named commander of the Algiers-Sahel sector, which roughly corresponded to the territory included in the rebel ZAA. Godard, Colonel Trinquier (one of Massu's regimental commanders), and their officers and troops progres-

[41] See J.-R., Tournoux, *Secrets d'Etat* (Paris, 1960), pp. 147–149, for a succinct play-by-play report of the event.

[42] Colonel Godard would subsequently enjoy a remarkable career, figuring prominently as the military negotiator in the events of January 24–31, 1960, as a putschist in April 1962, and subsequently as a leader in the Secret Army Organization. See ahead, Chapters XIII, XV, and XVI, *passim*.

sively strangled the rebel supremacy through an unabashed use of the methods of the enemy. Interior dissensions and the failure of fund-collecting also disturbed the insurrectional apparatus.

In January 1957 there had been more than two hundred victims of indiscriminate bombing. The FLN's strangulation of corporate municipal activity among the Muslims had been all but complete. A general strike was announced for January 28. The relentless efforts of Massu in compelling merchants to keep their shops open — at the risk of plundering if they followed the consigns of the FLN — frustrated the strike attempt. From then on, the credit of the ZAA began to wane; FLN orders for boycotts and economic sabotage were only imperfectly carried out. The slow but inevitable deterioration of the rebel network proceeded. On September 24, Colonel Godard personally received the surrender of Yacef Saadi after a honeycombing of the Casbah and a series of events too strange for fiction. By mid-October the autonomous zone of Algiers was dead, and the terror had been effectively lifted.

Without an understanding of the crucial importance of the battle of Algiers little that follows seems either proportionate or logical. A drawn-out war has its emotional amplitudes and periods, its flux and reflux. The pent-up energy released by the citizens of Algiers, including the Muslims of the Casbah — whether spontaneously or not — on May 13, 1958, and thereafter was the direct psychological reflex to the apprehension caused by the terror of the preceding year. The intensity of the one excess established the dynamism of the other. Within the vast irregular war of Algeria a minute war of Algiers was being fought — its ultimate prize being the destruction or protection of the central nervous system of the French administrative and military network.

Had the terrorists triumphed in Algiers in 1957 by forcing the two communities over the brink into inflamed and unrestricted civil war — as they came close to doing — the total perspective of the conflict would have been changed unpredictably, and might have caused the French to lose heart and abruptly relinquish the territory, as had happened in Tunisia and Morocco.

On the other hand, Massu's triumph over the rebel network supplied kinetic energy to the pacification and a false euphoric sense of eventual victory. The tight and irretrievable involvement of the urban civilian population — who, like the Muslims, now lacked representative institutions through which to express themselves — in the complicated business of war and politics was made final.

As a result of the victory of Algiers, the French military command

and informed activist segments of the civilian population now believed that they had within their grasp the means and conviction to defeat the enemy anywhere at his own game — *la guerre révolutionnaire*. From this point on, dogmatism in theories of war and activism in civilian politics became linked and interwoven and took on a common vocabulary centering around the slogan *Algérie française*. Soldiers and civilians, the latter often more "military" than the former, now set in motion the extraordinary series of events that would for years keep Algiers at a boil and shake Paris periodically. For a time and in certain ways a local but powerful perversion of the *rapprochement Armée-Nation* commenced to operate. Even when a light is destined to be extinguished, the broken filaments sometimes touch for a few moments and burn brighter.

Appendix to Chapter X

TORTURE

Tant d'habiles gens et tant de beaux génies ont écrit contre
cette pratique, que je n'ose parler après eux. J'allais dire qu'elle
pourrait convenir dans les gouvernements despotiques, où tout
ce qui inspire la crainte entre plus dans les ressorts du gouvernement; j'allais dire que les esclaves chez les Grecs et chez
les Romains. . . . Mais j'entends la voix de la nature qui crie
contre moi.

— *Montesquieu, on the subject of torture,*
De l'Esprit des Lois, *VI, xvii*

THIS BOOK is not a study of the ethics of the colonial wars fought by
the French or of any other wars. But the issue of torture has been unceasingly raised by many in the West, and it cannot be dismissed without comment. It is, indeed, part and parcel of the hyperconfusion of
values in which the French Army found itself in Algeria and is inseparable from the basic military problem.

If one takes the position that the forces of morality or history or both
operated inexorably on the side of the Algerian nationalists, then he
will have relatively less difficulty in excusing the cruel and unjustified
acts committed by the FLN in waging their revolution. If, on the other
hand, he is historically committed to the proposition that Algeria should
have remained French, he will make contrary apologies. But the truth
is not clear at all. Neither side exhibited an excessive concern for human
dignity or a praiseworthy respect for the innocents during the course of
the struggle.

This was nothing new, as some of the contending polemicists would have the public believe. All civil wars, in particular (and Algeria qualifies in some respects), have a way of being unsparing and remorseless, fraught with the extremes of honor and dishonor. The waves of reciprocal violence are more automatic and more terrible. Also, in the modern era of ideological conflict, the gulf between customary humane scruples and the conduct of violence has grown perilously wide for the civilized conscience. Our restraints magnify the shock of our excesses more than they did in previous ages. As Jean Bloch-Michel wrote concerning Algeria, "The era in which we live is curiously two-sided. We have rarely seen so much political cynicism, and never so many scruples, whether expressed or merely felt. If we did not have these scruples, the war in Algeria would long ago have finished in napalm." [1]

Torture was the most vivid and serious of the charges raised by those who did not admire the French Army. Although many persons took a convinced stand on this issue, individually and without political attachment, the vanguard consisted of the Extreme Left (which saw *torture* as a dramatic means of attacking its hereditary enemies through a screen of heroes and martyrs) and the humanitarian wing of the Catholic Church (which tended to judge the issue on the principle that it was better for a man to lose Algeria for France than to lose his soul). The vigorous opposition to physical and moral affronts to human dignity in the Algerian War does much credit to the quickened conscience of the French intelligentsia, whose works and pronouncements were legion.

But the uses of both torture and terror in the Algerian conflict had their very pragmatic content, exclusive of legality and, unfortunately, of moral concern. *Torture* was used essentially to extract intelligence and forestall other violence; *terror* was an express part of campaigns of political intimidation designed to forward the cause of the rebellion. The one called forth the other, and it is impossible in many instances to say which was cause and which effect. The simple fact is that both existed abundantly. Neither the French Army nor the Armée de Libération Nationale nor, more lately, the Organisation de l'Armée Secrète had clean hands. A cool man, Raymond Aron, wrote: "It is true that pacification cannot be imagined without torture, just as the war of liberation cannot be imagined without terrorism." [2] A passionate man, Albert Camus, added:

[1] Jean Bloch-Michel in "Textes de la revue *Preuves:* L'Algérie devant la conscience française," *Preuves,* December 1960, p. 10.
[2] Raymond Aron in *ibid.,* p. 48.

I know: violence has its priorities. The long violence of colonialism explains that of the rebellion. But this justification applies only to the armed rebellion. How can one condemn the excesses of the repression if one ignores or fails to mention the license of the rebellion? And inversely how can one express anger at the massacre of French prisoners when he accepts the shooting of Arabs without trial? Each one fortifies himself with the other's crime to commit further ones. But with this logic there is no end to the interminable destruction.[3]

Both men wished desperately that the Algerian War could end, even if it meant granting independence, and their wish was eventually endorsed by the French people as a whole.

But the Army had another problem: it had been given the mission of winning this war. The Army was institutionally and emotionally involved in the outcome, and neither was the intellect of its leaders deflected by the reason of an Aron nor was their morality chastened by the preaching of the Universal Rights of Man at the Hotel Lutétia in Paris. The well-established fact that certain members of the French military service, on their own initiative or on orders from above, methodically tortured FLN sympathizers and agents contributed little to the unity of the Army and much to its anguish. The responsibility, however, went all the way to the top. There, the politicians issued broad orders to the generals, covered for them, or simply had no wish to know specifics.

The Catholic clergy were among the first to speak out. They had, after all, a moral stake in the conduct of their communicants and, as time went on, an ecumenical stake in the future of a new Algeria. The Catholics were by no means uniform in the condemnation of military malpractices (there were, after all, the "integrist" groups of the Extreme Right and men like the famous paratroop chaplain Father Delarue). Nevertheless, it was the Archbishop of Algiers, Monsignor Léon-Etienne Duval, who took the lead in denouncing, without reservation, all assaults on human dignity. The majority of the hierarchy followed, at a distance, spurred on by advance-guard laymen, like the staff of the weekly *Témoignage Chrétien*. By October 1960, the French Assembly of Cardinals and Bishops was bold to declare:

Whatever their source, acts of terrorism, outrages against human beings, violent procedures to extract confessions, summary executions, attacks on the innocent as a means of reprisal, all are condemned by God. Even to take advantage of legitimate rights or to insure the success of a cause considered just, it is never permitted to use intrinsically perverse methods, for they

---

[3] Albert Camus, *Actuelles, III: Chronique algérienne, 1939–1958* (Paris, 1958), p. 158.

degrade one's conscience and their one sure result is continually to set back the hour of peace.[4]

Depending in emphasis on the political position of the spokesman, Catholic moral denunciation usually extended to cover the range of barbarities on both sides. As we may perceive, this was one genuine answer to the problem — perhaps the best — but it was no solution for pacification or independence, which were, after all, the outstanding political and military questions. Thus, although the Catholic and humanitarian intervention undoubtedly did much to mitigate certain excesses of sadism and inhumanity, it could not satisfy the requirements of the adversaries.

In the fearsome oscillation of the terror-torture cycle (best described in chronological sequence by Germaine Tillion),[5] the critical question was not *who* was right but *what* was right. This, however, is an approach that desperately engaged combatants cannot allow. *They* must be right, and *what* is right is *what works*. We have already seen the pendulum of hysteria and exhilaration at work in the sequence from the Battle of Algiers to the events of May 13, 1958. It was thus with all the aspects of repression and rebellion.

From the perspective of "who was right," there is much to be said for the rebels. Both Albert Camus and Germaine Tillion discover a basic motive for the rebellion of November 1, 1954, in the Sétif repression of 1945, and other evidence points to the truth of this assertion. One observer in the French Consultative Assembly has provided the following description: "Evaluating at 1000 the average number of dwellers in a *mechta* and taking into account the fact that in the luckiest cases, half of these people were able to run away . . . we can estimate the real number of Moslem dead at between 15,000 and 20,000."[6] The French bore a heavy burden in Algeria for past sins committed in a time when simple massacre was held to be an efficacious means of pacification. Though the French Left (of all shades) does not like to admit the fact, it shared responsibility for such "colonial practices."

In November 1954, the forces of order acted in much the same way when they tried to suppress the disturbances of the young revolution, thereby helping to fuel it for the arduous years of its existence.[7] Patterns

---

[4] *Cahiers du Témoignage Chrétien: Les évêques face à la guerre d'Algérie* (Paris, 1960), p. 66. Cited by William Bosworth, "The French Catholic Hierarchy and the Algerian Question," *The Western Political Quarterly*, December 1962, p. 669.

[5] See Germaine Tillion, in *Preuves, op. cit.*

[6] P. Fayet, *Journal Officiel, Assemblée consultative provisoire*, November 7, 1945, p. 1382.

[7] See especially the Edouard Sablier report in *Le Monde*, November 3, 1954.

of atrocity were already well fixed in Algeria before they were rationalized in practice or defended by theory.

Then, as an example of generalized terror, the FLN massacres on September 20, 1955, in the Constantinois proved, if proof were needed, that neither side placed human dignity on a footing with tactical expectations. From then on, the game was worth the candle of untold and innocent human suffering. The thousand — and pointedly useless — incidents of savagery that followed will be recounted some day in a documented history of the rebellion and the repression. Fortunately, this is not my task.

However, the French Army is taxed particularly on two counts. The first can be disposed of swiftly, though not finally. It is that the Army never approached any concrete idea of how to break the particular cycle of atrocity begotten by the Algerian situation. In truth, the great idea never dawned. The events of 1945 were largely unknown to the Army of 1956, which was not composed of Maghrebian historians. These men, new in the field, saw only the situation as it pertained to them, not the eternal atmosphere, to which the politicians were equally blind. They bore with themselves, in addition, the emotional baggage of Indochina and the orders of their government. They were to innovate in many respects — some of them pardonable and some abusive — but the insight of radical moral mediation could not be granted to men of war whose perception of history was forming in a contrary sense. When General Paris de Bollardière grew anguished at the implicit orders to pursue torture in the region under his command and officially protested in 1957, he ran into a stone wall of incomprehension not only from General Massu but from the Fourth Republic government as well.[8] *His* war was not being fought, and his career was over.

The second, and most serious, charge one can make against the French Army is not that it responded against the FLN in kind (which is in the nature of things) but that it *institutionalized* atrocity. Here, again, the final judgment will have to await future history. Nevertheless, the existing evidence is not entirely charitable. Where does atrocity start, and what does it consist of? In this case, mainly of two things: torture for intelligence purposes and summary execution of prisoners against the law.

In a passionate letter to the magazine *Preuves,* elicited by the Bloch-Michel essay cited earlier, General Pierre Billotte, a Gaullist "of faith" who had never commanded in Algeria, wrote as follows: "Regarding torture, I am categorical: whatever its form and whatever its purpose,

---

[8] General Paris de Bollardière's difficulties are recounted in Colonel Roger Barberot's *Malaventure en Algérie avec le général Paris de Bollardière* (Paris, 1957).

it is unacceptable, inadmissible, condemnable; it soils the honor of the army and the country. The ideological character of modern wars makes no difference." [9] This statement of inflexible dignity provoked great reaction in the Army. General Massu, then a division commander, found it necessary to reply in a mimeographed document distributed to his unit: "Torture is to be condemned, but we would like a precise answer as to where torture begins." [10]

The question was more than metaphysical. Under what circumstances did an intelligence interrogation become an affront to human dignity? Once certain methods were accepted as legitimate, how easily could their scope be expanded until instruments of torture as old as the Inquisition and as new as the electron tube, brainwashing, and narcotic serums became also admissible? The smoke generated indicated that there was more than a little fire, as private and public eyewitness testimony multiplied. "The innocent [that is, the next victims of terrorist attacks] deserve more protection than the guilty," replied General Massu.

What was even more disturbing was the growing awareness that an articulated and systematic network of torture existed in the bosom of the French Army, or at least by its side. This organization bore the initials DOP (Dispositif Opérationnel de Protection); it combined police and military skills, and had for its mission the unearthing and destruction of the FLN's clandestine political arm, the OPA.[11] Centers in which this ominous organ operated were described and revealed. But its connection with the Army high command in Algiers was uncertain, inasmuch as it could scarcely have been formed without the tacit consent of the Ministry of National Defense.

The matter of summary execution was of no less significance. Throughout the years of the Algerian conflict the Army implored the government for the power to conduct a policy of exemplary capital punishment against alleged terrorists and other rebel agents. Refused the support of law and theory, military commanders often condoned summary execution in an attempt to discourage the proliferation of the rebellion and to break its networks. It goes without saying that the most ardent interpreters of *la guerre révolutionnaire* were in the forefront of the clamor. Colonel Antoine Argoud, Massu's Chief of Staff, who was

---

[9] In *Preuves, op. cit.*, p. 11.

[10] *Ibid.*, p. 14.

[11] The best existing analysis of the DOP and its activities, compiled from a variety of sources, can be found in Pierre Vidal-Naquet, *La Raison d'Etat* (Paris, 1962), pp. 9–50. In this volume the Comité Maurice Audin has put together a number of very interesting texts concerning the torture question. Vidal-Naquet's *Torture: Cancer of Democracy: France and Algeria 1954–62* (London, 1963) repeats much of the same material in more integrated form and is accessible to readers of English.

later to enjoy a prominent career in the paths of dissidence, put the matter thus in a note to Edmond Michelet, the Gaullist Minister of Justice, in November 1959:

In revolutionary war, the main objective is to gain everyone's commitment through the conquest of hearts and minds. This can only be done and sustained if justice plays its role adequately. In disposing of the terrorist — the one who acts in secret as well as the one who throws the grenade — justice should be exemplary. Examples are set through severity and speed.[12]

Continued Colonel Argoud, faithful to his lights: "There exists legislation for time of peace and for time of war. But we are neither in time of peace nor in time of war, but in a time of *guerre révolutionnaire.*" Practically the same language, deflected slightly to fit the mood and personality, can be found in the words of a Colonel Broizat or a Colonel Trinquier.[13] The right to mete out summary justice was at the base of the Army's demands on General de Gaulle during the "revolt of the barricades" (January 24–31, 1960).

"Between two evils," argued an anonymous note circulated among the officers of the 10th Parachute Division in April 1957, "it is necessary to choose the least. So that innocent persons should not be unjustly put to death or mutilated, the criminals must be punished and put effectively out of harm's way." [14] The note had a striking resemblance to words used earlier by the Reverend Father Delarue, chaplain and confessor to the 10th Parachute Division, and commended by General Massu to the officers of the North Algérois zone on March 19, 1957.[15]

The double-branched problem of torture and summary execution had thus already reached its apogee in the days of the Fourth Republic. In fact, the Gaullist regime, with mixed success, made positive efforts to curb the worst abuses after it came to power. "Yes," admitted Michel Debré to Jean-Marie Domenach, "there are tortures in Algeria, but that is because we have no State. When we get a State, you'll see — things will change." [16] André Malraux announced as early as June 24, 1958, that an end of such abuses was in sight.[17] General de Gaulle, in whose throat many of the "methods of modern warfare" stuck like a dry bone, issued the following instruction to his Minister-Delegate for Algeria, Paul Delouvrier, on December 18, 1958:

[12] Vidal-Naquet, *La Raison d'Etat, op. cit.,* p. 263.

[13] Cf. Roger Trinquier, *La guerre moderne* (Paris, 1961), pp. 38–42; also Colonel Broizat's letter to *Le Monde,* January 20, 1961.

[14] Vidal-Naquet, *op. cit.,* p. 117.

[15] *Ibid.,* p. 110.

[16] Declaration of Domenach in *Témoignages et Documents,* No. 13, May 1959. Cited by Vidal-Naquet, *op. cit.,* p. 29.

[17] See Albert-Paul Lentin, *L'Algérie des colonels* (Paris, 1958), pp. 69–70.

The government attaches very great importance to the rigorous regularization of all police operations and all consequent preventive or repressive measures. From this point of view, the responsibility of the chiefs charged with command should be total within the appropriate zones of exercise; no specialized organism, and *a fortiori* no individual, should have the capacity to act outside their authority.[18]

By this time, it appears, the "extraordinary methods" had become *institutionalized,* and they were not so easily dissipated, even by order of the government. The DOP concealed itself within a broader organism known as the Centre de Coordination Interarmées (CCI), which in turn enjoyed an autonomous and privileged relationship with the military command. The organizational connection of the CCI network with the police, the regular sources of intelligence, the *camps de triage et de transit,* and the resettlement operations is not entirely clear, but the evidence suggests a confirmation of the theory of parallel hierarchies. The CCI appears to have had the paradoxical role of serving as a communications channel for the generals' putsch of April 1961 (and facilitating the rising power of the Secret Army) and of unwittingly aiding the political spread of the rebellion by backfiring as a re-education agency among the Muslims.

The evidence of military malpractice under both Fourth and Fifth Republics is a morass, but no less real for being at many points impenetrable. Not unexpectedly, the validation of physical punishment as a technique of intelligence-gathering led at one extreme to individual excesses of sadism and score-settling and at the other to the implantation of a clandestine bureaucracy that touched military politics at many points and was inextricable from the general theory of *la guerre révolutionnaire.* At moments the government was too vacillating and at others simply too incompetent to strike at this problem. In such a situation during both Fourth and Fifth Republics the leaders had a tendency to plead innocence and ignorance for obvious motives of self-defense.[19] The careful verbiage of Pierre Guillaumat was characteristic of any government response: "Unhappily it is true that abuses, explained if not excused by the cruelty of the adversary, happen from time to time. But this involves isolated individuals and, in many cases, distant facts. Disciplinary or judicial sanctions are always imposed."

The problem was admittedly a drastic one for the consciences of individuals in both government and Army. Eventually it fed the seditious

---

[18] Vidal-Naquet, *op. cit.,* p. 32.

[19] See the statements by Maurice Bourgès-Maunoury to *Le Monde,* April 15–16, 1956; by Guy Mollet to the SFIO Federation of the Marne, April 14, 1957; by André Malraux in a press conference reported in *Le Figaro,* June 25, 1958; by Pierre Guillaumat, in a letter to *Témoignage Chrétien,* January 1, 1960.

OAS and was engulfed in it. But it would be wrong to infer that the practices described here gangrened the Army as an institution. In their worst manifestations, they combined the sterile horror of technique, and the curse of sadism and racism beneath the coverlet of warped theoretical justification. But being inadmissible, they were compartmentalized and secreted — known to all but apprehended by few, a dark cloud floating over the operational landscape. The extent of contamination may possibly be measured by a poll taken by the magazine *Le Vie catholique,* which asked of its respondents (327 ordinary soldiers, 201 NCO's, and 71 officers): "Tell us in five lines your worst memory [of Algeria]." Of this number, 87 mentioned "a scene of torture [known about, heard about, seen and sometimes, but rarely, practiced]." [20] At least 80 per cent of the men polled were practicing Catholics, which would lead one to suspect a greater than average susceptibility to react to moral issues.[21] I regard these figures as disturbing but not as conclusive.

At the same time, the history of war — indeed, twentieth-century war — makes it clear that the Algerian conflict was not exceptional for its atrocities,[22] though they were committed with great remorselessness on both sides, partly as a result of the ideological feelings of the practitioners. Neither side could justly accuse the other of disrobing itself of moral pretense, because the guilt was heavy on both sides. Fortunately, both sides were able to raise voices against these practices: for every French officer who said, despairingly, "I am a Catholic, but cannot enter a church any longer," [23] there was, hopefully, a Yacef Saadi repentant of his crimes.[24] The shallowest argument was the one, sometimes pro-

---

[20] Xavier Grall (ed.), *La génération du djebel* (Paris, 1962), pp. 10, 27.

[21] *Ibid.,* p. 41.

[22] Cf. two other descriptions of modern war:

(1) ". . . the proclamations of the German army in Belgium concluded: 'For all acts of hostility the following principles will be applied: all punishments will be executed without mercy, the whole community will be regarded as responsible, hostages will be taken in large numbers.' This practice of the principle of collective responsibility, having been expressly outlawed by the Hague Convention, shocked the world of 1914 which had believed in human progress." Barbara Tuchman, *The Guns of August* (New York, 1962), p. 257.

(2) "Civil Governors and other officials of the Civil Government, if they had been appointed by the Popular Front Government, were almost always shot [by the Spanish Nationalists, in 1936]. So were those who sought to maintain the general strike declared at the time of the rising. The wives, sisters and daughters of men executed sometimes shared their fate. Often they would have their heads shaved, and their foreheads daubed mockingly with some working class sign such as the letters UHP or UGT. Then they might be raped." Hugh Thomas, *The Spanish Civil War* (New York, 1961), p. 166.

[23] Claude Dufresnoy (ed.), *Des officiers parlent* (Paris, 1961), p. 56.

[24] See Germaine Tillion, *Les ennemis complémentaires* (Paris, 1960), pp. 31–67.

claimed by Western "liberals," which held that the "higher" European civilization was above such baseness and obliged to give battle under gentlemanly rules.

Perhaps there is no answer. License is obviously no solution. It could not pay off morally. But did it even pay off tactically? The accusation of "torture done with a curious ease" resounded around the world. In the real sense, "a plague on both your houses" settled nothing either. "I condemn the atrocities of both sides with equal severity," wrote a French sergeant.[25] So, too, must the historian; but in so doing, he cannot imagine that he is helping to make the rules for the next war any less savage. Finally, he cannot, in blithe disregard for the reciprocity of the terror, absolve the rebels, simply because "history was on their side."

[25] Grall, *op. cit.*, pp. 47–48.

XI

LA FÊTE D'ALGER[1]

The particular nature of the modern State, the complexity and delicacy of its functions, the gravity of political, economic, and social problems that it is called on to solve, make it the geometric locus of the weaknesses and worries of peoples, thus increasing the difficulties it must surmount to defend itself. The modern State is more exposed to revolutionary danger than one likes to believe.

— *Curzio Malaparte,* Coup d'Etat, the Technique of Revolution

Le regime ne se transformera pas de lui-même. Cela n'est jamais arrivé dans notre histoire. Il faut un pression de l'extérieur.

— *Charles de Gaulle, in about 1952, quoted by J.-R. Tournoux,* Secrets d'Etat

THE EXTRAORDINARY events of May 13, 1958, loosely referred to as a *coup d'état,* seem dazzling and many-stranded. For better or worse, this was one of those legitimately intoxicating days that, more often in France than in most other places, interrupt the natural unfurling of

[1] An acknowledgment is due at this point to two works, previously published in English, that analyze a number of aspects of the succeeding history: James H. Meisel, *The Fall of the Republic: Military Revolt in France* (Ann Arbor, 1962); and Edgar S. Furniss, Jr., *De Gaulle and the French Army* (New York, 1964). Neither treatment agrees fundamentally with the present one, and the difference is primarily a matter of focus. Meisel attempts to attribute the French Army's turbulence to fascism (p. 4), a vastly

humdrum history. The *treize mai* was not the pale shadow of a Fascist putsch; actually, it was a half-rehearsed explosion of mixed popular and proconsular romanticism. Its causes were wide and deep, immediate and long-standing; and of defined political principles it had few, collectively, except for the temporary exhilaration of anarchy and a generalized anathema of all civilian politics, from those of Lacoste to those of Thorez. In this respect it resembled the Poujadist protest of two years earlier that had garnered 2,500,000 metropolitan votes on the strength of the slogan: "Sortez les sortants."

The Morass of French Parliamentary Politics

The global background of the rush on the Governor-General's palace that led through an insurgency to a sweeping change of regimes in France itself is undoubtedly twofold. First, there is the extraordinary anguish of decolonization and its attendant wars, which has been discussed. Secondly, there is the accumulated political tension between the "inside" and the "outside" of French political life that was the surfeit of a decade of Fourth Republic mismanagement and abdication of responsibility. In his illuminating and clever book *Du Malaise politique,*[2] Nathan Leites describes the "game" of politics as it was played in the *couloirs* of the Palais Bourbon, the byzantine croquet of knocking away a staggering ministry at the strategic moment, the intricate canasta of melding a new combination in consultations at the Elysée Palace. If this was not precisely a reproduction of the "République des camarades," which time could not bring back despite the earthbound prayers of the Radical Party, it was a closed system that amused and rewarded those admitted to the "game" and frustrated and embittered those to whom places at the table were refused.

Unfortunately for the endurance of the Fourth Republic, the numerical constriction of the Center from Right and Left[3] was considerably

---

oversimplified view in my opinion. Furniss, chiefly unsympathetic to the difficulties of the Army and to General de Gaulle *except in his dealings with the Army,* judges events mainly by the criterion of Atlantic defense; his book is, however, a useful and skillful commentary on the connection between France's strategic problems in Europe and her internal civil-military disorders. Neither author wastes more than a paragraph or two on Indochina, without which the performance of the Army is surely incomprehensible. Both books are gifted presentations of consensual American attitudes toward colonialism, military revolt, defense, alliances, etc. — Meisel's basically political in argument, Furniss's basically strategic.

[2] Translated as *The Game of Politics in France* (Stanford, California, 1958).

[3] The legislative elections of January 2, 1956, returned an Assembly of 150 Communists and 52 "Poujadists," thus establishing an antidemocratic opposition of 200 members and dangerously constricting the "gouvernementaux."

augmented by problems of interest and conscience attached to the Algerian War and colonial withdrawal. This nibbled away at the coherent majority needed by any government. On the Left the fifteen dyed-in-the-wool Mendésistes, the miscellaneous deputies who followed François Mitterrand, and an increasing number of "minoritaires" within the SFIO [4] found it impossible or unconscionable to support the "hard" Algerian policy of the government and Lacoste. And on the Right, the Gaullists (Républicains Sociaux) were fervently pledged to bring the regime down, while a "quarantaine" of the loosely governed Indépendants, encouraged by their loosely governing leader Senator Roger Duchet, were often unwilling to concede the slightest measure of social or political evolution to the colonial territories or admit the possibility of either clandestine or official contacts with the Algerian nationalists. Other political groups also had their Algerian attitudes and Algerian interests.

The Mendésiste-Mittérrandiste Left consistently voted against the government on all Algerian issues and much else besides; the Right Wing, as previously described, chimed in whenever any policy smacked of a too "liberal" orientation, like Bourgès-Maunoury's famous *loi-cadre* of 1957. The Socialists chafed beneath their discipline, and there were a few desertions of individuals, some of whom would later form the core of the dissident Parti Socialiste Unifié in 1960. The Mendésistes were not necessary to the government majority; the "quarantaine" of Indépendants, however, were, and it was their desertion that prompted the downfall of both the Bourgès-Maunoury and Gaillard governments and, mechanically, the effective end of the Fourth Republic.

When, on April 16, 1958, Gaillard was resoundingly rejected by a vote of 321 to 255, it was a combination of "outsiders" and "insiders" zealously devoted to the "game" of politics that brought him low. Besides the Communists and the cohorts of Mendès-France, there were the Gaullists (excepting Jacques Chaban-Delmas, who, as Minister of Defense, had done much to prepare for the Gaullist succession, and had the sense of tact not to vote to overthrow his own government), the Poujadists and other agricultural Rightists, and the significant "quarantine" of Indépendants, swollen now to a "soixantaine," but excluding such republican stalwarts as Paul Reynaud and André Mutter, who would later suffer threats of assassination as the "Resident" (a euphemism: he never got there) Minister for Algeria in the ephemeral Pflimlin cabinet. In the amazement of retrospect, one extracts the curious names of Modibo Kéita and Sékou Touré,[5] then deputies of

---

[4] Mayer, Depreux, Philip, Savary, Verdier, etc.

[5] Later these men became the heads of state of Mali and Guinea.

the French Republic, as supporters of the staggering bourgeois regime of the young *radical de gestion,* Félix Gaillard.

An aftermath of *treize mai* much commented on by the critics of the "system" was the skill of the informed "insiders" in preserving their places in the "new" Republic despite the fact that many secondary figures were swept out of office.[6] The revolution, if revolution there was, was made in Algiers by a mob of disgruntled "territorialists." But it was paralleled and confirmed in the *métropole* by the systematic breakdown of the old system, and by intense pressure for the reform of political and constitutional mores. Here the lead was taken by the furious defenders of the "nationalist" Right and the technicians and other apolitical "corporatists"; its success was, however, ensured by the relative apathy of the leftist "outsiders," who also prayed that things would change, and that Thermidor, in this case, would precede the Terror. Still, when the dust had cleared, General de Gaulle had depended for his republican mandate on the opportune and opportunistic support of the "insiders" — Pinay, Mollet, Pflimlin. It was an act for which the *ultras* never forgave him; increasingly, from this point on, they would fling his civil disobedience of June 18, 1940, in his face.

De Gaulle himself had probably hoped for a rally of the wartime Resistance — excluding the Communists — around his person, and for this reason the immediate defection of Mendès-France came as a heavy blow. Actually, by now — except among some of the Gaullist conspirators, who had been considering the acquisition of power since the days of the "Rally" — the Resistance was dead and just as phony as the trumped-up souvenirs of the Front Populaire that enlisted Edouard Daladier and a number of Socialists in a lugubrious if large "republican" procession from the Place de la Nation to the Place de la République on May 28, 1958.

Behind the Explosion of May 13

Those who carried the day in Algiers, before they were elbowed from prominence by more "reliable" persons, were not only "outsiders" but unknowns.[7] Many had first reached the surface in the

[6] Returned: Mollet, Pinay, Jacquinot, André Marie, Pflimlin, Robert Schuman, Maurice Schumann, Max Lejeune, Bidault, Lecourt, Gaillard, Reynaud, etc.

Defeated: Most of the Communists (Thorez excepted), Mendès-France, Daladier, Moch, Edgar Faure, Defferre, Morice, Bourgès-Maunoury, Teitgen, Colin, Mitterrand, Laniel, Pineau, etc.

Later elected to the Senate: Duclos, Mitterrand, Edgar Faure, Defferre, Colin, etc.

[7] André Baudier, named to the Algiers Committee of Public Safety by virtue of his early presence in the Governor-General's palace, when asked whom he represented, replied theatrically: "La foule."

Poujadist ferment of 1956; the Borgeauds, the Schiaffinos, the Quilicis were absent. One doubts that the "canned" profile of Pierre Lagaillarde was to be found in the files of the leading Paris newspapers on May 14.

The civilian counter-reaction to Massu's lifting of the "terror" and the people's confidence in their own resources and contempt of the government in Paris put a mob at the disposal of anyone who cared to step forth to lead it. The Douglas Fairbanks-like exploits of Lagaillarde would suit the occasion.

But a certain element of premeditation and excuse had to exist. Lieutenant Colonel Trinquier, Massu's adjutant, had set on foot his civilian Dispositif de Protection Urbaine, which would play a large part in the uprising. This was the first concerted example of "activist" concentration in revolt against the regime, if one excludes the more particularized "political" mob action of February 6, 1956, mounted mainly by the Poujadists and the veterans, and the various small intrigues that were a perpetual feature of settler discontent in Algeria. The Army had created the Dispositif, but scarcely measured the consequences of its action and was illy prepared to receive a captive administration when it was delivered by Lagaillarde's "universitaires" and other cohorts.

There is no doubt that the Army deeply shared the distress of the immediate causes of the uprising. One was the incident at Sakhiet, which had wide international repercussions. On February 8, 1958, the French Army had extended its operations beyond the Algerian border to attack an important supply base of the ALN, which lay only a few hundred yards inside Tunisia. No doubt exists that French planes patrolling the border had been fired on from this point; however, the aerial assault launched against the village took the lives of numerous innocent civilians, as the International Red Cross was able to testify. Tunisia indignantly protested the violation of its territorial rights before the UN and the world, and termed the incident wanton slaughter. The French Army fell back on its "right of pursuit" as a legal justification for the action. The Gaillard government in Paris half disowned, half countenanced the attack.

The United States and Great Britain, both appalled and diplomatically embarrassed by the event, offered their "good offices" in the dispute to prevent it from being taken to an international forum. Tunisia accepted rather eagerly, and France grudgingly. Gaillard had little room for maneuver, in any case, because he depended on the United States for military equipment and France was enduring one of her periodic foreign exchange crises.

The United Kingdom appointed Harold Beeley, an experienced

and senior Foreign Office official, and the United States named Robert Murphy, its French expert, to smooth the situation between the contending parties. The latter appointment caused heavy resentment among the Gaullist opposition and other former Resistance elements in the Army, who remembered all too well that Murphy had been President Roosevelt's accredited representative with Vichy. Murphy and Beeley held numerous consultations with the French and the Tunisians, making slight progress, as Gaillard fell from office and the French governmental crisis ensued. The Tunisians demanded indemnities and guarantees; the French wanted international control of the Algero-Tunisian border to prevent line-crossing. The "good offices" committee languished out of existence without reaching a solution, in the wake of the *treize mai*.

In the meantime, heated charges of "foreign interference" and "abandonment" had resounded through civilian and Army circles in French Algeria.

The problem of "internationalizing" the Algerian War was a knotty one. The French, for obvious reasons, preferred to consider it a civil war, on which grounds they could defend their rejection of all UN debate and allied interference in the pursuit of the conflict. But in the case of significant foreign intervention on behalf of the rebels, they would not have hesitated to invoke Article 6 of the NATO treaty, which specifically included Algeria in the Atlantic defense perimeter, thereby calling on obligatory allied military support. Even though the existence of the "privileged sanctuaries" of Morocco and Tunisia had probably sustained the rebellion, French thinking was that more was to be lost than gained in "internationalizing" the war, particularly since they were not in a position to read the law to their Anglo-Saxon comrades. The Sakhiet incident raised the question of internationalization anew. However, this, too, would be buried in the Algiers uprising and the speculative anticipation of de Gaulle's new policies.

The pot boiled over as a result of two closer and more concrete causes of the May 13 uprising. The first was the summary execution of three French soldiers in reprisal for the execution of *fellagha* terrorists. It was the mass demonstration in their behalf around the Monument to the Dead in Algiers and the emotional climate produced by the event (when General Salan, the Superior Commander, came to lay a wreath and was received with shouts of "Vive Massu") that led directly to the assault on the Governor-General's palace. The second cause was more orthodoxly political than visceral. It was the deep suspicion surrounding the intentions of the premier-nominee Pierre Pflimlin, regarding a general military cease-fire.

These are the words from Pflimlin's declaration of May 10 that disturbed the insurgents. In his search for a majority, he promised to

— Establish the means for a cease-fire containing reciprocal guarantees;
— Define the guarantees pertaining to the elections that will take place after the total establishment of calm, so that the will of the people can be expressed in safety and liberty. The government will allow the presence of neutral observers belonging to authentically democratic countries.[8]

Cease-fire, when total military victory would be only a matter of time, given the proper support of the Army by the government? The indignation of the European settlers swelled, and much of the Army was disquieted.

Robert Lacoste, a politician and not a revolutionary, was disquieted, too. He had noted the deterioration of political stability in his proconsulate, and when he was called back to Paris for consultations with René Pleven, who had preceded Pflimlin as a premier-candidate, he had made no bones about the fact. He had left Algiers after broadcasting his counsel for calm to the restive population:

After having given a fine example of patriotic wisdom, good sense, and heroism in resisting a provocative and barbarous terrorism for months, from now on Algiers should give the example of a calm and united will and nobly push destiny forward in order, restraint, and solidarity.

We must take care not to confuse agitation and action, not to let great and noble feelings be led astray by political factions in search of followers.

Don't forget that the mobilization of people on the streets, in order to be useful, should be reserved for solemn moments or hours of great peril. This is not the case today.[9]

In response to Lacoste's caution, thousands of European Algerians demonstrated silently and sullenly in the streets on April 26, manipulated by the skill of Léon Delbecque, who was Chaban-Delmas's attaché in Algeria and the liaison man for Jacques Soustelle, his USRAF (Union pour le Salut et le Renouveau de l'Algérie Française), and the Républicains Sociaux (Gaullists). This was the dress rehearsal for the popular uprising that was supposed either to forestall the Pflimlin investiture or to register the mass fury of French Algeria if it were carried by the "parliament of cowards." This planned action was later postponed until after the results of the vote at the Palais Bourbon would be known; the seizure of the initiative by Lagaillarde, Robert Martel, and others, however, upset this "Gaullist" strategy.

[8] *Le Monde,* May 11, 1958.
[9] *Le Monde,* April 27–28, 1958.

Plots: Gaullist and Other

Books have been written about the obsessive atmosphere of "complot" preceding May 13.[10] Actually, the causes for the downfall of the regime were, as we have seen, much deeper than the mere content of the blows rained on it by the insurrectional activity of the malcontented "outsiders." That plots existed in variety and competition with each other is really a symptom and not a cause of the collapse of the France we have been describing. The Fourth Republic fell because, in the last analysis, few — even those who justified its defense with formulas of "republican legality" and "fascism shall not pass!" — were prepared to defend it. If the system that passed unwept into history in 1958 had persuaded its legions of functionaries, administrators, gendarmes, and politicians of its right to survive, it is doubtful that the intrigues of Jean-Baptiste Biaggi or Robert Martel or Generals Chassin and Cherrière or even Delbecque could have prevailed against it.

In the closing days of the last government of the Fourth Republic, Robert Lecourt, the Keeper of the Seals, was feverishly working over a project of constitutional reform incorporating many of the features that would later be inaugurated with the constitution of the Fifth Republic. By contrast, when that document was finally made public, many of the more radical provisions constantly advocated by Debré and others in their writings and public statements were passed over or muted, in the interest of — continuity? reality? Despite the Algiers coup and the ensuing intoxication of the Forum, despite the sharp break with some of the policies and politicians of the past, despite the founding of a new Republic — there is a substantial measure of continuity between the old and new, the tarnished and mint replicas of French government. In many ways, then, the Fourth Republic spun the Fifth out of its dying entrails.

Clearly, there were two differences. One was that the symbol of something universally despised had been jettisoned. The other was that General de Gaulle, who would deliberately supersede all the institutions he had swept aside or brought with him, had returned to power in a plebiscitary state. The metropolitan plebiscite would become the strongest answer to the howlings of an Algerian mob, and it would vex and perplex beyond belief an Army that still sought legitimacy in its fundamental attachment with "the Nation."

What counted in the end was the flexible Gaullist "plot." From at least 1956 on (the end of Soustelle's Governor-Generalcy and the date

[10] Reported notably in Serge and Merry Bromberger, *Les treize complots du 13 mai* (Paris, 1959).

of his founding of the USRAF) the partisans of the Liberator fought a determined battle to topple the regime, as they had in the period 1947–1952. Allied to them — at least temporarily — were a host of other figures, often of little public importance on the political scene, who deplored the feebleness of France's parliamentary system and desired strong government. As in the Resistance, these conspirators covered a Right-Left spectrum, from the near-Fascist Jean-Baptiste Biaggi to rather left-wing authoritarians like Maxime Blocq-Mascart. Senator Michel Debré was the spiritual force and ideologist of the movement (like René Capitant in the earlier period of the "Rally"); Roger Frey was the organizer; Chaban-Delmas was the diplomat with the legal government; Soustelle was the parliamentary tactician. A majority of the leading figures in the collection of cliques that had determined to bring General de Gaulle to power had been by his side in the wartime Resistance; most of these had also filled key positions in the anti-regime Rassemblement du Peuple Français and some retained connections with its shrunken successor party, the Républicains Sociaux.

The Gaullist plot set no date for the seizure of power; in fact, the more sober of the conspirators hoped that power would come by default, as was ultimately the case. Gaullism as a creed depended on the solidarity of the French people, and not on the divisive intervention of putsch or civil war. No one understood this principle better than the General himself, who remained broadly aware of the subversive efforts on his behalf but never gave them his explicit approval. The plan for the restoration of Gaullism may be said to have consisted of six basic elements.

First of all, there was the pervasive anti-regime propaganda and administrative *noyautage,* inspired primarily by Debré, with his local newspaper, *Courrier de la Colère,* and his wide range of valuable contacts. Gaullism infiltrated the administration long before it invested the Palais Bourbon; numerous high civil servants were turning willing ears to the expedient of the General's strong government before the blow fell. In other words, by May 13, 1958, the men who "ran" France were conspicuously out of sympathy with the government that gave them their orders and the policies it made.

Secondly, there was the matter of influencing the government itself. The "Gaullists" wanted not only to overthrow the government but to establish a policy of strong leadership, constitutional reform, and revamping of administrative services. Moreover, they wished, for the sake of the country, to encourage some continuity between the regime that they were pledged to bring down and the one that they desired to raise in its place. To this end, they worked through their own minister, Chaban-Delmas, and through others like Lacoste who were sympathetic to some of their views. The infrequent personal interviews that General de Gaulle held with the politicians at Colombey were influential in this regard.

Thirdly, there was the strategy at the parliamentary level. This area of operations, dominated by Soustelle, was directed at precipitating government crises at specified moments and creating that inevitable tailspin from which the regime, numerically powerless to invest a government of the Right, could not recover, being finally compelled to cede to new solutions. To this end, Soustelle — because of the paucity of Républicains Sociaux — required the co-operation of non-Gaullist sympathizers like Georges Bidault, André Morice, and Roger Duchet, with his "quarantaine" of Indépendants. The rallying point for this anti-regime coalition was *Algérie française,* and its core of organized strength was not any political party but the USRAF, even though pure Gaullism based most of its opposition to the regime on the grounds of constitutional breakdown, rather than on its failure to find an Algerian solution. This ambiguity in the bosom of Gaullism was to loom large in the coming years. Soustelle's parliamentary tactic was, in the long run, the one that succeeded for de Gaulle — though under the threat of military intervention and by no means in the way that the deputy from Lyons had hoped.

Fourthly, there was the question of liaison with the Army. This was not so easy as the casual observer might suppose. De Gaulle, himself an unorthodox military leader, who, as chief of the Free French, had never advanced beyond the rank of brigadier general ("Who would promote me?"), had extracted obedience but never adulation from his forces. The old aristocrats of the prewar Army rather despised him as a *parvenu* that history had thrust on them; the younger officers, trained in the jungles of Tonkin and the compulsory stockade lectures of "Uncle Ho," regarded him as outdated, a grand wax mummy from the past. Still, his role in the war and history had been little short of glorious — France's only recent glory — and his prestige in the nation was not underestimated by the realists. For the bulk of the Army, de Gaulle was a viable alternative, if no strong government without him (the famous "Government of Public Safety": Soustelle-Bidault-Morice-Duchet) could be formed. Most of the "nonpolitical" officers of the Army of this period, like Massu, were incipiently Gaullist. Moreover, the General commanded the loyalty of "Europeans" like Maurice Challe (at the time a member of the General Staff), and had particularly active and ardent advocates in the person of General André Petit, Ely's adjutant,[11] and of General Grout de Beaufort, also a member of General Ely's cabinet. De Gaulle captured the loyalty of the Army at a crucial moment, when it was unprepared to offer any surrogate. "Perhaps the Army made a mistake," Massu was later to lament before the German journalist Hans Kempski in January 1960. But, for the present, the General had collected the obedience of a somewhat dubious Army. The celebrated toast of Colonel Trinquier was never fulfilled: "Néguib est au pouvoir; vive Nasser!"

Fifthly, there was the conviction of the people, the masses, to be reckoned with. De Gaulle was known to all and admired as a legend by many; little effort seemed necessary in this sphere. The mailbags arriving at Colombey and in care of President René Coty at the Elysée as the crisis deepened confirmed this judgment. The more the politicians were spat on at large, the more the lonely General was esteemed, rather in spite of the composition of his entourage. And it was correctly predicted that the people would follow without "education" and consultation. Michel Debré, the author of *Ces Princes qui nous gouvernent,* was the first to know that the power in France did not proceed from the people, in any case.

Finally, there was that mixture of disaffected citizenry called Algeria, or, in the inaccurate but popular rendering, "colons." It was no secret that they would strive to make a revolution for some purpose, probably aided and abetted by elements of the Army. The problem was to canalize the dissent into Gaullist paths before it took a chaotic, centrifugal direction. This was the task of the young and ingenious Léon Delbecque.

Delbecque operated in Algeria as the emissary of the Minister of Defense, Jacques Chaban-Delmas, the ex-officio parliamentary leader of the Républicains Sociaux. Robert Lacoste, the representative of the legitimate government, had sought on several occasions to have Delbecque recalled for his subversive activities, always without result. Is is even reported that Lacoste — with consequences he could not have foreseen — gave rather a free rein to other more radically "activist" elements in the hope of neutralizing Delbecque. Yet, to complete the enigma — which is perhaps not so dense if one regards the personalities and not the mechanics — Lacoste was on excellent terms with General de Gaulle (in one of his end-of-May statements de Gaulle was to refer to Lacoste, "qui est de mes amis") during this period and sought his advice on several occasions.

[11]Not so blind a follower of the General, however, that he would not conspire with General Challe in April 1961. See Chapter XV, p. 319.

Delbecque, Soustelle, and "Fraternization"

Delbecque labored under extreme disadvantage in trying to convert European Algeria to Gaullism. The settlers' sentiments stretched back to the time of the war, when the bulk of the territory had been either Pétainist, like Alain de Sérigny, or Giraudist. De Gaulle's left-wing reforms of 1945–1946 had not pleased the Europeans; neither had the earlier declarations of Brazzaville. The Algerian settlers looked on the General as the collaborator of Thorez, whose party had now given its blessing to the struggle of the *fellagha* for independence. But Delbecque had two capital trumps, which he played with great acumen after his personal leadership of the coup had been forestalled.

One of these was the magic name of Jacques Soustelle, Gaullist of the first order. Soustelle, under suspicion as a man of the Left when he came as Mendès-France's appointee as Governor-General at the beginning of 1955, had finished as France's most popular proconsul in Algeria. The crowds had escorted him back to his ship, singing "Ce n'est qu'un au revoir." Soustelle had determined to meet his rendezvous, but not until he had educated metropolitan France to the need of keeping Algeria French and, moreover, of making it French. To this end he had founded the USRAF and preached the doctrine of *Algérie française* from one end of the *métropole* to the other while the Front Républicain was ruling France. The masses anxiously awaited the return of Soustelle, who was expected to take over the haphazard rebellion and direct the destinies of the territory from his old seat in the Gouvernement Général, vacated by the opportune departure of Lacoste. Delbecque knew well how to capitalize on the claim that he was "the personal representative of Jacques Soustelle," a talisman against which no lesser magic could prevail.

The second event that played into Delbecque's hands was the "miracle of fraternization,"[12] the arresting spectacle of masses of Muslims and Europeans joining hands fraternally on the Forum on May 16, 1958. Enthralled enthusiasts of *Algérie française* attributed this event to spontaneity; jaundiced critics assigned to it ominous pressure on the natives by the *paras* and the officers of the SAU of the Casbah. The truth lies somewhere in between. Persuasion was used by the SAU at the behest of General Massu and Colonel Godard, commander of the Alger-Sahel sector, but there is also little doubt that the "fraternization" represented a flicker of hope in Muslim breasts that some apocalyptic recognition of equality — not necessarily the equality of integra-

---

[12] For further comments on "fraternization" and "integration," see p. 227 of this chapter and pp. 303–304 of Chapter XIV.

tion—had struck the exhilarated Europeans and would be guaranteed by the Army. The unifying factor, which really made fraternization possible, was the imminence of General de Gaulle on the horizon, the one Frenchman who genuinely commanded the respect of his Muslim compatriots, the man from whom they hoped and expected much, the *marabout* compared to whom, at least for the time being, Ferhat Abbas was some kind of bourgeois pygmy. Algerian realists recognized without difficulty the hinge on which the electrifying sight of Franco-Muslim amity turned. Immediately Delbecque's prestige as Algeria's leading Gaullist shot up; once the concept of integration was proposed as the first premise of the revolutionary syllogism, only General de Gaulle could sustain it. A few days later, on his arrival, Jacques Soustelle would warmly preach that brand of integration which he had devised in the famous plan submitted to the Edgar Faure government in 1955 and which Guy Mollet, coming to power, had left in its folder—an integration older and more respectable in its origins than the slogan that the Psychological Action Services had "discovered" on the model of Ho's *Doc-Lap*. But, long as his credit carried, Soustelle could not form the bridge between Dunkerque and Tamanrasset. The euphoria of integration was to be effectively abolished for all but the most optimistic on the anniversary of the *fraternisation* in 1959, when the Europeans failed to rally to the holiday. And, above all, de Gaulle had had his doubts.

Such, then, was the substance of the plot that came to power by legal means, after a series of menaces directed against the waning strength of the existing regime, at the beginning of June 1958. It had the immense advantage of a charismatic leader. He fell for a few days into the unfamiliar role of parliamentary chief, then demanded and got "pleins pouvoirs" and sent the Assembly on a six-month holiday. At the same time he received the power to rewrite the constitution: Debré and a committee of experts set straightway to work on this project.

The other plotters, thwarted in the *métropole,* cemented their control on Algiers and bided their time. According to their view, the "Néguib" experiment would, sooner or later, have to give way to "Nasser" if the political evolution did not square with their announced convictions. Their first effort was consequently directed toward committing General de Gaulle himself, through the intermediary of Jacques Soustelle and others. On the General's first triumphal tour through Algeria in the summer of 1958 the activists urged a grudging "Vive l'Algérie française" out of him at Mostaganem; they would later regard this phrase as an inalienable contract that he had made with the peoples of Algeria.

Secondly, the partisans of May 13 tried to strengthen their grip on the military command. Among the leading military figures around Algiers they were to find numerous sympathizers; in these confused days of May–June 1958 it was often the intemperate elements of the Army that gave the lead to the civilian hotheads. The apogee of both civil-military co-operation and *action psychologique* was reached in the period between the coup and the referendum on the new constitution and the structure of the French Community. It is important to see how this situation came about.

The Committee of Public Safety

When Pierre Lagaillarde led his cohorts into the Governor-General's palace on May 13, there was no effective legitimate power in Algiers besides the Army. Robert Lacoste, the "lame-duck" Resident Minister, knowing that his mandate would not be renewed by the next Fourth Republic government and torn between positive overtures by the "activists" and his congenital Socialist discipline, had fled his fief and returned to the Palais Bourbon to take part in the debate preceding the Pflimlin investiture. The officials of his cabinet, headed by his second-in-command, Maisonneuve, and the prefects of the various regions were in no position to run the country. The responsibility and the choice of methods fell to the Army, and quick decisions had to be made.

The scene of chaos inside the Governor-General's palace immediately after its capture was indescribable. The rioters, with Lagaillarde at their head, had swept aside the halfhearted CRS and made their way through a cordon of the sympathetic paratroops of Trinquier's 3rd Colonial Parachute Regiment unmolested. Suddenly, after breaking through the gate with a truck, they found themselves in the citadel of power, cheered on by a bewildered but enthusiastic crowd below. Sacking commenced, and hundreds of dossiers were flung out of the windows. Lagaillarde described his impressions of the occasion as follows:

I ran up the stairs. I realized I could do nothing all by myself. We had to get everybody we could inside. Stones were hitting the windows. The tear gas was filtering up from one floor to the next. I bumped into people screaming, women crying. I climbed to the fourth floor and went into a front office. A guy was standing there. I told him to get out, and I climbed through the window to the ledge. There again, I felt like a man all alone. Below, because of the gas, the mob would advance, then retreat, like slow breathing. It was weird-looking. I could even pick out my wife. As many as possible of those people had to get inside. . . .[13]

The case of this strange, ardent French Algerian is far from simple. A lawyer, born of Gascon parents who were themselves both lawyers, he, like his mother and father, had appeared before the court in Algiers to defend Messali Hajd's MNA terrorists as late as 1955. The bearded leader's great-grandfather had died on the barricades in 1848 as a republican deputy. However, revolted by the horror of the FLN atrocities, Lagaillarde had gone off as a reserve second lieutenant in 1955 to fight for his patrimony against the *fellagha,* and had swung increasingly to a right-wing position. Upon his release from active service, Lagaillarde returned to the University of Algiers — ostensibly to prepare his doctorate of laws — and plunged with a will into student politics, finally being elected president of the Federation of Students. This, and his heroics before the palace, earned him a seat on the Algiers Committee of Public Safety in the feverish hours that followed the assault.

Lagaillarde found himself with a few others in the offices of Lacoste's *directeur du cabinet* and also face to face with the crowd outside, which heard his exhortations with difficulty from the height of his balcony. Upon the arrival of competent military officials, especially General Massu, commander of the 10th Parachute Division, whose headquarters were in the Algiers suburb of Hydra, the immediate thought was to form a Committee of Public Safety, which would telegraph Paris forthwith demanding the refusal of the Pflimlin investiture and the formation of a "Government of Public Safety." Massu, having to reflect quickly on the contingencies involved, gave his approval with General Salan's acquiescence and agreed to become the president of the Committee of Public Safety. Civilians who happened to be present in the palace were appointed willy-nilly to the organization with little regard to their reputation or whom they represented. This solution was hastily imposed by Lagaillarde in order to forestall the dominance of Delbecque, who, for the moment badly outmaneuvered, had still failed to arrive with his supporters. Later, however, Delbecque and other "Gaullists" would assume places on the Committee, as well as influential persons like Alain de Sérigny and, after the "miracle de la fraternisation," a number of reliable bourgeois Muslims such as Sid Cara. A handful of military officers — Colonels Thomazo, Ducasse, Trinquier and Captains Engels and Marion — were placed on the Committee from the outset by the hurried choice of Massu. Finally, to cap the production and thwart the designs of Lagaillarde, the young and

---

[13] Brombergers, *op. cit.,* pp. 175–176.

fiercely partisan Gaullist from St-Etienne, Lucien Neuwirth, would later be made the official spokesman for the Committee.

These details hastily dispatched, General Massu set to work to draft the famous "moi Massu" telegram that would scandalize the government in Paris, create the convinced impression of Fascist or praetorian putsch in left-wing circles, and send the crowds before the palace into an avalanche of approval when its contents were read to them.

Actually, General Massu, the strong man of the hour, was completely *hors jeu* as far as the plot was concerned. The "activists" had hesitated to make any contact with him, knowing his reputation to be that of a loyal, apolitical officer, one who would be disinclined to countenance any political challenge to the legitimate authority. Delbecque's group had hoped to make use of Massu's popularity by persuading him to rally officially to Gaullism, but only once he had been faced with a *fait accompli*. Although Massu was obviously a key piece in the puzzle and the one officer who could command the fervent and unanimous loyalty of the *Algérois,* he could not be touched by direct overtures; there was no doubt, in any case, where the *Algérois* stood vis-à-vis Paris.

The pre-insurrectional contacts were therefore limited to known friends of the coup, many of whom had a rather prodigious ability to influence their fellow officers. Not all of these contacts were, to be sure, in Algeria, and there was a considerable amount of conspiratorial information passing back and forth from the *métropole.* The most comprehensive network of military contacts was achieved by the Gaullist forces. Among those who had some inkling of the course developments were likely to take in Algeria were: Generals Petit and Grout de Beaufort; General Cogny, the commander in Morocco; General Miquel, commander of the military district of Southwest France, which included the major paratroop training centers; and General Allard, commander of the Army corps of Algiers, and his Chief of Staff, Colonel Thomazo.

General Salan, the Superior Commander in Algeria was, like Massu, kept out of the plotting, though for somewhat different reasons.

Together with other sympathetic colonels, Colonel Thomazo was, in many respects, the linchpin for the Army's implication in the May 13 coup. He fraternized indiscriminately with both the Gaullist and the activist plotters and gave every indication of extending the official sanction of his position to whatever anti-regime camarilla he came into contact with. Colonel Thomazo was a devoted disciple of the theories of *la guerre révolutionnaire;* his superior, General Allard, had given an impassioned exposition of the Communist plan for world domination before the gathered military plenipotentiaries of SHAPE in the previous year.

It was inevitable in the light of the subversive rivalry over the seizure of power in Algiers that the Army itself would become somewhat distributed between the different sets of conspirators — conspicuously those whose aim was to bring General de Gaulle to power and those of the neo-Fascist and corporatist Right (such as Martel, Martin, Doctor Lefèvre, and Joseph Ortiz, who was just now making his appearance in the background) who wished for an authoritarian government of the "pur et dur" stripe. This, indeed, is in part what happened. But surprisingly, the major trump of the "activists," as it turned out, would be General Salan himself.

Raoul Salan

Salan is not an easy figure to analyze. Beside him, the actions and motivations of a Massu are almost crystal-clear. Perhaps to explain General Salan's psychology I must begin by describing him as a military figure with loose moorings — a temporizer, a man of intellect and great military skill, a cerebral and introspective officer whom the irony of history placed at the head of a passion-intoxicated "secret army" that had no qualms about its means. It is no less ironic that this general, who was destined for fanaticism neither by his politics nor by his religion, should have lived and intrigued in exile under the stigma of a death penalty imposed by a French military tribunal.

I might also explain much by saying that Salan, the most-decorated officer in France at the time he was stripped of his functions and honors, perceived the anguish of the Army most acutely by reason of his experience and intellect. It is perhaps the short distance from greatness so fatalistically embedded in Salan's personality and the frustrations it must have produced that drove him on his wild and errant course after nearly a lifetime of superlative military service. Fellow officers, less charitably, described Salan as far gone on the opium habit he had contracted in the Far East.

Salan, the reader will recall, became Supreme Commander of the French Expeditionary Force in Indochina following the death of de Lattre in 1952. During the period of his command he fought local operations and minor skirmishes, knowing full well that decision in Tonkin hinged more on the politics of Paris than on any sweeping military plans he could make on the spot. General Navarre, his successor, was not so convinced, and he managed to lose the war for his pains, though his failure must be attributed to numerous circumstances beyond his control. However, the hesitations and temporizations of General Salan in Indochina became rather a pejorative legend in French Army and some civilian circles after that war.

When Salan arrived in November 1956 to take command of the military forces in Algeria from General Lorillot, he was received not with enthusiasm but with the label "le bradeur d'Indochine." The fact that he had the reputation of being a "republican general," with alleged associations with the Radical and Socialist parties and French Freemasonry, did not improve his position. Scarcely two months after his arrival some freewheeling activists fired two shells from a home-made bazooka contrivance through the outer wall of his office, killing his aide-de-camp on the spot and sparing the Superior Commander only because he had been called upstairs for a consultation with Lacoste.

Another source of frustration was the constant awareness that his junior Massu possessed extravagant public popularity, which never failed to be embarrassing to Salan when functions demanded that the two appear together. Only the severe loyalty and soldierly discipline of the subordinate saved the situation. On May 13, Massu would defer to the uncomfortable Salan before accepting his mission as president of the Committee of Public Safety, and he would do all within his immediate power to prevent the ground from being cut out from under his superior.

There was, however, one pre-insurrectional link that made General Salan a distant party to the machinations of the activists. This was his honorary presidency of the powerful group known as the Anciens d'Indochine (veterans), which he relinquished to General Chassin only at the time of his assumption of the Algerian command. The Anciens had the greatest capacity of any movement to put demonstrators into the Parisian streets, and were adroitly maneuvered in the currents of anti-regime politics by their secretary-general, Yves Gignac, a former noncommissioned officer with the Expeditionary Force. Salan's sponsorship of this group merited him important metropolitan contacts in the activist milieu and reciprocal liaison with their counterparts in Algeria, some of whom had disliked him enough a year earlier to attempt his assassination.

Salan's position was aided by his ambiguous legitimacy. It would seem at first glance that Salan's appointment by a government of the vanishing Fourth Republic could rebound only to his disadvantage; but in the confused atmosphere of Algiers, where deception and time-phasing assumed great importance in the strategy of capturing the *coup d'état,* Salan's legitimacy gave a paradoxical advantage to the force that could make use of it. The turbulent events of May 13 had occurred when Gaillard's was still the *interim* government. A hasty phone call to Paris from the Governor-General's palace while the dossiers rained from the windows had confirmed Salan in his functions, with the express approval of Gaillard, his Minister of the Interior, Bourgès-Maunoury, and the premier-nominee, Pflimlin, who was about to face the investiture debate. Moreover, in the absence of Lacoste or any equivalent civilian authority, Salan's jurisdiction was extended to cover administration of the whole territory. General Salan, quite literally besieged by the insurgents, had, by edict of the legal government, become *le pouvoir* in Algeria.

Two bad mistakes in policy were now made by the harried Fourth Republic. The first one was Gaillard's preliminary verbal directive, later confirmed by Pflimlin, that assigned Salan complete jurisdiction over civil functions. Later, when the government learned that the zones of Constantine and Oran had the ghost of a chance of being preserved for the regime by loyalist elements, attempts were made by telephone to limit Salan's authority to the Algiers zone. Salan and his immediate entourage would later claim that express written orders to this effect had never arrived from Paris.

The second mistake was on the part of the new Premier, Pflimlin, after his investiture, which had taken place in the confused swell of heated gossip about the nature of the Algerian coup. In a rather impassioned speech before the Assembly, Pflimlin maladroitly described his legal deputy Salan as a "factious general." This was probably, under the circumstances, an irremediable error. At any rate, it was not long before Salan, hand in glove with the plotters, was corresponding feverishly with the metropolitan military conspirators like General Miquel and General Descours (commander of the military region of Lyons) and issuing the orders and operations plan for "Résurrection." This program called for the military seizure of the *métropole* by paratroop drops in the Paris area and action by the Second Armored Group, under the command of Colonel Gribius, from its base at Rambouillet toward the capital. General Challe and his Chief of Staff, General Martin, were to furnish the needed transport planes.

With Salan decisively conquered for the cause of the insurrection it became a question of which part of the insurrection he would serve. The Lagaillarde-Martel elements tried to ensure that he would serve their purposes by cultivating him at a moment when the Gaullists had not yet come forward. There was, in fact, extremely bad blood between Salan and Delbecque and a deep suspicion on the part of the military commander that the promised arrival of Jacques Soustelle was in part designed to eliminate his effective authority. When Soustelle finally came, after his picturesque escape from Paris in the trunk of a borrowed car and subsequent flight from Geneva incognito on May 18, his activity proved to be much more restrained than General Salan had feared. Finally, the persuasive interventions of General Petit with superior officers in the Algerian military command convinced Salan that the political wave of the future was Gaullism. Thus he yielded to the realistic imperative and became, at least officially, the agent of the Liberator.

Since the Gaullists, and apparently the General himself, never quite trusted Salan after this series of incidents, they sought an opportunity when he might be conveniently removed from his key position. In December 1958 he was called back to the *métropole* to assume the Inspector-Generalcy of the Armed Forces, and he was subsequently neutralized a month later by being transferred to the command of the military district of Paris. He retired shortly afterward from active service in embitterment and chagrin.

But, in the meantime, Salan was hierarchical chief in Algeria, possessing not only the military command (raised from "Superior" to "Supreme") but effectively the civil administrative powers that Lacoste had vacated, that Mutter could never assume, and that General de Gaulle would nominally assign to his own person when he came to power. The ascendancy of Salan meant also the ascendancy of the Army, even beyond the position of privilege it had known in the days of Lacoste, and, incidentally, the zenith of influence of the purest advocates of the tenets of *l'action psychologique*. The most extreme effects of the "intoxication" went unchecked in these months, and the various agencies of psychological action were permitted to reorganize for maximum effectiveness.

Corsica and the Collapse of the Fourth Republic

Before describing the aftermath of the investiture of General de Gaulle, it is necessary to record briefly one significant event. This is the occupation of Corsica, on May 24, 1958, by forces of the insurrection from Algiers, led by Colonel Thomazo.[14] It was the action that broke the back of the Fourth Republic and led to the peaceful parliamentary acceptance of a Gaullist government. Corsica — taken with consummate ease and without bloodshed — demonstrated infallibly that the government could place no confidence in its own troops or in the re-

---

[14] For an enthusiastic account of the Corsican coup, see Pascal Arrighi, *La Corse: atout décisif* (Paris, 1958).

sources of the Navy or Air Force. It also showed, by evidence of the popular reaction, that the political malaise was by no means limited to Algeria. The occupation of Corsica was a cheap, humane, and effective way of showing the Fourth Republic that it must pack its baggage and depart — a semi-inadvertent masterpiece of strategy. To have launched "Operation Resurrection" first could have had bloody and vicious consequences: the arming of civilians (including the Communists) and probably civil war. Corsica confirmed what Algiers had maintained.

In Paris itself during the period, the atmosphere was one of ghostly unreality. Police trucks filled with CRS, whose reliability was in doubt, lined the Place de la Concorde and the Left Bank quais. People came and went on weekends, and there was "business as usual." General de Gaulle motored in from Colombey to spend his usual day a week in his office on the Rue de Solférino. Finally he met secretly with Pflimlin and with the presidents of the two legislative chambers, André Le Troquer and Gaston Monnerville, and issued his famous provocative statement: "I have initiated the regular process necessary for the establishment of a republican government." [15] But otherwise, "Operation Resurrection" or not, the weather was splendid, and the thought of bearing arms in defense of the Republic was very distant from the minds of most people.

The Leftists managed their one grave rally in the form of a procession through East Paris, and the anti-regime forces countered with a puerile demonstration of auto horns klaxoning "Algérie française" — three shorts and two longs — on the polite Champs Elysées. Otherwise, very little happened, except in small groups and behind closed doors. Beneath this superficial calm, however, political crisis was quickening, and vulnerable persons out of sympathy with the new developments, such as Mendès-France, were blatantly threatened with violence and found themselves in a position of great insecurity.

Intoxication

Meanwhile, Algiers was "intoxicated" with the new element of *fraternisation* and the daily sojourn of crowds on the Forum to listen to this or that speaker of either community extol the paradisiacal virtues of *Algérie française*. The arrival of Jacques Soustelle caused immense excitement. Not wishing to get too much in Salan's way, the bespectacled deputy set out almost immediately on a speaking tour of the other

[15] Declaration of May 27, 1958.

Algerian cities, where events had somewhat belatedly followed the pattern of the territorial capital, and Committees of Public Safety and the usual scaffolding had been formed.

The *fraternisation* itself, most pronounced in Algiers, involved the inevitable consequence of co-opting Muslim representatives to the innumerable "corporatist" committees and functions, the "parallel hierarchies" that sprang up with extraordinary prolixity in the wake of the *treize mai*. Women unveiled themselves with unlikely profusion in the public squares, and bewildered Muslims circulated in Army trucks waving an indescribable number of banners and placards at their uninitiated compatriots. Still, Marshal Bugeaud's ideal of "un seul et même peuple" was at best distant, despite the assembly-line press releases of the Psychological Action and Information Service.

Concurrently, the vertical and horizontal committees took root, not perhaps very deep root. An admittedly unsympathetic observer describes this chaos of organisms following in the wake of the coup:

All Algeria was soon "gridded" [*quadrillée*] with a network of local or regional Committees of Public Safety, on the one hand, or professional committees (corporative hierarchy), on the other. To achieve this second goal, the colonels appealed with clever demagogy to certain assimilationist and integrationist traditions of the laborite Left. In any case, there exist today vertical Committees of Public Safety in numerous professional bodies, and notably among the gasoline workers, bank employees, dockers, fishermen, natural gas and electricity workers, and railwaymen. The taxi drivers, always quite boisterous, have at their head an officer charged with directing and, in extremity, calming them. . . . These professional committees successively organize "Corporative Nights" on the Forum: Gas Night, etc. (The most spectacular sight was, on May 27, the Labor Union Night, when, in an apotheosis of prefabricated enthusiasm, a Committee of National Labor Unions was created.)[16]

The conviction grew that everything in Algeria was psychologically tractable. For example, a broadside entitled "Bulletin d'Information et de Liaison du Comité d'Entente et d'Action des Anciens Combattants et Cadres de Réserve d'Algérie" stated:

War consists of imposing one's will on the adversary. Formerly it was imposed by natural violence. Today it is possible through psychological violence.

For the moment, to the extent that no organic structure exists and each person is reduced to his own resources, it is possible to "teleguide" people's minds from the outside. Psychological war becomes possible. Since others practice it without scruple, if we wish to defend ourselves, it becomes necessary.

By nature, a democracy has no ability to wage an efficient psychological

[16] Albert-Paul Lentin, *L'Algérie des colonels* (Paris, 1958), p. 66.

war. In the sphere of the armed forces the problem is different, for this is an authoritarian system. Only the Army has been able to develop psychological war because its structure lends itself to it.[17]

Until the referendum, the fever mounted: the "parallel hierarchies" multiplied in Algeria, creating every imaginable kind of fraternal and professional ligature; "psychological action" among the Muslims was rampant; and the exponents of "avant cela, rien — après cela, tout" were the ministers and missionaries of the new sovereignty. These convictions resounded throughout the vocal part of the Army, and were echoed in full volume by the civilian activists. One thinks almost of 1793, and the intoxicated peasants of Provence crowning Reason with fireworks and flowers.

While the colonels exposed their theories in Algiers to groups of ardent younger officers and an astonished international press, one could believe that the war against the FLN had almost come to a standstill in the interests of the intense propaganda campaign. In truth, the Algerian nationalists were astonished and pushed badly off balance by this extraordinary display of frenzy and enthusiasm. This was the beginning of the end of their active military power.

A military order of the period[18] demonstrates the character and intensity of the Army's efforts. It also plainly shows the limitations of *action psychologique* as such, and the massive recourse to the reputation of General de Gaulle, with which the Army sought to bewitch the natives:

It is useless to insist on the vital interest France has in the success of the referendum. Its failure would irremediably compromise the policy of *renovation* undertaken since May 13. Therefore, it is important for the Army, the possessor of civil and military power in Algeria, to undertake a vast campaign of propaganda so as to obtain:
— a massive participation in the referendum.
— a very strong majority for the proposition "yes."
The psychological action campaign should be launched immediately. The objective of the first phase will be to condition the population. . . .
Photographs of General de Gaulle should be displayed everywhere; they will be ordered and distributed by the Z.S.A. command.
The symbol of the "V" imposed on the Cross of Lorraine should be indelibly affixed (with tar or paint) in numerous places, even in the most distant *douars,* so as to strike the imagination of the masses.

[17] Dated May 12, 1958. Cited by Claude Choublier, "L'Arme psychologique entre les mains des colonels," *La NEF,* July 1958, pp. 27–33.

[18] Note de service N° 1247/Z.S.A./5 — that is, the Zone Sud-Algérois, commanded by General de Pouilly and occupied by the 20th Infantry Division. This was an uncharacteristic and isolated aberration by the very traditionalist Henri de Pouilly, who would appear as the loyalist, if Fabian, commander of the Oran army corps during the *putsch des généraux* in April 1961.

All sessions of *action psychologique* should speak of General de Gaulle.
Here are some themes to develop:
From now on, General de Gaulle is the head of France.
General de Gaulle means Peace.[19]

De Gaulle Temporizes

De Gaulle was a traditional, but nevertheless capital, trump for psychological action. The Army, working their fingers to the bone for three separate days (September 26, 27, 28), would extract greater than 60 per cent participation in the referendum for the adoption of the Constitution of the Fifth Republic (which meant Algerian reaffirmation of French sovereignty) and an extremely elevated proportion of "yes" votes (about 95 per cent). The former figure is obviously the more significant, given the conditions of close surveillance under which the vote was conducted in most communities. Although it is improper to say that the referendum proved the native loyalty to France, it did show that the French Army was equipped to marshal and protect the bulk of Muslims in a political election. Actually, at this time it is probable that most Muslims were still caught between the conflicting currents that had torn their country apart, and were waiting to see which wind blew the freshest.

For a frantic few months after the May 13 coup, it appeared to be the French wind. Thereafter, the illusion was gradually and fatally dispelled, until by the end of 1960 it was apparent that the majority of the Muslims had rallied to the FLN.

But even at the height of the "intoxication" a few warning flags were timidly signaled from Algeria in the form of letters or oblique statements to newspapers like *Le Monde*. One of these, from the Constantinois, stated, *inter alia:*

> The Army can impose by its prestige (which is real among the Muslim veterans and a certain number of people over thirty), or, more exactly, impose itself, because it has power and force. . . . The non-European population may then appear to "cede," but the "choc psychologique" of the recent events has already for the most part lost its influence.
>
> Concerning the "young people" (between twenty and thirty years of age) they generally continue to be ardently "nationalist." . . .[20]

In spite of this skepticism, it is clear that General de Gaulle continued to enjoy very great popularity in the Muslim community; he was abundantly aware of the fact and knew how to make use of it. In an

---

[19] Quoted from Lentin, *op. cit.*, p. 79.
[20] *Le Monde*, July 1, 1958.

interview with Pierre Laffont, deputy from Oran and publisher of the moderate daily *L'Echo d'Oran,* he was later to say:

> The fraternization of the two communities was not made on May 13 with M. Lagaillarde. It was during the days following that the Muslim people fraternized with the Europeans on the Forum. And this came about because someone started to shout the name "de Gaulle." Fraternization was done in my name and owing to my name.[21]

The fact is that the Muslims expected de Gaulle to bring peace, of one sort or another — which was, amid the turmoil of obscure politics, Criterion Number One. De Gaulle did not bring peace, but he did gradually adopt positions that hinted at his "liberal" policies of the future. He swiftly antagonized the activist groups, and gradually alienated wide segments of the professional Army.

De Gaulle's policy, however, took time and could be transacted only at a pace consonant with what the realities of the situation would bear. The extremists had great dynamism and some military capability, and rather than disbanding the subterranean networks they had prepared for the insurrection, they multiplied and strengthened them. In Algeria the "parallel hierarchies" and the Committees of Public Safety flourished, while in metropolitan France several activist groups, under the sponsorship of Gignac and the Anciens, joined to form the Mouvement Populaire du 13 Mai, with General Chassin as president. The Gaullists were effecting similar amalgamations, cleverly using the vast network of publicity and propaganda they had created for the referendum to advance the fortunes of the newborn Union for the New Republic in the legislative elections of November. Until the country had spoken, it would have been highly dangerous for de Gaulle to interfere very much with this hyperpolitical scaffolding; moreover, he was partially surrounded by the very men who had created it, even though he had also called Mollet, Pinay, Pflimlin, Jacquinot, Lecourt, and other "traditional" politicians into his first cabinet.

The Army, too, was in a rather artificial flush of unity, which would not endure. Those not involved in the plot were grateful for not being sanctioned or shoved aside; those implicated in the *treize mai,* its preparation, and its aftermath — confirmed for the time being in their regency of the Algerian territory — were disposed to think that events had taken a decisive and favorable turn. Over all of this ruled the sensitive and sagacious General Ely, who knew his Army like the palm of his hand, having been recalled by de Gaulle from his brief, voluntary banishment in the last days of Pflimlin.

[21] Cited in *Le Monde,* May 2, 1959.

At this point, the high command of the Army confirmed its political interest. General André Zeller, the new Chief of Staff of the Army (*armée de terre*), spoke in his General Order Number 1 of the Army as "the best guide of the nation" which had to consecrate itself to "the grand task of renovating France, which has fallen to it." Elsewhere, General Challe opined that "the Algerian War is the prefiguration of a continental conflict," and Marshal Juin favored the "constitution of a National Defense Front" to counter subversive action.[22]

The summer of 1958 was the apogee for the Army: a flush of power mingled with self-confidence. Civil-military contacts multiplied in Algeria, with the officers commanding the spectacle either directly or from the wings and, above all, arbitrating between the obscure groups that the *treize mai* had thrust to the surface. As an SAS officer in the commune of Ksar Sbahi recounts:

> Officers became administrators, lawyers, or economists, while the gendarmes wielded the trowel or recopied the electoral lists. . . . In return, the Administration was relegated to the rank of taking orders. The subprefect became the "assistant for civil affairs" of the "colonel commanding the sector, executor of civil powers in the arrondissement." Meanwhile, the Army tried to set up a para-administration which would be its political emanation: this was the experiment of the Committees of Public Safety.[23]

But the French in Algeria soon became aware that General de Gaulle, whose nominal monopoly of the new regime was becoming more actual every day, disapproved of the backwash of the tide that had brought him to power, and particularly the perception of the war that was common to the Army in Algeria. General Massu is reported to have had to inform the Committee of Public Safety of Algeria and the Sahara: "General de Gaulle and his ministers do not attach the same importance as the Algerians to *la guerre subversive*. They do not think that propaganda constitutes a psychological weapon." [24]

There was a shake-up in the SAPI. The Lacheroy-Goussault team in Algiers broke up in September, with the former returning to Paris to assume a chair at the Ecole Supérieure de Guerre and the latter being sent to take command of the sector of Guelma, in the South. Their replacement was Colonel Jean Gardes, whose palmiest days were still ahead.

There was one still, small gesture that more accurately predicted the conscious course which the government would try to impose on events.

[22] The preceding was cited by François Mitterrand, "Le parlement et l'armée," *La NEF*, July–August 1959, p. 37.

[23] Lieutenant Lion, "Témoignage d'un officier S.A.S.," *l'Armée*, August 1960, p. 29.

[24] J.-R. Tournoux, *Secrets d'Etat* (Paris, 1960), p. 403.

On October 12, 1958, General de Gaulle ordered all military officers to withdraw from their positions on the Committees of Public Safety. The civilian activists ranted at this peremptory blow struck at their convenient *rapprochement* with the Army; but the officers, led by General Massu, obeyed.

PART FIVE

ALGERIA AND BEYOND

XII

REVOLUTIONARY WAR
IN THE MÉTROPOLE

Nous allons quadriller la métropole.
— *Attributed to an enthusiastic*
student in Algiers, circa June 1958

By the time the Fourth Republic fell to powder, many French civilians had adopted the Army's manner of analyzing revolutionary war and had become sympathetic to its desire to keep Algeria French. This was not yet the unpopular war it was later to become in the Gaullist period. At the core of this civilian sympathy could be discerned various groups collectively described as "activists" who were prepared to defend the thesis that the principles of revolutionary war could be extended to interpreting metropolitan politics. The bulk of the Army shied away from this conclusion or paid it no heed, but its most vocal spirits — with the dynamism of the *treize mai* behind them — directed the energy born of anguish in a political direction and formed innumerable links with the "activists," many of them passing by way of Algiers. The military problem was thus irreparably expanded.

La guerre révolutionnaire taught that metropolitan France was the base that had to be protected at all cost against the enemy. Who, then, was the enemy in the *métropole,* and why was it qualified as such? The answer depended, of course, on which group of conspirators might be chosen to answer the question. The most extreme replies discovered not only the networks of the FLN and the Communists in this category but also the majority of the politicians of the Left and Left-Center, the progressive and humanitarian journalists and political scientists like Maurice Duverger, Pierre-Henri Simon, and Hubert Beuve-Méry, most of the government "technicians" and administrators, those who had any admiration for the United States or the UN, the "liberal" wing of the Catholic Church, the nonpolitical Army officers, the intellectuals almost without exception, the *gaullistes de gauche,* and virtually anyone — men like Georges Bidault possibly excepted — who had had anything to do with the Fourth Republic. By this logic, all these groups were anti-national, saboteurs of "Christian, Western, and Mediterranean values"; once the deceivers were unmasked, the healthy core of "la Nation" would wake from frivolous slumber and rescue itself from perdition.

At no time did a very alarming number of Frenchmen hearken to these imprecations. Nevertheless, the exponents of extremism were vocal, persistent, and well financed, able to hold their own and more against sterile leftist complaint (which had become routinized and shallow), and aided immeasurably by the fact that the majority of "la Nation," far from being susceptible, simply did not care. The rise of political extremism was also fed by a general wave of French neo-nationalism that probably, in 1958, found the majority of the country on the side of the Algerian pacification and the policies of the Army. Finally, the extremists of a political bent (that is, the exponents of a "pur et dur" regime) were often able to make common cause with other disgruntled elements in the body social: frustrated agriculturists, the *petit artisanat* that had formed the nucleus of the Poujadist movement, and, in general, the bulk of the forces of the subsidized and underdeveloped parts of France (*pays arriéré*) that had an economic ax to grind. Moreover, their liaison with the veterans' groups gave them the constant ability to put demonstrators in the streets.

Mutations of the Right in Postwar France

The basic connection between the Right in French politics and the wave of revolutionary activism surrounding the Algerian War cannot be seriously challenged. But, as René Rémond reminds us in his excellent study, there are Rights and Rights in France, manifestations of the historical symbolism of a long national existence and often opposed to one another.[1] Myths of great tenacity confront changing environments and pass into new forms.

Because of the experience of the years 1934–1944 the Right had undergone undoubted mutations; this was one of the striking discontinuities between the Third and Fourth Republics. In 1958 the most massive party of the Right (the Indépendants) was almost dogmatically wedded to republican forms and to the techniques of flexible parliamentary bargaining and coalition. The word "moderate" was fulfilled with a vengeance; sometimes only the senescent Church schools issue served to distinguish the conservatives from their colleagues of the Radical center, and sometimes not even that.

But if the domestication of French conservatism had largely been achieved and if the "royalist" Right and the Right of social privilege had now virtually disappeared as serious political forces, at least three newer "Rights" were showing muscle. The first of these was the Right of the backward rural areas, strong south of the Loire and in the West — the clientele of Pierre Poujade and Henri Dorgères. Once a source of Napoleonic support and of Boulangism, this was not a totally new Right; but modernization had multiplied its howls. Frenchmen of this strain still hoped, though not too optimistically, to make time stand still through their foolhardy, abusive, understandable — and sometimes brave — obstruction.[2] Their significance is in the mentality of archaism that they shared with the Algerian settlers.

The second Right was an ultratechnical or neo-Right, deeply affected by modern currents of international politics, the threat of war, and ideological formulations. Far from being an anarchic Right like Poujadism, this philosophy endorsed strict state control and supported the ideal of authoritarian government. Now seemingly Fascist, now endorsing the corporatism of Salazar, now alleging its affinity with the Catholicism of the Crusades, the neo-Right never centered on a single illustrative historical example. It had no Moscow or Peking to bow to with reverence; Lisbon and Madrid could scarcely suffice, but Paris would indeed be a prize. This Right was "new" and "modern," but it wore, for the demands of the occasion, a host of traditional disguises. It exalted the Family and the Nation, craft and skill as against labor, authority against liberal meandering. But its intention was clear: to rule by all the resources of the modern totalitarian state, the control of

---

[1] For a history and geography of the French Right, see René Rémond, *La droite en France de 1815 à nos jours* (4th ed., Paris, 1963).

[2] See Stanley Hoffmann, *Le Mouvement Poujade* (Paris, 1956), esp. pp. 11–25, 209–250.

the media and information, the condensation of legal technicality, the suffocation of parliamentary delay. By hazard, Algeria became the adopted child of the French neo-Right. This was the Right on whose platform the professional officer and the civilian activist most often met.

The third Right is by far the most difficult to describe. It was the "Gaullist" Right, which some would not call a "Right" at all. Gaullism, after all, is primarily a mood, primarily the sacrifice of independent judgment to faith in a totemic and legendary figure. The UNR deputy, elected in 1958 by proclaiming *Algérie française* up and down his *arrondissement,* who later praised the virtues of *Algérie algérienne,* was perhaps as much a fideist as an opportunist. But there were definite strands reaching back into the past that identified Gaullism as a rightist frame of mind.[3]

General de Gaulle's "rightism" did not mean that he had made his peace with Vichy, although he accepted Vichy as a symptom of a much deeper French psychological crisis. It is also clear that de Gaulle regarded himself as the savior of all France, and not just the half that had aided his cause during the war. His earlier mission had been to conquer; it was now to reconcile.

Though various partisans of the General, from time to time, labeled themselves *gaullistes de gauche,*[4] deeper historical reasons prevented the label from being persuasive. The Gaullist penchant for a strong executive and for state aid to Church schools seemed to identify the party position historically with the Right, and this is where most of its votes were found.

Two crucial issues further divided the contemporary Right. The first of these was the manner in which the State should be organized and what role it should play. On this point the Gaullists themselves were split, while the traditional "Indépendants," who favored a liberal economic and political society, and the various "activist" groups of the authoritarian neo-Right had virtually no doctrine in common. The second issue concerned independent versus French Algeria. The right-

[3] The Resistance had had its distinct rightist heritage of old-line nationalists, Cagoulards, etc. Also, the entire tone of de Gaulle's RPF experiment in the late 1940's was corporatist and anticapitalist. Previous Vichyite elements could find in the "Bayeux Constitution" of 1947 hints of the Pétainist past and a theory that was certainly preferable to the offerings of the traditional parliamentary parties. Finally, personalist rule (Napoleon I excepted) has generally been considered a "rightist" phenomenon in postrevolutionary France.

[4] One of the most interesting of the uniformly unsuccessful candidacies of the *gaullistes de gauche* (at that time called the Centre de la Réforme Républicaine) in 1958 was that of Colonel Roger Barberot in South Paris. Barberot had served under the famous General Paris de Bollardière in Algeria (the complainant against inadmissible practices of torture), and had described his experiences in a book called *Malaventure en Algérie avec le général Paris de Bollardière* (Paris, 1957).

ist tendency was to wish to preserve national territory for a host of patriotic or self-interested reasons, but those of the Gaullist Right, burdened with the consequences of seconding government policy, had finally to rally to the General's "liberal" solution, perhaps more out of prudent solicitude for their political future than out of substantive conviction.

The coalition of "Rights" that captured the French state in June 1958 was negative, having little in the way of common purpose and no common vision of the nation. Though much of the description to follow is concerned with rightist turbulence, one should not forget that the cause — Algeria — begot its own special peculiarities.

Muslim Terrorism in France

The war in Algeria was duplicated by a grim, incessant war in France that fed rightist accusations and whetted lawless appetites. Here, a far-reaching FLN network of terrorism and funds collection preyed upon the 400,000 or more Algerian unskilled laborers resident in metropolitan France. The primary object of the nationalist network was to sustain the revolution through monthly "donations" of 3000 francs (old-style) per individual over sixteen years of age. There was significant competition here between the FLN and the remnants of Messali Hajd's once-powerful organization, now labeled the Mouvement National Algérien. Most of the overt violence on metropolitan soil was perpetrated by the Algerian nationalists against each other or in kamikaze-type attacks against local commissariats of police; occasional instances of industrial sabotage were also recorded. This carnage, especially in the proletarian quarters and industrial suburbs of Paris, grew so ominous and distressing to Frenchmen in general, no matter what their political tendency was, that even Thorez had to lend his weight to the universal outcry against the terror.[5]

The following figures describe the *petite guerre* waged in the *métropole* more eloquently than anything else: in 1957, the Algerian terrorism was responsible for 779 deaths and 2725 wounded; in 1958, the comparable figures were 900 and 1500, respectively; from January 1 through June 15, 1959, 237 and 421. The terrorism was enjoying a recrudescence in 1959; deaths were recorded as 36 in January, 37 in February, 56 in March, 55 in April, 61 in May. In the latter two months

---

[5] Thorez's words: "The methods used by the FLN in France have not served . . . the just cause of the Algerian people, which has always enjoyed the understanding and political support of the French revolutionary workers. If the FLN thinks it is alerting opinion, it is wrong. It mobilizes opinion against it. Far from gaining sympathies, it loses them." Quoted from Michel Déon, *L'Armée d'Algérie* (Paris, 1959), p. 50.

the number of deaths, for example, included six Europeans, hit more or less by accident as passers-by.[6] In the same period of 1959, at least 4300 Algerians were arrested by the police in the *métropole* as agents of one or the other nationalist networks.

According to the testimony of Maurice Papon, the Prefect of Police of the Seine, in the year 1959 his services alone (Parisian) made 40,000 patrols, 112,000 verifications, and 69,000 interrogations. This led to the arrest of 800 fund collectors, 541 members of shock groups, more than 400 cell members, 9 zonal chiefs, 1 chief of a "superzone," 1 federal chief, and 2 *willaya* commanders. The police seized 53,000,000 francs of funds and 242 automatic pistols. Police action was further accentuated in early 1960.[7]

By late 1961, the FLN was able to control demonstrations in the Paris streets, resulting in violent contact with the Secret Army and the forced aerial deportation of Algerians in October of the year. This fever reached its pitch on nationally significant anniversaries and especially during the voluntary hunger strike of the captive leader Ben Bella, which was aimed, successfully, at winning him a political regimen of detention.

The principal nationalist organization — which was often, at least until 1961, challenged forcefully by Messali Hajd's MNA — was known as the Fédération de France du FLN. It was an organ of the Algerian Provisional Government (GPRA), directed through intermediaries located on Swiss and German soil. Like the ALN in Algeria, it was divided into six *willayas,* or military commands, the two most important being Willayas 1 and 2, covering the suburban Paris and Paris areas. Each *willaya* itself was further subdivided into two "superzones," and then into zones and regions. The region was the smallest organic whole, and a closely controlled pyramidal structure applied within it. From top to bottom its subdivisions were known as districts, sectors, *kasmas,* sections, groups, and cells. The cell was composed of three individuals, with one being in charge of the two others.

This normal hierarchical structure was doubled by the characteristic "politico-military" administration, which included special "committees of justice," "committees of sanitation," "committees of aid to prisoners," and so forth. Each region also possessed a specially armed "shock group" and, of course, numerous funds-collection groups. Each superzone was accorded two companies of thirty-one men each of the Organisation Spéciale (OS), whose missions were acts of assassination

---

[6] *Le Monde,* June 30, 1959.
[7] *Ibid.,* May 18, 1960.

and sabotage. The OS was directly attached to the GPRA without the intervention of the customary hierarchy.[8]

It was natural in such conditions that the government police services should take measures resembling the Algerian expedients in an attempt to curb the disorder. One such action was the creation of the SATFMA (Services d'Assistance Technique aux Français Musulmans d'Algérie), which were installed in the *métropole* in late 1958. According to a newspaper report,[9] they comprised twenty-one military officers, of which fourteen were assigned to the Paris area. The further increase of these services was envisaged, and this seems to have happened.

The SAT, albeit in a very different setting — the *bidonvilles* of metropolitan France — were designed to function in a manner similar to the SAU. Dressed in civilian clothes, their officers were attached to the local prefectures of police with the task of assisting the Muslims in their dealings with the administration. In many cases there was little or no contact between the SAT and the regular municipal authorities, since, in numerous towns inhabited by Muslims, the latter were duly elected Communists.

According to the testimony of Maurice Papon and of Commandant Pillot, director of the SAT, the organization had, by the middle of May 1960, handled eighty-five thousand interviews with metropolitan Muslim Algerians who were seeking information or technical assistance.[10]

In the course of 1959 the question arose as to whether the creation of Muslim *harkas* in the *métropole* as adjuncts of the regular police details would not assist perceptibly in achieving normal contacts with the Muslims and in gathering intelligence about the activity of the nationalist networks and the identity of their agents. Aside from the financial, administrative, and political complications that argued against the creation of this force, the government went to vigorous lengths to deny that it had undertaken the formation of "*harkas* in mufti." Still, well-informed sources surmised that the government employed and depended on "Muslims of privileged status," that is, paid informers — of whose hostility toward the FLN the police could be certain — as sources of intelligence for their often uncannily alert raids into the Algerian demimonde.[11] "C'est la guerre . . ." commented an

---

[8] Information given by Maurice Papon, the Prefect of Police, to the deputies and senators of the Seine. *Le Monde*, May 19, 1960.

[9] Eugène Mannoni, in *Le Monde*, November 14, 1959.

[10] *Le Monde*, May 18, 1960.

[11] *Le Monde*, November 14, 1959.

anonymous high official, when asked about these matters. "La guerre révolutionnaire," he might have added.

In any circumstances, the lot of an Algerian in industrial France was an unaccustomed one (most came from rural communities), and he needed all the advice and assistance he could obtain. He earned more than his trans-Mediterranean cousin and probably, in most cases, lived better, but he, too, was caught in the relentless vise of the revolutionary struggle and was quickly reached and manipulated by either the FLN or the MNA. Against the ubiquitous persuasion of these networks the French police could do little to assure the safety of the resident Muslims.[12]

The "Counterrevolution"

Internally, the Right reacted from 1956 on with increased passion.

One of the most interesting if farfetched theories that arose in the waning days of the Fourth Republic was the doctrine of the "Contre-Révolution." It was essentially an application of twentieth-century revolutionary technique by a more tradition-oriented and corporatist Extreme Right that distrusted the new methods of "parallel hierarchies" and the theories of the "psychologie des foules." Recalling ideas that went back beyond Vichy and Charles Maurras to Joseph de Maistre, this group held that the strongest impetus for counterrevolutionary action might be expected to come from the underlying forces of the natural society, "la Nation": the family, geographical subunits, professional and economic groups, administrative cadres. These entities were invited to enter into revolt against the existing state structure. But "to wish to hasten a taking of sides by the masses, to wish to convince them through an obsessional propaganda, is a dangerous error." One could say, then, that the group which was attempting to promote the "Contre-Révolution" was optimistic about the latent ability of the French nation to heal itself through the revision of its political structures — Dr. Bernard Lefèvre in Algiers was saying almost the same thing[13] — while the technicians and "psychologues" felt that renovation could be brought about only through psychological reconditioning based on quasi-Pavlovian methods.

The most novel portion of the theory of the "Contre-Révolution"[14] — which was elaborated *before* the coup of May 13, 1958 — was the idea

[12] See especially, Eugène Mannoni, "Du Maghreb à la Seine," *Le Monde,* April 19, 1960.

[13] See Bernard Lefèvre's, *Sur le chemin de la restauration* (Paris, 1959).

[14] See *Contre-Révolution: Stratégie et Tactique* (Editions Françaises et Internationales, Paris, 1958).

that the government of the Fourth Republic was itself, consciously or not, the agent of enemy subversion in the harshly dualistic spectrum of Good and Evil:

The analysis demonstrates that:
(*a*) the regime itself is intrinsically subversive — in essence and in spirit — in its inspiration as in its cadres — and therefore unreformable;
(*b*) in a subversive State, subversion implants itself through the law, then reinforces its grip on the country and breaks down the elements of opposition.
In consequence, it is necessary to:
Abandon legality to restore lawfulness.[15]

Sortir de la légalité pour rentrer dans le droit (the slogan of Louis Bonaparte), a motto that all too familiarly smacked of the action which, in the eyes of some, General de Gaulle had taken in June 1940, was soon to be turned against the General himself by the same elements when his regime gave evidence of progressively liberalizing its Algerian policy.

Like many of its competitors in disaffection, the "Contre-Révolution" professed a need to live in clandestinity despite the extensive manual of tactics that it bestowed on the outer world. "If the counterrevolution makes its doctrine known far and wide, it will be deformed by the Revolution and put at the service of a pseudo reaction." [16]

"National Catholicism"

If the ideas of "counterrevolution" were relatively bizarre and picturesque, a wider impulsion for change in a revolutionary and corporatist direction came from the movement known generally as "national Catholicism" [17] and, in particular, from Jean Ousset's monthly publication *Verbe,* put out by the group known as the *Cité catholique.* The significance of this *catholicisme dur* is multiplied by the fact that this and similar groups had an important number of adherents in the officer corps of the Army and had, to an extent, penetrated the services with activist cells. Unlike the "Contre-Révolution," it had no hesitation in recommending the methods of *action psychologique* as well as the more traditional tenets of *foi et croyance.* Colonels Goussault and Broizat, who played their individual parts in the vanguard of the military

---

[15] *Ibid.,* p. 101.

[16] *Ibid.,* p. 119.

[17] Two excellent and comprehensive studies of right-wing Catholicism are readily available: Madeleine Garrigou-Lagrange, "Intégrisme et national-catholicisme," *Esprit,* October 1959, pp. 515–543; and Jacques Maître, "Catholicisme d'extrême droite et croisade anti-subversive," *Revue française de Sociologie,* April–June 1961, pp. 106–117.

malaise, were reputed to be close to "national Catholicism," as well as a number of less conspicuous but more highly placed officers.

Even without the Algerian War, the French Church, its priesthood and its laity, was severely split in its diagnosis of the Communist menace and its attitude toward electoral policy and social reforms.[18] Probably, especially after the accession of Pope John XXIII, it struck a posture that was more liberal than not on the latter questions. It also had both clerical and lay movements that were, by any definition, leftist and socially oriented. Still, there was a considerable core of the clergy, including some upper hierarchy, that belonged to the Extreme Right. These were either so-called "Catholic *intégristes*" (favoring "harmonization" of Church and State) or "national Catholics." Both the "ultramontanes" and the "Gallicans," though proceeding from diverse historical traditions, possessed extreme tendencies that united on the question of anticommunism and "the defense of the West."

The reactionary wing of the Church constantly betrayed its historical links with the anti-republican past, but often in the guise of the "neo-Right" and the solutions of political corporatism.[19] It regarded the activity of communism as the paramount menace in all sectors and favored the adoption of some of the tactics and organizational structure of the adversary in order better to wage the battle against him. For purposes of liaison with the Army, with whose theories there had been considerable cross-fertilization, it was based primarily on the *Cité catholique* and the *Force psychologique* of the Catholic layman Georges Sauge, clustered around his Centre d'Etudes Supérieures de Psychologie Sociale. We shall consider these groups in order; both enjoyed the support of powerful figures in the Church.

In early 1958, just in advance of the coup, the magazine *Verbe* (organ of the *Cité catholique*) presumably renounced its revolutionary vocation and changed its subtitle to read "organ of ideological action for a Social-Christian order." The conjuncture betrayed a paradox that penetrated the very heart of much of right-wing Catholicism in France. Most of these groups, while in deadly opposition to "atheistic" left-wing solutions, had a deep hatred of the liberal bourgeois past. Their ideal, which many had hoped to achieve in the Pétain experiment, was the construction of a tight corporatist order in which social change

[18] For the Catholic electoral performance see René Rémond, "Les catholiques et les élections," in *Le référendum de septembre et les élections de novembre 1958* (Paris, 1960), pp. 99–118.

[19] In justice to the Catholics I should quote the following observation by Jacques Maître, *op. cit.,* p. 116. "Among the Protestants and in Freemasonry there are tendencies in many ways analogous to the Catholicism of the Extreme Right. In the Army, the impetus of *action psychologique* has not been monopolized by the Catholics."

would be patronized, but also paternalized. Neither "Rerum Nova-rum" nor any of the other progressive Catholic encyclicals were to be rejected out of hand; their instructions were to be used, however, in a very particular way. It was a vast distance from the *prêtres-ouvriers* to the cells of the *Cité catholique*.

Founded in 1946, the *Cité* had been since 1951 in the habit of holding national congresses. It enjoyed the support of General Chassin, General Weygand, Admiral de Penfentenyo, General Touzet du Vigier, and others.[20] It was characteristically organized as a cellular movement in semi-secrecy, each cell comprising from two to fifteen members. The upper hierarchy was composed of seventeen "regional networks" in France, with additional groups in the Maghreb and in the former French West Africa. Their study and action derived from the ideological lines traced out monthly in *Verbe*. In 1958, cells had been identified in the National Geographical Institute, the War College, the Advanced School of Aeronautics, the Naval Engineering School, and elsewhere. Apropos of the *Cité*'s activities in the services, one of its disciples, Captain de Cathelineau, wrote shortly before his death in action: "To create *Cité catholique* cells in the Army . . . is to make a national effort. Psychological action in the Army is the order of the day . . . and the essential goal is to oppose the Marxist faith with a national faith." Still, the *Cité*, according to its own admission, had only 3.5 per cent of its adherents in the armed forces.

Powerful sponsorship in the Church hierarchy assured the untouchability of the *Cité catholique*. Each year the bishop of the diocese where the national congress was being held received a letter from Cardinal Ottaviani, Pro-Secretary of the Vatican, containing "hearty welcome" and "encouragements." Other notable protectors were the Bishops Le Couëdic, Morilleau, Rupp (Auxiliary Bishop of Paris), Bressoles, Lusseau, the Most Reverend Abbot de Fontgombault, and the late Monsignor Marmottin, the Archbishop of Reims, who wrote to the movement on its tenth anniversary: "I was your advocate from the time I made your acquaintance; your spirit and doctrine so well suited my own views that I was immediately attracted by you."

Georges Sauge, one of the most curious figures in contemporary French activism and the principal inspirer of the "national Catholicism" movement, was once himself a Communist (of no importance) in his youth. This was a capital element of his psychology and, in a sense, ranged him with other ex-Marxists of the Koestler variety who perceived the most insidious menace of the movement to be in its dia-

---

[20] For this and following information, see " 'Verbe,' revue de la Cité catholique renie les principes de la révolution," *Le Monde*, July 9, 1958.

lectical versatility. Tall, good-looking, and (despite a slight impediment) a forceful speaker, Sauge carried his message across France and Algeria with exuberant energy and, at the behest of the military, delivered innumerable lectures on communism in the higher service schools.

From 1957 on, Sauge directed the so-called "Centre d'Etudes Supérieures de Psychologie Sociale," whose platform was: "To save society from the Communist whirlwind, inspire a reawakening of public opinion through knowing how to oppose the realist [sic] mystique with the Christian mystique. To increase this agitation until the Christian reawakening which will save Man and humanity." [21] His major work, a book called *Echec au communisme*,[22] was largely a confrontation of Christian and Marxist quotations, and an elucidation of the strategy and tactics of combating Marxism on the spiritual and physical planes.

In the wake of the explosion of May 13, 1958, Sauge expressed himself as follows in a circular addressed to leading ecclesiastical and political figures in France:

These days which shook Algiers can instigate a movement that History will preserve as a providential sign in favor of the Franks [sic] and of their civilizing mission in the service of God. *Gesta Dei per Francos*. This is why we have founded, on May 13, 1958, the feast of Saint Joan of Arc [sic], the "force psychologique" that we are proposing to you.

Sauge's background and personality led to his speedy cultivation by the Army's Psychological Action Services, which dispatched him on frequent missions to Algeria before the May 13 coup. He became friendly with Colonels Lacheroy and Goussault and others. With the ex-Poujadist deputies Le Pen and Jean Dides he spoke to a gathering organized by the Front National des Combattants on February 11, 1958, in the Salle Wagram. He was privy to the arrangements for the coup in Algiers. Later he was sent by the Army to the 8th Military Region (Lyons) to deliver lectures to the Reserve Officers Corps on the subject of *action psychologique*.

For all his Christian vigor, Sauge was not an especially humble man. "My superiority over the Catholic hierarchy," he is alleged to have said once, *à la* St. Augustine, "is that I knew the Devil before frequenting God and his saints."

Sauge's *Force psychologique* was intended to create kinds of "parallel hierarchies," with bases constructed at the level of neighborhoods,

[21] This and the other remarks attributed to Sauge are found in the article "Le National-Catholicisme," *Express*, February 19, 1959.

[22] Published in Paris, 1958.

labor unions, and professional groups, capped by a twelvefold regional directorate. According to the report of the hostile *Express*,[23] the majority of Sauge's adherents (no quantity was ventured) were "priests, squires of the western provinces, young officers of the active Army, old colonels of the Reserve, students in search of a patriotic ideal." Apparently, with its emphasis on social factors, the movement also attempted to raid the liberally oriented Catholic Action groups.

Sauge's career subsequently knew its ups and downs. He was one of the eminent anti-Communist types dispatched on an involuntary vacation to Corsica at the time of Khrushchev's visit to France. But he traveled later to Rome and had the honor of being ennobled and decorated by France's distinguished Cardinal Tisserant, a high Vatican official.[24] And his contacts with the Army did not lapse.

The success of movements like that of Sauge and the *Cité catholique* among elements of the professional Army could be attributed to four essential factors: (1) their mutual view of the political situation and the importance of "French Algeria"; (2) a similarity of strategic approach in the struggle against world communism and a joint appreciation of the counterdoctrines involved; (3) the existence of a remnant of the "old" Catholicism which historically united Church and Army against the depredations of the bourgeois state; (4) the spiritual grip of a simplified and "primitive" but convinced Christian faith on a substantial number of serving soldiers, and their identification of this allegiance with the national interest of France. This attachment is a phenomenon which has by no means run its course.

"National Communism"

Partaking of the same atmosphere as the "national Catholicism" groups but appearing nominally on the Left rather than the Right was the interesting movement of "national communism." Rallying around the group *Patrie et progrès,* it had no powerful sponsors but depended for its dynamism on a small but ardent clientele that favored drastic social change but detested Soviet communism and the parliamentary reformism of the social democrats in equal measure. Conditions of industrial peace and national renovation, together with a progressive and

---

[23] The *Express* article, which reproduces a good deal of material that had previously appeared in *Le Monde*, seems to confuse Sauge's movement with the *Cité catholique* and to attribute to Sauge a much more retrograde political attitude than objective evidence will support (hinting even at monarchism). Actually, Sauge's Catholicism leads toward a kind of technocracy of ecclesiastical *étatisme* with heavy nationalist but few royalist overtones.

[24] See *Le Monde*, June 10, June 15, 1961.

integrated Algeria, were to be enforced by a vigilant and social-minded Army. The inspiration of *Patrie et progrès* derived in part from the example of Marshal Tito's independence from Soviet domination. It never won a very large audience in either the Army or the nation, but it tended to appeal to some of the younger officers who, themselves frequently of modest origins and attracted politically toward the Left, were committed to the ideal of social justice in Algeria.

If national communism did not make much of a dent in Army circles, it at least constrained one of the orthodox explicators of the doctrine of *la guerre révolutionnaire,* Commandant Jacques Hogard, to enter the lists against it in the pages of the *Revue des Forces terrestres.* Citing the opinion of Milovan Djilas, that "national communism is communism in decline," Hogard argued that there was no such thing as "national communism": there was only communism itself, universal in its pretensions, or there were other forms, none of them related to it.[25]

Ferment among the Veterans and Reserve

Behind the tempest in the regular Army in the days surrounding and following the coup of Algiers was the malaise spreading through the veterans' groups and the Reserve Officer Corps of the Army itself, which was being constantly repeopled with Algerian fighters whose contracts of service had expired.

In July 1958 the previously mentioned Anciens of Yves Gignac, now renamed the "Association des Anciens Combattants de l'Union Française," came together in a "national council" in the presence of such luminaries as Generals Salan, Massu, Mirambeau, and Chassin. At this meeting it was decided to regroup all members according to military district, thus creating, in effect, a large paramilitary organization that could second the aims of the Army.

Of perhaps greater significance was the increased activity within the Reserve Officer Corps that reached its apogee somewhat later, in 1959. Here, although the group as a whole included liberal elements, especially men of the professions, the Right Wing was most vocal and tended to control the organization and "politize" it. In April 1959 a first regional *carrefour* of the Reserve (UNOR) was held in Arras; Marshal Juin sent a message of compliments urging each delegate to "consider himself mobilized and become a propagandist and defender

[25] "La tentation du communisme," *Revue des Forces terrestres,* January 1959, pp. 28–29.

of the national cause." [26] Other "regional *carrefours*" led finally to a "national *carrefour*" of Young Reserve Officers (the majority of them lieutenants) held in the Palais de Chaillot in Paris on September 27, 1959, attended by most of the seven hundred young officers of the ten regions and, significantly, by General Fayard, the Inspector-General of Reserve Forces.

The *carrefour* passed, among other acts, a motion on *Algérie française,* couched in extremely vigorous language, and uncomplimentary references to General de Gaulle were heard throughout the meeting. The resolution stated in part: "The Algerian departments are an integral part of France and the Army has taken its oath that they will remain so." [27]

Lieutenant Poulle, the president of the Youth Committee of the UNOR, affirmed the organization's entire solidarity with the Army's combat in Algeria and denounced "the equivocation hanging over the fate of a province that is an integral part of the territory of the fatherland." This was one of the strongest remonstrances that had yet appeared against General de Gaulle in public military circles.

Reacting as might be expected to the initiative of the Young Reserve Officers, the Minister of the Armies expressed himself as follows on October 10, in a letter addressed to Lieutenant Poulle:

[I am astonished that these officers] believed that they were authorized to vote on a motion whose political character will not have escaped their comrades of the active Army or to implicate them in their resolutions. . . . Such an attitude is inadmissible, from the moment when the leader, in full knowledge of his act, took the decision. . . .[28]

Regarding the intervention of the reservist officers in politics, Maurice Mégret has put his finger tellingly on the essential problem, the real *leitmotif* of the controversy I have been describing: "Defense and its jurisdictional domain are competences of the state and not an attribute or extension of the armed forces." [29] This is a democratic tenet which the Army felt increasingly compelled to challenge.

Intellectuals and Soldiers

French metropolitan activism and its relations with the professional Army would be presented here in a distorted fashion if no reference

---

[26] See Vincent Monteil, "Corneille chez Kafka," in *Cahiers de la République*, November–December 1960, p. 48.

[27] Jean Planchais, *Le Monde*, September 28, 1959.

[28] Monteil, *op. cit.*

[29] "L'Officier de réserve, la défense, et la nation, II," *Le Monde*, June 28, 1959.

were made to its most dedicated and dogmatic opponent, the intellectual Left. As we have seen, this group entertained a profound distrust of all military prerogatives reaching deep into the historical past. The Army's pretension to represent the highest interests of the nation especially disturbed the intellectuals, who were themselves direct competitors for the possession of the national quintessence. In this dialogue *la Nation* and *l'Etat, la foi* and *la critique* seemed to confront one another across an unbridgeable chasm. The right-wing civilians relished and capitalized on this acute disharmony by representing the intellectual Left as a foreign or cosmopolitan irritant in the national body politic; the Left all too frequently rose to the bait by condemning the entire military caste out of hand or unctuously patronizing the few of its number that publicly reacted against their traditions or the conduct of the war. Press conferences, declarations, meetings, and manifestos by the self-satisfied members of the "republican Left" (which in this context usually means the leftist opponents of the current regime) proclaimed the criminal complicity of the leaders of the armed forces, enjoining the troops to mutiny or passive disobedience, and announced to the outer world that France's military organization was equivalent to a Fascist conspiracy. In reprisal, the "activist" wing of the Army minced no words about the desirability of curtailing free intellectual activity and imposing censorship for *raison d'Etat,* and it indiscriminately branded those who were unsympathetic to its ideals accomplices in the global Communist plot.

It was rare to find a reasoned analysis of this particular problem in France in the years 1957–1960; one could easily have gotten the impression that the battle was being waged exclusively between the Sartres and Jeansons and the Lacheroys and Trinquiers. However, it was obvious that one of the fundamental elements of reconciliation in French society would have to be an overlap of understanding between the country's intellectual and military groups, so often at each other's throats, for both would have much to say about the national destiny.

One of the most judicious résumés — albeit from the "intellectual" point of view — was Pierre-Henri Simon's article "Intellectuels et militaires" in *Le Monde,* which at least had the virtue of stating the problem soberly in the context of the civilian fear of military power and its uses:

By force of circumstance — eighteen years of uninterrupted war, of which twelve have been against the rebellion of formerly colonized peoples — the Army has been drawn into defining its role as one which exceeds the pristine military sphere and impinges on moral, administrative, and political action. Here is the most serious cause of conflict; for nothing seems more necessary to the officers than this surplus of power, more justified than the use they make of it. And nothing is more destined to frighten that enlightened and liberal sector of public opinion that regards military intervention in the domestic affairs of the State as the main peril for democracy.[30]

Thoughtful intellectuals of the stripe of the liberal Catholic Simon probably need not have feared the advent of military dictatorship in France, because the military organization was itself rent by cross-conflicts and powerfully tugged by its traditional reflexes of unity and obedience. It would have been better for these two elements to have attempted the exercise of mutual comprehension. But Algeria and the ancient scarecrows of Left and Right stood in the way.

The Evolution of "Activism"

Activism, if numerically weak in France, became, during these years, vocally and physically strong. It was armed both metaphorically and literally with the weapons of fifteen years' continuous colonial contraction and disgrace and the spectacle of a national political humiliation from which it was excluded or exempted. The most conspicuous feature of protest from the Extreme Right in all the democracies of the West has been its foundation on premises of petty nationalism and unreflective anticommunism. This was a particularly heady concoction in France, where both domestic politics and colonial policies misfired badly. But outside this sphere of negative solidarity there were virtually as many theories and manifestos as groups: the French Right was not only aggressive but aggressively demoralized in its own bosom.

Attitudes in the French Army, which had been the frustrated agent of policies it regarded as inept and sometimes treasonable, found their parallels in civilian circles in both Paris and Algiers, and there was a great deal of mutual communication, if little joint action. Despite the Army's meditation on the ills of France, the coup of May 13, 1958, found it badly prepared to transform its doctrines into concrete political action. The barrier of personalism that General de Gaulle was erecting between the forces of discontent and the executive machinery of the state further frustrated its designs.

A badly organized foray into classical politics under the title of "Patrie et Renouveau" in the legislative elections of November 1958 proved to be without echo when the UNR, brilliantly financed and publicized, demonstrated that it was the party of inheritance. The most spirited battles between the two groups were waged in the Bordelais and especially in Bordeaux city, where the well-entrenched

[30] *Le Monde*, January 29, 1959.

mayor Jacques Chaban-Delmas easily swamped his vociferous right-wing competitor, General Chassin. A few first-string activists, like Colonel Jean Thomazo and Jean-Baptiste Biaggi, were able to seize the UNR stirrups and ride to victory. Since that time, both they (now retired by the elections of November 1962) and the National Assembly as a whole have been neutralized in French politics.

Activism was least at home in traditional political channels, and its exclusion from them merely returned it to a more familiar and conspiratorial milieu. In the early 1960's it continued to weigh heavily on French politics through its negative capability for making common cause with other types of discontent. By the time of the *treize mai* it had formed complex and persistent lines of liaison with the Army, and had taken it opportunistically to its bosom. From late 1959 on, these lines would be gradually doubled in an atmosphere of mutual anguish at the practices of the new regime. Soustelle, Bidault, and others would desert the Fifth Republic to play their part in this heterogeneous opposition which reached its apocalyptic climax in the Secret Army. Circumstances that profoundly alienated the Army from the regime ensured that the military connection with civilian plotting would not be easily severed.

XIII

ON THE BARRICADES

Allons donc, l'armée m'est fidèle, à quelques mécontents près.
— *attributed to General de Gaulle,
January 23, 1960*

Nous avions confiance d'avoir l'accord des militaires.
— *Pierre Lagaillarde, at the
"trial of the barricades"*

On joue avec des hommes, pas avec des idées.
— *General Jacques Massu, at the
"trial of the barricades"*

"WE KNOW the gravity of our task, the gravity of this trial, its implications. People have wished to give this trial a name. Some have baptized it: the trial of the barricades. History will give it another name: the trial of *Algérie française,* for that is what is really at stake." [1] With these words, the *bâtonnier* Charpentier, one of the distinguished and controversial lawyers retained by the accused, inaugurated the defense of fifteen men[2] who were being judged by a military court in Paris

---

[1] This and subsequent references to the testimony of the "trial of the barricades" designate the extensive J.-M. Théolleyre report in *Le Monde* and will identify the date of the publication rather than of the hearing, by the following formula: *Trial,* November 6–7, 1960.

[2] Pierre Lagaillarde, deputy of Algiers; Jean-Jacques Susini, President of the Federation of Students, member of the executive committee of the FNF (Front National Français); Marcel Ronda, businessman, Army reserve captain, Secretary-General of the

for an alleged series of crimes ranging from rebellion to attempt against the security of the state. Four others in flight abroad were faced with the same, or more serious, charges.[3]

The "Degradation"

The Fifth Republic had marched to power by a sequence of volatile and indeed revolutionary declarations which had asserted without nuance that France would stay in Algeria and that the FLN would be brought to heel. The idea of negotiations was treason; no "peace of the brave" was envisaged by the emotional fraternity of May 16, 1958. Muslim and Frenchman, "colon," "petit blanc," and "indigène" would share in the fruits of the new Algeria, but with the unmistakable idea that a French Algeria was intended. Some "pieds noirs" (Europeans that were Algerian by birth) hid behind the suddenly convenient motto of integration, seeing in it a salutary means for triumphing in a revolutionary war and reverting finally to something resembling as closely as possible the *status quo ante*. Others sincerely shared the conviction that the lot of the Muslims would be swiftly improved in a French country ("a province like Alsace or Brittany"). Following this line of thought was the majority of the Army, many of whose officers had worked at close quarters with the Muslim population in the pursuit of the war and had come to feel a loyalty and obligation toward sweeping social reforms in their behalf. While these propositions did not torment the citizens of metropolitan France with the same urgency, they, too, had been in early 1958 at the high-water mark of their neo-nationalist fervor in support of the war.

Once General de Gaulle had successfully assured himself of the reins of power through vast popular support in the referendum of Sep-

UT's (Unités Territoriales); Auguste Arnould, President of the Comité d'Entente des Anciens Combattants; Jean-Marie Demarquet, former deputy (Poujadist); Fernand Feral, member of the Mouvement d'Assistance et de Protection; Jean Gardes, Army colonel, former chief of the Algiers Psychological Action Services (SAPI); Bernard Lefèvre, doctor and corporatist theoretician; Pierre Michaux, Professor of Medicine of the Faculty of Algiers; Jean-Claude Perez, doctor and member of the executive committee of the FNF; Jean-Marie Sanne, member of the executive committee of the FNF; Victor Sapin-Lignières, reserve major, President of the Interfédération des UT; Serge Jourdes, reserve lieutenant of the UT; Marcel Rambert, reserve lieutenant of the UT; Alain Le Moyne de Sérigny, publisher of the newspaper *l'Echo d'Alger*.

[3] Joseph Ortiz, café proprietor, President of the FNF, and acknowledged leader of the January 24 uprising (charged with complicity in assassination); Robert Martel, agriculturist, president of the MP 13 (Mouvement Populaire du 13 Mai); Jean Meningaud, lawyer, member of the Mouvement Nationaliste Etudiant, and spokesman for the Ortiz group; Jacques Laquière, lawyer, member of the executive committee of the FNF.

tember 1958, the legislative elections, and a series of trips and speeches in metropolitan France, it became evident that the heady policies shouted *ad nauseam* in the Algiers Forum in May and proclaimed incessantly by all the grand tenors of the uprising would be gradually modified beyond recognition. Then began what Jacques Soustelle was to call the "degradation," the shading off of the doctrines of May 13 into something that no Fourth Republic government could ever have attempted. Swiftly the euphoria of *la révolution par la loi* vanished from the *métropole* to be replaced by serious popular concern about ending the war and limiting the damage. General de Gaulle was anxious to bring his Army ("the finest since Napoleon") home to use as a lever in his ambitions for European leadership; he was not convinced of the elements of *grandeur* involved in smashing the *katibas* of the FLN, or in the primacy of subversive war.

Furthermore, through his farsighted series of actions in 1959, he had converted the former French colonies of Black Africa into a Community, beside which any trace of an "Algérie de papa" was an anomaly. Finally, international and UN pressure was disagreeable, and it limited France's range of action in other spheres. Consequently, with great deftness and, to be sure, ambiguity, he began to turn his Algerian policy along lines calculated to anguish and infuriate the colonial population and its allies. This evolution culminated in his offer of "self-determination" to Algeria on September 16, 1959, an event that failed to provoke an uprising in Algiers only because the plans miscarried.[4]

At the most refined level of national grand strategy, there have been essentially two schools of thought in France. The first of these, to which we could give the title "neo-Carolingian," believed that the nation's manifest destiny dwells in her continental European mission. At the maximum this bore all the implications of French *grandeur;* at the minimum it meant leadership in the "little Europe" movement.

The other approach would not be mistakenly titled the "neo-Roman." Just as the first perspective represented the logical historical heritage of the Frankish empire with its eastward opening, the second looked to both sides of the Mediterranean basin and beyond, to a "Eurafrican" sphere of action, reproducing a part of the experience of historical

---

[4] See the evidence presented by Serge and Merry Bromberger *et al., Barricades et Colonels* (Paris, 1960), pp. 37–60. The withdrawal of nine deputies from the UNR (Union pour la Nouvelle République) was supposed to be the match to light the fuse. In this case, Paris was more precipitous than Algiers, and the plan ("Véronique") miscarried through refusal of Army participation. This date also marks the beginning of the phenomenal rise of Joseph Ortiz.

Rome. This implied close entente between France and the Maghreb, whether through outright possession or through association. It also visualized closer ties with Spain and Italy.

It would be wrong to attach either point of view to a right-wing, left-wing political mechanism, for a conservative or a Jacobin might find himself at home in either camp.[5] But the evolution of the Algerian conflict ordained that the sentiments of the Right would outweigh those of the Left in the neo-Roman camp, just as General de Gaulle's personal reading of history sufficed to give his regime a neo-Carolingian inflection.[6]

General de Gaulle had announced to the nation on September 16, 1959, that self-determination for the Algerians was the only method worthy for France to follow. He stated, however, that this referendum could not be organized until either the Army's pacification had eliminated the military strength of the FLN or a cease-fire had created conditions for the return to peace. He suggested three possibilities: total *independence,* in which case France would sorrowfully wash its hands of the former territory; close *association* with France, obviously in the sort of arrangement he had previously envisaged for the French Community; or *Francization,* that is, assimilation or integration to the culture and politics of the colonial country — the Soustellian conception.

The implication was that the President of France strongly favored the second alternative. However, he refused to commit himself positively, to give any clear directives to the Army or to Delouvrier, the civilian authority in Algiers, or to permit parties or personalities to organize for the eventual defense of any of the three propositions. Moreover, he could not be induced to indicate the form of the referendum in which these questions were to be posed.

Algiers before the Barricades

Thus a heavy pall of uncertainty hung over Algeria in the third quarter of 1959, despite the attempts of the Premier, Michel Debré, to reassure the high command that General de Gaulle certainly desired

[5] For example, François Mitterrand, partly as a result of his cabinet experience with French Union problems, might have been labeled a "neo-Roman" in 1954–1956. See his *Aux frontières de l'Union française* (Paris, 1956).

[6] Deserving of mention also is the "little France" tendency, perhaps best expressed in the mitigated Europeanism and internationalism of Pierre Mendès-France. It would, however, be difficult to find any consistent proponent of the "little France" position. The names of Antoine Pinay and Raymond Aron come to mind, in different ways, as partakers of the tendency.

the maintenance of the French presence. The justice of this malaise must, however, be balanced against the allegations of immediate plot, which are not without substance.

There is some evidence of an evolution in Army thinking on the Algerian problem between the time of May 13, 1958, and the "self-determination" speech,[7] but it was perhaps due principally to a willingness on the part of previously neutral or inarticulate elements to express themselves on the liberal side of the question. At any rate, de Gaulle had been forced to give serious reassurances to the Army following the repercussions of the "peace of the brave" remarks of October 23, 1958. The Army's "liberalism" was more pragmatic and social than political; dynamic social improvements for the Muslims were often favored, not just for their own sake, but as a rational instrument for winning the conflict.

The Europeans of Algeria, on the other hand, formed an almost consistently united front in support of their patrimony from the earliest days of the rebellion. This solidarity was reinforced, as we have seen earlier, by the paramilitary habit that culminated in the formation of the Unités Territoriales (Home Guard) in 1956, following in the wake of mass terrorism by the FLN. In the urban centers practically all the UT's were European, but, especially after the launching of the slogan of integration, some Muslim units were formed in the countryside. The UT's were regularized by decree as adjuncts of the regular Army, depending on the command of the relevant military sector, and in some cases served in formal military operations. There was an unmistakable tendency, however, as government policy and the desires of the settler population drew further apart, for these forces to form a potential nucleus of the "counterrevolution" and to become subservient to the orders and propaganda of the activist leaders, a number of whom held positions of command in the UT's. The urban UT's of Algiers were in a particularly apt position to affect the evolution of a *coup d'état,* inasmuch as they were regularly employed for patrolling and security purposes or in accomplishing the tasks of the Psychological Warfare Branch (SAPI).[8]

Toward the end of 1959 many persons were simultaneously engaged

---

[7] The series of interviews with Army officers conducted informally in 1959–1960 by Claude Dufresnoy and collected under the title *Des officiers parlent* (Paris, 1961) is highly valuable as a symposium but cannot be regarded as a statistical reflection of military attitudes.

[8] Colonel Gardes, one of the defendants, was responsible in his capacity as chief of the SAPI to the Delegate-General, Paul Delouvrier, and to the military Commander in Chief, General Maurice Challe. The UT's were often used to put up posters with mottoes of psychological action directed toward both the Europeans and Muslims.

in the UT's and in the OPAS (Organisation Politique et d'Action Subversive), the paramilitary adjunct of Joseph Ortiz's FNF (Front National Français), whose emblem was the Celtic cross, borrowed from the officially outlawed Fascist group, the Jeune Nation. Moreover, it is certain that Ortiz's action had the tacit consent of General Jacques Massu, the superprefect of the Algiers department and commander of the local Army corps.

The rebels had essentially two problems in working through the UT's. One was the simple matter of obtaining weapons by way of sympathetic Army contacts; as we have already seen, only one tenth of the auxiliaries were susceptible to bearing arms on any given day. The second was the principle of organization. As originally constituted, the UT's were directly linked to the Army command in their sector and had no formal hierarchy of their own. In such a situation, the task of commanding them for subversive action was insurmountable. A providential solution appeared, under the benevolent auspices of Colonel Jean Gardes of the *cinquième bureau,* when, after lengthy negotiation and argument, the separate UT's were brought together in an "interfederation" under a single president in late 1959. The Army thought by this measure to ensure better control of its semimilitary auxiliaries in dealing directly with a single center of authority. As Colonel Godard was later to testify in support of Gardes:

> He was chief of the *cinquième bureau,* responsible to the Delegate-General and the Commander-in-Chief. In doing his job, he was led to assume contact with all the groups, the activists included. His orders were to set up an organization of UT's and self-defense so as to group together those of the two communities engaged in the struggle against the rebellion. Thus it was possible to orient opinion along lines that the military command favored.[9]

The man chosen for this delicate position was no stranger to military or subversive activity. He was Victor Sapin-Lignières, who had made no secret of his right-wing opinions and had personally organized and commanded the mixed Franco-Muslim UT of the Casbah of Algiers with great distinction. However, he swiftly lost control of the destinies of the Interfédération. His secretary-general, conveniently, was Captain Marcel Ronda, chief of the semiclandestine OPAS of Joseph Ortiz. After September 16, 1959, Ortiz moved swiftly to capture Sapin's Interfédération through his adjutant, with the result that the offices of the two organizations became merged. Sapin-Lignières denied complicity in this operation, but in view of his background and military experience it seems inconceivable that he could not have been a willing party. Covered by the sanction of military orders for most of the tragic

[9] *Trial,* December 15, 1960.

week of the barricades, Sapin carefully defended all prior activities that might have linked him to the fusillade of January 24: "It wasn't necessary for me to intervene [in the manifestation] as President of the Federation. . . . Generals Crépin and Gracieux left me a very wide berth." [10]

Still there remained the question on which would depend the success or failure of the rebels' operation: will the Army march with us? As on May 13, 1958, the plotters hoped that the *fait accompli* of an insurrectional movement would thrust the Army into a position of unambiguous choice, and that they would respond as before. On the other hand, certain high-placed officers clearly anticipated the occasion when the military forces might be led to intervene politically in order to forestall the government's action, and they wished to have tight control over the activist groups through a single liaison to prevent them from running amok. The burden of this liaison fell on the willing shoulders of Colonel Jean Gardes, General Challe's chief of Psychological Warfare. After the "self-determination" speech, Joseph Ortiz (in the words of Jean-Jacques Susini, "the man with the best political sense, a man of good sense, a realist, careful about staying in touch with the Army") [11] became the chosen civilian instrument of General Massu. Ortiz, on his part, promised Massu "to do nothing without the Army."

The Front National Français

This was to be a drama of Algiers city and not of the territory as a whole: a distinction of considerable importance. The elements of the

---

[10] General Crépin arrived from the Moroccan-border zone of Algeria as Massu's replacement as head of the departmental *corps d'Armée,* and functioned as such during the insurrection. According to Bromberger, "un taciturne, inventeur, et Compagnon de la Libération," he has been described as a Gaullist and loyalist, and his actions confirm this portrait as well as the intimations of his testimony given *à huis clos* during the "trial of the barricades." Crépin was later promoted and became Challe's successor as Supreme Commander, serving in this capacity until after the referendum of January 6, 1961. There are rumors that he quarreled with General de Gaulle over the character of the Army's participation in the second referendum. As a commander in Germany, he was staunchly loyalist in April 1961.

General Gracieux commanded the 10th Parachute Division (formerly Massu's and considered most *ultra*) during the week of the barricades. "Un Vendéen massif et fort courtois, comme le suggère son nom." Although he gave no active support to the Ortiz camarilla, his feelings went toward the insurrectionists out of sympathy for *Algérie française* and because of the more overpowering political attitudes of his staff. He was shortly afterward transferred out of Algeria and made Inspector-General of Airborne Forces.

[11] *Trial,* November 20–21, 1960.

Army sympathetic to the insurrection or at least unwilling to intervene to squelch it were fighting for a doctrine of war and for the honor of an eventual triumph in Algeria, in addition to their loyalty to the Europeans and desire to avoid bloodshed.[12] One sometimes even gets the impression that if this triumph could have been achieved, especially through the application of the doctrines of *la guerre révolutionnaire,* many of the most rabid colonels might not have worried much about the future political disposition of the country. On the other hand, many were most deeply involved for other reasons. Social justice and the vision of French "generosity" were more than mere abstraction. Countless officers gave freely of their spare time to assist in educational and charitable work. General Massu and his wife themselves adopted two Muslim orphans. The motives were mixed and various, often highly confused, often extraordinarily honorable.

The great majority of settlers were not Fascists of the Ortiz stripe, but their obsession with the fear of negotiations and the relinquishment of sovereignty often made them willing to support any political leader who promised deliverance. A typical, intelligent, and by no means unattractive, example of the settler reflex was Auguste Arnould, one of the defendants of the *procès des barricades.* He was not a subversive, but a leading war veteran and, in the opinion of observers at the trial, a *bonhomme* whose honesty and propriety could scarcely be placed in doubt. Arnould testified:

I can only tell you that what we said we did. For I no longer know what I said or did, or what my friends said or did. They all should be here. The situation was tense: assassinations, bombings, knifings. . . . I have the right to talk about it as a man with feelings without your calling me "political." Our future, our life. The manifestation of January 24 was on everybody's brain.

We'd seen others, even in Paris. A manifestation in Algiers? You want to know what that is? Put a loudspeaker-phonograph on a little car, drive through Algiers with a flag, playing *Algérie française.* You reach the Forum with a hundred thousand people behind you.[13]

But there were all sorts involved in the episode. Together with Arnould in the defendant's box sat the hotheaded Susini, who could say of his activities as early as 1957: "Already I kept saying that it wasn't a riot but a war starting, and that France would lose it if the state wasn't given the necessary means of action."[14]

---

[12] Relations seem not to have been so congenial in other cities and in the large towns, especially the heavily Muslim centers of Constantine and Bône. See Jules Roy, *The Algerian War* (English translation, New York, 1961), pp. 76–92.

[13] *Trial,* November 9, 1960.

[14] *Ibid.,* November 20–21, 1960.

One could indeed speak of an "Algerian intoxication," which many observers have noted. Almost without any conscious planning, the Algerian emotional perspective had been tortuously transformed into a creed. As the Brombergers have written, rather dramatically but not inappropriately, "In a boiler heated red-hot a pail of water does not put out the blaze. It unleashes the explosion, a spitting blast of fire. The pail of water hurled on Algiers was the recall of Massu." [15]

Massu, it will be remembered, had sanctioned the activity of Ortiz, the "tough" café owner with "good political sense," and had extracted his promise that he would take no action without the consent of the Army command. Ortiz himself was clever enough to recognize that he stood little chance without the Army. Massu has reported their relationship in the following oblique words: "The FNF represented an important structure for me, so I made use of it. It carried out missions. For example, Ortiz took care of the police work at the Saint-Eugène stadium. I didn't want to have to use soldiers, and they hadn't given me enough CRS [security guards] to go around." [16] With Massu gone, Ortiz could argue that he was relieved of his promise. Still, he obviously hoped and expected to have the Army with him when he launched the manifestation on January 24. In any case, despite discouraging reports from his friend General Faure, he feared that his men would take action by themselves if he did not order the launching of the demonstration.

At the time of Massu's recall, the membership of the FNF had swollen to an estimated 13,500 men.[17] In this number were, of course, many civil police and UT's who had some access to weapons. The evolution of the FNF and its military branch, the OPAS, is interestingly traced in the testimony of Robert Aublet, former chief of General Intelligence in Algiers. He may be regarded as a hostile, but not unobjective, witness. His statement is worth quoting at considerable length:

From the end of 1959 there was an intense fever in the FNF. People were recruited in all the cafés, of which there are a lot. So far the conversations ran only along the lines of eliminating all members of the administration who weren't strictly "integrationist." It's here we first catch sight of Dr. Perez, soon joined by young Susini. They held several meetings a day. These

---

[15] Brombergers, *op. cit.,* p. 8. According to reliable sources, General Ely had been informed from Algiers that the activists were plotting an uprising and that one of the possible triggers for mass action would be the departure of Massu. Ely is further alleged to have informed the government in this sense.

[16] *Trial,* December 18–19, 1960.

[17] See André Euloge and Antoine Moulinier, *L'Envers des barricades* (Paris, 1960), p. 12.

meetings were private, but you could still get in. From Bab-El-Oued they went to work on the Belfort district.[18]

There the meetings were shut tighter and [were] more clandestine. The cars parked quite far from the place of assembly, and people approached by slinking along the walls. A password was needed to get in. Lookouts were organized outside, sometimes by women. When it was over, the audience left in small groups spaced at three-minute intervals. Next, the propaganda reached the center of the city, finally spreading to El-Biar, Hussein-Dey, and the last neighborhood, Saint-Eugène, also organized by Dr. Perez. . . .

[The OPAS] was a shock organization formed of groups of ten men, four of which made a unit or sector-unit. The units were unevenly distributed: 45 in the northern quarters, 20 in the center, 30 in the southern. The uniform was a khaki shirt with an Army belt and shoulder strap. The chiefs wore an armband with the letters FNF or a Celtic cross. You could get into a shock group only after being investigated.

As for the mass of members, they were principally persons of the poorer classes, railway workers, small merchants, dock workers. However, attempts were made to enlist the liberal professions. Thus you could count seven doctors and twelve lawyers. On the other hand, there were virtually no farmers. The MP 13 [Mouvement Populaire du 13 Mai] had the monopoly here, and its position had not been shaken. I'm compelled to say in all loyalty that the great mass of these militants were waiting for a positive and definite statement confirming their future as Frenchmen on Algerian soil.

Now let's look at the goals. From October 1959 on, it seemed to me that the FNF orchestra was playing out of tune. We had contacts with the top and bottom of the hierarchy. At the top we knew what the leaders were thinking by what they said at the meetings. At the bottom we had agents, inspectors, who, themselves being *Algérois,* obtained confidences from the little people of Bab-El-Oued. At the top the dominant theme was the defense of French Algeria.

To do this, they wanted to make of the Europeans what the FLN had made of the Muslims. They had to arrange the revolution before a cease-fire.

The form of this revolution? It wasn't precise. The idea was that the regime would tremble when fifteen thousand people went into the street to demonstrate. That wasn't too serious. But there was already talk of hanging traitors, which was more disturbing, and of sweeping out all the politicians inherited from the previous regime. The base [of the movement] was more explosive. These people were very wrought up, talking of rubbing out certain persons, purely and simply, of pillaging and setting fire to the shops that didn't co-operate with the strike. You heard talk of killing on the spot whatever elected officials might refuse to take their place at the head of a procession. And then, more seriously, you heard talk of a "ratonnade." [19] The leaders of the FNF themselves grew disturbed. Ortiz even stated that he didn't know what his troops would do. I even received one of the chiefs

[18] Bab-El-Oued and Belfort were popular quarters of Algiers with a mixed Muslim and *petit blanc* population.

[19] *Ratonnade* comes from raton, a slang word for Muslim; hence it means "a generalized mob action by the Europeans against the Muslims."

of the movement who went as far as to tell me: "We will apply the death penalty to those who take it out on the Muslims." [20]

By the turn of 1960, Joseph Ortiz had succeeded in capturing the torch of activism from other militant subversive groups. The Army's attempt to control the FNF and other factions through a liaison committee of "mouvements nationaux" merely served as a convenient front for the former and a means of implicating the high command in the actions it contemplated. Ortiz's only serious competition, at least until Pierre Lagaillarde precipitously reappeared on the scene, was Robert Martel's MP 13, whose clientele was limited mainly to the farmers of the Mitidja. Martel had spread tracts denouncing Ortiz as a government double-agent, but the two men would find themselves seated at the same table in a private room of the Sept Merveilles restaurant when serious action was discussed on the night of January 23.

As the Brombergers have convincingly shown, there was no plot scheduled in advance for January 24, an arbitrary fact that would give the defendants considerable leeway in the military courtroom when they were brought to trial the following November. "Operation Véronique" had misfired the previous October owing to bad timing and the reluctance of the Army; another *coup d'état* was provisionally established for April, when de Gaulle would be traveling abroad, in the United States. But if January 24 was not a meticulously planned operation or a clear case of premeditated treason, it was unleashed by some very positive causes. The most significant of these was, of course, the recall of General Massu, whom the Europeans looked on as "the last general of May 13" and whose dynamism and authority stamped him as the guarantor of *Algérie française* as long as he should command.[21] Three other incidents, however, deserve mention.

Causes of the Rebellion

The first cause was the recrudescence of FLN terrorism among the farms of the Mitidja plain, at the very gates of Algiers itself, toward the end of 1959. General Challe's *katiba*-smashing had taken an exceedingly heavy toll on the interior organization of the Algerian liberation forces, which reverted to isolated bombings and assassinations, thereby giving reason to the theorists of *la guerre révolutionnaire*. Not only were the new atrocities horrible in content, but they led to increased

[20] *Trial*, December 14, 1960.

[21] Cf. Alain de Sérigny's remark, *Trial*, November 25, 1960: "For us, he [Massu] was the symbol of the struggle against terrorism in Algiers; he was also the symbol of *Algérie française*. . . ."

pressure on the Minister-Delegate, Paul Delouvrier, by the farmers for the unlimited right to bear arms, a policy the authorities could not admit. Furthermore, it was personally embarrassing and disheartening to Massu, a convert to the doctrines of subversive war, to have such events taking place within his administrative territory, his *igamie*. Mob action by the farmers, spurred on by Robert Martel, could be foreseen.

The second cause was the refusal of the government and Delouvrier to allow Georges Bidault, leader of the Démocratie Chrétienne and former head of government, to give a series of speeches in Algeria in the month of January. Bidault, who had already visited Algeria in December, had ambitions of extending his political action to a Muslim clientele, and he had obtained the prior blessings of General Massu. But Delouvrier issued an order banning Bidault from Algerian territory between the dates of January 12 and 22, 1960, an act that disappointed Massu and raised the general tension considerably. The reason was, of course, that General de Gaulle had refused permission to the politicians to agitate for the position of integration in the forthcoming "self-determination" referendum.

Finally, there was the interview, variously reported (for there is no authorized version), that de Gaulle held with the Algerian deputies Portolano, Lauriol, and Larradji on the same day as Massu's explosive conversation with the German journalist Kempski. At this time the Head of State is alleged to have told the deputies that he foresaw regulation of the Algerian question only through negotiations with the FLN and the partition of the country.[22] Upon the return of the three parliamentarians to Algiers, where the fever was already mounting as a result of the Massu incident, the story went through different versions and was printed for all to see both in Alain de Sérigny's *Echo d'Alger,* in the form of an editorial, and in the rival *Dépêche Quotidienne.*

Already, the Rubicon had been crossed as a result of Massu's extraordinary half-hour with Kempski, the reporter for the *Süddeutsche Zeitung* and former paratrooper. This incident is too well known to bear lengthy repetition. Massu, noted for his plain speech, had studiously avoided journalists during most of his regency in Algiers. He appears to have received Kempski only at the request of Delouvrier and, finding the reporter sympathetic, to have unburdened his political soul in front of him. Among the statements attributed to Massu were the following: "We no longer understand de Gaulle's policy. . . . If he has one, it surely isn't ours. . . . [On May 13] he was the only man at our disposal. But maybe the Army made a mistake. . . . The Army

[22] Brombergers, *op. cit.,* pp. 119–121.

has the strength. It hasn't shown it up to now. The occasion hasn't come up, but in a certain situation the Army would establish its power."[23] The "loyal Massu," disciplined general and Gaullist, had finally succumbed to the "Algerian intoxication." It had taken three years. Long after the repercussions of this incident, Massu apparently remained convinced that Kempski's visit was part of a plot in which the government had trapped him to force his recall. "Je me suis fait pigeonner" meant not only that he had been foolish but that he had been made the plaything of diabolical forces, conceivably the plotting of Guillaumat, or the Elysée itself.[24]

Although, according to the Brombergers, Guillaumat had once sought Massu's transfer — blocked by the agonized objections of General Challe, who foresaw an uprising on his hands — he rallied now to the support of a solution that would keep Massu in place. There would later be a formal denial of the interview by Massu and a few concessions by the government to the Army in Algeria, principally in the sphere of eschewing direct negotiations with the FLN. But de Gaulle was unsatisfied with Massu's mitigating statement and refused absolutely at this time, with respect to self-determination, to declare his support for the "solution la plus française." Insubordination had reared its ugly head, and Massu could not be sent back without giving the impression of a government capitulation. "Je vous garde," de Gaulle told the Cyranesque paratrooper at a fiery meeting in which Massu, still within the bounds of discipline, said a few things that could not have pleased the President of the Republic. Interventions by both Guillaumat and General Challe were to no avail. Massu could scarcely believe that the government had dared relieve him of his command, into which the loyal General Crépin ("a safe man") was about to step. Crépin, an old friend of Massu and fellow wartime graduate of the 2nd Armored Division, was not a disciple of *la guerre subversive,* although a veteran of the Orient. The dangerous interregnum between commanders in Algiers was assured by the activist General Faure, who had been placed under fortress arrest for his complicity in a Poujadist plot in 1956; but this time Faure, who, like Massu, had genuine traits of Gaullism beneath his seething discontent, showed little inclination to take up arms against the state.

[23] *Ibid.,* pp. 34–35, translating from the Kempski article.

[24] It was a fashionable theory that Kempski had been planted in Algiers by the connivance of Guillaumat and the French Foreign Ministry to lure Massu into an irretrievable trap. Colonel Gardes would declare (*Trial,* November 10, 1960): "I can state almost without reserve that the expenses of the trip and the hotel bills of Kempski were paid by the Delegation-General on the orders of the Ministry of Foreign Affairs." But, clearly, Massu walked into his own trap, if trap there was. Nevertheless, certain tantalizing mysteries shroud the Kempski visit.

The generals and many of the government's civilian counselors saw Algeria as a single grave problem perilously exacerbated by de Gaulle's stubborn refusal to reassure the Army with the concessions it wanted (a declaration in favor of integration and support of the Army's right to exact summary justice on the FLN and to control the self-determination referendum). De Gaulle, however, saw Algeria as a mere piece in the vast puzzle of French policy and international interests. Hindsight must grant that his conduct of affairs in the last week of January 1960 was characterized by very few false moves. This was either the point of change or the point of no return: since February 1956, French policy had, in a real sense, been dictated from Algiers rather than Paris. It was now time to turn the tables, as de Gaulle perceived, or they might never be turned.

Lagaillarde Enters Spontaneously

A final, at first almost extraneous, factor must be related in setting the scene for the drama of the barricades. This concerns the role of the Algerian deputy Pierre Lagaillarde, who had stormed and taken the Governor-General's palace almost single-handed on May 13, 1958, forestalling for a time the carefully conceived Gaullist coup of Léon Delbecque.

After his operatic exploits, Lagaillarde chose to be elected a deputy, and set off for the Palais Bourbon announcing that he would resign within a year if integration were not proclaimed. The year passed without integration and without resignation. Cut off from his popular and activist contacts in Algiers, Lagaillarde's local strength waned. The *ultras* rumored that he had been bought off by his parliamentary salary. When Lagaillarde returned to Algiers shortly in advance of the insurrection, he could count on perhaps only twenty or thirty followers. The student movement belonged to Susini, and the entire mechanism of uprising was in the possession of Ortiz, with whom, for personal, political, and temperamental reasons, Pierre was on the outs.

Innate qualities of leadership and military dispatch that contrasted favorably with the miasmal atmosphere of alcohol, stale tobacco, and indiscipline hanging over Ortiz's command post during the week of the insurrection were to win many loyalties for Lagaillarde, many recruits for his "fortified camp" (*camp retranché*) in the Algiers Faculties, and the good will and sympathy of large segments of the Army. Lagaillarde, unlike Ortiz, was a "good soldier," a man whom the regular forces could admire. He was not a Fascist, but merely a heated devotee of *Algérie française;* he could never have been accused of saying, "Tomorrow I will take power in Paris." In short, he complicated the task of settlement immeasurably, whether it was to be achieved by negotiation or assault.

Later, at the trial, Lagaillarde made the following rather telling points in his own defense: "A successful plot [he told the Court, comparing his action with that of May 13, 1958] is a return to legitimacy, but an impassioned protest that fails is transformed into a frightful plot." The defense, of course, made every effort to portray the insurrectional activities of January as a spontaneous angry reflex and not as a contrived operation. Lagaillarde went on to say: "We were conscious of having the agreement of the military. I had even been told of three telephone calls from Paris and that General Massu himself was in favor of a calm, orderly manifestation." [25] In effect, there had been three calls to Colonel Argoud:[26] one from Madame Massu and two from the General, the first recommending calm and the second directing Argoud to act according to his own judgment. The interpretations placed on these calls by the activists were undoubtedly excessive.

Both Lagaillarde and Ortiz manifestly counted on the support of the Army. They (and especially Ortiz) were familiar with the military milieu and, through Colonel Gardes at least, with the emotional map of the officer corps in the Algiers sector. Thus it might legitimately be asked why the Army, which was permeated with activists, partisans of *la guerre subversive,* "pieds noirs," and sympathizers of *Algérie française,* did not take decisive action on the rebels' behalf. The whole matter is critical, for here indeed is the hinge of fate that might have determined the destiny of the French state for a long time to come.

The Posture of the Army

Actually, the moderation and ambiguity practiced by General Challe at the outset and by his subordinates Gracieux and Argoud when his orders were no longer followed, though they pleased nobody, probably permitted the situation to evolve with minimum damage, especially after the shock of the January 24 massacre of the Plateau des Glières. At that moment several factors prevented a pro-activist Army from positively taking sides:

[25] *Trial,* November 17, 1960.
[26] Colonel Antoine Argoud, Massu's supercompetent chief of staff and an apostle of *la guerre révolutionnaire,* described by his superior as "un colonel qui en avait." *Trial,* December 18–19, 1960.

1. A desire to wait it out until the terms of General de Gaulle's speech, previously announced for January 29, were known.

2. A flickering jealousy toward Massu on the part of some of the other general officers who might otherwise be styled *ultras.* These commanders did not want to fight the battle of *Algérie française* over the issue of Massu's dismissal.

3. A widespread distrust of Ortiz, his manner, and his political professions.

4. The favorable nature of two capital concessions that General de Gaulle had granted the Army at the urging of Challe and Delouvrier after the sacking of Massu. These were: (*a*) a speedier means of bringing FLN terrorists and spies to summary justice; and (*b*) assurance that no direct negotiations would be undertaken with the FLN. The Army had been seeking these guarantees for a long time, and attached great importance to them. It is possible that this act alone forestalled Army complicity in the insurrection.

5. An agonized fear of precipitously dividing the Army against itself, the most formidable specter that had haunted the military forces since the days of Vichy. The "activists" had many supporters east of the Rhine and in the *métropole,* most of whom had seen Algerian service, but they were not ready or able to move. In Algeria itself many officers, such as Generals Olié and Gambiez, the corps commanders of the Algerian left and right flanks, were resolutely determined to defend the government.

6. Profound shock in Challe's headquarters at the news of the fusillade and the conviction (afterward substantially verified) that the insurgents had opened fire on Lieutenant Colonel Debrosse's *gendarmerie mobile,* which had advanced on the barricades with unloaded weapons carried in the regulation manner.

7. The failure of the insurrection at the outset to capture any significant government buildings or the transmitter of Radio Algiers, thereby providing a voice for their operations and facing Delouvrier with a difficult *fait accompli,* as on May 13, 1958, when a reluctant Massu had been compelled to form the Committee of Public Safety. Delouvrier made sure that these vital centers were protected by reliable troops, gendarmes, and CRS. In the interests of preventing further bloodshed, even paratroop Colonels Argoud, Dufour, and Broizat were unwilling to give the rebels *carte blanche* to occupy or assault any of these points.

The net result was that the Army imposed an uneasy and paradoxical *modus vivendi* on both the government and the insurrection for several days. This immobility, tempered by a good many afterthoughts, brought the rebellion slowly to its knees. Perhaps the most amazing thing about the rebellion of January 24 is that, in a large city of friendly partisans controlled by a sympathetic Army, it failed. This was to have immense implications for the future confidence of government policy in Algeria and goes far toward explaining the swift capitulation of the military-inspired insurrection of April 1961.

Events of the Rebellion

The chronological episodes of the "week of the barricades" are described briefly below:[27]

January 19: Massu's interview with Kempski. De Gaulle receives the three Algerian deputies.

January 20: Massu recalled to Paris. Fear in Algiers of his displacement. The "activists" know they must strike before a new commander and staff are in position.

January 21: De Sérigny's editorial in *Echo d'Alger,* "Se ressaisir," recounting de Gaulle's alleged remarks to the deputies. Rising tension and uncertainty.

January 22: Challe and Delouvrier fly to Paris for conferences. De Gaulle rejects all pleas to return Massu to Algiers. In Algiers, Lagaillarde seeks an agreement with Ortiz. The activists anticipate trouble; Challe's headquarters is deeply divided as to what countermeasures might be taken. Late in the evening Crépin arrives to assume Massu's command.

January 23: Ortiz, acting through the UT's, contemplates a general strike in Algiers with a demonstration. The *noyautage* of the UT's by the FNF is apparent. Ortiz meets with Colonel Argoud, who refuses Army support and insists on the value of the concessions Challe has brought back from Paris. Colonel Gardes is an active intermediary with the leaders of the *ultras.* Delouvrier addresses the city on the radio, asking for calm.

The 10th Parachute Division is recalled to Algiers from operations in Kabylie to preserve order; this represents a compromise, for the 10th Parachute Division is known to be largely pro-activist and immensely popular with the civilians. Two regiments (the 1st Foreign Legion Parachute Regiment, commanded by Colonel Dufour, and the 1st Colonial Parachute Regiment, commanded by Colonel Broizat) are known to be particularly sympathetic to the activists, as is Colonel Meyer, General Gracieux's chief of staff. On their subsequent arrival, the parachute regiments will be detached from the direct command of Gracieux and placed

---

[27] The events of this chronological section are established by cross-checking the trial testimony against the recapitulation of two works, previously cited, *Barricades et Colonels* and *L'Envers des barricades,* the two most reliable books on the subject. The author disclaims intentional responsibility for political judgments that later evidence may show to be in error.

under the orders of Colonel Fonde, a Loyalist and the subordinate of General Coste, who is responsible for the maintenance of order in the Algiers-Sahel sector. Liaison attempts between the regular and temporary commands will be unsatisfactory, and the regimental commanders will resent the new hierarchical structure. This rancor will have one particularly grievous consequence: the malco-ordination of the next day's attempt to clear the barricades, resulting in the mortal exchange of fire on the Plateau des Glières.

At the restaurant Sept Merveilles, Ortiz and his lieutenants plan the demonstration and strike for the next morning. Lagaillarde is determined to forestall them by occupying the Faculties first, and decides to take action in the middle of the night with a handful of about thirty men. The Faculties is in a strategic position for interception and extremely difficult to reduce by assault.

January 24: In the night of January 23–24, innumerable UT's that are on duty leave their service, taking their weapons with them. Lagaillarde is installed in the Faculties with weapons and ammunition seized from a casern. Miscellaneous UT's arrive to join his "fortified camp."

From seven in the morning on, the UT's circulate, spreading the news of the demonstration and general strike. Ortiz goes to install his headquarters in the offices of the Interfederation of the UT's, which is at the corner of the Rue Charles Péguy and the Boulevard Laferrière, overlooking the Plateau des Glières, where the afternoon's carnage will take place. The building has a balcony with microphones, from which various orators — especially Meningaud — will address the crowds. Colonel Gardes and his adjutant Captain Filippi will be seen on this balcony in the company of the leaders of the insurrection.

Propaganda is distributed throughout the city. There is still hope that the Army will join the activists and take matters into its hands, as on May 13, 1958. The demonstration before the Central Post Office is scheduled for 11 A.M. There are plans to occupy the key public buildings, which, however, Colonel Fonde will take special pains to protect.

The regular troops take up positions to control the demonstration. It is ardent, but much reduced in size from the crowds of May 13. Ortiz, from his balcony, requests that the demonstrators remain; however, toward the end of the day they begin to disperse somewhat. Ortiz negotiates with the high command, which sets a moratorium on the demonstration. Ortiz denies that he has the power to make it evaporate. In point of fact there are by this time a horde of UT's roaming central Algiers who do not seem to be under anyone's orders in particular. Lagaillarde's camp is calm, disciplined, and determined not to cede. There is bad blood between the two chiefs.

At the beginning of the afternoon, young demonstrators commence to build barricades with parked cars, paving stones, and other materials. This causes the fever of the occasion to mount considerably. Challe's command, seeing that the demonstrators will not disperse, makes plans to return the city to order. A three-pronged movement of troops converging slowly on the Plateau des Glières will brush the demonstrators aside. Colonel Fonde commands the operation. His forces will be the pro-activist regiments of Colonels Dufour and Broizat, and the loyalist *gendarmerie mobile* of Lieutenant Colonel Debrosse. The latter is given the frontal part of the operation, that of disengaging the crowd from the whole length of the Boulevard Laferrière. Verbal orders for the action are transmitted to Debrosse by Fonde and General Coste at 5 P.M. It will be H-hour at 6 P.M.

Malco-ordination between the three advancing units will produce the consequence that the *gendarmerie* arrives alone at the point of convergence on the Boulevard Laferrière. The parachute colonels will later claim that orders were transmitted ambiguously and that they were retarded by impediments along the course of the march, such as the barricades at Lagaillarde's Faculties. Dufour's regiment (the first to appear) will not, in fact, arrive until after the fusillade has burst out and will be instrumental in achieving a cease-fire. In the aftermath of the tragedy and at the trial, all three operational commanders will vigorously defend the justice of their position. However, it will be pointed out that Fonde's action — qualified as literal murder by Dufour and Broizat — has been commended by his superior officers, Coste, Crépin, and Challe.

At exactly 6 P.M. the *gendarmerie mobile* appears before the barricades of the Boulevard Laferrière, at the intersection of the Avenue Pasteur. From this point on, the testimony regarding the fusillade — which occupied a considerable portion of the "trial of the barricades" — is confused. It is generally established, however, that Debrosse's troops were carrying their weapons in the regulation manner and that these weapons were not loaded. This latter point is verified by the fact that the *gendarmes* were inspected before they went into action. Further investigations of the cartridges recovered from the scene of the calamity and the missing ammunition from the magazines of the *gendarmerie* personnel seem to show that the "forces of order" fired in self-defense. The sequence seems to have been that the demonstrators (probably UT's) first opened fire, perhaps in response to or perhaps before the launching of tear-gas grenades by the gendarmes, who were trying to clear a path for their march. It is established that there was firing on the gendarmes from the buildings above; it is not absolutely certain that any of these shots came from Ortiz's command post in the *Compagnie Algérienne,* although this is strongly suspected. At least one automatic weapon was employed against Debrosse's forces, who did not put any into action; this accounted for a good deal of the carnage. The terrible scene — with short intervals of cease-fire — took place in the failing light of the winter evening (bizarrely, the street lamps came on in the middle) in front of the offices of *Le Bled,* and lasted approximately forty minutes. The casualties would later be set as 22 dead (8 demonstrators, 14 gendarmes) and 147 wounded (24 demonstrators or civilians, 123 soldiers, 70 of them from bullets).[28] At about 6:45 P.M. (forty-five minutes late for his rendezvous) the jeep of

---

[28] Brombergers, *op. cit.,* pp. 243–244.

Colonel Dufour, preceding his 1st Foreign Legion Parachute Regiment, arrived on the scene. The Colonel's presence made the cease-fire definite. With
the approach of his troops and, almost simultaneously, those of Colonel
Broizat, it is recorded that the demonstrators burst into spontaneous applause. There were harsh words and recriminations between the parachute
colonels and Debrosse.

The fusillade produces the following consequences:

1. The hardening of the insurrection and the intoxication of the population against the government in Paris and its representative in Algiers, Paul
Delouvrier.

2. An aura of martyrdom and the spread of the contagion of rebellion.
However, there is as yet no unity of action between Ortiz and Lagaillarde,
and there are countless UT's roaming the city, acting without orders. Furthermore, the forces of the insurrection have still been unable to seize any
key public buildings such as the post office, the radio station, or the
Governor-General's palace.

3. A fleeting hope among the forces of the insurrection that the Army
leadership, especially the *paras,* will come over to their side.

4. A realization on the part of the military high command that there is
nothing to do but temporize. Military obedience can be retained only
through virtual immobility. Massu's (now Crépin's) staff, together with the
higher officers of the 10th Parachute Division, are insistent that no action
be taken against the rebels and refuse to carry out such orders. General
Gracieux advises that street warfare might cost as many as 1000 lives.
Colonel Yves Godard, head of the Sûreté, demands the replacement of
Colonel Fonde,[29] an action that is later taken.

At 8 P.M. Challe issues a communiqué over Radio Algiers that says in
part:

> The riot will not triumph against the French Army. I am having
> regiments from the interior brought into Algiers. Order will be main-
> tained with the agreement of the Delegate-General of the government;
> I consider the city to be in a state of siege. Any gathering of more than
> three persons is forbidden. . . .[30]

Receiving the news in Paris, the authorities are resolved that the military
command should press on with the assault of the barricades. But Challe
knows that this will be a deadly business and that military obedience, in
any case, is hanging by a thread; he continues to temporize. Colonel Dufour
goes to interview Ortiz, who is confident and feeling his oats.

A *de facto* compromise is reached that satisfies the operational military
commanders (who are sympathetic to the activists) for the time being: no

---

[29] "I had nothing against him, but on the psychological plane I judged that Colonel
Fonde's personality was not the kind that could smooth things over." *Trial,* December 16,
1960.
[30] Quoted from Brombergers, *op. cit.,* p. 243.

orders will be given to the Army to reduce the barricades; no attempt by the insurgents to seize any public building will be countenanced. The matter rests. The troops of the 10th Parachute Division (many of whom have friendly or amorous connections in Algiers) fraternize freely with the rebels.

Virtually all communications are cut between Algiers and Paris. General Ely (military chief of staff) and his associates are anguished by the developments, which are threatening to break the Army in two. A certain alarm begins to spread in Paris. General de Gaulle remains cool and intransigent, and possibly somewhat misinformed.

January 25: Ortiz extends his power in Algiers. The city is paralyzed by the general strike, except for the essential services. The European population is clearly almost unanimously on the side of the activists. Although the Delegate-General possesses nominal authority, he is becoming a prisoner in a hostile place. The Army remains the arbiter of the situation; it has not yet taken any step to allow the insurgents to extend their territorial jurisdiction. The majority of influential officers are still hoping that the events of the day before and the intractable situation will cause de Gaulle to shift policies and declare for "la solution la plus française." General Gracieux (but really his subordinates Meyer, Dufour, Broizat) possesses supreme military power; General Challe is progressively losing his grip over the obedience of his forces.

Harangues to the crowd continue throughout the day from the balcony of Ortiz.

De Gaulle's associates, especially Debré, are nervous. But the *métropole* begins to rally massively to the President's support.

Various contacts take place between the rebels and military command and back and forth between Paris and Algiers. Late at night Premier Debré flies to Algiers to investigate the situation personally.

January 26: Debré pursues his conversations with the leading military chiefs, and makes a brief tour of the barricades. The generals he interviews are, with different nuances, in favor of allowing the dust to settle before any direct action is taken against the barricades. The colonels are less reserved, demanding a reversal of government policy with a declaration supporting *Algérie française,* and raising the threat of a camarilla. Debré flies back to Paris disheartened.

In Paris, de Gaulle has conversations with his military and civilian advisers and, despite the discouragement of some, resolves not to give an inch to the insurgents.

In Algiers, the rebels and the crowd are in a tense state of excitement awaiting the developments of the Debré visit and expecting concessions on the part of the government or, in default of that, direct Army intervention. The discrepancy between Lagaillarde's disciplined camp and Ortiz's sloppy headquarters is already evident to the military. The fraternization on the barricades continues unabated and unhindered. Sapin-Lignières, the president of the Interfederation of the UT's, is placed under the orders of the

Army and instructed to regroup his random troops and recall them to discipline — a halfhearted, if not hopeless, task. The most pro-activist Army officers decide that military intervention for the purpose of influencing de Gaulle's policy is useless unless, as on May 13, 1958, the Muslims can be made to rally to the insurrection. Some orders to this effect go out to the SAU of the Casbah, but the effort is almost without practical result; in any case, Ortiz and Lagaillarde are unenthusiastic. Delouvrier informs Debré of the possibility of a Muslim demonstration. "D'accord," says the latter, "à condition qu'ils crient 'Vive de Gaulle!' " Neither result is achieved.

January 27: This is the most dangerous point of the rebellion. The rebels either misconstrue their real strength or know that time is working against them. De Gaulle, after a personal exposé from General Crépin, who has flown to Paris, agrees to support him in a certain measure of "gradualism." Delouvrier and Challe are extremely worried, as they feel control of events slipping from their hands. The colonels put considerable pressure on Challe to declare for the aims of the insurgents. The rebels take heart at the indecision of the command, but in truth they are themselves losing steam because of their immobility in Algiers and their failure to rally any appreciable support elsewhere. Loyalist commanders have the situation fairly well under control in most of the other parts of Algeria, and loyalist troops are already on the move to relieve the 10th Parachute Division in Algiers.

Nevertheless, the local atmosphere is one of fatigue and nightmare. Delouvrier considers making some dramatic gesture; he weighs the alternatives of resignation, surrender, or withdrawal, and opts for the last.

January 28: Delouvrier and Challe, no more in command of the situation in Algiers city, where the fraternization continues and the people are hostile to the government, withdraw to Air Force (loyalist) headquarters at La Reghaia, leaving responsibility for order in the hands of General Gracieux. This withdrawal, combined with Delouvrier's impassioned and perplexing speech, delivered at 5 P.M., constitute a capital psychological act.[31] Delouvrier's words, which move and confuse all — including Paris, the activists, the Army command — create a situation of ambiguity that has the effect of robbing the insurgents of the initiative. The citation of a part of this extraordinary address will indicate its almost hysterically sincere tone:

> My brothers of Algiers, the fate of Algeria, the fate of France, the fate of the free world are at stake here. If you follow me, Algiers will once again have saved Algeria, and for the third time France, and — what glory! — perhaps Europe and Africa. Follow me, follow me, I beg you, lending your weight all at once to de Gaulle and France. And you, rescued from the complex of abandonment, you will no longer be afraid of a referendum. In the weeks to come, Algeria will be freely and incontrovertibly French. By rejecting de Gaulle you lose yourselves, you lose the Army and France, too. In backing de Gaulle, who

[31] This speech is reproduced in full in Brombergers, *op. cit.,* pp. 361–369, and all following excerpts from it are translated from this source.

asks only your voices, you save the Army and its unity, and you bring France to you. You also win the Algerian war and you go to kill the FLN who waits chuckling in the shadows. . . .

Small wonder that Paris is profoundly shocked at the strange concatenation of mystical loyalty and unorthodox placation from the tired mouth of Delouvrier, and that Roger Frey, the Minister of Information, forbids its retransmission over any of the national radio stations. As for the insurgents, they are both spellbound and disturbed; for no one can quite fathom the intention of the Delegate-General's sibylline remarks. On the one hand, he has appealed for massive support behind the President of the Republic; on the other, he has uttered the mysterious "Alcazar" passage, which causes immediate comment:

> . . . I address myself to you, first of all, Ortiz and Lagaillarde, and you, Sapin-Lignières, chief of the UT's, and all those who are shut up in the Faculties as at the Alcazar of Tóledo, ready to die — I cry to metropolitan France that I salute your courage, children of the fatherland. You see, Ortiz, Lagaillarde, Sapin-Lignières, and all the others, you will succeed, you will succeed tomorrow if you hear me out today.

At least one thing is certain: the effect of the speech is stunning and electric, hitting at the *Algérois,* as Bromberger puts it, "like a punch in the stomach." The response of the activists, far from being conciliatory, is even impudent; but the wind has been taken out of their sails. It is hereafter clear that they can count on no military support. The most intransigent colonels, like Broizat, envisage the return of Delouvrier for negotiations with the insurgents. The government in Paris is, of course, perplexed, but de Gaulle has already placed the authority for taking appropriate military measures in the hands of the trusted Crépin; solidarity against the insurrection swells in the *métropole.* The loyalists are ready to pass to the offensive.

January 29: Tentative negotiations ensue between the two rebel camps and the emissaries of General Gracieux. Colonel Bigeard from Saida interposes his services as an intermediary. But the real negotiations of the day are those taking place opaquely among the higher officers of different nuance. The idea now is to promote an end to the insurrection that will not be a capitulation. Compromise measures are envisaged that will commit the government more firmly to the doctrine of *Algérie française:* the government refuses such solutions, including the formula of Sapin-Lignières that would restrict the referendum to a choice between integration and independence, eliminating de Gaulle's preferred policy of "association." Delouvrier returns to Algiers at 2 P.M., followed shortly afterward by Challe. General Ely arrives from Paris.

In the evening, de Gaulle makes his scheduled address to the French people. He appeals to reason, reiterating that self-determination is the only policy worthy of a democracy, lumps the activists and FLN together as groups trying to squelch this idea. He beseeches national unity behind his policy.

But he declares: "How can you [Frenchmen of Algeria] doubt that if, one day, the Muslims should freely and formally decide that tomorrow's Algeria is to remain closely tied to France, nothing would cause more joy to the fatherland and de Gaulle than to see them choose, among the solutions, that which would be *la plus française?*" [32]

A game of semantics? Perhaps the substitution of *serait* for *est,* with the qualifying conditional clause, would be sufficient in the eyes of history to guard the President of France against any charge of duplicity regarding his policy in the coming years. Perhaps there are legitimately different conceptions of what is "most French" (the Mendésistes and the Poujadists would surely disagree on the point). But at the time de Gaulle made his speech the phrase "most French" had come to be infallibly associated with the alternative of *intégration* (whatever that meant) in the minds of the European settlers.

January 30: Colonel Godard becomes the official negotiator of the Army with the insurgents. Discipline and determination are still evident in the Lagaillarde camp, but enthusiasm is fast deteriorating *chez Ortiz,* now that it is apparent that victory, even if bloody, will go to the "forces of order." The UT's and other sympathizers begin to leave the barricades. Amnesty is promised to all but "chiefs of the rebellion"; this will later become a point of heated dispute. Lagaillarde, after threatening a minor Götterdämmerung, weighs his sentiments in the midst of a crisis of emotion: "The Army has betrayed us. It will be emasculated. . . . The loss of Algeria, like it or not, will be the end of France." [33] At five o'clock in the afternoon there is a final spontaneous and affectionate rush of civilians toward the barricades: a swan song of sympathy.

January 31: It rains. The negotiations for the capitulation proceed. Gracieux gives up his temporary command of the Algiers sector to General Toulouse. There are many false starts and threats of violence during the day. The atmosphere remains tense. Godard conducts conversations with rebels from both camps. Lagaillarde releases all his troops who wish to go voluntarily; few take advantage. But it is evident that this will be the last night of the rebellion.

February 1: Ortiz vanishes before dawn, fleeing his command post and his responsibilities; his organization breaks up.[34] The problem is reduced

[32] The entire speech is quoted in Brombergers, *op. cit.,* p. 895.

[33] *Ibid.,* p. 409.

[34] This event quickly led to the widespread sentiment in some activist circles that Ortiz had been a double-agent of the government, entrusted with creating an incident to break down the resistance to an eventual policy of French relinquishment of Algeria. See Brombergers, *op. cit.,* p. 157, regarding Lagaillarde's earlier doubts. The hypothesis seems extremely unlikely, although certain points are not clarified, such as the repugnance of the OAS for Ortiz.

to receiving the capitulation of Lagaillarde. This is done toward noon, with salutes and military honors, a subject of much criticism in Paris. The former rebels are loaded in trucks after the "ceremony" and enlisted in the "Commando Alcazar" for a hundred days' service against the *fellagha*. The euphoria of this strange climax does not last long. Lagaillarde, the first to be indicted, is returned to Paris the next day. Others, like Susini and Dr. Perez, follow him. The "Commando Alcazar" will fight only one minor skirmish and win no decorations. Later, there will be juridical protests at the trial that the government reneged on its assurances, since only Lagaillarde and Ortiz (in flight) could be construed as "chiefs of the rebellion."

Highlights of the "Procès des Barricades"

Between November 1960 and March 1961 the defendants of the action of the barricades were brought to trial, some of them in absentia. Hindsight permits us the dramatic irony of knowing that the next plot (the "putsch of the generals" of April 1961) was being hatched while this spectacle was in progress. Perhaps the most revealing keynote was sounded by Jean-Louis Tixier-Vignancour, the ex-deputy of the Extreme Right from the Basses-Pyrénées, in his supple and impassioned summation for the defense:

If tomorrow in Algeria a new insurrection should break out, which would be the side of legitimacy? Obviously, it would be the side of the insurrection, for over the course of almost three years the regime has used all the popular mandates of Algeria to do exactly the opposite of the truth that was being expressed.[35]

Basically, there were four particular topics of interest on which this interminable trial focused. The first came to be known familiarly as the "trial within a trial," specifically the accusation and defense of Alain Le Moyne de Sérigny, publisher of the pro-activist *Echo d'Alger*, the city's largest daily newspaper.[36]

The basis of Sérigny's indictment was that he had aided the insurrection in a series of 162 articles and editorials over a period of about a month preceding its outbreak. He was tried under the provisions of an

[35] *Trial*, March 2, 1961.

[36] Born in Nantes but taken to Algeria as a small child, Sérigny made a fortune in shipping and later became a newspaper owner. An unrepentant Pétainist during the war, he was converted to conditional Gaullism a few days before the General's assumption of power in May 1958, publishing his famous editorial: "Parlez, parlez vite, mon général." Sérigny was also a late convert to the Soustellian idea of integration, a supporter of USRAF, and an ardent public defender of *Algérie française*. An influential participant in the coup of May 13, 1958, he later described his view of the events in a book of journalistic memoirs: *La révolution du 13 mai* (Paris, 1958).

obscure and ancient press law,[37] which to the objective legal observer could have little legitimate relevance to the case at hand. The defense also pointed out that the majority of incriminating articles (135) had passed successfully through government censorship, which had been in force during most of the period (January 9–31, 1960).

The arguments in the Sérigny part of the trial were long and involuted, but it soon became abundantly clear that there was little right on the side of the prosecution. Even the left-wing press, which roundly detested the defendant, attacked the charge with all might and main, knowing full well that a highly elastic justice of this sort might be turned on them at any moment if it should prevail against the Algerian *ultra*. No verdict was received with universally greater favor than Sérigny's acquittal at the end of the trial.

Yet it was plain, too, that the government had accomplished its real purpose by merely bringing him to trial, and that conviction (had justice been thus miscarried) would have been incidental. He had been forced to relinquish his grip on the *Echo d'Alger,* and had been detained awaiting trial for almost a year. This had cost the cause of *Algérie française* a capital trump in the propaganda battle.

The second aspect of the trial was the assignment of culpability for the fusillade of January 24. A tremendous weighing of testimony and statistical evidence on the sequence and pattern of this event characterized both the *instruction* and the trial itself. Commissioners and functionaries too numerous to mention succeeded each other on the stand for the prosecution, while the defense was scarcely less abstemious, if more original, in introducing its own witnesses and submitting the hostile ones to a searching cross-examination.

No eyewitness of the event gave a thoroughly satisfactory account of what transpired, and numerous flaws appeared in even the most prudent testimony. The defense was interested in showing: (1) that culpability for opening fire could not be ascertained; (2) that the military loyalists responsible for the planning of the clearance operation, especially Colonel Fonde, had been intent on provoking an incident; and (3) that the demonstrators, their patrimony threatened and the government disregarding their wishes at every turn, had been systematically forced to the point of crisis.

The task of the prosecution was more exacting and specific. They sought to persuade the military judges of the following points: (1) that the *gendarmerie* had covered the Boulevard Laferrière with unloaded weapons and according to precise regulations and orders; (2)

---

[37] Articles 59 and 60 of the penal code ("attentat contre la sûreté de l'Etat") interpreted in the light of the press law of July 28, 1881 ("provocations directes suivies d'effets").

that all proper care had been taken by Colonel Fonde in the preparation of the operation and the transmission of orders; (3) that the first shots had come from the side of the demonstrators; and (4) that the gendarmes had been fired on from above, from several directions, including the Ortiz command post, and that at least one automatic weapon had been employed by the activists.

Both the expert testimony and eyewitness evidence of the prosecution were obviously more convincing, if not thoroughly decisive on all points. The flight of Ortiz abroad suggested in part that he may have assessed his jeopardy realistically. Several witnesses corroborated specific souvenirs of the firing from the buildings. Above all, despite withering cross-examination, the damning testimony of Lieutenant Colonel Debrosse remained unshaken. Somewhat further removed from the event, the appearances of Colonel Fonde and General Coste were also impressive.

An otherwise lenient military court found the evidence persuasive enough to assign the death penalty to Ortiz, not only as the leader of the insurrection but as the responsible agent of the massacre.

The trial undoubtedly helped to define the climate of "activism" in Algiers. Activism under the banner of *Algérie française* meant many things. There were the neo-Salazarian, corporatist theories of Dr. Bernard Lefèvre, one of the defendants.[38] There were the more fanatic ravings of Susini, who had taken for his own the most intransigent vocabulary of dialectical historicism and transmitted this conflict of *le Bien* and *le Mal* to his followers:

I wanted to reconcile the movement of social emancipation which is upsetting the whole world and the fact of nationality. For myself and my friends I tried to combine these two currents that have shaken the twentieth century in a global synthesis. Each of them has to be modified, and then perhaps their positions will merge.[39]

There were the defenders of vested interests like Sérigny; finally, there were the "men of good will" like Arnould and, to a certain degree, Lagaillarde.

One of the interesting features of this gamut of opinions and doctrines held by different French Algerians — of which I have given only the broad lines — is that they were quite closely reproduced in the thinking of various elements of the Army. Every activist knew the

---

[38] "I pursued a double aim: to show [the impossibility of fighting against communism with capitalist methods] and to propose a new order that could avoid that failure. This was a return to the natural order, the constitution of a society based on living realities and not fluctuating ideas." *Trial,* November 13–14, 1960.

[39] *Ibid.,* November 20–21, 1960.

turnings and twistings of the fashionable military doctrine of *la guerre révolutionnaire,* and civilian action accommodated itself to these premises. The use of the terminology had become so habitual that when Dr. Jean-Claude Perez, Ortiz's chief organizer, challenged Commissioner Aublet's testimony during the trial regarding the formation and purpose of Ronda's OPAS, he had recourse to the familiar military doctrine:

> Monsieur le président, [if we had striven to form shock groups of the OPAS] we would thus have created in two months what others have taken twenty years to build in this country. I add that subversive action is exactly the contrary of shock groups. Either you have a political organization and subversive action or you have commandos for attack, not both. They just don't go together.[40]

The "trial of the barricades" amply revealed what many had known for a long time: that the French Algerians were more than a troglodyte body of dissidents; they were an indigestible element in the French body politic whose interests simply could not be reconciled to the national interest by any magic formula.[41] Furthermore, it was now plain that civilian-military contacts and bonds of opinion were often close, multiple, and dangerous, and that the primary loyalty of the military organization was itself at stake.

The Army on Trial

The Army, too, was on trial in the *procès des barricades,* and this fact was not lost on the high command, the government, and the military judges. An important segment of it sat in the defendant's box in the person of Colonel Jean Gardes, ex-chief of the Psychological Action Services in Algiers.[42] There was an individual case against Gardes, to be sure, which occupied a good deal of the testimony.

Specifically, we can isolate the following charges that constituted the sum of the indictment: (1) periodic associations of a suspicious nature with Ortiz; (2) the harboring of unsavory and anti-republican employees in the SAPI; (3) the failure to report the activists' state of mind just prior to the insurrection through proper command channels; (4) the appearance on the balcony of the Compagnie Algérienne with Ortiz, giving the impression that the insurgents had military support.

[40] *Trial,* November 15, 1960.
[41] See the excellent sketch by Joseph Kraft, "Settler Politics in Algeria," *Foreign Affairs,* XXXIX, No. 4 (July 1961), pp. 591–600.
[42] The SAPI was suppressed in Algeria, and its functions were assimilated to the appropriate sections of the *deuxième* and *troisième bureaux* as a result of the events of the "week of the barricades."

There is little doubt that Gardes was guilty of some of these charges, in spirit if not to the exact letter. However, the nature of his duties — particularly that of liaison with the "mouvements nationaux" — could be invoked as an extenuation. Moreover, Gardes had been called to Paris in the midst of the insurrection to answer directly for his actions before the Minister of the Armies and had been allowed to return to Algeria without sanctions. Thereafter, following a famous warning from General Challe,[43] he went immediately to Saida to relieve Colonel Marcel Bigeard and was not present in Algiers for a portion of the events. But in answer to the question "Do you think that Gardes misapplied your instructions?" Challe was reported to have said in his private testimony at the trial, "In a general way, yes." And Crépin is reported to have confirmed: "I have the moral conviction that Colonel Gardes knew everything but kept quiet about it." [44]

The capital feature of Gardes's presence in the courtroom, however, was not anything he had done or thought as an individual, but rather what he represented in the dramatic play of forces that had plagued the Algerian situation ever since the Army had arrived there in strength. Gardes was a symbol of military bitterness, and a particularly apt one. Perhaps the only more logical defendant would have been General Massu himself, who later, as a witness, would declare: "I wonder why I am not with them [the defendants], for, in the long run, my place is with them." [45] But Massu and others knew full well that his prestige made him politically untouchable.

The defense took particular care to show that it was the Army that was being impugned in the person of Gardes. One impressive military witness after the next, among them Marshal Juin, the dean of the Army and a "pied noir," stressed the cruelty of Gardes's indictment. General Mirambeau, an Algerian zonal commander, expressed the collective sentiment as follows:

We have an Army that defends itself magnificently, thanks to its knowledge of subversive war, and that will go on doing it for a long time. The Army suffers to see itself not understood, it suffers to see Colonel Gardes where he is! [46]

Eugène Mannoni, the correspondent for *Le Monde,* corroborates this impression of the psychological atmosphere prevalent in the Army of Algeria:

[43] "Gardes, my boy, you exaggerate, I don't care for that. If you still want a chance to take over the Saida sector, you'd better get going." *Trial,* February 22, 1961.

[44] *Ibid.*

[45] *Ibid.*, December 18–19, 1960.

[46] *Ibid.*, February 3, 1961.

Between the "activists," the all-powerful political expression of the European population, and the officers of Algiers there was maintained, despite a constant deterioration of relations, a community, if not of objectives, at least of feeling. Colonel Gardes made no mystery of it when he declared, in speaking of MM. Lagaillarde and Ortiz: "These were two men who 'cried' French." We know of other officers of Algiers, and not the least, who from the witness stand, will probably say (or at least used to say) what Colonel Gardes said from the box of the accused.[47]

Who was Jean Gardes, and how was he typical or atypical of Army sentiment? The son of a solid Parisian family — his mother owned the Restaurant des Ministères on the Rue du Bac, which was long savored as a political rendezvous, but of the Left-Center — he had cast aside bourgeois ideals and sought a military career. He returned, much decorated, from service in Indochina and later received an assignment in Morocco. After the events of May 13, he was posted to Algiers to take over the Psychological Action Services; he had, at that time, the reputation of being a mild Gaullist. But he was also a convinced disciple of *la guerre subversive*. In the trial, Gardes explained it as follows:

I saw [in Indochina] one more war, more and more global, more and more total, involving all possibilities. Negotiations were disastrous for us. We went into the territory of the Viet Minh simply to obey the law of the enemy. That's how it is in *guerre subversive*.

In September 1958, some of our chums had trouble: Lacheroy and Gousseaud [*sic*]. But General Salan asked Paris for me as their replacement. Paris consented.

I believe we are waging our last battle as free men over there. Here is my curriculum. I started my job at the *cinquième bureau*. . . .[48]

Gardes went on to describe the methods of his operation and the difficulties of achieving fraternity between the European and Muslim communities. This had been noted especially in the signal failure of the celebration of the first anniversary of *treize mai*. The Psychological Warfare chief then sketched out his policy of encouraging integration, rebutting some of the charges commonly made against his profession:

We often get accused of rapes of crowds and a lot of other horrors. But I have to say that at this time the federation of U.T.'s and groups of self-defense was conceived for the purpose of educating, not violating, anybody's feelings. My second proposal was the development of contacts between the communities, human contacts, what has been called "fraternization" and what France has, for a very long time, called "fraternity."

I made a civil proposition: that was to form a huge rally of the Muslim population, for there was a danger that it would get away from us. This is

[47] "Une exception ou un porte-parole," *Le Monde,* November 12, 1960.
[48] *Trial,* November 10, 1960.

what some have seen as a subversive organization. It was just a rally, a popular rally for progress and fraternization.[49]

Also,

It [the accusation] is really like subversive war. A little factor becomes everything. It's a questionable tissue of statement mixed with unverified information. Here is my statement. I never received at my home the general staff of the FNF and I state that no one can say so. I received Ortiz himself of course. . . . It was my job to make the contacts that were inaccessible to my colleagues.[50]

Two other matters were brought before the tribunal in connection with Colonel Gardes. The first concerned the activities of his employee, de Kerdaniel (described as "savant en complots"), who appears to have prepared, on behalf of the Psychological Action Services, provisional broadsides advocating the overthrow of the regime.[51] The second was the evolution of political activity in the so-called "centres sociaux," which, under the jurisdiction of the Ministry of Education, were designed for the purpose of raising the intellectual and technical skills of the Muslims. The defense taxed the government heavily for allowing the *centres sociaux* to become a hotbed of pro-FLN activity and the virtual appanage of the rebels' political arm, the OPA. The particular target for this assault was Delouvrier's liberal *directeur du cabinet,* Eric Westphal, who was practically accused of being a hireling of the enemy.[52]

A final point of investigation was the influential role of *action psychologique* played by the Army's weekly *Le Bled* and the regular radio broadcast over Radio Algiers, "La Voix du Bled." *Le Bled* was a weapon in the hands of the purveyors of the new doctrines and a thorn in the side of the government. "La Voix du Bled" was a regular radio program of the same nature. Colonel Gardes was charged with

[49] *Ibid.,* November 11, 1960.

[50] *Ibid.*

[51] General Mongin, on behalf of the prosecution, cited the following text, recovered from the offices of the Psychological Action Services (*Le Monde,* November 12, 1960, Théolleyre report): "We are witnessing the sabotage of the Army by the leaders in Paris. The moment is coming when it will be necessary to create a central revolutionary bureau in secrecy, which might be directed by Colonel Gardes and include MM. Sapin-Lignières, Rogier, and de Kerdaniel." This sounds to the present observer like a feebly amateurish piece of work, perhaps even a plant.

[52] See especially the testimony of Colonel Gardes (*Trial,* December 13, 1960) and of Colonel Ruyssen (*ibid.,* February 5–6, 1961). Also see General Massu's remarks about Westphal (*ibid.,* December 18–19, 1960). Germaine Tillion's definition of a *centre social* is as follows (*L'Afrique bascule vers l'avenir,* Paris, 1960, p. 165): "The purpose of the *centre social* is to furnish the population of a well-defined geographical sector with the total means of progress necessary to reach a higher economic level." These organizations were created by Ordinance No. 58-759 of August 20, 1958.

having prepared and authorized a broadcast on January 25 in praise of the Army's fraternization with the insurgents, called "La barricade unie." His reply to this charge at the trial was rather anodyne and unsatisfactory: "From the twenty-fifth on, there wasn't any more drama. You saw people sharing coffee, and that's all that was meant when we spoke of the 'barricade unie.' . . ." [53] The lawyers of de Sérigny and Colonel Gardes argued that time after time Paris, which had the authority and the means, had not intervened to check those acts which were now described as provocative.

As a witness on his own behalf, Gardes was straight, correct, and resourceful, the model of a good soldier; if he sometimes unwittingly fell into the jargon of *la guerre subversive,* he was never guilty of the near-parody that marked the heated interventions of Susini or the dogmatic testimony of Colonel Broizat.[54] Unquestionably, there were many serving officers who doubted the cherished theories of Gardes and the "psychological clique" but who admired the Colonel's bearing and his military record and could not have inwardly tolerated his being sent to prison. Gardes's distinguished career bestowed a kind of invulnerability on him and, in a sense, falsified some of the critical doctrinal and political issues that were at stake in the trial. Colonel Thomazo, the right-wing deputy from the *pays basque* and veteran of subversive war in Algiers, put it this way: "Gardes, the most upright, the purest of us all, the centurion-colonels. We used to call him the 'holy man.' In bringing him to trial you have incriminated the purest part of the soul of the French Army." [55]

Needless to say, Gardes was acquitted and liberated, just in time to take his place in the next plot against the regime. Sanctity and sedition were not necessarily unrelated in the views of Colonel Thomazo.

Two Armies? Two Frances?

In dealing with the aspects of the insurrection that touched the Army, the military judges had to walk a difficult tightrope. Dissatisfaction with government policy in Algeria was rampant. Some of it could be permitted to emerge in the testimony; but all hints of disloyalty had to be suppressed. For this would jeopardize the Debré government on both the Right and the Left. The outspokenness of Gen-

---

[53] *Trial,* November 27–28, 1960.

[54] See *ibid.,* January 15–16, 1961. Also J.-M. Théolleyre, "Un 'templier' des temps modernes," *ibid.,* and Broizat's voluminous letter in reply to the article just cited, *Le Monde,* January 20, 1961.

[55] *Trial,* February 4, 1961.

eral Massu, who testified in public session, did not help matters. In his deposition he went right to the heart of the doctrinal issue:

I think that a method is on trial here. . . . This war that we didn't choose must be fought and won. That's what we're paid for. And for this little-known war, the *cinquième bureau* was the vanguard and Colonel Gardes is one of those who had the merit of codifying this war. To conquer the objective and the population, and even that political weapon, the ballot, you had to reassure the people, and to reassure them you had to protect them, and to protect them, you had to group them. All in all, these regroupings were a necessity and if it was a little harsh, the people at least got a better standard of life.[56]

Undoubtedly, some of the most heated military incriminations of government policy and personnel took place behind closed doors. It may also be that the most violent sort of criticism was deliberately muffled because it might have jeopardized the success of the forthcoming "putsch des généraux" in Algiers. But perhaps the solid center of Army thinking that was still preoccupied with the vital issue of unity was best exemplified by a spontaneous utterance of General Gracieux during his testimony. Gracieux, considered a witness basically friendly to the defense, was pushed a little too far by Tixier-Vignancour, who wished him to agree that the trial was a case of persecution and political duplicity. "It is not my business to answer that," Gracieux snapped. "I say only that there are not two armies, but a single one that obeys. If there were two armies, I would no longer be wearing the uniform that I wear." [57] Events were shortly to discredit General Gracieux's analysis, ratifying the long-standing fears of the high command.

Beside General Gracieux's measured loyalty, there were the clearly exasperated utterances of Massu and a host of colonels. Finally, there was the clear expression of the loyalist position, notable especially in the words of General Coste: "My taste doesn't run to politics. To hear the term 'comité de salut public' is enough to make me shiver." [58] As the courtroom cleared after the final sentencing, few suspected that these lines would be sharply drawn in little more than a month.

After so much passion, so much verbiage, so many critical themes, charges, and countercharges, the sentences were considered lenient, ludicrously so by many. By November 21, 1960, all the defendants had been granted provisional liberty, which meant that they were no longer detained in prison. On December 4, Lagaillarde, Susini, Ronda, Feral,

[56] *Ibid.*, December 18–19, 1960.
[57] *Ibid.*, February 18, 1961.
[58] *Ibid.*, January 17, 1961.

and Demarquet took advantage of this opportunity to flee to Spain. Feral returned within a few days, the apparent victim of confusion, and Demarquet trudged back toward the end of the trial. The others remained in exile, evidently awaiting some future Algerian action in which they might participate. This flight seems to have influenced the sentencing more than the evidence of the trial. Lagaillarde received a penalty of ten years, Ronda of three, and Susini of two with suspension. Ortiz, absent since the last day of the insurrection, was sentenced to death; the other vanished conspirators, Meningaud and Martel, were to receive seven and five years, respectively. Those who had stayed to face the music came out unscathed.

The government had relied on the object lesson of the detention and public spectacle to make its point, and had tempered justice with considerable mercy in the sentencing (or, more precisely, in the prosecution pleas). But it had come out of the long ordeal in weakened condition. The defense had managed to turn the trial into a political debate, and had exposed many of the "paradoxes" of government policy. The Right was not appeased by the leniency of the proceedings; it was annoyed that they should have taken place at all. The Left was overtly contemptuous of them. Some of the legal anomalies of the Fifth Republic were revealed. The *procès des barricades* was probably an object lesson for no one, unless it was the government itself. But this was a government which, insofar as it was skillful, ruled by the skill of instinct and personality, and was not in the habit of receiving object lessons.

XIV

AGONIES OF THE
GRANDE BAVARDE

> Many are now of the opinion that no two things are more
> discordant and incongruous than a civil and military life. But
> if we consider the nature of government, we shall find a very
> strict and intimate relation between these two conditions, and
> they are not only compatible and consistent . . . but neces-
> sarily connected.
>
> — *Machiavelli, Preface to* Art of War

THE EVENTS of the barricades were a turning point in the regime's
relations with the Army. Solicitous of its fragile unity, the Army had
marked time during the week of January 24–31, 1960, and had finally,
despite the initiatives and temptations described earlier, served as arbiter
between the Fifth Republic and the hysterical Europeans of Algiers.
This had not, however, been an especially willing or profitable arbitra-
tion; it increased rather than mitigated the Army's own inability to
influence policy, and it restored a political power to Paris that had been
lacking since Guy Mollet's visit to Algiers on February 6, 1956. It guaranteed further crises between the regime and the Army, but it ensured
also — not least by demonstrating the metropolitan strength of de
Gaulle — that the outcome of any future crisis would most likely be
decided in favor of the government.

The Republic That "Knew What It Wanted"?

By 1958 the French Army, long trained to submit to civilian command and operate discreetly within a penumbra of silence, had discovered not only language but the gift of speaking with many tongues. The *grande muette* of former times had become an incorrigible *grande bavarde,* committing its thoughts, shotgun-fashion, to interviews and signed articles. This literary occupation of an Army eager to spew its pent-up feelings about politics, doctrine, and, above all, Algeria at an insouciant public, a scandalized regime, and a restricted but fascinated international audience served to confuse the problem of loyalty and discipline still further and to confirm frustrated elements of the service in the political vocation they had chosen.

What sort of a game had the regime been playing vis-à-vis its Army in the year 1959? Clearly, the motives and the psychology were confused, as confused in Paris as they were in Algiers. De Gaulle's intent to surround himself with the symbols of legal succession — the Mollets and Pinays — as well as the distances he now maintained between himself and former comrades like Soustelle, who had taken an out-and-out *Algérie française* position, seemed to indicate a preference for republican scrupulosity and a distaste for revolution. But they also provided greater latitude for the development of his still embryonic and empirical policies toward the absorbing colonial question, of which he considered Algeria a perfunctory part. For the Army, on the other hand, not only was de Gaulle's mixed entourage distasteful, but there was something fundamental, nothing negotiable, about Algeria.

On March 27, 1958, before coming to power, de Gaulle had received a delegation of the National Action Committee of Veterans' Associations (CANAC). In the minutes drawn up after the audience by Alexandre Sanguinetti, the Secretary-General of CANAC, and approved by all the delegates present, we may read the following:

The General knows that wide sectors of public opinion reproach him for not having made any statements about the nation's great problems in the last four years; he refrains from making them because he realizes that his words and the intentions expressed by them would immediately be deformed and used in a contradictory way by the different factions seeking power.

For example, if he stated that generosity and liberalism were needed with regard to Algeria and Africa, one faction would seize upon this to help bring about capitulation. If he dwelled on the need for the maintenance of the French presence in Africa, another faction would take advantage of it to refuse to approach any African problems through political solutions.[1]

[1] J.-R. Tournoux, *Secrets d'Etat* (Paris, 1960), Appendix D, p. 478.

Though by 1959 de Gaulle was himself *le pouvoir* and was ruling with instruments of his own choosing, he still faced the same delicate balance of pressures that had elicited his prudence a year earlier. And so he practiced, for better or worse, a politics of ambiguity, which some described as duplicity or betrayal. This pleased neither the Left Wing nor the Army.

The Left Wing, in typically doctrinaire fashion, never ceased to accuse the Debré government of coddling its Army and failing to recall it to discipline. But the government had to diplomatize with the Army, and it resorted to the abusive expedient of issuing ambiguous orders or none at all, and of encouraging lines of cleavage that would work to the advantage of its own power position. How distasteful this was even to military moderates one can imagine.

The process by which the Gaullist Fifth Republic burned its bridges with an Army that believed it had installed the new regime in power with an express mandate to fulfill the pacification of Algeria will remain somewhat in shadow until the dossiers spill out their secrets. However, the concrete grounds of accusation are well known. The first charge against de Gaulle was that of studied duplicity. Riding to power on a wave that mingled the revulsion for a degraded political institution with the nationalist enthusiasm centered around the phrase *Algérie française,* the General was held to have abused the sources of his power in a systematically unprincipled way. Frustrated men like Jacques Soustelle, writing from exile, would later attempt to search deep in the past for evidence:

It will probably long be asked whether, in May 1958, General de Gaulle had decided to abandon Algeria. What now appears certain is that during the first years of rebellion he adopted various and contradictory positions in conversations with those who came to see him in his retirement.[2]

Once de Gaulle had returned to power, Soustelle maintained, "the trickery was so skilled, so gradual (at least at the beginning), camouflaged with such astuteness, that it was difficult to penetrate." [3] So difficult, in fact, that Soustelle himself, never granted the coveted portfolio of Algerian Affairs, would not leave the cabinet until February 5, 1960, after the "week of the barricades." De Gaulle indeed had in his entourage men whose inclination was toward relinquishment of French sovereignty in North Africa (Olivier Guichard, Jacques Foccart, Bernard Tricot — names that would become anathema in military circles); but it is no less certain that the General made his own decisions. To

[2] Jacques Soustelle, *L'espérance trahie* (Paris, 1962), p. 7.
[3] *Ibid.,* p. 12.

reduce the barricades the President of the Republic had, to be sure, held out the tantalization of the "most French solution." But he had cunningly personalized and conditionalized the statement ("serait la plus française"). In a much later speech (before selected military officers at Strasbourg, on November 23, 1961) de Gaulle intoned what might be construed almost as an echo passage when he referred to "the [understandable but vain] hope . . . that simply by wishing it things could be changed from what they really are to what one desired them to be. . . ."[4]

The second fundamental castigation of de Gaulle was based on the charge of indecision and indirection. This is a different matter, which evades the logic of the first reproach. Even Soustelle touches upon it at some length: "At least the government could have taken a firm position, repeated a hundred times, in defining its goals of war and peace, so as to leave no more room for equivocation."[5] Claude Paillat, in his sensational indictment of de Gaulle's Algerian policy,[6] makes much of the "testament of strategy" which General Challe left behind him when recalled from his supreme command in Algiers in April 1960. This collection of documents allegedly outlined in expansive detail, and in ways toward which de Gaulle was known to be hostile, the conduct of counter-revolutionary operations, including heavy stress on psychological warfare. Paillat charges that, though the Challe papers were well known, de Gaulle never indicated the government's position by revoking the orders:

> The government . . . allowed the simultaneous edification of two doctrines, one for the use of the Army and the Algerians, the other for the use of the *métropole*. The [Challe] directives, far from being secret, could not have been more official. General de Gaulle never addressed the least criticism to the commander-in-chief over them. And when the latter left Algeria, the government did not take advantage of it to have them canceled. They remained in force under his successors.[7]

In fact, there is no doubt that the lines of command and information between Paris and Algeria had progressively broken down, so that one had to contend not only with opposition but with misunderstanding. Under the Fourth Republic the Army had resented all the inconveniences of feeble government and coalition politics. A collapsing cabinet or military credits refused by the Assembly could interfere annoyingly with the conduct of the war. Yet there were basically stable relations between Robert Lacoste, the Resident Minister, and Bourgès-

[4] Text contained in *Le Monde,* November 24, 1961. See Chapter XVII, pp. 360–361.
[5] Soustelle, *op. cit.,* p. 91.
[6] Claude Paillat, *Le dossier secret de l'Algérie* (Paris, 1961).
[7] *Ibid.,* p. 393.

Maunoury, Morice, and Chaban-Delmas, successively the Ministers of National Defense (especially the first two), between Lacoste and his military counterpart General Raoul Salan, and between General Paul Ely, the Chief of Staff, and the military commanders in the field. If the regime was often unable to provide basic political support for the military effort (witness the "bons offices" undertaking of the Félix Gaillard government in the Tunisian dispute of March 1958, which, more than anything else, was the mechanical cause of the fall of the Fourth Republic), it was still true that the conduct of the war had passed mostly into the hands of the Army and sympathetic civilian overseers.

Under the Fifth Republic, after the civil-military euphoria of the summer of 1958, this situation changed drastically. The major policies no longer were fabricated of the pieces of much-debated and much-communicated propositions but were imposed by fiat, often obscurely, and without warning or preparation. As Premier, Charles de Gaulle himself assumed the responsibility for defense matters and further subdelegated them to General Salan in Algeria. This meant, in one respect, a large concentration of power in the hands of the Algerian commander in chief; but, in another, it meant the breakdown of useful hierarchical communications with Paris. When de Gaulle became Head of State and Guillaumat and Messmer successively received the attribution of Minister of the Armies, the latter two frequently had little more hint of policy changes than did the nation at large. Neither, it seems, did Michel Debré. The television screen and radio set became official channels of communication. Field commanders had the President's speeches recorded on tape so that they could be studied minutely for the nuances that took the place of standard hierarchical directives. Of course, many officers sought for ways to misinterpret them, a ruse that might have been obviated by a more orthodox system of transmission. The wish remained father to the thought in Algeria.

It seems also that the government lacked, at critical moments, the precise information it needed to deal with the bewildering complexity of the Algerian affair. At the outbreak of the barricades insurrection Debré was forced to make a hurried and emotional night journey to Algiers to form an on-the-spot impression of the balance of forces, despite the fact that numerous military and political consultations had been held in Paris prior to his departure.

Winds of Change

When General de Gaulle posed the three alternatives of "independence," "Francization," and "association" in his famous self-determination speech of September 19, 1959, with a scarcely disguised preference for the last, no implementing directives followed the declaration. Colonel Gardes, chief of Psychological Action, launched an immediate campaign for "integration" (the more usual word for the second option) with the conditional approval of General Challe. Before a month had passed, he was abruptly called to order by Paul Delouvrier, the Minister-Delegate. Hints had been received from Paris: don't go too strong on the second solution. But hints were all; a succession of critical events passed, and still the equivocation was never entirely dissolved.[8]

The procedures by which de Gaulle effected his radical changes in Algerian policy did not respond to consistency or, in a real sense, to honor. But to the objective observer it is difficult to see that they did not conform to reality, to *raison d'Etat,* and to the demands of empirical finesse. De Gaulle had once written, years earlier: "The French military spirit is loath to recognize that the action of war wears an essentially empirical character. It tries unceasingly to construct a doctrine that would permit it to undertake this action *a priori*." [9] There is every likelihood that he applied the same standard to politics, and especially to that sector of public affairs where war and politics meet. But no one can affirm that, successful as they may have been, de Gaulle's actions were not destined to demoralize the French Army.

On the one hand, the regime was cautiously penalizing extremism and transferring "dangerous" officers from critical posts, not recognizing that its methods were having the effect of making loyal officers "dangerous" as well. On the other hand, it acquiesced in certain policies designed to placate the Army and hold it shy of the brink of rebellion. Chiefly, thanks to a fortunate inheritance from the Fourth Republic, it resorted to the Biblical expedient of leading a chosen part of the Army to the top of a mountain and tempting it.

In early 1956, unnoticed by all but the most careful observers, France had fought out the battle of whether or not it would develop atomic weapons.[10] The controversy was disguised in the Euratom debate in the National Assembly, which took place in July 1956, some five months after the investiture of Guy Mollet's "Front Républicain" government. Two lines of politics crossed in this conjuncture. In the first place, there were Mollet, some of his Socialist colleagues, and the virtual whole of the MRP, who believed in the creation of "European" institutions. Secondly, there was a large bloc on the Right that deplored France's

[8] *Ibid.,* p. 298.
[9] Charles de Gaulle, *Le fil de l'épée* (Paris, 1932), p. 98.
[10] See the parliamentary debates reported in *Le Monde,* July 1–July 12, 1956.

reticence from entering the atomic weapons competition, a government policy that had been formalized by Edgar Faure's statement of April 13, 1955:

It is necessary for France to become an atomic power. We should make rapid progress toward that realization. But we have decided to eliminate research devoted to specifically military uses. Consequently we do not intend to devote any study to the creation of an H-bomb or any other bomb. . . .[11]

Guy Mollet temporized without any great misgivings; three of his Radical colleagues, Félix Gaillard, Maurice Faure, and Maurice Bourgès-Maunoury, strongly favored France's entry into the field of military nuclear development. A numerically impressive coalition of the "Europeans" and the "belligerents" carried the Euratom treaty through the Assembly by a vote of 332 to 181. Both the ideal of "Europe" and the "independent deterrent" were mutually forwarded. Mollet's double-edged conviction on the subject was well expressed in these words:

The position of the government is the following: France agrees not to explode an A-bomb before January 1, 1961 [a pledge later contravened]. Considering the retardation of studies and manufacture, which the High Commissioner of Atomic Energy [Francis Perrin, who testified extensively in the debate] has evoked, this moratorium cannot set our program back.[12]

The evolution from this time is perfectly clear: France pursued her atomic research toward the production of a bomb. Jules Moch, Félix Gaillard, and others made this amply evident in statements and interviews in the two years following. When General de Gaulle (already on record from much earlier days as an exponent of the bomb) came to power at the beginning of June 1958, he found at least one situation tailor-made to his views that the previous regime had created. He incorporated the bomb and the supplementary idea of a *force de frappe* into his diplomacy and attempted to use it, incidentally, as a technical sop to the discontented Army of Algeria.[13]

Disputes arose in the military between the growing school of nuclear strategists (like Generals Charles Ailleret and Paul Stehlin) and the Algerian revolutionary war specialists, competing over resources, strategies, and political preferences. These technical polarities cannot very well be criticized except in the light of political events surrounding them. Since General de Gaulle was their fervent ally, the "nuclearists"

[11] *Le Monde,* April 14, 1955.

[12] *Ibid.,* July 12, 1956.

[13] See General de Gaulle's press conference of November 10, 1959, reported in *Le Monde,* November 11, 1959.

were apt to be found at the core of the government's support, while the "subversives" would furnish the kernel of the opposition.

On February 13, 1960, two weeks to the day after the capitulation of the barricades, the first French atomic bomb was exploded at Reggane, in the Sahara. This, too, was to prove a watershed in the regime's relations with its military forces.

At the same time that the government was holding out its nuclear blandishment to a suspicious Army, it was working much more subtly in another sphere to loosen the military grip on Algeria. This was a side effect and subsidiary intention of the "Constantine Plan," [14] announced shortly after the General returned to power as a means for dramatically raising the indigenous standard of living through investment, public works, education, and the creation of employment opportunities at rapid cadence.

The trained economists knew much better than the soldiers that the goal of trans-Mediterranean equality, if not an out-and-out pipe dream, was at best a very distant prospect. However, the Constantine Plan at least promised some progress against the dual specters of galloping pauperization and cruel demographic pressure. Conveniently, this would also be a means of releasing Algeria from the administrative grip of an ardent Army that had acquired *de facto* control over the province as a result of Lacoste's delegations of power of 1956, confirmed by government edict in June 1958.[15] The appointment of the technician Paul Delouvrier as Salan's replacement was intended to confirm the will of the government to concentrate on the sphere of economic reform. As we know, political events swiftly outstripped all but the preliminary effects of the Constantine Plan; nevertheless, it was disturbing to the Army to find itself challenged obliquely in an area where its power was especially vulnerable.

Ambiguity: The "Tour of the Mess Halls"

These problems, vastly magnified by the trauma of the barricades, were all festering in the hearts of the officers when the President of France, accompanied by Pierre Messmer (who had just replaced Guillaumat as the Minister of the Armies) and General Ely, set out on March 3, 1960, for his famous *tournée des popotes* ("tour of the mess halls") in Algeria. The junket was not the direct result of the insurgency

---

[14] De Gaulle's Five-Year Plan for Algeria offered at Constantine on October 3, 1958. The plan foundered badly in 1960 from want of confidence in the private sector.

[15] On this subject, see the highly suggestive essay by François Gromier, "Le 'trouble' de l'armée," *La NEF*, July–September 1961, pp. 5–18.

of January, since it had been previously planned to begin on February 5, but the events of Algiers underscored its urgency. It was of critical moment that *le pouvoir* should re-establish the lost contact with *la force.*

The impact of de Gaulle's impromptu speeches to the officers of a number of military posts — reported (ambiguously, some would claim) by a single Agence France Presse correspondent — was abundantly clear when the tour had ended. The difficulty is that it was clear to different persons in different ways, and that it would generate equivocation in the years to come.

For example, in defense of the now-classic argument that de Gaulle had betrayed both his previous positions and the national interest, the Army would later be able to point to such statements as:

There will be no Dien Bien Phu in Algeria. . . . The independence demanded by Ferhat Abbas and his gang is a farce. [Hadjer-Mafrouch, March 4]
After military operations come to an end, there will be a long time before we can proceed to elections. It will take years. Till then there is a duty to be done. The Army has only to accomplish its mission. [Redjas, March 4] [16]
The people who say "independence" commit an absurdity. Algeria can't go it alone. [Aumale, March 5] [17]

But the President had said other things, too. On March 5, he had cautioned the officers at Barika: "For the moment you are the sword of France in this place, but the day will come when it will be somewhere else. You always have to think of that. You are not destined to be the French Army in Algeria forever." [18] More significantly, he declared at Zafirete on the day of his departure (March 7):

France has not only got the Algerian problem on her hands. She has many others. We, the state, have to consider each thing in its place with relation to all the rest, Algeria included. I have been anxious to tell you this, *messieurs les officiers,* so that you will make no mistake. [19]

This is perhaps the closest thing one could find to the pure Gaullist theory of the Algerian situation in a nutshell. New days make new demands. But this statement went curiously unperceived at the time. For de Gaulle, France's position in the world depended on a calculation of dozens of factors; for much of the Army, all of France's honor, esteem, and success centered on a single issue — Algeria.

---

[16] This and the preceding are from *Le Monde,* March 5, 1960.
[17] *Ibid.,* March 6–7, 1960.
[18] *Ibid.*
[19] *Ibid.,* March 8, 1960.

De Gaulle also lifted the equivocation concerning his position on the self-determination referendum, which he had stated might be years away. He announced himself as favoring the third solution, *association* with France (apparently a part of his Community conception): "I believe that [the Algerians] will say [at the referendum], an Algerian Algeria tied to France." [20]

Maurice Duverger commented on the *tournée* in the following manner after its conclusion:

The *tournée des popotes* seems to have been designed to honeycoat a decision which certain officers will find bitter: the unequivocal condemnation of *intégration*. . . . It will no longer be possible for any *"x" bureau* to deform the thought of the Head of State in claiming to interpret it. It will no longer be possible to claim obedience to the government while continuing to promote *intégration*.[21]

The Army leaders were either unwilling to settle for this solution, or else the remark had passed over their heads. They were not now content to consider the Army a blind instrument of opportunistically shifting national policy, whatever de Gaulle's estimate of the situation might be. The new constitution made the President of the Republic the defender of the national territory, and stated that no part of it could be arbitrarily alienated. Besides, not only did the Army believe itself bound by solemn contract to the defense of the European population and, especially, its Muslim allies; it was also combating revolutionary war at the last outpost "in defense of the West." For the majority sentiment in the Army, colonialism was a dead issue and would never reappear again in its previous form. As an anonymous officer told a left-wing correspondent rather pointedly:

If M. Sartre throws in my face: "You are bastards because you have waged war against a friendly people," I would object, because this is wrong. We will always be ready to love and respect that people. We have risen instead against that enemy that is ours and yours, the one who, tomorrow, will stop you from being allowed to read and write. You are in peril of death and you don't know it. We know it for you and we are defending you.[22]

It was frequently said that the Army was no longer capitalist, not as capitalist as de Gaulle himself. Many of the officers most devoted to the proposition of *Algérie française* avowed how they detested the banks and the big capitalist enterprises, the apathy of the Champs Elysées and the selfishness of the *gros colons* of the Algiers suburbs. They equally

---

[20] At Azziz, March 7. *Ibid.*

[21] *Ibid.*, March 9, 1960.

[22] Cited in Claude Dufresnoy, *Des officiers parlent,* in the preface by Jules Roy (Paris, 1961), p. xii.

detested the French Left, which was sabotaging their effort with all the means at hand. If the Left would abandon its insane idea of Algerian independence and throw its weight toward the creation of social equity under French rule, then, according to one officer, "that day you would no longer be perverted intellectuals but would be our masters, for we are desperately looking for a Barrès. The Right offers us nothing but mountebanks." [23] But this was clearly an impossible proposition.

Still, this Army, like so many others affected by currents of modern history, persisted in thinking that it was bringing a revolution and not a *status quo* in its wake. "National communism?" Hardly, except among an insignificant number of the very young officers. But, rather, a kind of indefinable "national leftism" that would impose equity and the purity that a military officer absorbs as his own regimen through efficient technical means rather than political bargaining. Let us listen to the argument firsthand in the words of Colonel Antoine Argoud, Massu's former Chief of Staff and *éminence grise,* who was later to choose the side of direct rebellion:

You would be surprised to learn how much the majority of officers are "leftist." We have understood that you have to fight communism on its own ground; in other words, we can't put up with the privileges of the banks and the capitalists, etc. . . . If the Army had really been able to do what it wanted in Algeria, there would have been a radical land reform with expropriation of the big estates long ago.[24]

To be sure, not all of the officers were Young Turks, after this fashion. But it was perhaps the most dynamic of the attitudes one encountered. At the least, there was majority agreement on three points: (1) the Algerian War as the "defense of the West," against a *guerre révolutionnaire* playing into the hands of global communism; (2) a contract to protect the Europeans and the loyal Muslims, and a determination to fight the pacification out "for twenty years if necessary"; (3) the resolution not to suffer defeat, by political chicanery or any other means.

This made of Algeria an absolute, when de Gaulle would have it a dependent variable in the mathematics of international affairs.

Loyalists and "Conditionals"

Surely not all officers were potential insurrectionists,[25] nor did they — national Catholics, national socialists, anguished "pieds noirs," "psy-

---

[23] *Ibid.,* pp. xv–xvi.

[24] Claude Krief, "Portrait d'un colonel" (interview with Colonel Argoud, November 1960), *La NEF,* July–September 1961, p. 54.

[25] Girardet's careful description is *à propos:* "If the Army as a whole seems presently inclined to follow the old rules of subordination and obedience, that obedience is essen-

chologues," anti-Gaullists — stand much chance of completing a durable coalition with one another, as later events were to verify. But their morale was harshly shaken by the government's ambiguous progress toward negotiations with the enemy, and their sentiment was, at best, one of conditional obedience. Many of them would continue to be fence-sitters when the blow fell in April 1961.

When a modern democratic Army *almost* rebels against its government — especially one of concentrated power led by a charismatic figure of military origin — this is *at least* as significant as its failure to succeed in doing so.

The Army had its loyalists and qualified loyalists as well as its insurgents and qualified dissenters. Jean Planchais settles on the terms "liberals," "Gaullists," and "traditionalists," [26] and these distinctions will do as well as any others. The Gaullists, relatively few in number, were those who had been continuous admirers of the General from the days of the Liberation, when "support of de Gaulle had meant a commitment which engaged one's whole life without any immediate hope other than taking part in combat against the enemy," [27] through the deceptive days of the RPF and its aftermath. They were supplemented by some whose attachment to the General on May 13, 1958, had represented more than a tactical posture.

The "traditionalists" were those survivors of the old Army and a few younger descendants who believed in the principles of obedience and service, the legacies of the *grande muette,* and the desirability of no political involvement. The position speaks for itself.

Finally, the "liberals" were those officers most closely in touch with normal civilian politics and the attitudes included in that spectrum. To be a "liberal" in the Army might range from the admission of legitimate doubt regarding the dogma of *Algérie française* to overt socialism or Catholic left-wing humanitarianism. The essential distinction from the other groups was that "liberalism" based its loyalism to the government in part on a political attitude, and not on a personalist one or simply on the mechanism of command and obedience.

The majority of the officer corps may be appropriately described as "conditionalist." However, "conditions" had a habit of changing. The demonstrations of Muslim support for the FLN, reaching maximum pitch in the Algerian cities in December 1960 — just prior to the referendum on self-determination — probably did a great deal to convince

---

tially defined as one *that is subject to reflection*." "Pouvoir civil et pouvoir militaire dans la France contemporaine," *Revue Française de Science Politique,* March 1960, p. 33.
[26] *Le Monde,* March 11, 1960.
[27] *Ibid*.

many officers that the cause of integration was lost, whether through natural evolution or through the government's blindness, and that other consequences would follow. Not even at this point, though, did most of the Army contemplate the abandonment of the territory with any willingness. The argument now became that the Army must remain in all circumstances as the guarantor of the equal civil rights of the two communities. Many in retrospect now had regrets that they had held off in the Ortiz-Lagaillarde coup of January, when, despite the disagreeably "fascisant" tone of the rebellion, the time had probably been most propitious for backing de Gaulle into a corner.

There was another army, too, a forgotten army learning, like its seniors, the gift of self-expression. These were the draftees, the *contingent*, no longer an illiterate rabble like the Grande Armée of Napoleon but a representatively articulate body of French opinion. By the time of the barricades, the duress and attrition of the war were already beginning to weigh on these nonprofessionals. Although, coming from the most diverse walks of life, many of these young soldiers had discovered an unexpected fraternity and solidarity in the Army, increasing numbers began to question the sense and justice of the war. One wrote in a letter:

Isn't the balance equal between the interests of our countrymen and the aspirations of the Algerian people for independence? Some want to stay French, they want to protect their goods, they fear for their lives. Haven't we the duty to defend them? The others fight for the recognition of their dignity as Algerians, for the possession of goods in their turn, and for the exercise of powers which, thanks to us, they feel able to assume.[28]

Another stated, typically: "We've all learned that Algeria was a political plum. Ever since, I've been disgusted with politicians. The politicos are two-faced salesmen."[29]

Like metropolitan opinion, which they much more accurately reflected than the *armée de métier,* the draftees were becoming impatient with the excruciating protraction of the conflict, even if some of the professionals were "willing to fight it out for twenty years, if necessary." Like the nation, the rookies were inclined to place their faith in the one man who stood a chance of ending the war on any terms. This feeling would burst forth spontaneously during the "putsch of the generals."

At the time of the government's referendum on self-determination (January 8, 1961) a number of high-placed officers were infuriated by the government's scarcely concealed orders to use military pressure in

[28] Xavier Grall (ed.), *La génération du djebel* (Paris, 1962), p. 47.
[29] *Ibid.,* p. 101.

support of "oui," when the government had done all in its power to mitigate the Army's political activity in the opposite sense. This inconsistency provoked hesitations on the part of the Supreme Commander, General Crépin, and had more than a little to do with his transfer to a command in Germany shortly after the referendum. Crépin was undeniably loyal; but his conscience could not easily support political involvement when the majority of officers under his orders were greatly disturbed at playing the role of government's advocate. General de Gaulle recognized Crépin's Algerian service magnanimously but with a hint of innuendo in his letter of January 12, 1961:

My dear Crépin . . .

I fully recognize the type of abnegation which, in these circumstances, has had to govern the conduct of many persons. Second to none, I understand why and to what degree the profound transformation of Algeria, both within and in its future relations with France, is heartfelt among the soldiers. . . .[30]

Prior to this letter a group of sixteen retired generals had issued a manifesto urging support of the "non" at the referendum; they were answered individually by other retired or reserve officers, such as General Billotte and General de Larminat, who pledged loyalty to the government's program and took those to task who were already in verbal rebellion. The battle of the following spring was already being joined on the printing presses. This period also covered the "trial of the barricades" and was affected by the general feeling of apprehension throughout the officer corps caused by Colonel Gardes's indictment and the quasi-seditious testimony of many senior officers, up to and including Marshal Juin. It was at this point that Juin broke his "amitié cinquantenaire" with the President of France.

The Eclipse of Psychological Action

In the midst of these events, and reaching its apogee in the period just preceding the week of the barricades, *l'action psychologique* had run its course.

About a year after General de Gaulle had come to power — and after the psychological action of the Army had served its purpose in the first referendum campaign — the regime made positive attempts to limit the scope of the doctrine and induce the officers to comply with the new definitions. In taking this step, the government recognized the existence and applicability of *l'action psychologique,* but gave it very precise boundaries. Its position is contained in a significant "instruction

[30] Text in *Le Monde,* January 14, 1961.

sur les fondements, buts et limites de l'action psychologique," signed
by Pierre Guillaumat, the Minister of the Armies, on July 28, 1959. The
document is worth quoting at considerable length:

Psychological war is designed to harm the adversary. Its purpose is less
the conquest of territory than of the enemy population. Always an accompaniment to a "hot war," it is one of the principal forms of the "cold
war." As with other weapons, the limits imposed on its use depend as much
on the enemy's practice as on the elementary rules of warfare.

Quite to the contrary, *psychological action* has the mission of facilitating
the training and information of the fighting forces of the nation. Known
under a new name because it works with modern techniques, it seeks to
achieve something that has always been a chief preoccupation of the high
command: the strengthening of the morale of the combatant, in time of
peace as in time of war.

On the practical plane, this action aims to immunize the combatants
against the adversary's initiatives of demoralization, for which the people at
large are often the conscious or unconscious agents, and also to give them
concrete ideas about national realities, the evolution of different kinds of
conflict, the general organization of defense, and the role of the armed
forces.

Fortifying the determination and combative will of friendly elements, it
likewise encourages the active sympathies of others, which it cannot do
without in time of peace, especially in a period of cold war. . . .

The West is indebted to France in particular for having been able, over
the course of its history, to develop a certain number of values . . . love of
liberty, respect for the human person and its rights, support and glorification
of the national ideal.

These things that make life worthwhile, undisputed for the French of
European origin, preserve all their value for the French North Africans and
for all peoples of the Community that have been nurtured and penetrated
by French culture. With regard to these latter, we must apply ourselves to
implanting these notions in the contexts proper to their civilizations and
their particular ways of life.

Our behavior should be such that the spirit of teamwork and solidarity,
as indispensable in a regiment as in the factory or the fields, should never
in any way violate the rights of the person. . . .

It is appropriate to emphasize that if discipline and psychological action
are not mutually exclusive, they should be confused in neither their principles nor their methods. . . . Thus understood, psychological action as it
applies to the armed forces aims at nothing else but raising the morale of the
soldier and his unit, improving their cohesion, assuring their connection
with all elements of the nation, and inducing the citizen to participate with
free conviction in safeguarding France, the Community, and, in so doing,
the free world.[31]

The language of Guillaumat's directive constituted both a compromise and a clear warning to the "psychologues" of Algeria, endorsing

[31] *Ibid.*, October 3, 1959.

the broad lines of their preoccupation but recalling to them the national values that should form the substance of their effort. As an injunction it was perhaps a little abstract to deter these convinced practitioners of the "war in the social milieu." The *cinquièmes bureaux,* distressed by the trends of government policy and eager to create their diverse committees of liaison among the activist groups, finally lent themselves, in some cases, to complicity with the insurrectionists of January 1960.

As soon as the government had prevailed over the rebellion, it took the obvious step in its own defense, with the justification of the events of the preceding weeks: it ordered, by decree of the Council of Ministers, on February 10, 1960, the suppression of the psychological action organs of the Army. "Suppression" may be a slightly misleading word, for in Algeria these same functions were redistributed between the *troisième bureau* (Operations) and *deuxième bureau* (Intelligence). At least, the locus of power, the citadel, of psychological action was swept away.

To many officers, the *cinquième bureau* had seemed the cornerstone of the civil-military effort, the *bureau population* whose activities had cemented the two communities through the creation of social, medical, and youth centers; its dispersal threatened to produce a lapse of these contacts.[32] It had also taken upon itself a multitude of administrative responsibilities (with the SAS) in scattered communities. The latter prerogative was answered crisply by a Presidential directive of February 20, 1960, defining strictly the limits of the military authority and, at least on paper, returning the Algerian administrative system to what it had been before 1956. An immediate aim of the instruction was to discourage the Army from intervening forcefully in the prospective cantonal elections, as it had in other consultations. The order read in part:

By decree of June 28, 1958, the government prescribed that "by virtue of the present exceptional situation regarding public order in Algeria, the military authority will exercise the powers normally attributed to the civil authority."

Subsequently a variety of measures have tended to restore a normal balance of attributions between the civil and military authorities.

Henceforth, and by virtue of the decree of February 20, 1960, ordered by me at the proposition of the government, the civil authority will once more, in principle, exercise in the Algerian departments the whole of the attributions which are its normal prerogative. However, and by reason of evident necessities of public order, special dispositions shall remain or enter into force.[33]

---

[32] See *ibid.,* February 17, 1960.

[33] *Ibid.,* March 4, 1960.

The end of a long, dark tunnel? Scarcely, because the Army, which had become a kind of State within a state and was persuaded that it understood and administered Algeria better than the civilians, would not easily relinquish its grip on a territory where military precautions were still very well advised.

From the point of view of psychological action, the functions of the *cinquième bureau* were shared. These affairs were co-ordinated by a "Bureau d'études et de liaisons," a component of the Superior Command Interservice Staff, charged directly with the pursuit of *la guerre psychologique*. A "Centre d'information générale" was provided with the mission of "the conception and adaptation of ideas pertaining to information and human problems" — that is, it became the "drawing board" of psychological action. The *troisième bureau* was henceforth responsible for adaptation of directives relating to the indoctrination of the armed forces and population, for education, for the administration of the re-education camps for Muslims, for the organization of collective groups, and for the media of propaganda. The *deuxième bureau* received the attributions of "psychological intelligence" and the "control of persons."

The decentralization of the psychological services altered the convictions of some and probably exasperated others, but it lowered the point of direct political danger by subversion and may have cost the four generals a valuable channel of authority when they made their putsch in April 1961.

Utopia Turns Sour

As the year 1960 progressed, moreover, certain currents of conviction in the Army were perceptibly changing. Largely this was a function of realism, not of the abandonment of too long and too closely held ideals. Few officers relished the thought of relinquishing Algeria to the GPRA, but an increasingly large number realized that the end of their adventure was in sight and silently submitted to the imperative that they would not make war on the government to save an irretrievable situation, albeit with valor. The demonstrations of the FLN's grip over the Muslim civilian populations of Algiers, Oran, and other urban centers in the *journées musulmanes* of December 1960 and the retaliatory European *ratonnades* of the same month shook sentiment in the Army badly and dissipated the tenacious dreams of an "integrated" Algeria that might have remained. For the first time since Massu had cleaned out the Casbah there was real danger of generalized race war, and the Army, with its prevailing social sympathies, wanted no part of it. The FLN had won the "second battle of Algiers."

Previously, the Army's "social liberalism" and its doctrine had been all of a bloc. Theorists would have boiled both down to a desire for the reassertion of man "on the human scale," [34] since subversive war exalted the primacy of the individual in making judgments and involved his moral and ideological qualities, just as contacts with the Muslims "on an equal footing" seemed a vast progress in the sphere of fundamental human relationships. The events of December 1960 seemed to show that this basic connection had been severed. The brave scheme of friendship between the two communities had not come into the realm of the possible, and it seemed to some that the cause of this rupture might be discovered in the false or improper application of the principle of *la guerre révolutionnaire* itself.

In some circles, to be sure, there had been a continuous questioning of the foundations of ideological war, generally by those officers who would be impatient with any political doctrine.

The best, and most influential, document of this "guerrier" position was a long letter appearing in the *Revue militaire d'Information* in late 1959, signed with the *nom de plume* "Simplet" (otherwise identified as a colonel commanding a regiment in Algeria). "Simplet" attempted, among other things, to "demystify" the ideological interpretation of the Indochina War:

In the Indochina conflict there wasn't any action of revolutionary or psychological war, and I am persuaded that the young soldier of the Viet Minh who rose — and with what courage! — to assault our positions at Dien Bien Phu was thinking not of the triumph of international communism but of "kicking the foreigner out of the place where I belong." . . .[35]

Whether or not this was an oversimplification of the role of ideology in Indochina, or whether it had indeed been essential that the "young soldier" should possess the ideological conviction of his leaders, this is an attitude that deserves to be recorded in the spectrum of opinions that assailed and divided the Army in Algeria.

At an opposite pole from the "guerrier" position in the Army's strange dialectic of soul-searching was the following. "Why have we lost *la guerre révolutionnaire* in Algeria?" asked a young officer in an

[34] See François Gromier, "Une conception archaïque," *Cahiers de la République,* November–December 1960, p. 18: "The Army, for a time, found confidence in its destiny somehow proportional to the distance it adopted with regard to its present and former missions: it discovered or rediscovered 'man' through an ideological or moral screen, borrowed, it is true, from the theory of *la guerre révolutionnaire* of a new age. . . ."

[35] "Simplet," "Guerre révolutionnaire, guerre psychologique, ou guerre 'tout court'?" *Revue militaire d'Information,* October 1959, p. 99.

anonymous article in *La NEF*.[36] "Because *at no moment* have we waged *la guerre révolutionnaire*." For this young and very forthright mind, the war in Algeria had been fought purely and simply to protect the interests of the French settlers, their "statute of superiority which distinguished them from the Muslims." He maintained that the theoreticians of *la guerre révolutionnaire* had been so hypnotized by their interpretation of the struggle waged by the Viet Minh and by their theories of crowd manipulation that they had lost sight of the historical, sociological, ethnic, and religious differences that set the Maghrebian Muslim off from any other people. Between the two wars he drew the contrast: "Nationalist and Arab — Marxist and Asian."

The lieutenant's analysis of what ought to have been done did not diverge profoundly from current theories; he was adamant in claiming, however, that none of these things had been done:

In a war like this one, military victory can be a defeat . . . if it leads to nothing. To conquer, it would have been necessary to take the regrouped peoples in hand, rally them around the Army in the same fight. That presupposed that the Army had truly revolutionary objectives. But it couldn't have any, since it was at the service of an unrevolutionary state.[37]

Algeria — another revolutionary, subversive struggle lost because of the primacy of political over purely military factors. This was the candid and private admission of an increasing number of officers as the year 1961 progressed and Belkacem Krim was about to come to Evian. The quality of some of the bitterness had now changed, as with "Lieutenant X," who crisply commented: "Precisely because the military command . . . was able to take the widest initiatives, its responsibility is the greatest." But could the military command ever have attacked the banks, the large landholders? Colonel Argoud, at least, had thought not. The majority of the Army did not share the special, autocritical misery of "Lieutenant X." They found a solidarity of anguish in the conviction of metropolitan duplicity and turned with pain on the government, keeping uneasy silence or preparing to take arms against it.

[36] "Lieutenant X," "Pourquoi nous avons 'perdu' la guerre d'Algérie," *La NEF*, July–September 1961, pp. 20ff.
[37] *Ibid.*, p. 36.

PART SIX

LIQUIDATION

XV

A SWORD TO BREAK

Dans un Etat libre, le pouvoir militaire est celui qui doit être
le plus astreint; c'est un levier passif que meut la volonté
générale. . . . Généraux, le temps de la désobéissance est passé.
— *Comité de Salut public,*
Décret du 14 frimaire, an II

FROM THE beginning of the Third Republic forward, despite periods
of turmoil, France had never known an undisguised military coup.
To be sure, the "putsch" of April 22, 1961, had its disguises — chiefly
the assertion that it was aimed, not at seizure of power in the *métropole,*
but only at winning the war in Algeria and saving that territory for
the West (a cornerstone of Maurice Challe's argument). But it undoubtedly violated a tradition of military restraint that had resisted
political storms for three quarters of a century.

Nevertheless, significant elements of France's military groups had
actively wished for and plotted the downfall of the legal regime on
numerous occasions from 1955 on. Their schemes had been of either
the wishful or stillborn variety, or had been stolen from them by
civilians who were not sensitive to the controls of professional discipline
and fealty. The successful coup of Algiers in May 1958 had been made
by civilian activist elements and a well-organized "Gaullist" network,
often in competition with each other, and handed to the unprepared
Army as a kind of trophy. The "week of the barricades" had likewise

been a civilian performance, and had found the Army profoundly divided on the question of what action it should or could afford to take. Other more nebulous schemes were canceled for one reason or another, usually in the interest of that "military solidarity" which their execution threatened to shatter.

April 1961, however, was a purely military operation, planned and executed almost entirely in disdain for the civilian milieu; in this case, the Army was determined not to become the prisoner of the violent "types" of Algiers, but rather to be in a position to impose its own political surrogates when the need for regular administration arose. If the military, in consciousness of cause, were to shatter its own unity by launching a coup, it desired, above all, that the action be its own responsibility and that its own reasons and justifications be paramount.

In Algiers city, the operation was carried out smoothly at night by the elements of the 1st Foreign Legion Parachute Regiment (under temporary orders of Commandant Denoix de Saint-Marc), and there was no crowd scenario or *veillée européenne*. The civilians simply awoke in the morning to discover that the military command had changed hands, and with it effective power in part of the territory.

Background of the "Putsch"

The stage for the "putsch of the generals" is set by a number of particular factors besides the "malaise," which it was customary for all to refer to. First of all, there was the theory of the "incomplete revolution" of May 1958. To many, the "promises of the Forum" had not been kept; the fault was partly with the European civilians of Algeria, but in large measure it was attributable to the duplicitous policies of General de Gaulle himself and to the betrayal of trust or weakness by members of his entourage. Debré had seemingly gone back on a decade of recorded belief; the weekly *Carrefour* had been seized on May 28, 1958, by the dying Fourth Republic for containing one of his blasts, and was now being seized by his own government for the same reasons. Roger Frey and other "stars" of the Gaullist accession were now complacently serving the General's maneuvers to create at all cost an *Algérie algérienne,* which, because of the extreme polarization the war had created, could mean only an *Algérie musulmane.* Even Soustelle, following his essentially political vocation, was confining himself to oratory rather than action. Things had been better for the Army under the weak Fourth Republic; de Gaulle had betrayed them with strength, rather than feebleness.

Secondly, there was the atmosphere in military circles surrounding the "trial of the barricades," which concluded only in March 1961. Marshal Juin, Generals Massu and Mirambeau, a covey of colonels, and many others had deposed for the defendants and issued many damning criticisms of the government. Gradually, sedition was becoming convinced, persuaded; loyalty was becoming somnambulistic and dubious. For the first time a great many direct criticisms of the President of the Republic were heard. The Left Wing, attacking the government from opposite premises, helped to destroy faith in its guidance of affairs. Attempts by Debré to muffle the National Assembly in its exercise of its critical function together with economic unrest in both labor and agriculture compounded the shakiness of the Fifth Republic structure. While Colonel Yves Godard and others were plotting the insurrection that was undoubtedly intended to return de Gaulle to Colombey and shake the nation into accepting an authoritarian "Sixth Republic," the protest proved, in the last analysis, as before, to be only negative. The putsch would be quickly destroyed by a type of hesitation that, properly, could see no clear alternative and feared the step into the void.

The evidence developed in the wake of the putsch suggests strongly that the operation was hasty and ill-conceived. Because of deep antipathies and poor co-ordination the lines of action between Salan in Spain and Challe in the *métropole* were never tied together.[1] All in all, the generals — except for Jouhaud — stood in the dark, ready to command the stage on cue, while the colonels spun the plot. The almost amazingly haphazard and fortuitous actions of Air Force Generals Bigot and Nicot, who, while remaining ostensibly loyal, failed to reveal the existence of the insurrection to their superiors and gave General Challe the means to reach Algeria, do not square with any interpretation of a carefully planned action. Palace revolutions in the Middle East have normally shown a good deal more prudence and finesse than this. A large amount of knowledge in subversive action is usually attributed to Colonel Godard, who, more than anyone else, was the ringleader of the attempt; but one cannot honestly conclude in this case that the former head of the Algiers Sûreté produced any masterpiece. Nonetheless, as we shall see later, there were certain factors operating in favor of the rebellion.

Two events in particular seem to have rushed the conspiracy into action precipitously. One was, of course, the threat that the sinuous negotiations with the GPRA might lead to some major decision. At

---

[1] " 'Were you in contact with General Salan?' 'Absolutely not. He was in Spain, you know. I didn't know if he would be able to come. (Negligently.) He came, I think, on the morning of Sunday, the twenty-third.' " Challe's testimony before the tribunal (hereafter referred to as "Trial"), *Le Monde*, May 31, 1961.

all cost, it suddenly appeared necessary to set these undertakings off balance and, if possible, create a climate in which they could not possibly resume.

A second factor, which can scarcely be stressed too much, was the reorganization of the military command in Algeria. After the referendum in January a significant shake-up in key posts had occurred, with the Commander in Chief, General Crépin, eventually being assigned to Germany and being replaced by General Gambiez, who had been the loyalist commander of the Oran Army Corps during the events of the barricades. A tightening of discipline and hierarchies was indicated, and Gambiez had already made one *tournée* of his command with the objective of restoring faith in the government's direction. However, he had been in his position scarcely more than a month and had not yet had time to cement his control completely over his staff, his field commanders, and the various military agencies throughout the territory. Every day lost by the insurgents meant added opportunity for Gambiez to assert his authority, neutralize hostility, and bring certain waverers back to discipline. The reader will remember that one of the factors precipitating the insurrection of the barricades in 1960 was the fear that Massu's replacement, General Crépin, would be progressively able to stifle the pro-activist survivors of the staff of the Army Corps of Algiers, like Colonel Antoine Argoud.[2] For similar reasons, it appeared imperative to act in April 1961.

Maurice Challe and André Zeller

The trump card was Challe. This esteemed leader and former Commander in Chief in Algeria had only in January gone into voluntary retirement from his "gilded niche" at Fontainebleau (as Supreme Commander of Allied Land Forces, Europe). It was expected that a preponderant part of the French military forces, which would have turned a deaf ear to the instances of the unpopular Salan, would follow him. Without him, the military would have felt considerably less anguish in deciding to stay out of the plot, and the recourse would have had to be to civilian activists, many of whom by this time tended to idolize Salan as the foremost defender of *Algérie française.*

Challe's impact on the efficiency of the plot was paradoxical. On the one hand, his presence neutralized some of the effect of Salan and his newly formed Organisation de l'Armée Secrète[3] and perhaps muted

---

[2] Actually, Crépin and Argoud were on the best of terms.
[3] See Chapter XVI.

the vigor of the uprising somewhat. On the other hand, this assurance that Salan and his element would not be in the saddle of the insurrection greatly animated the participation of some units and their officers, like the 1st Foreign Legion Parachute Regiment, which played the leading role, and whose commander, Saint-Marc, "detested Salan." Challe lost no time in declaring what everyone believed of him: that he had "no political ambitions." Neither had André Zeller, and if Edmond Jouhaud had any, there was scant chance of their fulfillment. This left Salan, "le chinois," whose Madrid sojourn in the company of Lagaillarde and Susini had served only to reinforce the common notion that he was hopeful of some day arbitrating the French political situation. To the officer corps Challe was the nearest thing to a revered leader that they had had since de Lattre and the best guarantee that the insurgency would be sanctioned by military integrity.[4]

How and whether Salan intended to manipulate Challe in the event of success is not known; it was, and is, no secret that there is little sympathy of outlook and personality between the two ex-generals. Salan's abortive attempt to revive the coup on April 25 after Challe had sent his emissary Colonel Georges de Boissieu to Paris to announce his capitulation undoubtedly heightened whatever grievance previously existed. Before the tribunal Challe refused to answer a question pertaining to his personal relations with Salan. Still, he could later declare by letter to the President of the Tribunal on July 8:

Our [Challe's and Zeller's] two comrades Jouhaud and Salan, not having the same reasons [to surrender themselves] as ourselves, departed so as to remain free for future struggles against the *fellagha*. They left with my complete agreement.[5]

It was not surprising to find Generals Raoul Salan and Edmond Jouhaud at the center of any military plot directed against the Fifth Republic. Salan had long since crossed the Rubicon when he slipped beyond the border illegally and took up émigré life in Spain at the end of October 1960; Jouhaud — another member of the fraternity of *treize mai* — was a "pied noir" both by birth and conviction and did not disguise the fact, even if he was not an intellectual officer with tastes running to *la guerre subversive*. The presence of Colonels Lacheroy, Godard, Gardes, Argoud, and Broizat as motive forces in the preparation of the insurgency was entirely in the nature of events. But one

---

[4] For example, Challe testified before the tribunal that if Lagaillarde had come to Algiers (as was rumored), he would have ordered him into the Army so as to control him. *Trial,* May 31, 1961.

[5] *Le Monde,* July 13, 1961.

might be surprised to find Maurice Challe and, to a much lesser degree, André Zeller[6] in this company.

The case of Zeller is the easier to deal with. It is based on a singular manifestation of the "traditionalist reflex." The only one of the four "putschist" generals to issue from a military family — his older brother Henri had also been a general — André Zeller was never in any sense a field commander or a leader of men. His reputation was that of a planner and logistician, and his personality was strict, sometimes choleric, and, above all, dogmatic in a very traditional and very Alsatian way. Though allegedly a "republican," his opposition to the concrete military measures of the Fourth Republic was no secret, and the Front Républicain government kept him in an unimportant post until he reached the age of retirement for his grade in 1957. Despising the government, he nevertheless played no part in the *treize mai;* but de Gaulle called him back to service on July 1, 1958, to become Chief of Staff of the Army. Having had nothing to do in his previous career either with Algeria[7] or with the intoxication of *la guerre révolutionnaire,* Zeller now became, paradoxically, one of the stoutest defenders of the *ultras,* some of whom he placed on his own staff. He was finally retired for good in 1959, whereupon he took to vigorous agitation against the Algerian policy of the government. Choler, frustration, and old-style fervor seem to have been the principal factors in André Zeller's decision to join the putsch. As part of the "quarteron" of generals, he had a specific duty. Not the sort of man who could inspire the loyalty of wavering regiments — although he dictated the timorous capitulation of the unfortunate General Marie-Michel Gouraud, commander of the Constantine Army Corps — Zeller was to be the logistical brains of the operation. Had the insurgency continued over a longer period of time, this would have burdened him with the responsibility of arms and ammunition distribution, the procurement of air transport, and the critical problem of feeding and paying an Algeria that the *métropole* would have tried to starve into submission.

Challe gave the conspiracy wide sanction, and it was his presence that made many believe, in its opening moments, that it might carry

[6] Jacques Fauvet and Jean Planchais, in *La Fronde des généraux* (Paris, 1961), find Zeller's presence at the center of the plot highly explicable; he had, in fact, been rather outspoken in January 1960. But to this observer, his background would not seem ideal for the lure of dangerous adventure. In every way, André Zeller appeared more gifted in the production of *feuilletons* than of putsches.

[7] Curiously, Zeller had asked to be relieved of his logistical post on the staff of the Minister of Defense in 1956 because he opposed the breakup and "deconversion" of France's European Army for the purpose of fighting the war in Algeria.

the bulk of the Army with it. As Fauvet and Planchais point out, he had become the "patron" for much of a subaltern Army that had never even laid eyes on him personally. With the spectacular advantages that Challe brought to the coup, even those who were not sympathetic to his deeply convinced apolitism rode on his coattails and left no doubt as to who was in charge.

Maurice Challe, Salan's replacement in Algeria, was the first air general in the history of the French Army to have extensive ground forces under his orders. An affable Southerner, frequently smiling but short on *bavardage,* he was one of the few valid visionaries of the French Army who understood global military strategy and its complicated relationship to technique, hardware, and operations. He was not an intellectual, but a coolly instinctual mover of military chess pieces. He inspired confidence, loyalty, and even love in his subordinates. Following a plan originally constructed by General Salan and his staff, he had brought widely dispersed forces together with great acumen in a series of regional rollback maneuvers, beginning in the Oranie and moving east, which caused the military power of the ALN to plummet to an extremely low ebb. After his departure General Crépin continued this same type of attack with almost comparable success. It was principally due to the military skill of Maurice Challe that one heard the opinion voiced in Army circles in 1959–1960 that the Algerian revolution might be crushed, after all, by strictly military means so long as the forthcoming political solution implied justice for the majority community.

Like Massu and many others, Challe was not, however, an uncritical proponent of the primacy of revolutionary war, its power and omnipresence. He shared a more balanced appraisal of the military problem with his successor Crépin and with other associates who had formed the "European" perspective at SHAPE.

He clarified his attitude toward *la guerre subversive* considerably in an interview for the *Revue de Défense nationale,* given in January 1961, just after he left Fontainebleau and the military service, and published, with unconscious irony, in the April number. Asked by Claude Delmas: "In view of its struggles in Indochina and Algeria, wouldn't the French Army be in a position to contribute its experience in revolutionary war profitably to the whole of the allied armies?" — Challe replied with great prudence: "It is quite obvious that because of the risks of subversion that we face the experience gained by the French Army can be useful. But dogmatism, which is always an abusive schematization, must invite our suspicion. The Algerian War is not a simple geographical transposition of Indochina, no matter what lessons the FLN chiefs might have been able to extract from the action of those of the Viet Minh." [8]

Maurice Challe took two things away with him from Algeria. One was a deep conviction that the territory should remain French and that the Army and the regime were obliged to honor their pledge to this effect. The other was that in Algeria the French Army was, in miniature, engaging in a war that was not peripheral but crucial to the survival of the West and the prevention of the spread of communism — a tiny replica of the conflict that might some day break out in continental Europe. These unabridged feelings and the perception that the government was trapped in a chronic misinterpretation of the critical danger threatening France and the West are what prompted Challe to act in the company of unlikely collaborators in April 1961.

Central also was the belief that the war in Algeria could be won in the matter of a relatively short time if he could take the reins back in hand. At the time of his departure, some of his officers had been engaged in serious negotiations with the leaders of Willaya 4 (Algérois), Si Salah and Si Mohammed, presumably with the goal of the capitulation of this rebel command.[9] It is known that Si Salah traveled to Paris under safe-conduct in this connection and was received at the Elysée. What happened in the interview is unknown, but in June 1960 de Gaulle opened negotiations with the GPRA at Melun. Challe felt that a military victory had been deliberately sacrificed to political expediency, and that his efforts to bring about this conclusion had been frustrated by his recall. Oblique and minatory mention of the "affaire Si Salah" would later be made by the defense at the "trial of the barricades." This event may have helped to persuade Challe that he knew how to end the Algerian War, if indeed this argument was not merely a transparent excuse that he used to protect others at his trial.

Challe's personal plan, according to his testimony in the trial, consisted of: (1) taking complete charge of military operations in Algeria and pacifying the territory in three months' time; (2) dutifully presenting a peaceful Algeria to a grateful France; and (3) conceivably producing that "choc psychologique" in the *métropole* which would lead to a re-examination of policies and a change in regimes, with General de Gaulle motoring back to Colombey for the last time. For, if General Challe was apolitical, he was assuredly no longer a Gaullist

---

[8] Claude Delmas, "Interview avec le général Challe," *Revue de Défense nationale,* April 1961, p. 587.

[9] See Fauvet and Planchais, *op. cit.,* Annex Two, pp. 263–264. Also, J.-R. Tournoux, *L'Histoire secrète* (Paris, 1962), pp. 329ff.

now. Some of his entourage hinted at a military seizure of the *métro-pole,* but Challe disclaimed such intentions, both then and before the tribunal.[10]

How could such a cool and competent military commander have gained the impression that he could pacify all of Algeria in three months, feed and supply the territory from unknown sources, and hold the *métropole* at bay? This is one of the deep mysteries of the Challist psychology that has never been effectively explained. The evidence must suggest that Challe hoped for and evidently believed in the complementary putsch in the *métropole* that would have helped solve some of his problems. There were undoubtedly many hesitations, interceptions, and broken promises — things which the defense was prudent enough to keep secret at the trial in the hope that the vacillators might take courage some day in the future and that the unity of the Army would not be completely sabotaged by the revelations.

Challe hoped to carry with him the quasi unity of the Army, as de Gaulle, helped by the ministrations of Generals Petit and Grout de Beaufort, had done in May 1958. Instead, he carried only the frustrated minority. The presence of himself and another Air Force general, Jouhaud, in the center of the plot and two others, Nicot and Bigot, on the periphery — although this latter was unknown at the time — failed to rally the Air Force. And the Navy, led by the staunch apolitism of its Southern Mediterranean commander, Admiral Querville, remained indissolubly loyal to the regime. When Challe perceived that his forces were a wavering fraction rather than the vanguard of a new expression of solidarity, he submitted to the old axiom of "l'unité de l'armée" and ceded. There was little else to do for a man of his stripe. Salan, who had arrived from Madrid only on the morning of April 23, gathered the ruins into his arms.

Re-enter Salan

History will pronounce its judgment on the delusions of Maurice Challe. It may also justify his feeling that he was being betrayed. But historians will be more intrigued by Raoul Salan than kind to him, one suspects. From his base in Madrid Salan had been the most distin-

---

[10] The fact remains that at 8:30 A.M., April 22, France V (Radio Algiers), now in the hands of the insurgents, broadcast an address by Challe in which he said, *inter alia:* "The command reserves the right to extend its action to the *métropole* and re-establish a constitutional and republican order which has been gravely compromised by a government whose illegality must be obvious in the eyes of the nation." Psychological action? Challe's own view? No one can very easily say. This was his only significant departure from "apolitism."

guished activator of anti-regime agitation ever since his self-enforced exile. He never officially forsook his "republican principles," [11] but he was not averse to making common cause with the neo-Fascist refugees of the "barricades" insurrection and the supporters of Dr. Bernard Lefèvre's type of corporatist state. In short, he attempted to catalyze the anti-Gaullist opposition of all sorts, making paradoxical overtures to the Extreme Right, the frustrated peasantry, the workers, disgruntled parliamentarians, princes of the Church, and anyone who, neither Communist nor "fellow-traveling," was susceptible to making common cause against the practices of the Fifth Republic.

By a curious sequence of events conditioned by the Algerian disillusion over the aftermath of May 13, 1958, the "Mandarin" had become a kind of idol of the "pieds noirs" and activists in the war-torn territory. His relations with General de Gaulle had become more and more uneasy as the summer months had worn on; his contacts, on the one hand, with the Algerian plotters and, on the other, with the Anciens in metropolitan France could reassure the harshest critics of de Gaulle's New Republic. The characteristic cry "Ne partez pas, Salan!" had accompanied him at his departure from Algiers in November 1958. After his retirement he returned briefly with Madame Salan to live near Algiers. Delouvrier advised him that it would be better to leave. When General Massu froze himself in anguished but correct discipline after his famous explosion, Salan came to be considered that "general of May 13" on whom settler hopes could be founded.

His command of the putsch of April would have ensured the implication of civilian elements in the operation; his political *maître de pensée* had apparently, by this time, become the perfervid Jean-Jacques Susini, who had his role in the events of the barricades. Challe's supremacy, on the other hand, made it likely that the insurrection would remain military in conception and direction; a number of high officers at the trial, including Nicot, would maintain that they sanctioned the idea of the putsch because they felt that Challe's presence would neutralize the extremism of Salan. The point of crisis between these counterpressures came on April 25, when Challe decided on his capitulation and Salan was forced to decide quickly about whether to pass the rebellion into civilian hands by distributing arms to the population. Happily, it was too late in the day to attempt an action of this sort after the psychological impact of the departure of "le patron."

---

[11] See Salan's letter to Hubert Beuve-Méry, p. 341. Also Fauvet and Planchais, *op. cit.*, Annex Six, pp. 273–274 (OAS letter to the deputies of the National Assembly, dated January 24, 1961).

It is not necessary to elaborate the reasoning of the "putschist" colonels, who swam in conspiracy as if it were their private pond. One other figure who deserves brief attention, however, is General André Petit, the dedicated Gaullist diplomat of May 1958, whose acceptance of an army corps command [12] from Challe would later cost him his rank, honors, decorations, and five years of liberty. Petit testified as follows in explanation of his actions:

For me the conception [of honor] is first of all the integrity of the national territory. That is why in 1940 I overcame an inner conflict and joined the Resistance. That is also why I committed myself to the thirteenth of May, 1958. No one can ask the Army to be an Army that gives up, any more than the Pope can ask his clergy to become apostates.[13]

For Petit and so many others a harsh lesson awaited at the end of a long and, but for the last stretch, unconditionally straight road.

Metropolitan Reaction

The reason that the misshapen plot of April 22 was genuinely danger-ous is that it drew a singularly misshapen response. Despite its attempts to control all information pertaining to seditious activity and to in-filtrate the activist milieu with informers, the government was un-prepared for the swift action by which the paratroops invested the key points of Algiers city and effectively won political control for General Challe with very little commotion. To be sure, reports of potential trouble had reached General Gambiez, but these were of the sort that "one gets every week." General Saint-Hillier, commander of the 10th Parachute Division, dined unsuspecting with his rebellious subordinate Denoix de Saint-Marc on the very evening that the legions were preparing to roll. And there is something essentially comical about the peripatetics of Gambiez in his jeep, trying fruitlessly to stop the march of his insurgent troops.

In a totally unalerted Paris, elements of irony blossomed. Importuned by the sensitivities of the Moroccan government, the French had ar-ranged for the transfer of the ashes of Marshal Lyautey, the titan of colonization, from Rabat to a more permanent resting place in the Invalides. Couve de Murville, the Foreign Minister, and Messmer, the Minister of the Armies, had gone to the Moroccan capital to supervise this delicate mission, which provided a strange symbolism for the events

[12] Petit was later to describe this as a "mission provisoire."
[13] *Trial,* June 8, 1961.

that were to burst forth.[14] Maurice Papon, the Prefect of Police, was on vacation at a ski resort; Michel Debré was sick in bed. President and Madame de Gaulle, in the company of the visiting Léopold Senghors, passed the evening at the Comédie Française witnessing a performance of Racine's *Britannicus* (a play in which one character, Burrus, describes himself as "un soldat qui sait mal farder la vérité").[15]

The first reaction was a kind of panic and utter incredulity at Challe's involvement in the plot. No one in government circles knew very clearly which troops had remained loyal or exactly what had transpired in Algiers. After a phone conversation with the government announcing their impending capture (and the existence of the insurrection), General Gambiez and the Minister Delegate, Jean Morin, together with the Minister of Public Works, Robert Buron, who happened to be in Algiers for another purpose, were sequestered and finally imprisoned at In-Salah. A few hours later General Jean Olié, the Chief of Staff, and Louis Joxe set off by plane on a trouble-shooting mission to "put down where they could" in Algeria in an attempt to recall the waverers in Constantine and Oran to discipline and to outtalk the rebels.

As during the "week of the barricades," it is rumored that a representative number of high government officials were ready to disgrace themselves through compromise and fear of the consequences of the coup. In the confused earlier moments of the conspiracy one could well believe that a person of Challe's caliber would not have acted unless he were assured of the unquestioned support of a large part of France's military forces. It was not known at this time what frustrations Challe was having in his conquest of Algeria itself.

But the imperturbable General de Gaulle held firm, though with a trace more of tension than usual, as he had during the more protracted "week of the barricades," and his associates gained strength from his example. Again his reaction seems to have been that curious mixture of simplification, obstinacy, and self-assurance which had served him well in the past. "Françaises, Français, aidez-moi!" he exclaimed in his television-radio address of the evening of April 23. The *métropole,* itself massively confused, nevertheless crystallized its sympathies and rallied to the support of the Republic.

The "quartier des Ministères" never surrendered to the fictitious tanks of Rambouillet; in Germany, General Crépin seized hold of his com-

---

[14] De Gaulle, speaking at the official interment of Lyautey's ashes on May 10, 1961, quoted the Marshal significantly: "We can foresee that in a more or less distant time an evolved North Africa, having a life of its own, will break its ties with the *métropole.*" *Le Monde,* May 11, 1961.

[15] This fact is due, with gratitude, to the literary erudition of Professor Stanley Hoffmann.

mand with loyal vigor and had all possible troublemakers placed under surveillance or temporary arrest, among whom were Colonel Henri Dufour (commander of the 1st Foreign Legion Parachute Regiment during the "week of the barricades") and General Paul Vanuxem, a known *ultra* who later disclaimed any association with the putsch. The Southwest and the other military districts of France were, in their turn, assured.

Premier Debré, Gaullist incarnate, no longer *ultra,* had matured in fortitude since the previous plot, but had lost none of his talent for the histrionic. Shortly after de Gaulle's performance he addressed the country himself, evoking the threat of aerial invasion by the rebels ("airplanes are ready to launch or discharge paratroops upon various airfields preparatory to a seizure of power"), and enjoining the good citizens of the Ile de France

... to go [to Orly, Le Bourget, Villacoublay, etc.] on foot or by car [some would later snicker over this "bourgeois" touch] to convince these soldiers who are misled by their ponderous error. Good sense must come from the soul of the people and everyone must feel that he is part of the nation.[16]

These passionate remarks, in a certain sense, together with de Gaulle's appeal — which seemed a little more human, a little less lofty, than usual — provided the "choc psychologique" which the insurgents themselves had hoped for and so notably failed to achieve.

Republic or de Gaulle or peace? No one can say in what proportion the average Frenchman weighed his motives in showing his distaste for the putsch. But it was certain that *le pays réel* was desperately tired of the war, its cost, confusion, and personal tragedy — together with the *petite guerre* waged in the alleys of the metropolitan cities — and could have no love for those who wanted to prolong it in the interests of mystique, loyalty, or even sheer practicality. The reputation of a Maurice Challe meant little to the *cafetier* or *épicier;* the coup might have gained more sympathy if it had been led by Jacques Anquetil, the winner of the Tour de France.

The presence of Challe continued to be a grave worry to the government until the moment when the insurgency was ready to collapse and Georges de Boissieu crossed the Mediterranean bearing the white flag. As before, the burning question now became: if there was a danger of metropolitan attack, to what extent should the government permit the mobilization and arming of civilians? The Left Wing thundered for the creation of popular militias, and the Communist-dominated Confédération Générale du Travail was screaming for close labor union

---

[16] Quoted in Fauvet and Planchais, *op. cit.,* p. 199.

co-operation across the board, with itself presumably in charge. Actually, general strike action was effectively carried out "in support of republican liberty," but the anti-Communist Force Ouvrière and, to a somewhat lesser degree, the Confédération Française des Travailleurs Chrétiens shunned a too close association with their eager Bolshevist brethren. Even the Parti Socialiste Unifié kept certain distances; no Popular Front came close to forming in April 1961.

The government discreetly decided that if prudence argued for the formation of civilian militias, it would be best to commence with the membership of the local committees of the Union pour la Nouvelle République. The newspapers would carry pictures of some of these doughty volunteers struggling into battle clothes in the midst of the court of the Ministry of the Interior, while a dapper and officious Roger Frey (the Minister) looked on approvingly and a dramatic André Malraux harangued the patriots *à la guerre d'Espagne*. Happily, the plot was over before these civilians had time to take to the field.

Failure and Liquidation

There is little point in examining the Algerian events in great detail. Hesitation, incredulity, and the widespread refusal of the troops of the command to defect with their officers overcame the initial impetus of the putsch. Challe, by the action of the night of April 22, had gained control of the central area of Algeria; it was then a question of assuring the compliance of the eastern and western wings of the territory. By the time the rebellion was a day old, it had collected the allegiances of the 1st, 14th, and 18th Colonial Parachute Regiments, the 1st Foreign Legion Cavalry Regiment (chiefly the units of the 10th and 25th Parachute Divisions), and some other miscellaneous troops. On the other hand, certain army regiments as well as the marines under the command of Admiral Querville and most Air Force units had remained loyal.

In the Oranie, General Henri de Pouilly stalled and temporized under the verbal onslaughts of General Gardy and Colonel Argoud, but refused to submit to the law of the putsch, withdrawing his headquarters from Oran to Tlemcen to avoid becoming embroiled with the insurgents, in a manner reminiscent of Challe's own action during the "week of the barricades." The unhappy General Gouraud vacillated in the Constantinois and played a poor Pontius Pilate until General Zeller reduced him to tears and written submission. He later countermanded his defection in another order of the day, but his indiscretion was to cost him a penalty of seven years' imprisonment when the smoke had cleared.

All in all, what defeated Challe and his collaborators in Algeria was not so much the galvanization of any conspicuous pro-regime attitude among the superior officers, but rather a pervasive psychology of buck-passing up and down the zonal and sectoral military hierarchies, the attitude described by the French word *attentisme,* "wait-and-see-ism." Planchais covers this phase admirably:

Attentisme, much more than loyalism, among the leadership snuffed out the plot. The *attentisme* of Gouraud . . . the *attentisme* of many others who, in knowledge of the conspiracy, weighed its chances at the last moment and found them too light. The *attentisme* of those who, placed before the event, recalled that eleventh-hour adherences often pay off better than early pledges. Finally, the *attentisme* of a crowd of subordinates proceeding from a formal conception of discipline: each obeying his immediate superior, expecting a sense of direction from him.[17]

The common soldiers, finally, the element constituting the majority of any army but which this Army so characteristically divorced from its calculations, took courage from the indecisiveness of their superiors and began to express their loyalty to the regime. The putschist generals, sensitive to a measure of dissatisfaction among the *contingent,* had already planned to release these drafted soldiers progressively from service and return them to the *métropole,* replacing them with Algerian volunteers from the disbanded Unités Territoriales,[18] and they had hastened to announce this policy to the Army of Algeria. It did not placate the men or win their affection.

Interestingly enough, and disquietingly for the leaders of the putsch, the resistance of the *contingent* to their orders, which had reached wide proportions by April 24, assumed the industrial form of the sit-down strike rather than the military form of active disobedience. Later investigation would reveal that many of the popular leaders that rose to direct this action in the ranks had "syndicalist" experience, a number of them coming from the Jeunesse Agricole Chrétienne and the Jeunesse Ouvrière Chrétienne, left-wing Catholic movements. The Communists do not seem to have been much implicated in this activity — except at the airbase at Blida — despite the retrospective judgments of Maurice Challe; probably there was not time for authoritative Party directives to reach them, in any case. If the movement was largely passive, it was

---

[17] Jean Planchais, "Quelle est cette armée?" *La NEF,* July–September, 1961, p. 59.

[18] One boatload of the *contingent* actually cleared Algiers harbor before the end of the putsch. The recruits shouted back Gaullist slogans at their angry activist escort.

spontaneous and impressive — a reflection of the metropolitan war-weariness and a gesture of approval for de Gaulle's attempt to end the conflict.

Here again, the main "choc psychologique" seems to have been the General's radio broadcast, which some of the men were able to hear illicitly on portable sets and whose content they made known immediately to their comrades. Some would hereafter refer to the "victoire des transistors."

The Left Wing, with *l'Humanité, Express,* and *France-Observateur* all chiming in, was quick to trumpet the preservation of "republican legality" (a legality they severely questioned when the regime was not threatened from the activist Right) by the joint efforts of the "democratic Army" (the *contingent* as opposed to the *armée de métier*) and the vigilance of the workers. It is true that these two elements contributed significantly to the frustration of the Challists. But the whole truth concerning the failure of the conspiracy is far from being this simple, and the interpretation offered by the French Left is characteristic of its own brand of "intoxication" and repugnance for the professional Army as a corporate group. Here the ghosts of the ideal army of Jaurès and the FFI raise their forms briefly from history's interment to dance to the ancient ideological music of class struggle. What is more important, especially in view of the government's shaky reaction, is the *attentisme,* itself a psychological cloak hiding the fact that the French Army, despite anguish, was not ready to pass beyond the brink into parricide.

One could then ask, as many did in the aftermath: since the Army had not marched into insurgency behind Challe, whom would it ever follow along the course of rebellion?

The last hours of the putsch, so unexpectedly deflated when compared to the promise of the opening moments, were still not without their moments of legitimate drama. After a cursory agreement with Challe on ending the resistance, Salan, Jouhaud, Gardy, and the camarilla of colonels made their escape into the friendly djebels. Denoix de Saint-Marc calmed the sympathetic crowd around him: "For us there's only one solution left: to go and get ourselves killed." He did not manage this, for he followed Maurice Challe to Paris to prison, trial, and sentencing. "Le patron" placed himself under arrest; in compensation Morin, Buron, and General Gambiez were freed to become masters in their own houses again. Challe, clad in field jacket and sadly and a little philosophically puffing his pipe, was bundled onto the plane for the *métropole;* arriving there, this dog-tired hulk of a physical specimen tumbled pathetically down a flight of stairs but never lost his amiable dignity or the conviction that he had done the only thing that was left to do. Morin, in the company of the agile trouble-shooter Louis Joxe, passed between the solemn ranks of CRS to re-enter the Governor-General's palace, from which he had so recently been evicted. The 1st Foreign Legion Parachute Regiment rode out of Algiers in trucks toward their base at Zéralda and formal dissolution as a military unit singing Edith Piaf's famous "Je ne regrette rien" while the women of the city hurled flowers at them. The government had known how to defend itself. At what price?

The "Procès du Putsch" and the "Procès du Complot de Paris"

The mistake of the "trial of the barricades" was not repeated; the government had at least learned this much. Patin, the President of the Tribunal that judged the first high-ranking military cases, was alternately suave, forceful, and ironic, and he knew his dossier well. The grand tenors of the "activist" bar of Paris had no chance to shine; their military clients had determined to submit to their lot quietly without making a political spectacle of the defense. The testimony and the judgment were speedy, occupying only two months (June–July 1961). One thing the defendants did not mask was the malaise of their profession, which, if it had become a commonplace feeling, was nevertheless a constant tincture of venom in the French body social. Said Challe: "The unity of the Army can now be found only in its hopelessness." He evoked the breadth of this feeling; stung by Patin's remark, "Lots of colonels are in prison who wouldn't have gone along if you had not been there," he replied in measured tones: "Maybe, but I can also say that if a certain number of officers, especially young ones, had not called me, I would not have gone." [19] In truth, this interaction was fatal and inevitable. As Colonel Georges de Boissieu, Challe's former Chief of Staff, said of him: "This is a man who left his mark on me. The evolution of his thinking is limpid. He is clean of any hint of ambition. He wanted to take up the Algerian business where he had left off." [20]

Defendant after defendant and witness after witness evoked the Army's feeling of playing the dupe for the regime's (both Fourth and Fifth Republics) ambiguous and contradictory policies. "Fifteen years of hope," said Commandant Saint-Marc, who looked the model officer despite his one serious transgression, "turned out to be fifteen years of

---

[19] *Trial*, May 31, 1961.
[20] *Ibid.*, June 1, 1961.

deceit." [21] Others echoed the feeling until President Patin, exasperated and ironic, finally declared: "Whatever country it is, the Army always takes power to maintain order." [22]

One dramatic incident which carried with it perhaps the dim shadow of reconciliation deserves passing mention. When twelve junior officers of the 1st Foreign Legion Parachute Regiment were being judged, they rose as a man to salute their former superior, the convicted Saint-Marc, as he took the stand in civilian clothes to testify. They then refused the same courtesy to General Gambiez, who proceeded to argue before the court for a just measure of clemency and tolerance. When Gambiez had concluded,

The President turned toward the accused. "Any remarks?" At that moment the twelve men rose with a single motion, as they had done for Commandant Saint-Marc.

For several seconds witness and defendants confronted each other face to face. When General Gambiez moved away, the lawyers stood up in their turn.[23]

Before a different tribunal (in the "trial of the plot of Paris") it was a witness, General Boyer de Latour, who saluted the accused. President Robert glared at him and said, "You could salute the defendants a little less and the tribunal a little more." "I acted according to my conscience," the General replied. "The tribunal appreciates your attitude as is fitting, be sure of that." [24] Boyer de Latour, like the distinguished General Valluy, Challe's predecessor at Fontainebleau, though not involved in the putsch, had made no secret of his sympathy. Valluy's own judgment, which found many echoes, was the following:

If I had been mixed up in this business closely or distantly I would have told them: what you are doing is totally unreasonable, mad in fact, but I can't help sharing your spirit.[25]

Finally, when a series of harsh but not unanticipated sentences had been passed on the major defendants, which could not have failed to shake the Army, the clever *bâtonnier* Charpentier saw his opening and warned the court: "You can still recapture that Army which by new condemnations you run the risk of forcing into opposition, exposing yourself to the creation of new seditions." [26] The tribunal, dealing with serious charges, to be sure, had perhaps gone far enough in effacing

[21] *Ibid.*, June 4–5, 1961.
[22] *Ibid.*, September 14, 1961.
[23] *Ibid.*, July 9–10, 1961.
[24] *Ibid.*, September 17–18, 1961.
[25] *Ibid.*, June 1, 1961.
[26] *Ibid.*, July 27, 1961.

the leniency of the *procès des barricades*. It seemed to reflect on Charpentier's point; hereafter the verdicts were tempered with the mercy of suspensions.

The most significant sentences (those without suspension) were the following:

Condemned to death in absentia:[27] Reserve Generals Raoul Salan, Edmond Jouhaud, and Paul Gardy; Colonels Antoine Argoud, Joseph Broizat, Jean Gardes, Yves Godard, and Charles Lacheroy.

Condemned to criminal detention.

15 years: Reserve Generals Maurice Challe and André Zeller; Air Force General Pierre-Marie Bigot, commander of the Fifth Air Region.[28]

12 years: Air Force General Jean-Louis Nicot, vice chief of staff of the Air Force.

10 years: Commandant Elie Denoix de Saint-Marc, interim commander of the 1st Foreign Legion Parachute Regiment.

8 years: Colonels Masselot (18th Colonial Parachute Regiment) and Lecomte (14th Colonial Parachute Regiment).

7 years: General Marie-Michel Gouraud, commander of the Constantine Army Corps; Colonel Charles de La Chapelle (1st Foreign Legion Infantry Regiment).

6 years: Commandant Georges Robin, commander of the parachute commandos.

5 years: General André Petit, commander of the 7th Light Mechanized Division.

Of the subsequent "trial of the plot of Paris" in September, which dealt with the machinations begun by Colonel Godard and subsequently guided by Colonel Vaudrey that were allegedly directed against the seat of government itself, little needs to be said. The plot was feeble and rudimentary; in the trial, charges of surreptitious meetings and the passing of OAS literature were aired, but the one fact that stood out was that this was a lamentable conspiracy.[29] The sensation of the trial

---

[27] Symbolic in a sense; if the fugitives were again to come within the reach of French law, they would have to be retried. General Jouhaud provided the first illustration; General Raoul Salan, the second.

[28] Particularly heavy penalties were imposed on peripheral accomplices, which could, in part, be regarded as cautions to others concerning the location of the boundary of sedition.

[29] The star of this trial was none other than General Jacques Faure, who, within his proper legal rights, refused to testify before a tribunal composed of inferior officers. On September 22, 1961, Faure and Colonel Roland Vaudrey were sentenced to ten years' imprisonment. Vaudrey escaped to Algeria to join the OAS.

was the publicity surrounding the famous *"carnets* of Colonel Godard," which, allegedly in the Colonel's own hand, implicated other plotters by code name. Photostats of the notebooks were mysteriously communicated to the newspaper *Le Nouveau Candide,* which published and commented on them; these documents formed part of the trial dossier. Colonel Godard denied authorship of the *carnets* from his foreign sanctuary; it is barely possible that the whole episode represented a tactic of *action psychologique,* introduced by the OAS to create apprehension and notoriety.

"Les Reins Cassés"

The government steered a clearer course through the trials of 1961 than those of 1960. But it rode rather roughshod over an already divided and demoralized Army, which, if it could not receive any feasible consolation for its disappointments, needed understanding and productive dialogue with the regime. This danger of driving a nerve-shattered institution to the wall, evoked in Charpentier's remarks at the trial, was an expedient with which the government had a close and necessary flirtation. Even so, no penalty against the putschists and the institution as a whole could have been severe enough to please a cantankerous and frustrated Left. After the Challe and Zeller verdicts, the Parti Socialiste Unifié announced righteously:

The scandalous clemency toward men who went to the brink of plunging France into civil war will provoke anger among the soldiers of the *contingent* and the workers. It will not fail to produce a bad taste with the Algerians [GPRA], with whom negotiations are under way.

Only a regime based on popular support would have wished and been able to punish the chiefs of the rebellion implacably.[30]

The effects of the trial on the Army itself were undoubtedly paradoxical.[31] Military men became conscious, as never before, of their differences and their isolation not only from the country but immutably from a regime from which they had expected understanding and which they believed they had carried to power. Time and again at the trial one saw not only that there were just the two armies of loyalty and disobedience, but that these were sometimes armies separated also by the thin line of thought and deed. If some marveled at the brazen foolishness of the putschists in view of their probable chances for success, many more endured crises of conscience for not having stood up

[30] *Le Monde,* June 2, 1961.
[31] See especially, Maurice Duverger, "L'Armée et le Procès," *Le Monde,* June 11–12, 1961.

to be counted on the side of *Algérie française* at the day of reckoning. Maurice Challe took a part of the soul of the Army with him to prison, dishonored and stripped of its decoration. There was now perhaps less anger, less *fougue,* more genuine metaphysical bafflement. A painful silence fell over the Army. One heard: "Nobody has spoken of politics for the last six months." "We've been kicked in the gut" (*On a les reins cassés*).

Once one postulates *Algérie française,* a great deal else must follow.[32] If the military rebels made a grave error in their postulation, the reasoning from that point on was not necessarily illogical. To restore the effectiveness of the military instrument and bring angry brothers back together under arms, it was necessary for the government to cut into the heart of the cancer and teach or bludgeon the Army to believe that it must abandon what had become its faith or its opiate. Here the government failed because it could not dismiss a mountain of prior equivocation and maladroitness or penetrate the essential psychology of the situation.

On the other hand, misery sometimes has its escape hatches. The terrible polarization wrought in Algeria by the FLN and the OAS activists had left the Army, like it or not, breathlessly swinging in the middle as a kind of constabulary moderating force. The excision of the "colonels" and general separation of the true *ultras* from active military influence had somewhat the same effect. In Algeria, the Army had been forced toward a new and decisive rendezvous with the pure interests of law and order.

This, however, did not exclude rancor and bewilderment. For there was no moratorium on thoughts about "fifteen years of deception," about communism and the defense of the West, the reform of the *métropole,* and the "pledge of May 13," of the plight of the loyal *harkis* when the GPRA took over Algeria, and of the dreary prospects of reintegration to a country that they loved but whose territory they dreaded as a permanent domicile.

[32] For an extraordinary exhibit of this point, see Jean Cau's interview with the right-wing deputy Alain de Lacoste-Lareymondie in *Express,* March 1, 1962.

XVI

THE TIME OF THE PLAGUE

A partir de ce moment, il est possible de dire que la peste fut notre affaire à tous. Jusque-là, malgré la surprise et l'inquiétude que leur avaient apportées ces événements singuliers, chacun de nos concitoyens avait poursuivi ses occupations, comme il l'avait pu, à sa place ordinaire. Et sans doute, cela devait continuer. Mais une fois les portes fermées, ils s'aperçurent qu'ils étaient tous . . . pris dans le même sac et qu'il fallait s'en arranger. C'est ainsi, par exemple, qu'un sentiment aussi individuel que celui de la séparation d'avec un être aimé devint soudain, dès les premières semaines, celui de tout un peuple, et, avec la peur, la souffrance principale de ce long temps d'exil.

— *Albert Camus,* La Peste

Peuple jardinier, toujours une eau sainte arrosera tes terres. Peuple; peuple qui ne recules devant aucunes pestilences.

— *Charles Péguy, "Le porche du mystère de la deuxième vertu"*

THE HISTORY of the last year of French Algeria cannot yet be written. Perhaps the task will some day fall to a man who, like the Dr. Rieux of Camus's classical account of plague in Algeria, has lived through the crisis with open eyes and open notebook and an unusually deep fund of humanity. Here was the visceral explosion of a long ordeal and cruel misunderstanding which mounted until whole cities were seized by dread and false rumor, terrified and determined to exact terror, driven to despair by the punishment of seeing a creed and patrimony wrenched away by the forces of history. Who can do the tragic scene justice?

In the midst of this chaos of a "secret army" and populations frenzied by the doom or jubilation of the inevitable was the nervous and baffled Army, allegedly pursuing a war that had by now been declared a war without victory, but that could not be stopped until men could sit for months around a table deciding on the peace that would take its place. Suddenly, one could wonder why so many had been allowed to die or why the dying could not stop. As the controversial Corsican deputy Pascal Arrighi asked the National Assembly on March 21, 1962: "To reach this point [that is, Evian], were so much blood and so many tears needed?" [1] And yet the brutal subversive war in the cities was to cost the bleeding territory over five thousand lives between the months of January and June 1962.

Formation of the Secret Army

Seven years of war in Algeria had not brought deliverance to the European Algerians or the exhilaration of triumph to the French Army. *La guerre révolutionnaire,* with its corollary of the "control of the population," had been a dismal failure so far as the Muslims were concerned, for their support of the independence movement had now swollen greatly in amplitude and ostentation. Either *la guerre révolutionnaire* was abstract and inapplicable, or the French Army had waged it imperfectly, or, as "Lieutenant X" insisted in his bitter article, it had not been waged at all. A commanding reason for the failure of the method, however, was probably the insuperable paradox of the "French fish trying to swim in Algerian water."

With the creation of the Organisation de l'Armée Secrète (OAS), following the so-called "Madrid agreements" of February 1961 concluded between Raoul Salan and others, the aqueous climate was suddenly more favorable to the French subversives. For it was now a matter of trying to capture the souls of their own population, first and foremost, and of using them in a revolutionary manner. The "psychological" colonels who followed Salan and went into hiding in Algeria or took alien refuge following the collapse of the putsch of April 22 had a more fertile laboratory in which to test their theories than they could ever have dreamed of when they came out of Indochina. After its demise in the fighting in Algeria, psychological action, with all its

---

[1] The entire National Assembly debate on the Evian agreements is of interest; see *Le Monde,* March 22, 1962.

accoutrements of terror, conspiracy, and "parallel hierarchies," was suddenly again in the ascendant as France veered toward the chaos of civil war.

The Secret Army was both a consequence and a cause of the extreme polarization of the preceding Algerian situation. The demonstrations and riots in both the Muslim and European camps that attended the preparation for the self-determination referendum of January 8, 1961, blasted an unbridgeable chasm between the two communities, and thrust the regular Army — with its ideas of fraternity and social equity — into the curious position of a "third force" between the nationalists and the settlers. The OAS, on the other hand, from the time of its formation, became the parliamentary agent of the settler psychology in Algeria.

Too weakly articulated to be of vital consequence in the "putsch of the generals," it nevertheless supported the April 22 coup without disclosing its liaisons and affiliations too damagingly. Three days before the outbreak of the insurgency, in its tract *La Voix du maquis,* it sought to undermine the loyalty of the police and CRS of Algiers:

Police, CRS, you who belong to the forces of order, know that the moment of choice draws near. Remember what happened to the *miliciens* [of Vichy]: ten thousand of them were shot for thinking they could have double-dealings with the fatherland. Today, for there is still time, take sides resolutely. Sabotage the orders of the infamous regime. Transmit false information to your treasonable superiors. Organize your own networks of resistance. Stand ready to join the nation's Army at the hour of the uprising.[2]

In general, one can distinguish very neatly between the OAS affiliates and the other conspirators of April 22: the former escaped to continue the subversive struggle they had chosen to wage, while the latter (like Challe, Zeller, and Petit) gave themselves up and were returned to the *métropole* to stand trial.

The OAS represented the intersecting axes of military and civilian complicity. Thus it was particularly dangerous and was assured of wide contacts, the availability of practically all existing activist networks, access to weapons and explosives, and the possibility of significant financial support. Swiftly the OAS gathered under its wing the diverse anti-regime groups of the Right that had so frequently squabbled among themselves. Its liaisons reached not only into the embittered Army, but to certain sources of Catholic Church power — through such intermediary agencies as Jean Ousset's *Cité catholique* — to business and finance, to the veterans' groups, and to the National Assembly

[2] *Le Monde,* April 21, 1961.

itself, where eighty deputies identified their sympathies on November 9, 1961, by voting for the "amendement Salan."[3] It was conveniently fronted by such polite *Algérie française* organizations as the Comité de Vincennes of Georges Bidault, Jean Dides, and Jean Le Pen and by the activity of Jacques Soustelle, who exiled himself voluntarily to northern Italy during the summer of 1961; it was supported explicitly by such publications as *Rivarol* and somewhat more discreetly by others like *Carrefour*.

Structure and Capabilities of the OAS

By the fall of 1961, the OAS was apparently structured along lines familiar to anyone who had read the special number on "La Guerre Révolutionnaire" of the *Revue militaire d'Information* (February–March 1957), put together by Lacheroy and his team. Both Algeria and the *métropole* were divided into zones (apparently four in the latter case), sectors, subsectors, districts, and cells. There were parallel organizations for making military and political contacts; these, however, overlapped to a degree. Specialized units were formed to carry out the functions of funds collection, propaganda and psychological action, intelligence, terror *au plastic,* and justice (that is, assassination). The latter elite was reputedly directed by Jean-Jacques Susini. Susini himself enjoyed close relations with General Salan. In assigning victims the dossiers and experience of Colonel Godard, who had headed the Sûreté in Algiers during Salan's incumbency, proved to be particularly useful. Thirty small shock groups were organized for action in the Algérois.

General Paul Gardy and Colonel Godard were announced to be Salan's direct deputies commanding the Algeria-Sahara region. General Edmond Jouhaud, prestigious in his native fief of Oranie but not a practiced tactician in *la guerre révolutionnaire,* was given that area to supervise. Captain Pierre Sergent was allegedly the Commander in Chief of the Secret Army in the *métropole*. At the top of the pyramid sat Salan, enthroned somewhere in Greater Algiers, flanked by the dogmatic theoretician Susini and by Colonel Jean Gardes, an efficient courier and elusive traveler.

After a year of growth, the OAS network and its structure were impressive, even if its own claims of strength were clearly inflated for purposes of propaganda and "intoxication." Political assassinations — of such men as Commissioners Gavoury and Goldenberg, Commandant

---

[3] An amendment on reducing the duration of military service, which solidified and identified the regime's right-wing parliamentary opposition.

Poste, Colonel Rançon, and General Ginestet — were carefully controlled on explicit orders from above. Finances were fed not only by forced contributions *à la FLN,* but from a remarkable — and as yet largely undisclosed — variety of sources in France and other countries, some of them impeccably well connected. General Salan's famous letter, written from prison on May 4, 1962, to the unidentified treasurer of the Secret Army, authorized the transmittal of 100 million ("old") francs to "the man replacing me" (Georges Bidault).[4] At the same time, a large measure of security was maintained against the attempts of the French government to topple the structure. As might be expected, this was much more successful in Algeria, where hidden complicities and double agents aided the subversive group massively, than in the *métropole,* where the general population was hostile. A certain autonomy in the activity of the hierarchies and an extreme vigilance against allowing details of the organization, its operations and its membership, to circulate internally where they did not pertain made it difficult for government agents to penetrate the OAS or move against it integrally. Suspects brought in by the police for questioning were carefully schooled to reveal only what they believed to be already known; plans, headquarters, and places of meeting were changed at the slightest hint of compromise. Needless to say, the structure and catechism of the OAS resembled those of the FLN on many points. However, there was never such a thing as a monolithic OAS. The Secret Army was, in reality, a congeries of groups, each having its own myths and political ideals.[5]

In Algeria by the fall of 1961 it was estimated that the OAS enjoyed the active or passive support of about 80 to 90 per cent of the European population, that it had the *droit de cité* in Algiers, Oran, and probably Bône, and numerous efficient contacts elsewhere. However, it had made no appreciable dent in the countryside, where, without the consent of the French Army's troops of the *quadrillage,* the "French fish" was unable to swim.

But the complex structure of the European quarters of the city was a swarming culture for subversion. The channels of intelligence were almost entirely in the hands of the OAS, and its terrorists could and did appear in broad daylight without likelihood of frustration or cap-

---

[4] The text of the letter was published in *Express,* May 31, 1962. See also the note entitled "Bidault, chef suprême de l'O.A.S.," allegedly quoting an order diffused on April 1, after the arrest of Jouhaud but before his own capture (No. 32/OAS/106), in which Salan named Bidault his heir apparent.

[5] See Paul-Marie de la Gorce, "Histoire de l'O.A.S. en Algérie," *La NEF,* October 1962–January 1963, p. 174.

ture. Complicities in the police, the bar, and the medical profession made the task of the government especially trying: a wounded terrorist sent to a hospital under police guard was apt to slip away in a mysterious sedan after he had received medical treatment. Strikes, miniature demonstrations, and obedience to specific slogans were continually invoked to prove not only the strength but the authority of the OAS in urban Algeria, to dismay and vex the government in its negotiations with the GPRA and pretensions of controlling the territory, and to serve as cumulative dress rehearsals for the *grand jour*. Although race war against the Muslims was at first severely repudiated by Salan, it began to increase in 1962 as the fortunes of the OAS began to decline. The result was a critical re-examination of the organization's earlier strategy. A plan to launch a direct attack on the administrative capital of Rocher-Noir on January 4 aborted; it had been intended to make Algiers "fall like a ripe fruit." The introduction of government secret agents and special police commandos ("barbouzes") into the explosive situation infuriated the European settlers and threatened to discountenance the Army, which was being progressively withdrawn from the territorial *quadrillage* and regrouped as a potential constabulary on the outskirts of the cities.

When the inquiring reporter Alain Jacob of *Le Monde* asked these Europeans to describe their reasons for attachment to the OAS and what they expected of it, their answers were diffuse and vague. A student summarized the general attitude:

If de Gaulle and the FLN reach an agreement, that means the FLN will more or less take power. We know what that means. We have to have something solid to fight this with.[6]

But many Europeans conceived, often fatuously, of different outcomes ranging from a sort of Algerian South Africa to an independent state formed in collaboration with the FLN and implying organic minority protection. ("Why not a government with our own people: Jouhaud, the Bashaga Boualem, and Ferhat Abbas?")[7] Partition, either negotiated or enforced by arms, was a frequently voiced solution.

In the *métropole* the OAS possessed numerous agents and generous sources of finance, but it was essentially operating in an alien milieu.

---

[6] Alain Jacob, "L'O.A.S. telle que la voient les Européens d'Algérie," *Le Monde*, November 16, 1961.

[7] *Ibid.*, November 15, 1961. Abbas was considered by the Europeans to be more reasonable than his successor, Ben Khedda; the Bashaga Boualem was an independent but pro-French feudal Muslim leader, elected a deputy in the 1958 National Assembly and later a Vice-President of that body.

Its activities, rarely synchronous with those of Algiers, were the more spectacular for being isolated and unsustained. As the source of grave incidents in all parts of France — especially in the capital — the Secret Army appeared to implant cores of strength in the Toulouse region (to which many French North Africans had moved in recent years) and in the strongly Catholic departments of Brittany and the Vendée. The interservice officers' training school of St-Cyr-Coëtquidan became a hotbed of OAS activity, and many members of aristocratic families dwelling in the area became implicated in the networks of the Secret Army. The government police forces were able gradually to penetrate and uncover these metropolitan operations in the Rhône Valley, in the Southwest, and finally the West, and to limit, if not quench, the effectiveness of the subversives. A major success was recorded with the revelation of the Bosquet-Boutmy network in September 1961.[8] Another came with the capture and confession of Count Horace Savelli in March 1962; this scion of a family that had given two popes to Christendom admitted himself to be "Marceau," the leader of the OAS in the West of France. Finally, in early April 1962, the French services arrested Captain Sergent's adjutant, Lieutenant Daniel Godot, who would later admit participation in numerous arms thefts and acts of assassination.[9] Among the documents discovered with Godot was one entitled "The participation of the *métropole* in the last phase of OAS action." This plan envisaged in detail the implementation of three stages of subversive action: (1) paralysis of Gaullist power; (2) creation of a climate of generalized insecurity; (3) total paralysis of the country. Needless to say, the ambitions of the Secret Army were far in excess of their capabilities in this case; 90 per cent of the French people were about to say "oui" to the Evian agreements.

As the published names of agents and provocateurs multiplied, the French judicial process staggered under a fantastic burden of instructions and trials. A guess about the numerical extent of the dissidence might be based on the "non" vote of the referendum of April 8, 1962 (nonapproval of the cease-fire accords signed with the GPRA at Evian on the preceding March 19). This position enlisted the support of 1,795,000 persons (9.3 per cent of the number voting) in the *métropole*. Though this was a stunning electoral success for de Gaulle, the considerable numerical strength of a resourceful, well-heeled, and embittered Right was nevertheless revealed.

[8] Bosquet was one of the reporters for the extreme right-wing weekly *Rivarol;* Boutmy had been a right-wing Senator.

[9] Godot would, notably, confess involvement in the attempt on the life of Yves Le Tac, brother of the Gaullist deputy Joël. See *Le Monde,* April 11, 1962.

Factionalism

By the late spring of 1962, with the abolition of French rule in Algeria assured, the seizure of power in the *métropole* became the unique end of the cohorts of the Secret Army. The OAS leadership had split earlier on this point, at least insofar as it affected tactics. During the fall of 1961 a dispute developed between the so-called "Madrid group" and the official leadership, based in Algiers and headed by Salan. The "Madrid group" were Pierre Lagaillarde, and Colonels Argoud, Lacheroy, and Broizat. Aside from whatever personal jealousies may have existed, the two groups appeared to disagree over the desirability of launching a metropolitan putsch in concert with an attempt to seize control of a part of Algeria. Salan and his staff allegedly demurred from the idea of the double-pronged attack, in the belief that a successful action in Algeria could impose a "period of reflection" on the *métropole,* during which de Gaulle's literal power would crumble and be forced to cede to a "more realistic" government, which then would have to recognize the *fait accompli* of European sovereignty in a part of Algeria.

Moreover, it seems certain that Salan wished the entire governing apparatus of the OAS to be located on French or Algerian soil so as to emphasize the Algerian vocation of the organization and exhibit solidarity with the European settlers; the "Madrid group" preferred the idea of foreign sanctuary and a potential government-in-exile *à la FLN.*

It is reported that the controversy grew so heated that Salan, through his personal emissary in Madrid (Captain Marcel Ronda, one of the defendants of the "trial of the barricades"), intervened with the Franco government to expedite the neutralization of the "Madrid group." *Embarras de richesse:* The Debré government was seeking the same favor. With an enviable totalitarian speed, the Caudillo responded handsomely by packing the troublesome tourists off to the Canary Islands, on October 26, together with Joseph Ortiz, who was shunned by the others. He received in return a prompt roundup in Paris of some Spanish republicans that had been causing him distress. Colonel Argoud would return from his exile to participate importantly in the final actions of the Secret Army.

According to the plan that Salan and his adjutants seem at one time to have endorsed and were unable to implement, events would have gone as follows:[10]

[10] See Jacquet Fauvet, "D'un putsch à l'autre," *Le Monde,* October 20, 1961.

1. At the most favorable psychological moment, the OAS would seize Oran and Algiers and as much as possible of the coastal territory in between. Its main effectives would be the reanimated Unités Territoriales and, especially, the veterans of the Dispositifs de Protection Urbaine, originally set on foot in 1957 by Colonels Godard, Trinquier, and Vaudrey to combat *fellagha* terrorism. The neutrality of most of the Army would be counted on, and the "pied noir" members of the civilian police would be expected to follow. This base, which might be called "la République française d'Algérie," would be held indefinitely, to the frustration of the *métropole*. Europeans and loyal Muslims would be regrouped in the territory.

2. A waiting game would be played with the regime in order to show its impotence in settling the Algerian affair. Strenuous propaganda efforts would be made to create a temporary coalition of the dissent — activists, peasants, politicians, even workers — whose unremitting pressure would lead to de Gaulle's collapse. If extreme polarization produced civil war at this juncture, the OAS would be prepared to cross that hurdle. If, on the other hand, some type of parliamentary regime were the successor government, the OAS would count on imposing its strength there also.

3. In this case, recognition would be accorded by the government of France to the *de facto* partition of Algeria. The Army would be little inclined to follow orders to move against this European enclave if it could preserve order and enforce its own legitimacy. And popular feeling in France, conceding a measure of right to the settlers, would rally to the settlement if it meant peace and oppose any initiatives of reconquest.

The Army and the OAS

The Army in Algeria faced an extremely complicated problem of conviction vis-à-vis the OAS. On the one hand, the smart and frustration of the putsch of April still lingered on; the service as a whole had been sanctioned through the suppression of the rebellious regiments, and knew it. The malaise could not be effaced by penalties and a sharp recall to discipline. Comrades of old whose ideas had seemed logical once upon a time were in prison or had joined the ranks of sedition. Resignations and voluntary retirements were mounting. The "oath of May 13" and the possibility of protecting the loyal Muslims were being swiftly jettisoned by the government. The Army, which had fought the FLN for seven years and had a very low opinion of its constructive capabilities, could never become attached to the idea of handing it a territory that it probably could not feed, administer, or distribute justice in.

At the same time, a number of mechanical details were operating progressively against the Army's visceral feelings. The core of anti-regime resistance in the Réserve Générale had been fragmented by the measures taken in the wake of the putsch. Two divisions of troops were alerted for return to metropolitan France by order of General de Gaulle. Unreliable commanders had been posted elsewhere, especially to Germany, where it was felt that they could do the least harm. The influence of civilian activists in Algiers with efficient Army contacts, like Alain de Sérigny, had been muted; either one was now clearly in hidden subversion or one held his tongue. The Army command in Algeria had been, as far as possible, placed in the hands of unconditional loyalists who would not permit their subordinates even the excuse of *attentisme* in the execution of orders.

Finally, although served and commanded by former military officers (of the civilians only Susini and Dr. Perez held high positions), the OAS was not an entity designed to appeal to the military reflex. It committed incessant brutal acts which the Army had to hazard itself and its own unity to curtail. It provoked race war between European and Muslim, which went deeply against the grain of most professional officers. It was penetrated in the lower echelons by the most dubious type of civilian, including professional murderers. It was the idol of the "pieds noirs," toward whom many members of the Army had by now acquired certain reservations. After April 24, 1961, Challe and others had not fled to the *maquis* to join it. Most fundamentally, it forced the Army, against its wishes and most basic strategic lessons, to fight a war on two fronts.

Anxious to confide all key posts in Algeria to proved loyalists and, if possible, Gaullists, the regime cemented its grip on the territorial command structure. For Superior Commander of the Joint Forces of the 10th Military District (no longer could a "Commander in Chief" be countenanced) it chose General Charles Ailleret, who had waveringly opted for obedience as a division commander in the Northeast Constantinois at the time of the putsch. Ailleret, a *polytechnicien* and frequent writer on questions of atomic strategy in the military journals, had interests and tastes paralleling those of de Gaulle. His rise had been appropriately meteoric: from colonel in 1958 to divisional general at the turn of 1961 and to general of the army less than a year later. De Gaulle was running out of generals and thus not uncharitable to the ones on whom he could count. Ailleret's mission was: (1) to snuff out all "intoxication" in the Army; (2) to preserve order; and (3) to prepare Algeria for the transfer of sovereignty. Ailleret and Jean Morin, the Delegate-General, set up their headquarters at the newly constructed and heavily guarded "administrative capital" of Rocher-Noir, at a sufficient remove from the seething anarchy of Algiers.

Ailleret moved to the attack on September 20, 1961, in a notable order of the day, where he wrote:

> While pursuing the struggle against the rebellion, in which they are fully joined, and while opposing any racial manifestation wherever it comes from, our armed forces should also:
> — Assist the forces of the police charged with neutralizing the so-called OAS.
> — Recover the arms, ammunition, and equipment stolen from the Army that is held by the subversives.
> — Oppose any propaganda aiming to justify revolt and violence.
> — Protect the people against extortions of funds based on terror and against bombings.[11]

Thus the Superior Commander made it plain to all officers and men under his orders that they were expected to execute the regime's directives with dispatch and thoroughness or leave the Army. Trimming and oblique loyalties would not be countenanced. This statement, treating the OAS as an enemy, removed a previous equivocation. For scarcely a week earlier, the activists had distributed a clever tract among the officers, urging their neutrality if not their support:

> In the case of a new popular explosion, two solutions confront you:
> — To place the whole or a part of your men behind the military chiefs who direct the movement without hesitation. You will merit the respect of all Algeria.
> — Or to refuse to join the movement, deterred by the scruples that we understand or uncertain of the reactions of your men.
> In this last hypothesis we ask you to refrain from entering this dispute which sees Algiers and Paris opposed, not to contravene the will of the Algerian people, but to continue the struggle against the *fellagha* and to avoid any clash between Europeans and Muslims.[12]

Many officers were now robbed of their "neutral" option by the order of the day.

The Army would obey without enthusiasm, for police tasks were always distasteful. At any rate, by March 1962, in an atmosphere of mounting bloodshed with worse events in prospect, the high command had little choice but to bring the Army into the cities and try to stop the massacre by trying to create a "quadrillage qui bouge." [13] That

---

[11] *Ibid.,* September, 21, 1961.

[12] *Ibid.,* September 16, 1961.

[13] See (*Le Nouveau*) *Candide,* March 8–15, 1962, especially the article "L'Armée obéira-t-elle?"

this tactic was only in part successful should be attributed not to the disloyalty of the Army but to the reticence of the government to grant Ailleret the powers that Massu had once enjoyed. But the great majority of the Army — excluding the *activistes de foi* — were by now desperately fatigued by missions for which they had been neither equipped nor trained. The continuation of the nightmare suddenly seemed more agonizing than the experience of its worst conclusion.

The Army had demonstrated *en masse* that the OAS could count neither on its support nor even on its sympathetic neutrality under normal circumstances. The grip of the regime was too tight on the military forces, and the literal content of the daily acts of the subversives was too abhorrent to tempt the Army into sedition. Consequently, it was only through the encouragement of anarchy and race war that the Secret Army might hope to turn the tide in Algeria and impose its solution of partition on the war-torn country while creating "paralysis" in the *métropole*. The Secret Army took this gamble and, in failing to achieve a single one of its primary objectives, lost it.

Attempts on de Gaulle's Life

Since the government's conduct of Algerian policy — and, indeed, all foreign and military policy — depended ultimately on the whims and insights of a single person, the Chief of State, there was a very great temptation to induce chaos by removing him. On the evening of September 9, 1961, assassins scarcely missed blowing up the General's car with dynamite on Route Nationale 19 at Pont-sur-Seine. The character of their contact with the OAS was real though oblique. However, on September 15, in a letter forwarded from Algiers to Hubert Beuve-Méry, the publisher of *Le Monde,* General Salan had the following to say:

Hasn't one pushed ignominy a little far in alleging that I, Raoul Salan, twice commander-in-chief in the face of the enemy, could have been the instigator of an attempt to murder the Chief of State? I shall not tarnish my past and my military honor by ordering the assassination of anyone whose own past belongs to the history of our nation.[14]

Salan's *haut-le-corps* caused Beuve-Méry to comment crisply: "Better if the ex-commander-in-chief had left off there. Or rather if he had taken advantage of this occasion to disavow completely the criminal acts of the groups claiming allegiance to the Secret Army."[15]

---

[14] The full text of Salan's letter is reproduced in *Le Monde*, September 20, 1961.
[15] *Ibid.*

On September 20, the government (through the Delegation-General of Algiers) would release an extraordinary photostated document dated September 11, purportedly from Colonel Gardes, showing that the OAS was plotting the murder of the President, even if not involved in the attempt at Pont-sur-Seine. Astonishingly enough, it also brought to light the allegation frequently made afterward in right-wing circles that the whole affair had been a put-up job:

This is a show staged by Foccart, the Elysée, etc. . . . Who benefits from the crime? De Gaulle and his acolytes. Let the arrests take place. That's what I think. We have to counterattack the Gaullist propaganda on the radio. It's pretty stiff right now. Still, we mustn't draw up any leaflets indicating that we don't intend to liquidate him. The day the O.A.S. acts there's going to be a dead man. End of message. Fleur [code name of Gardes].[16]

One more Chinese box in the strange history of France to be put beside the theft of the Revers Report, the bazooka attempt against Salan, the Massu-Kempski affair, and a host of others.

On August 22, 1962, there was another unsuccessful attack on the President as he drove to the military airport at Villacoublay with Madame de Gaulle. Preliminary reports, without tangible evidence, sought to implicate Jacques Soustelle in the plot. The constant danger of the decease and lapse of *le pouvoir* finally led Roger Frey, the Minister of the Interior, to envisage extraordinary police measures to ensure the security of the state during the perilous interregnum that threatened to come at any moment.

Apocalypse

What might happen in the event of a successful OAS attempt on the life of the President of France at a time when Algeria still hung in the balance was problematical. However, a number of important documents captured in Greater Algiers and the Constantinois by the forces of order amply revealed the main lines of subversive action. One order of considerable interest, labeled the "instruction Salan" and dated February 23, commenced with the following words:[17] "The irreversible is about to be undertaken." It continued notably with the following observations and instructions:

On the situation:

The population: I believe that the population of the large urban centers has reached a high enough degree of structure and organization to be

[16] *Ibid.,* September 21, 1961.
[17] *Ibid.,* March 20, 1962.

considered a valuable tool. In the countryside this stage is far from achieved. . . .

The Army: It is not impossible that upon the declaration of the cease-fire . . . certain military units led by young cadres will decide to cross the line and enter the struggle. . . .

The *maquis:* In their present state our *maquis* are far from being a tool for determining the outcome. I demand that the projects under way be speeded up. . . .

On the intention:

Regarding the preceding elements, I propose:

(*a*) To smash the adversary's maneuverability and oblige him to modify his plans in whole or part.

(*b*) To that end, to create one or more new situations phased in time. These situations should seek to draw the population into opposing the orders and decisions of the legal authority. They should prevent the exercise of executive action.

(*c*) To make our maneuverability more flexible in the light of our two possibilities. On the one hand, the [secret] army with its option of the *maquis.* On the other, the population taken as an army in the first stage and later as a mass and human tidal wave so as to exploit the chances of maneuver and the *pourrissement* which should be produced.

(*d*) Faithful to the line of conduct which I have set forth many times in my instructions, I want no sudden *coup de force,* I don't want us to box ourselves in locally; in short, no determined putsch.

(*e*) Finally, it would be preferable if, to the greatest extent possible, the *métropole* could be associated with this plan in a practical and positive way. . . .

At the end of this document, these were some of the precise orders:

— Systematic firing on the *gendarmerie mobile* and the CRS.

— Concern for the use of all means that the streets provide such as gas pumps.

— In the case that the Muslims advance in a mass, the European population will be asked to remain in a defensive position. It will be stationed at points judiciously chosen by armed defense units that can protect the population with their fire power if the forces of order prove impotent to control the uprising.

— Not all these actions will be necessarily led by formal commandos; the "armed population" will participate integrally.

— Upon order of the regional commands . . . the crowd will be thrust into the streets at the moment when the situation has developed in a sufficiently favorable sense.

— In all cases, everyone, at all echelons, must understand clearly that it is not a question of precipitous action, a *coup de force,* but rather of a campaign protracted in time and space, and that this campaign can and must be decisive.

Other captured orders served as psychological annexes to the global plan just quoted. Still another document of mid-February, noting that few Muslims had been compelled to adhere to the Secret Army, recommended that:

> We must make our attack on the Muslim intellectuals [liberal professions], which are an essential mainstay of the rebellion, and I think particularly of the doctors, dentists, and pharmacists. Each time that any of them is suspected of sympathy [for the FLN] . . . he must be struck down. We must create the condition in which the French presence is a vital necessity for all activities of daily life.[18]

The major schema, once decided on, was very simple. Provoke massive Muslim retaliation against the Europeans by concerted terrorist commando attacks against their population. Force the police services and the Army of the urban *quadrillage* to intervene and, in so doing, to have to decide between the protection or the slaughter of the Europeans. Force the Army, once committed to the European cause in some violent general skirmish, to honor its decision by issuing a pronunciamento against the government, insisting on the right of partition (which would cause the Evian talks to collapse), if not the territorial integrity of French Algeria.

It is indeed a miracle that this plan fell so far short of achievement. Algiers was the first of the great cities to know that it would fail. Two months of a sickening effervescence and a mounting casualty rate culminated in heavy violence against the Muslims in the mixed quarter of Bab-el-Oued on March 23 (four days after the signature of the Evian agreements). The forces of order quelled this massacre by the judicious use of arms and fire hoses and imposed strict surveillance and *quadrillage* on the frenzied Europeans.[19] The casualty rate after the pitched battle was approximately fifteen dead and sixty-six wounded among the military forces and a slightly higher number among the enraged civilians. This single action did not stifle the OAS in Algiers, but it lowered the peril point and served as an illustration for some of the combats to come. It also prompted the government to move in troops and impose the "quadrillage qui bouge," at the express orders of Debré.

But the apocalypse of the OAS was not to be reached in Algiers, the scene of so many crises of both Algeria and the French regime; it was rather in Oran, the most European of the Algerian cities (200,000) and, ironically, the fictitious setting for Camus's plague, where the subversion and civilian panic would rise to their greatest heights of frenzy. Here the OAS had established systematic control since the beginning of 1962; the forces of order, except for police and second-category troops, remained poised on the outskirts of the city for the event of

[18] *Ibid.*
[19] *Ibid.,* March 24, 25, 26, 1962.

uninhibited violence. An anonymous officer writing to *Le Monde* at the same time as the bloody incident of Bab-el-Oued described how the situation had deteriorated:

> Beginning in January 1962, the grip of the OAS on the 200,000 Europeans of Oran began to be felt. By the day of the cease-fire it was absolute. Why?
>
> First, because the cause of *Algérie française* is still that of the vast majority of Europeans. But also and especially because the civilian and military power — nonexistent for several weeks — could not cope with the subversive action.
>
> The Army is practically invisible. . . .
>
> The CRS make patrols. . . .
>
> The mobile gendarmes have among them a certain number of "pieds noirs."
>
> The state police is, in its large majority, obedient to the orders of the OAS.
>
> The civilian intelligence agency has, for a long time, been cut off from all sources of information. . . .
>
> In the Army, complicity has abated, but it still exists.[20]

To relieve the situation, or at least to hold it in equilibrium, the government had sent the tough-minded General Joseph Katz to assume command of the newly created Autonomous Zone of Oran. Upon the death of the chief of the Oran Army Corps, General Ginestet, from OAS bullets in the last month of French Algeria, General Katz assumed temporary command of the whole region. Oran would prove the tough nut to crack until the very last hours of the functioning of Christian Fouchet's High Commission and the dusk of French Algeria.

There were now for the first time not only indications of the Army's lack of solidarity with the settlers but overt demonstrations of it. On March 10 in Algiers several hundred soldiers of the 9th Zouave Regiment demonstrated in the court of their casern, crying "Down with the *pieds noirs*." The OAS commandos extended their terrorist attacks from the CRS and gendarmes to the regular Army in some instances, provoking a further deterioration of old bonds of sympathy already heavily strained by the horror of race war. On March 26, in Algiers, a massive crowd of civilian OAS sympathizers demonstrated in the streets in a manner reminiscent of the vast spectacles of previous times; the government, however, had absolutely prohibited all mass demonstrations. Ordered to fire on the advancing demonstrators, the young soldiers of the *contingent* delivered a fusillade against them, leaving fifty Europeans dead.[21] Agonized at what they had done, some fell into tears or hysteria while the dispersing demonstrators howled at

[20] *Ibid.*, March 23, 1962.
[21] *Ibid.*, March 27, 1962.

them in disbelief. But this particular peak of horror did not throw the Army into the OAS camp; rather it authenticated the perilous balance of the existing situation. In Oran the OAS and the forces of order remained tensely at sword's point up to the declaration of the Algerian Republic, following the referendum of July 1.

The Evian Agreements

The accords signed at Evian on March 19 established the mechanism whereby the transfer of sovereignty between the Republic of France and the GPRA was to take place.[22] Thus, the point was reached that Salan had earlier described as "the irreversible." Executive power in the interim between the signature and the projected referendum, later scheduled for July 1 (framed thus: "Do you want Algeria to become an independent state co-operating with France as defined by the declarations of March 19, 1962?"), was to be ensured by two organs operating jointly at Rocher-Noir. The representative of evaporating French sovereignty was to be a High Commission led by Christian Fouchet, former Ambassador to Denmark and an unswerving Gaullist; it would maintain responsibility for foreign affairs, the defense and security of the territory, justice, currency, and foreign economic relations. In addition, a Provisional Executive was named under the presidency of Abderrahmane Farès, the former President of the Algerian Assembly. Its competences included the preparation of the referendum, the direction of internal public affairs, the administration of the Algerian civil service, and the maintenance of order. Its governing body was to be composed, in equal number, of representatives of the French government, the GPRA, and non-GPRA Muslims. Farès, arrested a few months earlier for complicity in FLN funds collecting (residing in France, he had favored Algerian independence but never adhered to the rebellion),[23] was liberated in a manner typical of the exigencies of colonial politics and dispatched to Algeria to assume his new functions. Farès had once declared that he "would never play the El Glaoui in Algeria."[24] In his new and extremely difficult role he did not resemble the

[22] The full text of the Evian declarations was published by *Le Monde* on March 20, 1962. An English translation of the official text, "Texts of Declarations Drawn Up in Common Agreement at Evian, March 18, 1962, by the Delegations of the Government of the French Republic and the Algerian National Liberation Front [*sic*]," is supplied by the Ambassade de France, Service de Presse et d'Information, New York.

[23] It is conceivable that Farès's arrest was intended to allow him to share somewhat in the mystique of the rebellion and thus equip him as an "interlocuteur valable."

[24] Quoted from Claude Delmas, "Les hommes arrêtés représentaient la tendance la plus 'égyptienne' du F.L.N., et la plus militaire, "*Revue de Défense nationale,* December 1956, p. 1247n.

aged Rif chieftain of Morocco, but rather lent patience and moderation to the shambles he had peremptorily and provisionally inherited. He would have a capital part in restraining the last excesses of the OAS as the end of French sovereignty approached.

At the same time, France's blue-chip political prisoner Ahmed Ben Bella and his companions Mohammed Khider, Hocine Ait Ahmed, Mohammed Boudiaf, and Rabah Bitat were liberated by the government and returned with the halo of martyrs to the maelstrom of Algerian and Arab politics, with consequences that are too fresh and too extensive to relate here.

The forces of order for the transitional period in Algeria were to be under the ultimate command of the Provisional Executive; the High Commission (that is, the French) could intervene "in the last resort." The ALN forces from neighboring Tunisia and Morocco under the orders of the chafing Colonel Houari Boumedienne were not to be introduced at this stage; the security troops, numbering forty thousand and eventually sixty thousand, were to be drawn from the police and regularly constituted military units operating on Algerian soil, in equitable proportions. The French Army and rebel commanders in the *bled* were to arrange the problems of provisional authority between them.

Thus, what remained of the *quadrillage* was broken. The French Army's mission of seven years had been surrendered at the stroke of a pen. Its Muslim auxiliaries, the *harkis,* were placed in immediate danger, despite specific assurances for their protection. An estimated ten thousand would perish in the first six weeks of Algerian Algeria.

But the OAS danger had not passed — it could do its work by destroying the literal authority of the Executive and by creating a chaos in which the referendum could not take place. The nationalists, still regarding the Secret Army threat as very grave, were reluctant to take any action of their own for fear of upsetting the Evian agreements, and were determined to exert all available pressure on the French forces of order to deal with the problem before the transfer of sovereignty. This the French Army could not be compelled to do, especially by its late enemies.

The French Army was sick and numb from the seven years of bloodletting and political adventure in pursuit of a cause for which it had risked its future — for nothing. The order of the day that General Ailleret (who was about to be replaced as Superior Commander by Air General Michel Fourquet, an unconditional Gaullist) issued at the conclusion of the agreements had a particularly hollow ring to many of his subordinates:

The mission is . . . fulfilled. The Army can be proud of the successes won by its arms, of its valiance and sense of duty shown by both its regular and conscripted soldiers, of its assistance to the peoples so sorely tried by events.

Its role here is not finished. It should, by its presence and, if needed, through its action, contribute to the prevention of disorder, no matter who might try to unleash it once again.[25]

Transitional events had made of a once proud, if overspirited, fighting force a transitional Army — a crippled and cursing police. It had now been ordered to risk itself to preserve order for its enemy, then to haul down the flag and depart.

The Trials of Jouhaud and Salan

The spasm of violence accompanying the publication of the Evian agreements in Algeria was quickly fueled by the capture of General Edmond Jouhaud on Sunday, March 25, in the center of Oran, in a heavily armed sortie by General Katz's forces of order into a principality where the Secret Army made the law. The infuriated Oranais reacted violently to the seizure of their chief, who, if not the most indispensable member of the OAS directorate, was himself a "pied noir," and a prestigious figure in his community.[26] Rushed to Paris, Jouhaud was swiftly retried (the previous condemnation to death *in absentia* for the putsch of April 22 had been quashed in accordance with French law at the moment he came within the grasp of the authorities). The Air General's defense was unelaborate and straightforward, evoking notably the vacillations of the regime and his own dedication to the cause of his native territory, French Algeria. When he was sentenced to death by the High Military Tribunal on April 13, it came as no surprise to anyone, although some wondered if Jouhaud's life could not be traded for a mitigation of OAS terrorism in the face of the inevitable.

Another extraordinary judicial event came in the following month. On April 16 a commando of the forces of order had invaded an apartment in Algiers and seized General Salan, his wife, daughter, and aides, after tracking his comings and goings for a month. Salan, furnished with false papers that identified him as Louis Carrière and with dyed hair and mustache, was sped heavily guarded to a tense confrontation with General Ailleret, then returned to the *métropole* to prison and trial. All felt that his fate was sealed, and that he and Jouhaud would shortly fall before bullets of a French firing squad.

---

[25] *Le Monde,* March 20, 1962.
[26] *Ibid.,* March 27, 1962.

Few, however, reckoned with a conjuncture of circumstances exceeding even the drama of the OAS or of Salan's own brilliant and errant career, a pattern traced in the wily and lucid language of Tixier-Vignancour, which would rehabilitate the theory (valid in law if not in politics) of the regime's duplicity vis-à-vis its subordinates in Algeria. One would be led to ask: what circumstances in the chaos of modern times are not extenuating?

On May 15, Raoul Salan, with the natural white restored to his hair and his mustache removed, stood before the same military court (with the difference of one member) which had shortly before voted for the death of Jouhaud. The crimes of which he was accused — infraction of Articles 86, 87, 91, 95, and 99 of the penal code — were sufficient, if sustained, to have him executed many times over. They concerned his implication in the military putsch of April 22, 1961 (for which he had, once before, been sentenced to death), and his leadership of the Secret Army. But aside from any dry statement of the charges or even of their supporting chronology, Raoul Salan stood accused, in the eyes of most Frenchmen and by world opinion, of planning and commanding the grisly Algerian bloodbath which numbered its victims, many of them innocents, in the thousands.

"I am the chief of the OAS. My responsibility is therefore total," [27] Salan told the court in his opening statement of defense, which went on to trace meticulously the evolution that had led him first into dissent, then subversion. General Valluy, one of the most effective witnesses on behalf of the accused, was later to suggest to the tribunal: "Perhaps we hold in our hands persons, who, being the most moderate, avoided the worst catastrophes, but who will not tell you this." [28] "Moderate" or not, compared to the Godards, the Susinis, and the Argouds, General Salan would not base any part of his defense on the argument that his "moderate" orders had been misconstrued by subordinates. In so choosing, he was wise, for the point could not have held.

After his first remarks, Salan chose to keep silence for the rest of the trial, though he followed the proceedings intently. This curious and complex personality remained in shadow and did not inform the hearings; the Sphinx would not give up its secret.

Instead, Salan's defense, which from the point of view of pure technique must be accounted one of the most brilliant in French judicial history, was led by a "quarteron" of attorneys — the workmanlike Le Corroler, the candid Mennuet, the sympathetic "pied noir" Goutermanof, and, finally, the protean and effervescent Tixier-Vignancour.

[27] J. M. Théolleyre trial report, *ibid.*, May 17, 1962.
[28] *Ibid.*, May 19, 1962.

They called almost eighty witnesses on behalf of the accused, among them the widow of Marshal de Lattre, a number of parliamentarians, a Franciscan friar, several military figures, Dr. Georges Salan (the Gaullist brother of the Secret Army leader), Robert Lacoste, François Mitterrand, and Michel Debré. The appearance of several witnesses demanded by the defense, including General Challe, was refused.

The prosecution, after rehearsing the evidence of the putsch anew, depended on the obviously informed testimony of General Ailleret, Morin, Jannin, who had been Prefect of Police in Algiers from March to December 1961, and others to score its points concerning the operations of the OAS. The intent was: (1) to develop the direct responsibility of Salan, as commander, for the crimes committed by the subversives; (2) to underscore the ghastly character of the crimes; (3) to leave no doubt that the OAS was a treasonable organ. Speaking of the sequence of atrocities, Jannin, who had not even experienced the worst moments of 1962 himself, said notably: "It would take me hours to speak of all those murders, which give an impression of delirium."[29]

The defense could not renounce General Salan's part in the frenzy, quite obviously; it might not even be able to justify it on its own grounds; but it would, piece by piece, attempt to construct a larger context reaching back into the Fourth Republic, to Indochina, to the *affaire du bazooka*[30] and to May 13, 1958, in the effort to show that Salan had followed a meticulous straight line, whereas the regime, acting in the sense opposite to the orders it had given its military agents, had duplicitously sought another solution. For this demonstration, the witnesses were cleverly chosen: some to establish Salan's strength of character, some to affirm his loyalty to republican principles, some to dramatize the distress of the Algerian settlers, some to portray the anguish of the Army, some to document the regime's duplicity or to implicate it unfavorably in certain episodes (like Mitterrand, called to comment on his knowledge of the suppression of the bazooka affair, or Debré, challenged on his own part in the matter). Salan, explaining why he undertook to organize the Secret Army, had declared: "When one has known the France of courage, he can never accept the France of abandonment." Now the echo came back from his brother and political adversary:

General de Gaulle has granted all my wishes, but in so doing he has abused and ulcerated those, like my brother, who had seen in him the guardian of *Algérie française.* . . . When, on May 15, 1958, Raoul appealed to General

[29] *Ibid.,* May 17, 1962.
[30] See Chapter XI, p. 223.

de Gaulle, it certainly wasn't so that he might deliver Algeria to the FLN, but rather that he would guard it jealously for France.[31]

In short, while the prosecution pleaded fact and the irrefutable existence of criminal stains that not even the cleverest argument could wipe off, the defense was pleading motive and the desperation proper to a man ordered, in effect, to write his own death warrant or abandon his ideals. "I had been — on May 13 — the dupe of a frightful and sacrilegious comedy," said Salan. "If," he continued, "the allies had lost the war and General de Gaulle had been brought before a High Military Tribunal . . . the Germans would have screamed for his head just the way the FLN is demanding mine today." [32]

It remained for Portolano, the Algerian deputy ("Unité de la République"), to sketch in the plain language of passion, the sentiments of the Europeans, for whom Salan had become a savior and de Gaulle a demon:

They are mad with rage, they are mad with panic, and panic, don't you see? . . . is divided into two branches: that which leads to flight and exodus, that which rebounds into rage. . . . Jupiter has driven them mad.[33]

The defense did not neglect to evoke at length the equivocation of the bazooka affair, even if it made no startling revelations. It also provided an extensive dossier of orders and letters of approval by de Gaulle in favor of Salan's conception of *Algérie française* — including a previously undisclosed note to the defendant of October 24, 1958, containing the words, "we should not let Algeria go. . . . They [the FLN] will be admitted only to discussions concerning the cease-fire, and this will necessarily imply the surrender of rebel arms to the military authority." [34]

The prosecution's summation, delivered by Advocate-General Gavalda, was flowery and tempestuous, full of humanity's reprobation of the OAS terror. Addressing the ashen-white subversive leader directly across the courtroom, Gavalda thundered:

. . . Are you not fearful that when the hour comes . . . God Himself, confronted by your unpardonable obstinacy [in failing to ask forgiveness for your crimes], will forget the promise which the beloved disciple has passed on to us: that God Himself will not deign to wipe the tears from your eyes? [35]

---

[31] Théolleyre, *Le Monde*, May 20–21, 1962.
[32] *Ibid.*, May 17, 1962.
[33] *Ibid.*, May 22, 1962.
[34] *Ibid.*, May 25, 1962.
[35] *Ibid.*

The three lawyers for the defense, in their summation, preferred a simpler, if no less stunning, language, without recourse to the theology that had previously informed some of the arguments on both sides. Mennuet made a concise mechanical statement of Salan's adherence to the "straight line" policy which had been traced out for him. Goutermanof, in colloquial but not ineloquent terms, evoked the nightmare that the Europeans were experiencing as a result of France's renunciation of Algeria; his peroration, addressed to the defendant's box, left much of the court and the accused himself in tears — the tears which, according to the prosecutor, God Himself would not wipe off.

It remained for Tixier-Vignancour, with measure in his voice but with each word glittering with hidden pitfalls and subtle remonstrances, to construct a tableau of the events of the past six years, to examine de Gaulle's motives and Salan's distress. De Gaulle, said the brilliant right-wing barrister, had come to power with the intention but not the strength to give Algeria its independence. Thus, to arrive at that goal, he had usurped the force of *Algérie française* and tricked all but a handful of his closest collaborators — Debré, Guichard, Frey — by practicing his duplicitous gradualism. Salan had been the unknowing victim of this intrigue; even knowing, he could not have become a party to it, because:

What is permitted, what is authorized to a statesman, ruse, feint, these normal, well-known, and customary weapons of the statesman, can be neither accepted nor used by the man of war.[36]

Finally, the succinct bravura passage: "Machiavelli never insisted that those who could not guess his game should be put to death."

Tixier-Vignancour reseated himself after a final flight of prose, in what would at least prove an academic triumph. His interpretation of French history may have been wildly errant. It was at least forceful, and it was a version of events that General de Gaulle would not effectively challenge by labeling the coup of May 13, 1958, an "undertaking to usurp," as he did in his address of July 8, 1962.[37]

General Salan, exercising his prerogative of speech for the first time in days, rose for a final "Vive la France" and a plea to God to spare his life. Within a few hours, to the stupefaction of all, his wish had been granted when a majority of the tribunal found extenuating circumstances to the charges and sentenced him to perpetual detention.

Express provided the following interpretation of how the thunderbolt had been thrown:

[36] *Ibid.*

[37] See *Le Monde,* July 10–11, 1962. The speech was properly qualified in all but the most Gaullist quarters as "un discours stupéfiant."

Despite the secret deliberations of the High Military Tribunal, the members of the entourage of General de Gaulle appear convinced that the decision to grant extenuating circumstances to Salan was made by five votes to four. Those allegedly in favor: Generals Gelée and Jousse, Admiral Galleret, and Professor Pasteur Vallery-Radot. Those allegedly against: the three magistrates of the High Tribunal, including President Bornet, and General Gilliot.[38]

Why had this court acted as it did, when all had acknowledged in advance that Salan's life was not worth a sou, that the court was responsive to the wishes of the Executive? Why had the court saved Salan and failed to save Jouhaud? Some suggested that in sparing Salan, the tribunal was implicitly guaranteeing Jouhaud's life as well. Some, relying on an interpretation of the vote similar to that which *Express* had printed, pointed out that Salan's fate had hung on the one exchanged member of the panel, General Gelée. Had the facts of history been too big, too confused and errant, to condone Salan's execution for the blood-guilt of his OAS? Had it been Goutermanof's sincerity that had saved him? Tixier-Vignancour's relentless artifice? The deposition of Georges Salan? That of General Valluy or of Portolano? Had it been guilt feelings about the *force majeure* of a personalist and arbitrary regime? Had it been a fight for the existence of the judicial process independent from the whims of the Executive?[39] Had it been a temporary coalition of solidarity against *le pouvoir* — what Salan had incidentally sought for his OAS in his letters to ecclesiastics, parliamentarians, and even to Guy Mollet, what would be asserted shortly afterward in the "manifesto of the Europeans"?[40] No one could say very clearly how these elements were represented in the total equation that had preserved life in Salan's body.

In the amazement of the Salan verdict, all that the League of the Rights of Man, speaking through its President, Daniel Mayer, could find to say was: "Hereafter the death penalty should no longer be applied to anyone."[41]

The regime was furious and scandalized at the verdict, and moved highhandedly to reconstitute the tribunal and extend its sway over the judicial process. A neo-Fascist and "fascisant" Right leaped with scarcely concealed transport over what it regarded as a personal victory. "What could be expected from a regime born in the mud of the

---

[38] *Express*, May 31, 1962. Not mentioned: Henri Hoppenot.

[39] Edgar S. Furniss, Jr., in *De Gaulle and the French Army* (New York, 1964), has some penetrating and apposite comments on the relations of the French judiciary and executive under de Gaulle.

[40] A declaration signed by 293 deputies, protesting de Gaulle's foreign policy, on June 14, 1962.

[41] Quoted by *Le Monde*, May 25, 1962.

thirteenth of May?" thundered the PSU and the Communists. "Scandal and consternation," cried François Mauriac, the authentic *gaulliste de foi*. "Action," blustered some; "reconciliation" pleaded others.

Aftermath

The problems remained. The OAS remained, now forcefully in the hands of the colonels; the FLN remained, ready to come into its kingdom with results that few could foresee. The refugees of Algeria, torn between conflicting advice to stay and fight (from the colonels) or to depart, *sauve qui peut,* and survive (from their party, the "Unité de la République") gave themselves up to the terror or landed penniless in Marseilles and other southern ports by the tens of thousands each month.

The Salan trial was not the trial of the French Army, as the *procès du putsch* had been. Neither did it contain the innuendoes of the possible uses of military power against the regime, like the *procès des barricades*. Instead, the Army sat on the side lines, a bemused spectator, and played no active role, except for confirming what the prosecution made no effort to conceal: that Salan's military career up to the end of his service as an active officer had been brilliant and unblemished. But the Army's separation from the issues of the Salan trial was somewhat circumstantial and illusory. If Salan — no more than Jouhaud, Gardy, or the rank of colonels (Argoud, Godard, Gardes, Château-Jobert),[42] who were continuing to make subversive war on the regime in Algeria — did not, like Challe, carry away a piece of the soul of the Army in his sedition, he was, nevertheless, a crucial victim and protagonist of the civil-military malaise. He was not the "patron," but he was still remembered as "the republican general," the man whom Guy Mollet and his left-center coalition had been able to trust in Algeria. And in each one of the "hundred or so" *soldats perdus,* many officers could recognize their own images, give or take just a little more fanatic ardor, a little less discipline, a few more contacts and opportunities. Indeed, a few *ultras* against whom no charges had been officially made, like Colonel Henri Dufour, former commander of the 1st Foreign Legion Parachute Regiment, rallied to the OAS during the spring.

The character of OAS action, now riding on the swell of its fanaticism, began to change perceptibly. The referendum of April 8 had ratified the Evian agreements and provided the mechanism for the later vote that

---

[42] Colonel Pierre Château-Jobert defected to the OAS in the fall of 1961. He was given operational command of eastern Algeria.

would authenticate Algeria's independence.[43] Despite the capture of its primary leadership, the Secret Army fought desperately to foil the arrangements, to create a civil disorder in which no meaningful consultation could be held. The French Army could not and would not be massively used to quell this tumult and break the *anti-quadrillage*. The Provisional Executive, holding only transitory authority, could offer the olive branch and little else. And the FLN, still militarily weak in Algeria, was anxious to prove its seriousness and peaceability until the day when it would govern in its own name; any hint on its part of breaking the Evian agreements might easily lead the French Army to take the action of enforcing partition, which many preferred now that the ideal of integration had been shattered. The situation remained unbearably tense — and bloody — throughout April and May, with the outcome fragile and dubious.

But just as the protagonists of the Evian agreements were racing against time as they aimed for a July 1 independence referendum, time was running out on the subversives. Their clientele, the European population, was losing heart and fleeing the stricken land, clogging the funnel of available transportation to the *métropole*. Some went so far as to predict that half a million would leave; the French repatriation services had figured on 160,000.[44] Terrorism might reach its apocalypse of "scorched earth" and destruction of records and immovable property, but there would be no "human wave," as Salan's earlier plans had envisaged.

Colonel Antoine Argoud, who had escaped from the Canary Islands in February, came to the fore with the advent of full subversion and the dwindling chances for sabotaging the Evian agreements. Salan's capture reiterated his position and that of Godard as tactical leaders. And the OAS "second strategy," that of all-out political war against the regime, began to gain the ascendancy with the prospect that the Algerian operation might have to be liquidated. Argoud made a surreptitious *tournée* of the French military posts in Germany in April; half a dozen of his contacts, including General Gribius, were subsequently sanctioned by the government. The reflux of the OAS, or what was left of it, on the *métropole* now had to be seriously envisaged.

[43] See de Gaulle's speech of March 20, to Parliament: "Thus it seems necessary to me that the nation itself should sanction a vast and profound transformation and confer on the Chief of State and the government the means of resolving, with the shortest delay, the problems that will arise."

[44] So many were encamped in Marseilles by July 1962 that the predominant Socialists feared that one of their major fiefs might be transformed into a right-wing city. Nor were the Communists themselves idle among these thousands of displaced unemployed. These fears proved substantially groundless.

There had been rumors attending the first Salan interrogation that the OAS leader had admitted to a serious rupture with the "colonels" in determining basic strategies. "They are interested only in settling scores," he is alleged to have told his questioners.[45] This was subsequently denied by Salan's lawyers. In any case, General Valluy's assessment about "the most moderate" of the leadership may have been correct. By the turn of the month of June, those most politically aware in what remained of the OAS leadership, like Susini, were beginning to perceive the despair of the senseless battle they were waging and to make overtures in the direction of some kind of "peace with honor." A dignified letter made public on June 5 by General Jouhaud, over whom the sentence of death was still hanging, urged the OAS to cease its combats and did much to pierce the atmosphere with a ray of reason.

The grand directorate of subversion had been passed back to Europe from Algeria, and precisely, according to the weekly *Express,* into the hands of Georges Bidault,[46] who had fled France and was making contacts feverishly in the countries along her eastern border. For Susini, Perez, and Colonel Gardes (allegedly, the "reasonable" faction), there was little left to do but liquidate on as favorable terms as they could manage; Argoud was apparently in the Bidault network, but they were, ungratefully, *hors le coup.*

During the first half of June, Susini made overtures to the Provisional Executive and the FLN through the medium of such men as Jacques Chevallier, who had suddenly acquired stature as an "interlocuteur valable." The ex-chief of the Student Federation demonstrated his residual strength by imposing a near-perfect cease-fire on his own troops in Algiers while discussions were in progress. Conscious of the great need to halt the bloodletting and anxious to reassure the remaining Europeans (as Ben Khedda himself had tried to do), Dr. Mostefai, one of the FLN members of the Provisional Executive, lent himself with prudence and comprehension to the talks. Abderrahmane Farès, who, as non-FLN, could foresee a modest political future in any case, was unstinting with his good offices. Finally, even though Roger Frey had earlier declared, on behalf of the French regime, "The government will never negotiate with a band of criminals,"[47] Christian Fouchet, the High Commissioner, lent his earnest efforts to the deliberations, hoping to salvage what could be salvaged of Franco-Muslim amity and avoid the implementation of any scorched-earth policy.

[45] *Le Monde,* April 24, 1962.

[46] Salan's contact with Bidault was to lead a furious government to reinstitute criminal charges against him after the judgment and sentencing of May 24. No new trial, however, came to pass. Jouhaud's sentence was later reduced to life imprisonment.

[47] Statement of February 9, 1962. Quoted by *Le Monde,* February 11–12.

These talks resulted in the so-called Susini-Mostefai agreement of June 17,[48] which was ratified by the rapid cessation of OAS turbulence in Algiers and most other parts of the territory and, more tardily, by the written acquiescence of General Salan on June 22.

Until practically the last moment, the die-hards held out in Oran and continued the terror, including some scorched-earth activities such as blowing up oil tanks. They did not accept the inevitable until two days before the referendum on June 29. Their reluctance can be attributed not only to their subversive purity but also to their reasonable fear that the FLN was itself seriously divided on the question of accepting the legitimacy of the Susini-Mostefai agreement.

On July 2, 1962, Algeria passed to the GPRA with its conflicting tendencies (of which a coalition of the Ben Bellists and Boumedienne's "foreign legion" of the ALN seemed temporarily to have the upper hand), and into provisional turmoil. Over five hundred Europeans disappeared in the chaos, which the OAS had done so much to ensure and the personalist factions of the FLN so much to perpetuate. "Well, you will suffer," General de Gaulle had allegedly told Lauriol, the Algerian deputy. Perhaps there had been no other way. About 200,000 unrepatriated members of the French armed forces remained in their caserns, dumb and impotent, watching the spectacle. Algeria was not, after all, Indochina.

The Godards, the Susinis, and the Perezes escaped, vanished. Where would their next incarnation be? Already Argoud had turned up in Europe by the side of Georges Bidault and became, apparently, the dominating tactician of the latter's Conseil National de la Résistance (sic), a title that sent horrified shivers of laughter through the Gaullists. Both men published interviews in the conservative Brussels daily *La Dernière Heure,* and were observed flitting like bats along the channels of the clandestine *émigration*. Were they attempting to feed a European neofascism, itself as integrated as the Common Market, with headquarters in the same city? [49] Many feared this to be the case.

In early March the left-wing Catholic weekly *Témoignage Chrétien* had published a special thirty-page "dossier" devoted to the problem of renascent fascism in Europe and the developments that might aid its growth. Here, notably, Joseph Rovan evoked the contribution of technology to fascism; Maurice Duverger traced the subtle affiliation be-

---

[48] A lengthy account of the mechanism of these contacts by Alain Jacob appears in *Le Monde,* June 15, 1962. The text of the so-called agreement was broadcast by both the FLN and OAS with slight textual differences, and may be found in *Le Monde,* June 18, 1962.

[49] See "Pourquoi le piste des colonels passe toujours par Bruxelles," [*Le Nouveau*] *Candide,* July 8–15, 1962. The French police later seized Argoud in Bavaria.

tween fascism and a mushrooming technocracy ("a 'technical' dictatorship almost foreign to the population which must submit to it"); and Jean Planchais wrote of the continuing problems of the Army — the "fragile loyalism constantly unbalanced by the propaganda and pressures directed at it by military and civilian activists." [50]

Could a de Gaulle, guarding life and limb, prevail above these menaces? Would history retain the substance of Tixier-Vignancour's subtle attacks or the high-flown compliment of François Mauriac: "De Gaulle, the great Druid oak, powerfully enrooted on top of the brush and brambles of Right and Left . . . where nothing that is fascist has even been able to do more than vegetate?" [51] Above all, the General was interested in French power, not personal compliments.

But finally, there was not just the problem of France and her future institutions at stake; there was the tangible effect on the lives of the 13,000,000 Algerians, both Europeans and Muslims. They had endured frightful ordeals; they had generated others. They had known the full rigor of the plague — a plague that demoralized with slogans, that killed with unremitting stealth and terror, that robbed and impoverished, that reduced life to formulas too simple for life, that turned the hourglass of morality every half hour. They would yet have to conjure with the results of this contamination.

[50] Summarized in *Le Monde,* March 11–12, 1962.
[51] "Bloc-Notes," in *Le Figaro littéraire,* week of June 15, 1962.

XVII

EPILOGUE: THE ARMY, THE STATE, AND THE NATION

> The best lack all conviction, while the worst
> Are full of passionate intensity.
> — *W. B. Yeats, "The Second Coming"*

THERE IS a photograph worth many words that was radioed to the American newspapers by United Press International on the occasion of General de Gaulle's speech to a selected group of eighty generals and admirals and two thousand other officers at Strasbourg on November 23, 1961. Against a bleak landscape of houses — or perhaps they are barracks — that fade out impressionistically in the distance two men in the heavy military dress of winter clasp hands.[1] They are the President of the Republic and his host for the occasion, the commander of the Military District of Strasbourg, General Jacques Massu. The first wears an expression of hope, dignity, and comprehension; the other, the sinewy air of stubborn and painful loyalty, with just a hint of Gascon *malignité*. Let us make of the occasion a symbol. No one can divine exactly what may lie behind these masks. But on the reconciliation of these two forces — the lonely General leading his ancient country like a young, uncertain bride along the stony paths of history and the savagely indignant but enormously disciplined officer swallowing his

---

[1] The photograph was reproduced in the *New York Times*, November 24, 1961.

hurt like a draught of forgetfulness — seemed to depend the chances of civil-military stability in France.

De Gaulle at Strasbourg

With his flair for the dramatic, for making the gesture, de Gaulle had corralled his bewildered cohorts at Strasbourg, the city that guards the Rhine and looks both ways at Europe. It was also the seventeenth anniversary of the liberation of this place by the brilliant action of Leclerc's 2nd Armored Division, the cream of the Army of the past, which de Gaulle had made out of nothing. He would know how to evoke these sentiments and souvenirs in a cold climate far from the "furnace" of Algeria.

Most of the officers obeyed the summons to come to Strasbourg with heavy hearts and teeth clenched. They knew full well that if Algeria was a depressing bit of unfinished business for de Gaulle, it was a transaction that he could not be dissuaded from carrying through. They expected him to reiterate this, telling them paradoxically that they could, nevertheless, be proud of their military victory over the Algerian nationalists. They came expecting him to materialize brilliant vistas for the French Army of the future, modernized, technologized, and endowed with nuclear weapons, passing in easy cadence from the meager equipment of the djebels to spectacular accoutrements fit for the Rhine.

The General did, in fact, touch these points, but not in quite the way anticipated. Instead of praising a heartsick Army for the victory it knew it had not won, he said simply: "The French Army has fulfilled its task with courage and honor." Psychological discretion similarly governed the rest of his address. "If he had only told us this two years ago," a number of his auditors were to lament afterward. If de Gaulle had only laid his cards on the table. But could he have? Had de Gaulle himself understood the full meaning of his policies and the course of their evolution from that vantage point of the summer of 1958? The remark dropped at Mostaganem and the unfortunate *tournée des popotes* of March 1960 would seem to indicate otherwise.

De Gaulle made a statement that was worded carefully — and cloudily, when one compares the classic candor of his usual prose — on the alliance of *action psychologique* and sedition:

Certainly, everyone — and especially myself — can grasp why, in the minds and hearts of certain soldiers, there could have been born some other brand of hope, indeed the illusion, that simply by wishing it things could be changed from what they really are to what one desired them to be in the ethnic and psychological sense. But once the State and the nation have chosen their path, military duty is spelled out once and for all. Outside its guidelines there can be, there are only lost soldiers. But in it the country finds its example and its mainstay.[2]

The speech was delivered out of doors. Beneath the balcony where the orator stood with his microphones, rank on rank of officers were fixed solemnly at attention, their emotions concealed in the convenient military decorum. Far off, in Algiers, Oran, and cities and villages throughout Algeria other officers sat by their radios. The reactions were, as might be expected, mixed. Some were relieved that equivocation had been further swept aside; for a part of the Army had never gone so far as to insist on *this* directive or *that* directive, but merely on *some clear directing*. Many others, however, continued to torture themselves with the paradox they perceived between this recall to discipline and de Gaulle's own act of "civil disobedience" of June 18, 1940. Challe, etc. (1962) : de Gaulle (1962) :: de Gaulle (1940) : Pétain (1940) was the magic equation. Still, the speech had not pulled many punches, and these officers were no longer so sure of what they wanted to believe as in the past.

Perhaps the modernization and nuclearization of the armed forces was a deceit of sorts, but in adversity it was undeniably attractive. It was also a resumption of the rhythm of French military development that had been abruptly halted in 1956 to make way for the Algerian emergency. As a distinguished analyst of French politics commented, "you don't take Algeria away from the Army and then bring them home to shoot popguns."[3] It was possible that a portion of the ultranationalist rancor that had made much of the Army wish to guard Algeria as a sacred and inalienable parcel of French soil could be diverted to the defense of France's claims to rank as a major strategy-making power in the Western alliance. This was a point on which de Gaulle and the Army could agree. As the General had never ceased to declare in his press conferences and speeches, and as Louis Joxe had put it in 1959: "France thinks that she should be summoned not only for *Kriegspiel,* not only for planning, but also for the preparation and decision of world strategy."[4]

This implied possession of the bomb, whatever its minatory and diplomatic uses might prove to be. It was not just that "since eventually it will become possible to destroy France from any spot in the world, our force must be made capable of acting anywhere on earth."[5] It was

---

[2] *Le Monde,* November 24, 1961.

[3] Professor Stanley Hoffmann.

[4] *Le Monde,* October 22, 1959.

[5] De Gaulle, in a speech to the Ecole Militaire, November 4, 1959, cited in *Le Monde,* November 5, 1959.

that history does not retrace its steps or offer voluntary aid to the purblind and shortsighted. Nuclear technology had swelled enormously in fifteen years; the moralistic renunciation of these consequences, in the view of de Gaulle, could jeopardize forever France's pre-eminent role, to which the cycles of history entitled her.[6] France had done much for the world; she could still do much, but she must tilt with the times, by using the maximum of power at her disposal. For, in the words of Saint-Simon,

A system which the centuries have built and destroyed cannot be re-established. The destruction of old doctrines is complete, radical, and irrevocable. They will always be remembered with gratitude and veneration by all true thinkers and all people of probity for the innumerable and eminent services they rendered civilization during the long era of their maturity. But henceforth their place is only in the memory of true friends of humanity, and they can make no claim to vigor.[7]

For de Gaulle and for many others it was inconceivable that France would slowly degenerate to the status of a sunny Portugal, "where people sometimes went on holidays."

Already in March of the year a considerable military reorganization had begun to take place, directed not so much toward stifling the potential of sedition, but toward giving France's forces responsible and efficient direction for the new tasks confronting them. The publicity concerning the reorganization had been fairly well submerged in the atmosphere of the putsch. Its chief effects were: the separation and functional delineation of military, industrial, and administrative responsibility for national security policy; the strengthening of the role of the Minister of the Armies and the simplification of the chiefs of staff under his direction.[8]

As for the cherished notions of *la guerre subversive,* de Gaulle's progressively relentless policy of seeking an Algerian settlement posed the ultimate and harsh question: In what territory would France ever again be compelled to wage such a war? Guiana? Martinique? Réunion?

But Algeria was not settled as de Gaulle spoke at Strasbourg, though there were intimations that some important news might arrive by New

---

[6] Cf. Charles de Gaulle, *Mémoires de Guerre,* Vol. III, Tome 1, *Le Salut* (Ottawa, 1960), p. 303: "Vieille France . . . allant et venant sans relâche de la grandeur au déclin, mais redressée, de siècle en siècle, par le génie du renouveau."

[7] Henri de Saint-Simon, *Oeuvres de Saint-Simon et d'Enfantin,* VI, "Système Industriel" (Paris, 1861), pp. 50–51.

[8] See *Le Monde,* March 25, 1961; also April 2–3, 1961. For a chart of the reorganization, see *Revue de Défense nationale,* May 1961, pp. 919–922, and June 1961, pp. 1121–1122.

Year's or shortly after. The OAS was girding itself, stepping up its activity, making sure of its forces. An undeclared civil war in grand subversive style was the war the newspapers wrote about and, in a real sense, the only war that France was fighting — since ALN activity had diminished after the terrorist outbreak of midsummer. The capital psychological strategy of the OAS was to try to destroy the "mythe de Gaulle" in metropolitan minds, to represent him as senile, doting, failing in power, incapable of clear judgments, monomaniac, reminding one strangely of the words of William Blake in another context:

> The dead brood over Europe, the cloud and vision
> descends over cheerful France;
> O cloud well appointed! Sick, sick, the Prince
> on his couch, wreath'd in dim
> And appalling mist, his strong hand outstretched'd
> from his shoulder down the bone,
> Runs aching cold into the sceptre, too heavy for
> mortal grasp. . . .[9]

But de Gaulle, aging, bowed, and with weak eyesight, gave no evidence of the failure of nerve or indecision of Louis XVI. If he was losing some grip on the scepter, this was because of other inevitable inroads into his power. But no Mollet, no Pinay really wished for the return to Colombey until the Algerian crisis had been settled or proved itself intractable by the standards of all human reason. In January 1962 it did not seem that the test would be long delayed; the government would not be long in having to cope, and cope desperately, with what de Gaulle had once labeled "les équipes diverses de la hargne, de la grogne et de la rogne."[10]

At this critical point my chronicle is over. The pattern of the past is traced; the future will issue from it as the wiser or more foolish offspring of violence, frustration, and misunderstanding. The task is now to summarize the quality of this experience.

Summary: What the Army Saw

The French Army was neither the spoiled and rebellious adolescent nor the glorious herald of national renovation that its critics or its advocates claimed. It was a very specialized national corporate group subjected to extreme pressures arising from the complexity of both French and global politics. As we have seen, it had a long history of divorce from the productive wellsprings of the national life. The divorce

[9] William Blake, *The French Revolution*, Book I.
[10] Speech of *quatorze juillet*, 1961.

became an intensely bitter alienation because of a continuous postwar sequence of debilitating colonial struggle for uncertain and ambiguous goals and because of no less constant clashes with vacillating civilian authority and a poorly informed and mistrustful public. The government failed abysmally to give the Army direction; the Army gradually assumed, and then was tempted to usurp, prerogatives of the government. The Army began in Indochina by the pursuit of national objectives as they were set forth for it in Paris, amid the debris of changing governments, by Moutet, Coste-Floret, and Letourneau, the successive colonial ministers. When the government was laggard in the support of its goals, the Army attempted to sustain them, reinterpret them, and, much later, to invent new ones.

In the meantime, the combat leaders had confronted a strange kind of enemy, one who, with his comparatively meager resources, was committed to a total conflict featuring several novel allocations of social strength and the fabric of a powerful ideology. They compared this masterful unity of action — this "rapprochment armée–nation," if one pleases — with the reticent, venal, and desultory methods of their own government. After devitalizing defeat — and for some imprisonment, for others the quickened sense of betrayal — they did not fail to conclude that a national housecleaning was in order and that an agonizing strategic reappraisal, extending to all spheres of the military art, was dictated. Almost at the same time, Morocco and Tunisia were lost, and Algeria exploded.

The implications of the Army's complex attachment to Algeria, its mission there, its sense of accomplishment, and its longing for victory are too fresh to need retracing. In this maelstrom the logic of subversive war and sedition, of alienation and action, fashioned itself into something that history will probably judge as an immense illogic. I have tried to show how this came about, how it continually threatened to pass the French nation into statelessness, how, paradoxically, some of the best of the military ideal could be the mirror image of a rebellious nightmare. I have done this in order to understand, and not to judge, although there are sides to be taken and none can refrain from taking them.

Not only was the age of colonization — a brief age, in terms of the wrinkled crust of the earth — passing out of existence, perhaps for all time, but the specter of the Cold War lay heavy over the world. Part of the French enemy was within, and this hostile force became magnified many times in the eyes of those who, in discovering resemblances between communism and other political positions, deduced identity and captivity. Compromise, in all its forms, became impure and unworthy of the mighty but intangible "Christian, Mediterranean, and Western values."

As for the enemy without, according to the same vision he was potent and monolithic. His tentacles reached into everything that was inchoate, everything that was neutral; he knew how to flatter the sensitivity of the downtrodden; he drew the unsuspecting to him and consumed them. He knew well how to fight the multiform battle he was waging, and he could teach others. The sources of his strength could be learned, technically if not morally re-created, and unleashed against him. In Algeria he was reaching a covetous arm around Western Europe; that arm had to be cut off. But it could not be severed with a big blow; it had to be done in little snippets, and furthermore with Algerian scissors.

France, guarding the gates of the West in Algeria, needed a government that knew how to wield these scissors and to keep them sharpened. When the desired government came, it showed no comprehension of the problem. It broke the scissors; whereupon, an angered "French Algeria" and parts of the inconsolable Army turned the broken scissors against the government itself.

A neat theory, that of *la guerre révolutionnaire,* complete enough to persuade and even to intoxicate, because, like all powerful persuasions, it contained some striking elements of truth.[11] But it was the implication that it passed for the entire truth which aided in tearing the French military society asunder.

War and Ideology

It was probably no accident that the real demands of fighting a subversive or irregular war occurred in conjunction with a deep if unbalanced questioning of ideological problems. In embryo, and certainly in miniature, the combination was being re-created in the United States, as isolated "activists" and a few military personnel began to attack national policy and to deride the liberal fabric of national life at a time when Cuba, Laos, and Vietnam disturbed the equanimity of the country. "John Birchers" and "Minutemen" are far from threatening to cast a pre-eminently stable and democratic state into its "Second Republic," but the character of their antagonism is close enough to the early souvenirs of the French experience to suggest that we have been dealing here with tensions that are only in part national. With a certain

[11] But see Maurice Duverger, "L'Amérique et la guerre subversive," *Le Monde,* August 11, 1961. He maintains that theories of subversive war now in the ascendant in the United States operate from the opposite premise. By this logic, it is because of lingering colonialism and its effects that the march of communism is facilitated.

Algerian solution achieved, the torch of subversive war has seemingly been passed to the next runner. Perhaps he can avoid singeing himself if he is prudent about the way it is borne. A multiplication of new books and essays on the subject indicates that the "years of mediation" have begun in America.

The "psychologue" mentality — or as its advocates would prefer, the "centurion" mentality — is never entirely absent from the realms of the human psyche and is apt to become magnified in periods of great stress, particularly when the stakes are high and the criteria of success and failure are controversial. Its incidence and mechanism is a problem for the psychologists to investigate. But we may perceive some connection here with what Robert Jay Lifton has described as the "psychology of totalism" in his illuminating study of Communist Chinese methods of "thought reform" and their effects on personality.[12] One "totalism" is a good psychological defense against another if it is devoutly held, and the clash of "totalisms" generally leads to their intensification. Comparatively few French officers in the period about which I am writing were born or manufactured "totalists," but it is these persons who launched the new doctrines and became most politically engaged, dragging numerous others in the wake of their enthusiasms: another instance of Mao's "fish in water" principle. A wise Army will guard against its voices from the deep, its "notes from underground."

A wise government and a wise Army, together with the other productive plural activities of a nation, will work hand in hand to preserve, transform, and re-create vital institutions and legitimate lines of authority in an age of fluidity and unrelenting challenge. Since armies are the ultimate recourse of the state in times of critical emergency, it will be important to examine the view they tend to take of the situation and the paradoxes of the role they are asked to play. For armies are faced with novel pressures amid our present crisis of the unknown and the intractable.

The Civil-Military Dilemma

All armies operating in free or relatively free societies betray significant similarities; they grind a fairly common grist from their mills. Conflicts, after all, are not nearly so diverse as the types of states that wage them. This means that training, professional indoctrination, and military organization are also roughly the same wherever we look, and that severe changes in any of these components are normally caused by

[12] Robert Jay Lifton, *Thought Reform and the Psychology of Totalism* (New York, 1961).

alterations in the technical role of an Army rather than by a questioning of the fundamental bases of military society. Once accepted by the professional military milieu, the grocer's son and the aristocrat's son are apt to form a striking similarity of attitude, which they could not have achieved in any other earthly context except religious orders.

Armies dwell in oscillating relationships with the historical entities of State and Nation. In some countries we can observe that the State (which is really an allegory of the government apparatus) and the military forces enjoy a harmonious existence; in others, like France, a troubled one. Sometimes   one thinks here of pre Hitlerian Germany — the military is able to become a sort of state within the State. Finally, especially in the underdeveloped countries, the guideline between Army and State may scarcely have been drawn or had time to function naturally.

Never, though, will an Army renounce its vital connections with the Nation — another abstraction, which normally is intended to represent the organic and historical values of the fatherland or national territory, of which any given "State" may be only a transient and perishable image. The concept of Nation, as we have seen too often and too unhappily in the past, can often be distorted in the interest of racial supremacy or territorial aggrandizement. On the other hand, it may be quite pristine and exalted. Sometimes it is both, depending on who is viewing the issue.

Peaceful civil-military relations are most assured in those countries where an Army's conceptualizations of the abstractions State and Nation tend to coincide — in other words, where the perishability of the State is somehow linked to the exhaustion of the vital resources of the Nation itself. Democracy in the United States and Scandinavia, for example, had wide acceptance as part and parcel of the "national style." In France this type of consensus has never existed, and powerful protest groups on the Right and Left have periodically arisen to challenge this association of truly "national" values with the premises of the State.

If, as in France, an Army has come by stages to entertain a profound distrust of national political institutions, its tendency will be to appeal over the head of its nominal master, the State, to a higher referee, the Nation. In a normal democratic system the military force will be an instrument of the regime. But if it feels it has been abused, it will tend to consider itself coequal with the regime and attempt to appeal to a higher loyalty, which it will accuse the regime of having betrayed. Colonel Château-Jobert, later to pass into sedition, had recalled this point to Guy Mollet after the lecture given by the latter before the Institute for Advanced Studies of National Defense in 1960: "The Army is at the disposal of the State for the benefit of the Nation." [13] This view will necessarily be divisive to a military group, because the normal mechanism of command and obedience requires a concrete hierarchy of individuals and cannot be sustained by inspirational recourse to a set of invisible ideals that invite a variety of interpretations. Only the State can supply the flesh and blood that conditions obedience; the Nation cannot. Right or wrong, justified or not in taking anti-regime action according to this model, an Army will tend to forget that institutions and, indeed, ideas are made for man, and not vice versa.

In the democratic consensus, it would seem that an Army had no right to expect anything of the State but constitutional observance. Civilian control of the armed forces is an established principle that exists, at least formally, in all democracies. However, the wide extension of the activity of regimes into the realm of foreign affairs and the hair-raising perils of incompetence in this jurisdiction have alerted military groups, conscious of their role as the "last resort of the nation," to the possibility that national survival might be gambled away by weak leadership or endemic feebleness in the normal political process.

This is not to say that military groups are customarily more visionary than their civilian counterparts; it may happen, however, that they believe themselves to be. Furthermore, they know that they are bound by the trusted command mechanism, and not by the perplexing and knotted ligatures of the civilian process. They have confidence in their efficiency and ability to avoid vitiating compromise. But this leads also to a distrust of politics and a generalized unwillingness to take power except *in extremis* or to hold it indefinitely. The traditional ideals of duty, honor, order, and discipline constitute a strong focal point of resistance against misconceived adventure in the political realm. However, when an Army crosses the Rubicon of sedition because of what it conceives to be intolerable pressures, it will fling these abstractions in the face of the regime and will appeal to its higher authority, the Nation. The State will be held guilty of dereliction of duty and abuse of confidence.

What a military group principally demands of the State is that it create the political conditions in which the widest margin of national survival is assured and the maximum power of the nation sustained. Civilian and military estimates of these criteria will frequently differ, with a consequent accrual of tension between the two groups. In case of war the military expects the full support of the civilian agency and an involvement in its decisions; it has a natural horror of being squandered

[13] Quoted by Claude Paillat, *Le dossier secret de l'Algérie* (Paris, 1961), p. 374.

in "dubious battle" or being made a stalking-horse for the regime's political errors.

A military group feels instinctively that it is the best judge of the nation's security interests, regarding this prescience as a part of its *raison d'être*. It therefore frequently seeks, not control of the State or power for its own sake, but, rather more negatively, a "right of veto" over major policy decisions of the civilian regime. A wise democracy will therefore allow its military hierarchy certain safety valves and platforms for opinion so long as this remains consonant with the principle of civilian control.

It is when a regime's policies seem to the military group to be leading the nation toward decay and despair or when the breakdown of state machinery threatens the survival of the unit that an Army is strongly tempted to political intervention. The quality of an outside challenge may well determine how this intervention is made and on what bases it is justified.

In France, military intervention in politics was a consequence not only of institutional disorder but of the severe external pressure of decolonization seen through the ideological screen of the East-West struggle. The question here is not that the Army, if it came to power, would refuse to place the State in "safe" civilian hands, which is the undoubted tradition of the country, but that the activist leaders of the Army have had very positive, if not discursive, opinions as to what type of state they would like to build, partially as a result of their experience in warfare.

Before the advent of nuclear technology and the rise of revolutionary armies in the new states it was fashionable and, indeed, feasible to regard military groups as belonging to the Right of the political spectrum. "Far Right" is perhaps an even better term; for, except in the United States and a handful of other countries, the military answered to precapitalist siren songs and was fundamentally out of sorts with even the "loyal" Right of industrial democracy. This historical irritation with the plural forms of modern capitalist society has abated among those officers who are involved with technology, but elsewhere it persists, although deflected in new directions.

The reasons for this phenomenon are not hard to locate if we simply consider the military regimen, the military way of life, which is incompatible in the extreme with the complex compromises of the world of affairs and their reflection in the civilian political process.

This incompatibility has, in the past decade, led armies in France and in some of the underdeveloped nations to exhibit a hostility toward the premises of plural capitalism and to wish for something more rugged, direct, and unambiguous. At the same time — unlike their traditionalist counterparts of the past — they have accepted certain egalitarian tenets of the Socialist Left (1) because the perplexities of ordering civilian society were not their direct concern; (2) because the armies themselves had shown an unmistakable trend toward "democratization" on the basis of social origin; and (3) because the efficacy of promoting social justice among populations in an area of combat had been frequently demonstrated as a military criterion. This modified "leftism" of military groups had never, in any case, prevented their making timely coalitions with the "nationalist" Right; by nature they are always themselves more "nationalist" than "Socialist."

Together with a frequent preoccupation for social justice — increasingly felt to be a *sine qua non* of national solidarity in a troubled world — armies are deeply concerned with technique, or a desire to make politics apolitical, to avoid the compromise, waste, and delay of the liberal process. Like the "technocrat" class, they are apt to become attracted to what Engels, in *Anti-Dühring,* called "the administration of things" rather than "the government of persons." They are not intoxicated by the passion of the *couloirs* or the election meeting but disposed to regard these things as frivolous survivals of the past. Here again, the inspiration is nationalism and "national efficiency."

Every Army of today, from the smallest to the greatest, must in some sense construe its mission and requirements in the light of the East-West conflict and the existence of thermonuclear weapons. The need to deal with this ponderous but shifting situation creates nervous pressures for any military group and widens and intensifies the existing areas of quarrel between the military and civilian leadership.

The prospect of a continuous Cold War of, let us say, sixty or seventy years is not a sanguine one to the military mind, which rebels at not being able to do anything forceful to alleviate the national peril. The Cold War, then, though it affects military groups in a wide variety of "national" ways, makes all of them more volatile, alert to controversy with the civilian leadership, and frustrated by the apparent insolubility of many of their most pressing problems.

Liberalism and "Cold War"

The Western democracies are the evolving products of the liberal political conventions of the eighteenth and nineteenth centuries; many of the emerging nations have shaped their written constitutions in roughly the same image. But today it is increasingly questionable, in an "era of total war," whether these sacrosanct and, to be sure, highly worthy forms are adequate to meet the challenges that threaten the existence of nations. Federations, consultative mechanisms, and economic unions have arisen to oppose this dilemma externally. But interior reform of the democratic mechanism has not been carried out to a very high degree in the West. The habit of institutions and their time-sanctioned relationships is very compelling. But the question is one of adequacy.

Many precious values have come out of the play of liberal institutions, and it will be exceedingly imprudent to discard any of this heritage inadvisedly. Moreover, the vital dynamism of states is not advanced through the sacrifice of organic *idées fixes* and the adoption of repugnant and contrary values, even if there are challenges that encourage such a choice. Yet the dispassionate fact is that customary institutions and their normal functioning have been transcended at many points by the exigencies of modern peril. This has been frequently authenticated by pragmatic revisions but has rarely been writ large in constitutional or statutory terms.

A major organizational problem of the age seems to be that of achieving a comfortable structure within the state bureaucracy for the needs of national defense. Leaders of the defense forces themselves have been among the first to be touched by this realization. Civil-military relations will probably tend to readjust themselves within revised statutory structures if the Cold War continues, and we can see only very darkly what form this might take in order to be compatible with the indispensable values of the past.

But democracy, if it is to survive in time-tested or experimental forms, cannot tolerate the imbalance of unrepresented elements within its citadel seeking ways of renovation that do not command the consensus of the community. Military groups sometimes dash themselves on the ideological rocks attempting to prove their national purity and representativeness; in so doing, they may alienate themselves even further from the *pays réel* that they profess to clutch to their hearts. Yet their claims and remonstrances in a world preoccupied with survival must not be thrust aside with a yawn or branded as puerile and self-seeking by intellectuals and politicians who cannot see beyond the transient political harmonies that have assured their own places in the system.

In France, history conspired to swell the intensity of the civil-military dilemma. A nation, rich in ideas and often noble in their execution, rich in men and often inspired in their use, and, above all, rich in the bounty of civilized experience, came up against one of the "miserable predicaments" [14] of modern times. It had not proposed this problem; neither did it seem able to dispose of it. The end of the Algerian war pulled the curtain on the drama, but it did not remove the actors or the properties from the stage.

[14] The phrase is George Kennan's.

XVIII

POSTSCRIPT: DE GAULLE'S "GREAT LEAP FORWARD"

> . . . What seest thou else
> In the dark backward and abysm of time?
> If thou remember'st aught, ere thou cam'st here,
> How thou cam'st here thou may'st.
> — *William Shakespeare,* The Tempest

IT WAS NOT that de Gaulle had deliberately set out to exterminate the centurions in a game of political warfare. But he had robbed them of their existence, their substantiality. Gone were the giddy and anguished days of the North African legions — *para*-heroes in their leopard-spotted battle clothes with their funereal songs, all the other tough and ardent troops fresh from emotions that few wars grant. Having crushed an Army's dreams with a calculating policy, de Gaulle was extending the prestige of technique and matériel as an olive branch. There were some who, distant from the scene, snickered at the Liberator's pretensions of creating a national striking force, "capable, if necessary, of acting alone"; there were others who deplored the vitiating waste in Western armament and the confusion in Western strategy. Still others foresaw that de Gaulle, or de Gaulle's successor, might be persuaded to place these new forces reliably within the Western system of defense after patient negotiations and concessions. But few speculated that because of Algeria and its antecedents some very different germ might have been planted in the French Army.

At the national parade on July 14, 1962, where the President of France kept a rendezvous with his sullen hoplites, one already perceived a changing Army, which had less music, less of the heroic or "folklorique." An Army of mass and equipment was gradually replacing the exotic fraternity of 1958 with its *harkis,* spahis, and fervent sky-jumpers. It was not yet the impassive omnipotence of Red Square, to be sure; but some watchers thought they caught a glimpse, in the train of the march, of the unimaginable silhouettes of — nuclear bombs. This was bravura grudgingly exchanged for the image of power, neither sad nor gay, but under rigid orders and commanded to crush not only an enemy but its own most proximate hopes and nightmares.

The parade of 1962 was the first fulfillment of the government's "program law relating to certain military equipment" of December 8, 1960, and of the reorganization of the Ministry of the Armed Forces and the central military command of March of the following year.

De Gaulle and French Power

"France is once more becoming a world power," General de Gaulle had declared to the assembled officers of Redjas, Algeria, on March 4, 1960. Many officers subsequently refused to see how France could recapture her position of world power by systematically withdrawing from historical positions of strength. But for de Gaulle, the retrenchment and re-equipment, the restaging of improved force on the critical base of Western Europe were vital; Algeria, whatever one's personal feelings, was a wasteful peripheral war that had to be liquidated. With this liquidation went a part of the soul of the French Army.

Even if the Army suffered, the Western allies — who had placed their own ambiguous pressures on the war in Algeria — were prepared to welcome these battle-tested forces of France back into the shield of NATO. But the President of France, struggling for leadership in a Europe that would be very different from the much-proclaimed "Atlantic Community," appeared to have other uses for his military power. He would employ it instead as the nucleus of a new "third force" that would seek an existence independent from its American ally and progressively conquer all other types of "Europeanism" that stood in its way. De Gaulle saw a more unified Western Europe whose character would respect the flavor of the individual member states, evolving along a way strewn with the residual history of the nations. The emerging entity could play its role only if, consonant with its obligations, it exercised maximum autonomous power over the issues of its own destiny. And the primary issue was defense — which could not be perpetually ceded to the control of an ally on another continent.

This attitude was neither universally hailed by all Europeans nor treated with much comprehension in the United States. De Gaulle himself did little to help matters by indulging in periodic historical speculations, such as the now-famous statement in his press conference of November 10, 1959:

No doubt the sort of equilibrium that exists between the atomic power of the two camps is for the moment a factor of world peace. But who can say what will happen tomorrow? Who can say that, for example, some sudden advance in development, especially for space rockets, will not provide one of the camps with so great an advantage that its peaceful inclinations will not be able to resist it?

Who can say that if in the future, the political background having changed completely — that is something that has already happened on earth — the two powers having the nuclear monopoly will not agree to divide the world?

Who can say that as the occasion arises the two, while each deciding not to launch its missiles at the main enemy so that it should itself be spared, will not crush the others? It is possible to imagine that on some awful day Western Europe should be wiped out from Moscow and Central Europe from Washington. And who can even say that the two rivals, after I know not what political and social upheaval, will not unite? [1]

Did de Gaulle really expect that France would have to "go it alone" some day? One might suspect, rather, that his purpose was primarily to apply pressure to coalition politics, to use the menace of "French irresponsibility" to gain acquiescence in an increased French responsibility. The political fragility of NATO confronted by the intransigence of one of its leading members called to mind Marshal Foch's celebrated *boutade:* "My admiration for Napoléon has shrunk since I found out what a coalition was."

It was possible that de Gaulle's plan was not beyond his scope of action; however, in the eyes of his enemies, it smelled of blackmail.[2] In the bosom of his own Army, one of its side effects had been to teach the "Africans," for the first time, the virtues of NATOism, and to teach the seigneurs of Fontainebleau that they were threatened on their flank as well as their front by the creeping action of *la guerre subver-*

---

[1] Quoted by the *New York Times*, November 11, 1959, from General de Gaulle's press conference of the preceding day.

[2] The strength of this interpretation in the National Assembly was demonstrated on June 14, 1962, when Maurice-René Simonnet of the MRP read to the deputies the so-called "manifesto of the Europeans," which had the names of 293 of the legislators attached (an absolute majority). The 293 agreed on little else, however.

sive. For NATO the dawning came late that the Algerian War had been not only a "guerre à retardement" in matters of matériel but a "guerre de révélation" in matters of grand strategy and political understanding. The American preoccupation with Asian commitments and hemispheric problems, arriving simultaneously, lent great-power backing to this judgment. Maurice Challe, in prison, remained the "patron" of this newly harmonized strategy, just as Paul Ely had been its modest crystallizer, years earlier.[3]

Neither a Georges Bidault of the *petite émigration* nor a Jacques Soustelle, *persona non grata* in Italy, would one day catalyze the Army's sentiments against *le pouvoir.* Nor would any other civilian ranting, however self-righteously, against the *fait accompli* of Algeria. The Army, sharing the same distress, showed itself to be more realistic than its allies in mufti. If it retained a political vocation in the future, this urge would proceed from the Army's own fluctuating assessment of its strategic tasks and missions. From the juvenile excursions into the realm of "pur et dur," the Army had perhaps matured to a real understanding of a global mission accepted in concert with other free nations and free armies. Recently it had given much evidence of mastering its own morbidity, by bowing to the inevitable, by retaining independent judgment in silence and discipline, if with crossed fingers.

The Algerian settlement of July 1962 had undoubtedly removed the excuse and temptation for overt sedition. But otherwise the Army's future political course was problematical. The demon of the djebels could not be exorcised by the command to forget.

The "Armée de Demain"

The reorganization of the defense structure in 1961 had tightened the government's reins over the services, while at the same time pointedly separating the functions of Intelligence (now attached to the Secretariat Général de la Défense) and Operations (the responsibility of the Etat-Major des Armées). This meant that some of the co-ordination essental for plotting had been broken down. It meant also that so severe a division of responsibility had been created as to handicap French forces almost prohibitively if they had to fight a war. On the other hand, the separation seemed tailor-made for purposes of advanced planning and reconversion of units and matériel.

With the cessation of the Algerian responsibility, into the key positions at the head of the double pyramid went, respectively, Air Gen-

[3] See General Ely's book, *L'armée dans la nation* (Paris, 1961), especially the preface and pp. 57–103.

eral Michel Fourquet, the absolute Gaullist of the last days of Algiers, and General Charles Ailleret, the assiduous student of atomic questions. The regime's grip over its Army seemed assured as never before. It was widely noted that both Fourquet and Ailleret were *polytechniciens,* that is, graduates of France's difficult and highly regarded "grande école," the Polytechnique. Many *polytechniciens* had entered the officer corps in the 1930's. Thus the Army, by both natural and extraordinary causes, was passing into the hands of its technical engineers, who had, according to one commentator, "l'âme plus sèche mais la tête plus solide." [4] The Gaullist logic and the promotion of generals, even if the one had a certain impetus from the other, had produced a useful conjuncture.

What was this "Army of tomorrow" that Generals Fourquet and Ailleret were charged with fabricating? It had been announced in a much-remarked article by Pierre Messmer, which appeared in February 1962.[5] Even though the language was in the neutral tone of the technician, no one doubted that the inspiration had come from above. It was not a trial balloon, but an order.

The points of greatest interest in Messmer's essay are the following:

1. "Since, in any possible future conflict, France will not be the aggressor, the French armed forces must be able to respond, *alone or whenever possible with our allies* [italics added], to threats directed at us." [6]

2. France's armed forces were to be reorganized into three major components: the nuclear striking force, an operational force armed eventually with tactical nuclear weapons, and a regionally based home-defense force adapted to internal territorial operations.

3. Military expenditures were to increase during a five-year period at a rate roughly paralleling the expected growth of the gross national product.

4. Military personnel would be reduced as a consequence of the cost of the new weapons and other factors. Whereas the Navy and Air Force would enjoy slight numerical increases, the Army would be steadily cut back from about 700,000 to 450,000 officers and men. There would be a higher proportion of officers (39 per cent) in the "Army of tomorrow," and they would have a higher degree of technical training.

[4] Jean Valluy, "Réflexions sur l'armée de demain," *Revue des Deux Mondes,* July 15, 1962, p. 168.

[5] Pierre Messmer, "L'Armée de demain," *Revue des Deux Mondes,* February 15, 1962. Subsequent references are made to the translation, "The French Military Establishment of Tomorrow," *Orbis,* Summer 1962, pp. 205–216.

[6] *Ibid.,* pp. 205–206.

5. Budgetary and research and development emphasis would clearly fall on the development, construction, and installation of nuclear weapons and their delivery systems. The ICBM's would be operational before 1970, as well as a nuclear-powered submarine. The deterrent force would not be subject to the "political and military limitations that weigh on nuclear explosives of American origin." [7]

Many of the judgments expressed under the pen of Messmer were undoubtedly correct, and many others, if controversial, needed to be stated bluntly. But, taken as a whole, the article replied to a conception of French power that many regarded as dangerous or utopian. With social troubles erupting in France, with the peasants in periodic fiscal revolt, with the vexatious problem of the repatriated European of Algeria to be dealt with (160,000 had been predicted by July 1, but closer to 900,000 would eventually arrive), there were hints that the French budget could not support de Gaulle's ambitious *force de frappe*. Valéry Giscard d'Estaing, the Minister of Finance, spoke sanguinely of the possibility that in 1963 the government might have to "open necessary credits while fully respecting the balance of the public finances." But others thought that the margin was perilously small and could become smaller, especially if French economic growth were to fall below the estimated yearly 4 per cent.

In the month of July, Messmer found his military challenger in the person of retired General Jean Valluy, former commander of Allied Land Forces, Central Europe, writing also in the respectable *Revue des Deux Mondes*. There is reason to think that General Valluy had taken the pulse of many of his military contacts and was not writing simply as a private person.

À tout seigneur, tout honneur, the General began in substance, thanking the "technical minister" for finally laying his cards on the table. Then Valluy began to demonstrate that these matters were not purely and simply technical. He evoked the political fact of the Soviet menace (always more important to de Gaulle's detractors than to his sympathizers) and the folly for any nation of the Western alliance, even the United States, to believe that it was really capable of acting "seule." He warned:

Our friends will put up with us for a while . . . as long as possible, but now their patience is sorely tried, and one fine day we shall all be joined or shall all blow up. Shall we then have to draw up a new detailed report of "fraternités perdues"? . . . shall we find ourselves armed with a tool

[7] *Ibid.,* p. 213.

of national combat which is imperfect and laughable, and expelled from a collective system which we shall have done our part to render impotent? [8]

Then there was the Army itself — not just a collection of robots whose clothes and armament could be changed at a command and whose experience and judgment could be erased by the stroke of a pen. Some of its most promising officers had left in disgrace; now others were leaving in disgust. "To proclaim that the best are gone would be an extreme simplification," wrote Valluy with prudence. "Excellent ones remain, but they have all passed through a traumatic experience." [9]

An Army in Doubt

The Army of tomorrow might turn out to be an unswervingly obedient one, chary of politics, rigorously under the orders of the national government and the faithful executor of its wishes. The temptation of new matériel and the challenges of nuclear capability might conquer many spirits. But it was possible that the germ of Algeria had begun to grow and could not be aborted. This was a question for the years and the political succession to settle. Behind the rank of *polytechniciens* now taking command there was a mass of younger officers whose lives had been deeply etched by the experience of "quinze années d'abus de confiance." They might not rebel; they would not forget.

For the moment military feelings lay unresolved beneath historical scar tissue. Whatever the Army's mood, it was performing in obedience and discipline; a strong policy, however disagreeable, was better than none at all. By the force of fate, the Army was emerging from its "nuit coloniale," but one could not be sure how things would look to it in the daylight.

There was an undoubted appeal for many in the relatively grandiose conception of the *force de frappe* and the emphasis on independent national defense. The fact that the nation itself seemed to support the Gaullist conception of French power was not a negligible influence. And, after all, when the General had announced his referendum for direct popular election of the President, had he not taken contemptuous leave of the Assembly and gone off to watch the military maneuvers in the Auvergne?

De Gaulle had overcome many formidable obstacles. The nation, against all predictions of the experts, had given him the parliament of his choice in the elections of November 18 and November 25, 1962. But

[8] Valluy, *op. cit.*, p. 164.
[9] *Ibid.*, p. 168.

uneasy moments lay ahead. If, as many believed, the *force de frappe* proved a strategic white elephant bought at prohibitive cost, the military repercussions might be severe. Also, it turned out by January 1963 that Giscard's amiable economic estimates had been on the wishful side. Social restiveness was growing, with damaging strikes in the coal mines and elsewhere. But, of greater importance from the military point of view, the *force de frappe* was squeezing the conventional Army out of the picture, creating interservice tension and disturbing previously loyalist and traditionalist elements. For its entire history, the French Army had seen the leaders of the ground forces dominant in the councils of the military establishment; now they were being displaced by the nuclear and missile technologists, and their commands were being shaved to the bone. Messmer had foreseen a gradual reduction of effectives to 450,000, but less than a year later the Gaullist deputy Sanguinetti was talking about less than half that number.[10] The unspoken fear — though Messmer had denied it — was a policy of the "dégagement des cadres," the selective forced retirement of military personnel in order to hasten the cutback. Economic and social pressures on the regime were conspiring to force this solution. France seemed to be entering a period of "bigger bang for the franc."

These were radical prospects for an organization still gnawed by its wartime souvenirs. They had the possibility of touching many more than the blue-ribbon "soldats perdus," a large number of whom had deserted, been sanctioned, or resigned voluntarily.[11] A small, highly mobile conventional force would probably be preserved out of what had once been the flower of the French Army. Other than that there would be the nuclear elite and a large network of territorial reserves.

A recent poll taken in the Army highlighted some reactions.[12] It revealed a widespread suspicion of the new military technology. Old ideas about the probability of subversive war had not died out. The gap between the Army and the Nation was still deeply felt, and was blamed on the government and the press.

Much more interestingly, the majority of respondents were reported as thinking that French nationalism was dead, that it had lost its last battle in Algeria. Many, still infected by the obsessive conviction of

---

[10] *Le Monde,* January 25, 1963; see the parliamentary debate on the military budget in the same number.

[11] See Jean-Louis Guillaud, "Les Soldats perdus," *La NEF,* October 1962–January 1963, pp. 116–117. The abrupt and discreet retirements of General Olié, the Interservice Chief of Staff, of General Gambiez, the former Superior Commander in Algeria, and of General Stehlin, the Chief of Staff of the Air Force, none of them "soldats perdus," were significant straws in the wind.

[12] *Ibid.,* p. 124.

la guerre révolutionnaire, would willingly transfer their allegiance to a context larger than France, such as Europe. They resented the *force de frappe,* not only because it was Gaullist and threatened their careers, but because it seemed to weaken Western cohesion. If this was true, it meant that the flame of General Challe still burned in the hearts of many officers.

"Some day a discouraged Army will probably take sides," predicted General Valluy.[13] The writer was obviously an extreme partisan of his own feelings, but he was not alone in this respect. De Gaulle had already accomplished feats believed to be impossible by the well-informed. But the French Army would still have choices to make, if not this year, then in years to follow. An army simultaneously nourished on nightmare and drastic change might lack stability. At the beginning of 1963, some of the perils of its choices had not yet emerged, while others leaped before the eyes of all.

[13] Valluy, *op. cit.,* p. 169.

BIBLIOGRAPHY

Many of the observations contained in this work have been verified by or at least compared with the experiences of persons close to the situation. However, there has been no extensive reliance on such interviews, since they are as apt to be misleading as profitable, and the means were not, in any case, available for a systematic pursuit of sociological methods.

Journalistic commentary on all phases of the history of the French Army's perplexity has been closely followed and collated. Limitations of space clearly forbid the gargantuan task of listing all press articles that have been useful. The writer would like to call special attention to the coverage provided in *Le Monde* by its excellent staff of correspondents, especially Jacques Fauvet, Robert Guillain, Alain Jacob, Jean Lacouture, Eugène Mannoni, Jean Planchais, J.-M. Théolleyre, Pierre Viansson-Ponté, whose names appear often in the footnotes. I have also consulted, with regularity, the dailies *Le Figaro, Combat,* and *Paris-Presse,* as well as the weeklies *Express, France-Observateur, Carrefour, Témoignage Chrétien,* and [*Le Nouveau*] *Candide.* General, though not week-to-week, reference was made to the military weekly *Le Bled* during its period of operation, and to the FLN weekly *El Moudjahid* and the Tunisian *Jeune Afrique.* I have made a selective, but by no means comprehensive, examination of such publications as *Verbe, Contacts,* and *Itinéraires* and other right-wing Church and military organs.

Particular attention should be called to at least five special numbers of reviews devoted to the French Army and its various problems. Composed of articles written from various points of view, they are, taken together, an excellent small library of French military doctrine and politics:

"La Guerre révolutionnaire," special number of *Revue militaire d'Information,* February–March 1957.

"L'armée française," *Défense de l'Occident,* November–December 1958.

"A la recherche d'une armée perdue," *Cahiers de la République,* November–December 1960.

"L'armée française," *La NEF,* July–September 1961.

"La guerre d'Algérie suivie d'une histoire de l'O.A.S.," *La NEF,* October 1962–January 1963.

The following bibliography is itself selective:

BOOKS

Abbas, Ferhat, *La nuit coloniale,* Paris, 1962.

Alleg, Henri, *La Question,* Lausanne, 1958.

Alquier, Jean-Yves, *Nous avons pacifié Tazalt,* Paris, 1958.

Argoud, [Colonel] Antoine, *Sans commentaire* (testimony given in closed session at the "trial of the barricades,") Paris, 1961.

Aron, Robert, *Histoire de la Libération de la France, juin 1944–mai 1945,* Paris, 1959.

—— and Georgette Elgey, *Histoire de Vichy, 1940–1944,* Paris, 1954.

——, François Lavagne, Janine Feller, and Yvette Garnier-Rizet, *Les origines de la guerre d'Algérie,* Paris, 1962.

Arrighi, Pascal, *La Corse: atout décisif,* Paris, 1958.

Azeau, Henri, *Révolte militaire: Alger, 22 avril 1961,* Paris, 1961.

Barberot, [Colonel] Roger, *Malaventure en Algérie avec le général Paris de Bollardière,* Paris, 1957.

Bassot, Hubert, *Les Silencieux,* Paris, 1958.

Bedjaoui, Mohammed, *La Révolution algérienne et le droit* (Preface by Pierre Cot), Brussels, 1961.

Behr, Edward, *The Algerian Problem,* London, 1961.

Berque, Jacques, *Le Maghreb entre deux guerres,* Paris, 1961.

Boudot, Pierre, *L'Algérie mal enchaînée,* Paris, 1961.

Bromberger, Serge, *Les rebelles algériens,* Paris, 1958.

—— and Merry Bromberger, *Les treize complots du 13 mai,* Paris, 1959.

——, Georgette Elgey, and J.-F. Chauvel, *Barricades et Colonels,* Paris, 1960.

Buis, Georges, *La Grotte,* Paris, 1961.

Camus, Albert, *Actuelles, III: Chronique algérienne, 1939–1958,* Paris, 1958.

Catroux, [General] Georges, *Deux actes du drame indochinois,* Paris, 1959.

Chieu, Ngo Van, *Journal d'un combattant viet-minh,* Paris, 1955.

Clark, Michael K., *Algeria in Turmoil,* New York, 1959.

Cole, Allan B. (ed.), *Conflict in Indo-China and International Repercussions, 1945–1955,* Ithaca, 1956.

Contre-Révolution: Stratégie et Tactique, Editions Françaises et Internationales, Paris, 1958.

Cosyns-Verhaegen, Roger, *Les armées irrégulières dans l'évolution des Etats et de la Société,* Brussels, 1960.
————, *Théorie de l'action subversive,* Brussels, 1960.
Debré, Michel, *Ces princes qui nous gouvernent,* Paris, 1957.
de Félice, Philippe, *see* Félice, Philippe de.
de Gaulle, Charles, *see* Gaulle, Charles de.
de la Gorce, Paul-Marie, *see* Gorce, Paul-Marie de la.
Delmas, Claude, *La Guerre Révolutionnaire,* Paris, 1960.
Delpey, Roger, *Soldats de la boue, I: La bataille de Cochinchine,* Paris, 1961.
Demain . . . L'Armée française (anon.), Paris, 1963.
Déon, Michel, *L'Armée d'Algérie,* Paris, 1959.
Despuech, Jacques, *Le Trafic des piastres,* Paris, 1953.
Devillers, Philippe, *Histoire du Viet-Nam, 1940–1952,* Paris, 1952.
Dinfreville, Jacques, *L'Opération Indochine,* Paris, 1952.
Domenach, Jean-Marie, *La propaganda politique,* Paris, 1950.
Dresch, J., P. Stible, *et al., La Question algérienne,* Paris, 1958.
Dronne, Raymond, *La révolution d'Alger,* Paris, 1958.
Dufresnoy, Claude (ed.), *Des officiers parlent* (introduction by Jules Roy), Paris, 1961.
Duverger, Maurice, *La cinquième République,* Paris, 1959.
Ely, [General] Paul, *L'armée dans la nation,* Paris, 1961.
Euloge, André, and Antoine Moulinier, *L'Envers des barricades,* Paris, 1960.
Evénements survenus en France de 1933 à 1945, Assemblée Nationale, Session de 1947, Vol. I (*Témoignages et Documents*), Paris, 1951.
Fall, Bernard, *Le Viet-Minh, 1954–1960,* Paris, 1961.
————, *The Viet Minh Regime,* Ithaca, 1954.
Fauvet, Jacques, *La Quatrième République,* Paris, 1959.
———— and Jean Planchais, *La Fronde des généraux,* Paris, 1961.
Félice, Philippe de, *Foules en délire: Extases collectives,* Paris, 1947.
Furniss, Edgar S., Jr., *De Gaulle and the French Army,* New York, 1964.
Gamelin, [General] Maurice, *Servir,* 3 vols., Paris, 1946–47.
Gaulle, Charles de, *Le fil de l'épée,* Paris, 1932.
————, *Mémoires de Guerre,* 3 vols., Paris, 1954–1959, and Ottawa, 1960.
Gendarme, René, *L'Economie de l'Algérie,* Paris, 1959.
Giap, Vo Nguyen, *People's War, People's Army,* New York, 1962.
Girardet, Raoul, *La Société militaire dans la France contemporaine, 1815–1939,* Paris, 1953.
Gorce, Paul-Marie de la, *The French Army,* New York, 1963.
Grall, Xavier (ed.), *La génération du djebel,* Paris, 1962.
Griffith, [Brigadier General] Samuel B. (trans.), *Mao Tse-Tung on Guerrilla Warfare,* New York, 1961.
Groussard, [Colonel] Georges-André, and [Colonel] Georges Loustaunau-Lacau, *Consuls, Prenez garde!,* Paris, 1952.
Guernier, Eugène, *La Berbérie, l'Islam, la France,* Vol. II, Paris, 1950.
Guevara, Ernesto, *Guerrilla Warfare,* New York (Monthly Review Press edition), 1961.
Guillain, Robert, *La fin des illusions, Notes d'Indochine: février–juillet 1954,* Paris, 1954.
Hoffmann, Stanley, *Le Mouvement Poujade,* Paris, 1956.
Hostache, René, *Le Conseil national de la Résistance,* Paris, 1958.

Jaurès, Jean, *L'Organisation socialiste en France: l'Armée nouvelle*, Paris, 1915.

Jeanson, Colette and Francis, *L'Algérie hors la loi*, Paris, 1955.

Jeanson, Francis, *Notre guerre*, Paris, 1960.

King, James E., Jr., *Limited War in an Age of Nuclear Plenty*, L57-154, Industrial College of the Armed Forces, 1956–1957.

Kraft, Joseph, *The Struggle for Algeria*, New York, 1961.

Lacoste, Yves, André Nouschi, and André Prenant, *L'Algérie: passé et présent*, Paris, 1960.

Lacouture, Jean, *Cinq hommes et la France*, Paris, 1961.

——, and Philippe Devillers, *La fin d'une guerre, Indochine 1954*, Paris, 1960.

Laniel, Joseph, *Le drame indochinois*, Paris, 1954.

Lartéguy, Jean, *Les Centurions*, Paris, 1958.

Le Bon, Gustave, *La Psychologie des foules*, Paris, 1895.

——, *Les lois psychologiques de l'évolution des peuples*, Paris, 1894.

Lefèvre, Bernard, *Sur le chemin de la restauration*, Paris, 1959.

Leites, Nathan, *The Game of Politics in France* (translation of *Du Malaise politique*), Stanford, California, 1958.

Lentin, Albert-Paul, *L'Algérie des colonels*, Paris, 1958.

Leroi-Gourhan, André, and Jean Poirier, *Ethnologie de l'Union française*, Vol. II, Paris, 1953.

Lifton, Robert Jay, *Thought Reform and the Psychology of Totalism*, New York, 1961.

Lyautey, [Marshal] Louis H. G., *Lettres du Sud de Madagascar, 1900–1902*, Paris, 1935.

——, *Lettres du Tonkin et de Madagascar*, 2 vols., Paris, 1920.

Macridis, Roy, and Bernard E. Brown, *The De Gaulle Republic*, Homewood (Illinois), 1960.

Malaparte (Suckert), Curzio, *Coup d'Etat, the Technique of Revolution* (trans. Sylvia Saunders), New York, 1932.

Mandouze, André (ed.), *La révolution algérienne par les textes*, 2nd edition, Paris, 1961.

Mao Tse-tung, *Collected Works*, 4 vols., New York, 1953.

Matthews, Ronald, *The Death of the Fourth Republic*, London, 1954.

Mégret, Maurice, *L'action psychologique*, Paris, 1960.

——, *La guerre psychologique*, Paris, 1956.

Meisel, James H., *The Fall of the Republic: Military Revolt in France*, Ann Arbor, 1962.

Mitterrand, François, *Aux frontières de l'Union française*, Paris, 1956.

Mouillaud, Maurice, *La mystification du 13 mai au 28 septembre*, Paris, 1958.

Mus, Paul, *Viet-nam: Sociologie d'une guerre*, Paris, 1952.

Navarre, [General] Henri de, *Agonie de l'Indochine*, Paris, 1958.

Nora, Pierre, *Les Français d'Algérie*, Paris, 1961.

Paillat, Claude, *Le dossier secret de l'Algérie*, Paris, 1961.

Pagniez, Yvonne, *Choses vues au Viet-nam*, Paris, 1954.

——, *Le Viet-minh et la Guerre psychologique*, Paris, 1955.

Paret, Peter, and John Shy, *Guerrillas in the 1960's*, New York, 1962.

Passeron, André (ed.), *De Gaulle parle*, Paris, 1962.

Pickles, Dorothy, *The Fifth French Republic*, New York, 1960.

Planchais, Jean, *Le malaise de l'armée*, Paris, 1958.

Procès d'Edmond Jouhaud, Le (stenographic reproduction), Paris, 1962.

Procès de Raoul Salan, Le (stenographic reproduction), Paris, 1962.

Procès des Barricades, Le (stenographic reproduction), Paris, 1960.

Procès du putsch d'Alger et du complot de Paris, Les, (stenographic reproduction), ed. Maurice Cottaz, Paris, 1962.

Reiwald, Paul, *De l'Esprit des masses,* Paris, 1949.

Rémond, René, *La droite en France de 1815 à nos jours,* Paris, 1954; 4th ed., Paris, 1963.

Réscapés de l'enfer, Les, Paris, 1954.

Reynaud, Paul, *Au coeur de la mêlée,* Paris, 1951.

Ribeaud, Guy, *Barricades pour un drapeau,* Paris, 1960.

Rovan, Joseph, *Une idée neuve: la Démocratie,* Paris, 1961.

Roy, Jules, *The War in Algeria,* New York, 1961.

——, *La bataille de Dien Bien Phu,* Paris, 1963.

Sainteny, Jean, *Histoire d'une paix manquée,* Paris, 1953.

Sauge, Georges, *Echec au communisme,* Paris, 1958.

Sérigny, Alain de, *La révolution du 13 mai,* Paris, 1958.

Servan-Schreiber, Jean-Jacques, *Lieutenant en Algérie,* Paris, 1957.

Simon, Pierre-Henri, *Contre la torture,* Paris, 1957.

Soustelle, Jacques, *Aimée et souffrante Algérie,* Paris, 1956.

——, *L'espérance trahie,* Paris, 1962.

Sulzberger, Cyrus L., *The Test: De Gaulle and Algeria,* New York, 1962.

Susini, Jean-Jacques, *Histoire de l'O.A.S.,* Paris, 1963.

Tanham, George K., *Communist Revolutionary Warfare,* New York, 1961.

Tchakhotine, Serge, *Le viol des foules par la propagande politique,* Paris, 1939.

Thérive, André, *Essai sur les trahisons* (Preface by Raymond Aron), Paris, 1951.

Tillion, Germaine, *L'Afrique bascule vers l'avenir,* Paris, 1960.

——, *Les ennemis complémentaires,* Paris, 1960.

Tournoux, Jean-Raymond, *Secrets d'Etat,* Paris, 1960.

——, *L'Histoire secrète,* Paris, 1962.

Trinquier, [Lieutenant Colonel] Roger, *La guerre moderne,* Paris, 1961.

Trotsky, Leon, *The History of the Russian Revolution* (trans. Max Eastman), 3 vols., New York, 1932.

Vidal-Naquet, Pierre, *La Raison d'Etat,* Paris, 1962.

Weber, Eugen, *Action Française,* Stanford, 1963.

Werth, Alexander, *France, 1940–1955,* New York, 1956.

Weygand, [General] Maxime, *Mirages et Réalité,* Vol. II (*Mémoires*), Paris, 1957.

Whitaker, Urban G., Jr., *Propaganda and International Relations,* San Francisco, 1960.

Williams, Philip, *Politics in Post-War France,* 2nd edition, London, 1958.

——, and Martin Harrison, *De Gaulle's Republic,* London, 1960.

ARTICLES AND DOCUMENTS

Allary, G., "L'armée et les intellectuels," *Défense de l'Occident,* November–December 1958, pp. 132–138.

Argoud, [Colonel] Antoine, "Répercussions de l'évolution de l'armement sur l'organisation et l'emploi de forces terrestres," *Revue des Forces terrestres,* July 1955, pp. 19–32.

Bardèche, M., "L'armée et la nation: La fin du mythe de 'la grande muette,'" *Défense de l'Occident,* November–December 1958, pp. 151–159.

Beaufond, [Lieutenant Colonel] de, "L'officier de guerre psychologique," *Revue des Forces terrestres,* October 1957, pp. 97–102.

———, "L'opération de guerre psychologique," *Revue des Forces terrestres,* July 1957, pp. 137–142.

Beloff, Max, "The Sixth of February," in *St Antony's Papers,* No. 5, New York, 1959, pp. 9–35.

Bloch-Michel, Jean, *et al.,* "L'Algérie devant la conscience française," supplement to *Preuves,* December 1960.

Bosworth, William, "The French Catholic Hierarchy and the Algerian Question," *The Western Political Quarterly,* December 1962, pp. 667–680.

Bourdet, Claude, "Les hommes de la guerre," *Les Temps modernes,* August–September 1953, pp. 419–428.

Brichant, Bernard, "La conduite des hommes et ses techniques psychologiques," *Revue militaire d'Information,* December 1956, pp. 40–60.

"Building the New Algeria: Role of the Specialized Administrative Sections," Ambassade de France, Service de Presse et d'Information, September 1957.

Cailloux, R., "Où en est l'armée française?", *Défense de l'Occident,* November–December 1958, pp. 3–12.

Calliès, [General], "Le problème algérien," *Revue militaire d'Information,* August 1956, pp. 35–43.

Castex, [Admiral], "Les enseignements de la guerre d'Indochine, *Revue de Défense nationale,* December 1955, pp. 523–538.

Chassin, [General] Lionel-Max, "Du rôle idéologique de l'armée," *Revue militaire d'Information,* October 10, 1954, pp. 13–19.

———, "Vers un encerclement de l'Occident," *Revue de Défense nationale,* May 1956, pp. 531–553.

Choublier, Claude, "L'arme psychologique entre les mains des colonels," *La NEF,* July–August 1958, pp. 27–33.

Collinet, Michel, "Le saint-simonisme et l'armée," *Revue française de Sociologie,* April–June 1961, pp. 38–47.

de Beaufond, *See* Beaufond, de.

Delmas, Claude, "Interview avec le général Challe," *Revue de Défense nationale,* April 1961, pp. 577–594.

———, "La rébellion algérienne après l'arrestation des chefs du F.L.N.," *Revue de Défense nationale,* December 1956, pp. 1463-1474.

Desjours, [General], "La pacification dans le secteur de Blida," *Revue des Forces terrestres,* October 1959, pp. 29–44.

de Navarre, Henri, *see* Navarre, Henri de.

de Rocquigny, *see* Rocquigny, de.

De Soto, J., "Pouvoir civil et pouvoir militaire," *La Défense Nationale,* Paris, 1958, pp. 87–132.

Dogan, Mattei, "Les candidats et les élus," *Les élections législatives du 2 janvier 1956,* Paris, 1957, pp. 425–466.

Domenach, Jean-Marie, "L'armée en République," *Esprit,* November 1958, pp. 632–642.

Doumic, R., "L'armée et la formation de l'opinion publique," *Revue militaire d'Information,* July 1956, pp. 14–16.

Etcheverry, [Batallion Chief], "Réflexions sur la guerre subversive d'Algérie," *Revue des Forces terrestres,* July 1959, pp. 41–48.

Fall, Bernard, "Indochina — The Last Year of the War," *Military Review,* October 1956, pp. 3–11.

Galay, N., "Partisan Warfare," in Basil Liddell Hart (ed.), *The Red Army,* New York, 1955, pp. 153–171.

Garrigou-Lagrange, Madeleine, "Intégrisme et national-catholicisme," *Esprit,* October 1959, pp. 515–543.

Girardet, Raoul, "Pouvoir civil et pouvoir militaire dans la France contemporaine," *Revue française de Science politique,* March 1960. Translated as "Civil and Military Power in the Fourth Republic," in Samuel P. Huntington (ed.), *Changing Patterns of Military Politics,* New York, 1961, pp. 121–149.

——, "Problèmes militaires contemporains. Etat des travaux," *Revue française de Science politique,* June 1960, pp. 395–418.

——, *et al.,* "Essai de prospective militaire," *Cahiers de la République,* November–December 1960, pp. 31–41.

Gorce, Paul-Marie de la, "Histoire de l'O.A.S. en Algérie," *La NEF,* October 1962–January 1963, pp. 139–192.

Gottmann, Jean, "Bugeaud, Galliéni, Lyautey: The Development of French Colonial Warfare," in Edward Meade Earle (ed.), *Makers of Modern Strategy,* Princeton, 1941, pp. 234–259.

Grand d'Esnon, [Battalion Chief], and [Captain] Prestat, "L'endoctrinement des prisonniers de guerre dans les camps du Viet-minh," *Revue des Forces terrestres,* October 1956, pp. 31–46.

Gromier, François, "Le 'trouble' de l'armée," *La NEF,* July–September 1961, pp. 5–18.

——, "Une conception archaïque," *Cahiers de la République,* November–December 1960, pp. 15–30.

Guillaud, Jean-Louis, "Les soldats perdus," *La NEF,* October 1962–January 1963, pp. 116–124.

Hoffmann, Stanley, "Protest in Modern France," in Morton A. Kaplan (ed.), *The Revolution in World Politics,* New York, 1962, pp. 69–91.

Hogard, [Commandant] Jacques, "Guerre révolutionnaire et pacification," *Revue militaire d'Information,* January 1957, pp. 7–24.

——, "Guerre révolutionnaire ou révolution dans l'art de la guerre," *Revue de Défense nationale,* December 1956, pp. 1497–1513.

——. "Le soldat dans la Guerre révolutionnaire," *Revue de Défense nationale,* February 1957, pp. 211–226.

——, "Stratégie et tactique du Communisme," *Revue des Forces terrestres,* October 1959.

——, "Stratégie et tactique dans la Guerre révolutionnaire," *Revue militaire d'Information,* June 1958, pp. 23–36.

——, "Tribune des lecteurs: De la guerre subversive à la guerre révolutionnaire," *Revue des Forces terrestres,* July 1958, pp. 168–171.

——, "La Tentation du Communisme," *Revue des Forces terrestres,* January 1959, pp. 23–32.

J. G., "L'organisation de base de l'Armée de Libération Nationale," *Les Temps Modernes,* October–November 1960, pp. 531–537.

Jousselin, J., "Y a-t-il un problème de l'armée?", reprint from *Le Semeur,* December 1960, Paris, n.d.

Kelly, George A., "Revolutionary War and Psychological Action," *Military Review,* September 1960, pp. 4–12.

———, "The French Army Re-enters Politics, 1940–1955," *Political Science Quarterly,* September 1961, pp. 367–392.

———, "The Political Background of the French A-Bomb," *Orbis,* Fall 1960, pp. 284–306.

———, "Algeria, the Army, and the Fifth Republic: A Scenario of Civil-Military Conflict," *Political Science Quarterly,* September 1964, pp. 335–359.

Kerr, Walter, "The French Army in Trouble," *Foreign Affairs,* October 1961, pp. 86–94.

Kraft, Joseph, "Settler Politics in Africa," *Foreign Affairs,* July 1961, pp. 591–600.

Krief, Claude, "Portrait d'un colonel," *La NEF,* July–September 1961, pp. 51–56.

Labelle-Rojoux, R., "Moral de l'armée, moral de la nation," *Revue militaire d'Information,* July 10, 1953, pp. 14–15.

Lacheroy, [Colonel] Charles, "La Guerre révolutionnaire," *La Défense Nationale,* Paris, 1958, pp. 307–330.

———, "Scenario-type de Guerre révolutionnaire," *Revue des Forces terrestres,* October 1956, pp. 25–29.

Lacoste, Robert, "Rôle de l'armée dans l'action psychologique," *Revue militaire d'Information,* July 1956, pp. 10–11.

Lenin [Vladimir Ilyitch Ulyanov], "Partisan Warfare" (trans. and ed. by Regina Eldor and Stefan T. Possony), *Orbis,* Summer 1958, pp. 194–208.

"Lieutenant X," "Pourquoi nous avons 'perdu' la guerre d'Algérie," *La NEF,* July–September 1961, pp. 19–38.

Lion, [Lieutenant] "Témoignage d'un officers S.A.S.," *l'Armée,* July 1960, pp. 21–29; August 1960, pp. 26–40.

Loquin, J., "La doctrine de la guerre révolutionnaire," *La NEF,* July–August 1958, pp. 25–26.

Mac-Carthy, [Lieutenant Colonel], "L'armée française et la politique," *l'Armée,* February 1960, pp. 30–40; March 1960, pp. 38–48.

Mairal-Bernard, [Commandant], "Cinquièmes bureaux et septième arme," *Revue des Forces terrestres,* January 1958, pp. 77–92.

Maître, Jacques, "Catholicisme d'extrême droite et croisade anti-subversive," *Revue française de Sociologie,* April–June 1961, pp. 106–117.

Mégret, Maurice, "Fonction politique de l'armée," *Le Défense Nationale,* Paris, 1958, pp. 133–182.

Messmer, Pierre, "L'armée de demain," *Revue des deux mondes,* February 15, 1962, pp. 481–493. English translation in *Orbis,* Summer 1962, pp. 205–216.

———, "Notre politique militaire," *Revue de Défense nationale,* May 1963, pp. 745–761. English translation in *Military Review,* August 1963, pp. 24–34.

"Milites," "Enquête sur la Défense nationale," *Hommes et Mondes,* April 1955, pp. 1–21; May 1955, pp. 153–176.

———, "L'Algérie n'est pas l'Indochine," *Revue militaire d'Information,* April 10, 1956, pp. 40–44.

Mitterrand, François, "L'armée dans le système," *La NEF,* July–August 1958, pp. 16–18.

———, "Le parlement et l'armée, *La NEF,* July–August 1959, pp. 33–38.

Monteil, Vincent, "Corneille chez Kafka," *Cahiers de la République,* November–December 1960, pp. 43–52.

Navarre, [General] Henri de, "Les données de la défense de l'Indochine," *Revue de Défense nationale,* March 1956, pp. 271–279.

Nemo, [Colonel], "A la recherche d'une doctrine," *Revue militaire générale,* March 1958, pp. 335–358.

——, "La guerre dans la foule," *Revue de Défense nationale,* June 1956, pp. 721–734.

——, "La guerre dans le milieu social," *Revue de Défense nationale,* May 1956, pp. 605–623.

Nouguès, J., and G. Galzy [Battalion Chiefs], "A propos des enseignements de la guerre d'Indochine," *Revue de Défense nationale,* April 1956, pp. 427–435.

Paret, Peter, "La Guerre Révolutionnaire," *Journal of the Royal United Service Institution,* February 1959, pp. 59–69.

Pinto, Roger, "La France et les états d'Indochine devant les accords de Genève," *Revue française de Science politique,* January–March 1955, pp. 63–91.

Planchais, Jean, "Crise de modernisme dans l'armée," *Revue française de Sociologie,* April–June 1961, pp. 118–123.

——, "Journalistes et militaires," *Revue militaire d'Information,* September–October 1957, pp. 108–112

——, "Quelle est cette armée?", *La NEF,* July–September 1961, pp. 57–63.

Poirier, Lucien, "Un instrument de guerre révolutionnaire: le F.L.N.," *Revue militaire d'Information,* December 1957, pp. 7–33.

Rémond, René, "Les catholiques et les élections," *Le référendum de septembre et les élections de novembre 1958,* Paris, 1960, pp. 49–118.

Richter, Melvin, "Tocqueville on Algeria," *The Review of Politics,* July 1963, pp. 362–398.

Rocolle, [Colonel], "Méthodologie de la guerre subversive," *Revue des Forces terrestres,* April 1958, pp. 53–60.

Rocquigny, [Colonel] de, "Le terrorisme urbain," *Revue militaire d'Information,* February 1958, pp. 77–83.

Schmuckel, [Colonel], "Contre-guérilla," *Revue des Forces terrestres,* April 1956, pp. 5–24.

"Simplet," "Guerre révolutionnaire, guerre psychologique, ou guerre 'tout court'?" *Revue militaire d'Information,* October 1959, pp. 97–102.

Souyris, [Captain] André, "L'action psychologique dans les forces armées," *Revue militaire d'Information,* October 1958, pp. 34–45.

——, "Les conditions de la parade et de la riposte à la guerre révolutionnaire," *Revue militaire d'Information,* February–March 1957, pp. 91–111.

——, "Un procédé efficace de contre-guérilla," *Revue de Défense nationale,* June 1956, 686–699.

Tabouis, [General], "La lutte psychologique en Algérie," *Revue des Forces terrestres,* April 1957, pp. 29–40.

"Texts of Declarations Drawn Up in Common Agreement at Evian, March 18, 1962, by the Delegations of the Government of the French Republic and the Algerian National Liberation Front," Ambassade de France, Service de Presse et d'Information, New York.

Tournoux, Jean-Raymond, "A Proletarian Army," *The Reporter,* XXII, No. 4 (February 18, 1960).

Tréanna, Dominique, "Les évadés du paradis viet-minh," *Hommes et Mondes,* April 1955, pp. 78–87.

Trinquier, [Lieutenant Colonel] Roger, "Contre-guérilla," *Revue des Forces terrestres,* July 1956, pp. 128–134.

Valluy, [General] Jean, "Réflexions sur l'armée de demain," *Revue des deux mondes,* July 15, 1962, pp. 161–171.

Weil, P., "Armée et fonction publique," *La Défense Nationale,* Paris, 1958, pp. 183–204.

Williams, Philip, "Algerian Tragedy," *Encounter,* January 1961, pp. 5–15.

———, "The French Army," *Encounter,* December 1961, pp. 30–37.

"Ximenès," "Essai sur la guerre révolutionnaire," *Revue militaire d'Information,* February–March 1957, pp. 11–14.

"XXX," "L'armée française et la guerre psychologique," *Defense de l'Occident,* November–December 1958, pp. 43–57.

Zeller, [General] André, "Armée et politique," *Revue de Défense nationale,* April 1957, pp. 499–517.

[The following works, which were not in my hands in time to affect the writing of *Lost Soldiers,* will be of interest: General Paul Ely, *Mémoires,* Vol I: *L'Indochine dans la tourmente* (Paris, 1964); Peter Paret, *French Revolutionary Warfare from Indochina to Algeria* (Princeton, 1964); and General Jean Valluy, *Honneur et Patrie: Nation et Supranation* (Paris, 1964).]

INDEX